To Lou with
best wishes
from Marilyn's brother

David Comstock

The Nevada County Chronicles 1851-1859

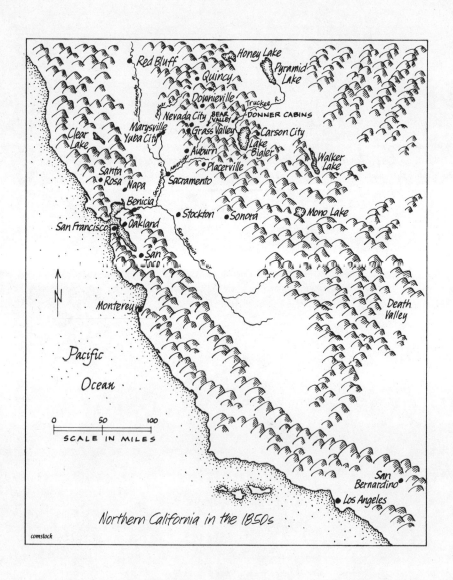

Northern California in the 1850s

The Nevada County Chronicles

Brides of the Gold Rush

1851-1859

David Allan Comstock

Comstock Bonanza Press

GRASS VALLEY • CALIFORNIA

PUBLISHED BY COMSTOCK BONANZA PRESS

18919 WILLIAM QUIRK MEMORIAL DRIVE

GRASS VALLEY, CALIFORNIA 95945

MANUFACTURED IN THE UNITED STATES OF AMERICA

FIRST EDITION

LIMITED TO TWO THOUSAND COPIES

Permission to quote from William Speer letter granted by Scholastic Inc., publishers of *From Canton to California* by Corinne K. Hoexter, copyright 1976 by Corinne Hoexter. Permission to quote from letters of Noel Follin granted by the University of Oklahoma Press, publishers of *Purple Passage: The Life of Mrs. Frank Leslie* by Madeleine B. Stern, copyright 1953 by University of Oklahoma Press. Permission to reproduce Indian festival poster and photo of Wema granted by Peter Shearer.

LIBRARY OF CONGRESS CATALOGING-IN-PUBLICATION DATA

COMSTOCK, DAVID A.

BRIDES OF THE GOLD RUSH, 1851–1859

(THE NEVADA COUNTY CHRONICLES)

BIBLIOGRAPHY: P. 429.

INCLUDES INDEX.

1. NEVADA COUNTY (CALIF.)—HISTORY.

2. NEVADA COUNTY (CALIF.)—GOLD DISCOVERIES.

3. NISENAN INDIANS—HISTORY.

4. INDIANS OF NORTH AMERICA—CALIFORNIA—NEVADA COUNTY—HISTORY.

I. TITLE.

II. SERIES.

F868.N5C655   1987   979.4'3704   86-73171

ISBN 0-933994-05-2

To Janet Haseley, Frances and Jack Long,

Hubert and Inez Miller,

and Fred and Doris Searls;

without their invaluable assistance and encouragement
these chronicles could not have succeeded half so well.

CONTENTS

MAPS AND CHARTS

PHOTOS

DRAWINGS

Aaron A. Sargent, 1827–1887 (California State Library photo).

William M. Stewart, 1825–1909 (California State Library photo).

INTRODUCTION

*C*ALIFORNIA'S THREE LARGEST cities in the 1850s were San Francisco, Sacramento and Nevada City. The last named was a prosperous gold mining community in the foothills of the Sierra Nevada. Five miles to the southwest lay the equally prosperous but less densely populated town of Grass Valley. North, south, east and west of these towns were dozens of smaller communities with such exotic names as Rough and Ready, Humbug, French Corral, Blue Tent, Gouge Eye, Red Dog and Orleans Flat.

One hundred and thirty years later the corporate limits of Nevada City are nearly the same as they were in the 1850s, and her population has not increased noticeably, although Grass Valley and the surrounding countryside have grown at a steady and rapid rate since about 1970. Nevertheless, within a dozen miles of Nevada City there are pockets in the forest where modern utilities do not exist, and people like myself still improvise their own heat, light, power and water resources.

Many stories have been told about people who passed through this area in the 1850s and later, but until now there has been no comprehensive description of them or their times. Nor have I read an account of any real or fictional western mining camp whose inhabitants even slightly resembled those at Nevada City. When I first peered into the archives and saw the rich array of characters whose notable careers began in this most

Niles Searls, 1825–1907 (Fred and Doris Searls photo).

Addison C. Niles, 1832–1890 (Frances G. Long photo).

cosmopolitan of mining camps, I realized I had rediscovered a forgotten world.

These were the formative years for many ambitious young men and women who later played important roles on a much larger stage. I have in mind such people as William M. Stewart, who embarked on a law career at Nevada City which carried him to the United States Senate for five terms as the representative of the state of Nevada, and who claimed authorship of the text of the fifteenth amendment to our Constitution. Or Aaron Sargent, whose law career also began in Nevada City—he served in the House of Representatives in the 1860s and the U. S. Senate in the 1870s and was our diplomatic minister to Germany in the 1880s. Another senator whose career started at Nevada City was George Hearst, who never studied law but amassed a fortune in gold and silver mining.

I also have in mind their wives: Ellen Clark Sargent, who invited Susan B. Anthony to share their home at Washington D.C., the better to lobby for passage of her women's suffrage amendment, which Senator Sargent sponsored. After their husbands died, Phoebe Apperson Hearst (who never lived in Nevada County) and Ellen Sargent founded San Francisco's Century Club, providing a forum for Julia Ward Howe and others to speak to the women of that city. When Mrs. Sargent died in 1911, political reformer Hiram Johnson spoke at her memorial service in San Francisco's Union Square.

Another advocate of women's rights was the wife of Dr. William J. Knox. After his death in 1867, Sarah Knox organized the woman's suffrage association at San Jose and lobbied for a bill to permit women to hold educational offices in California. The wife of James Churchman helped Zachary Taylor's daughter elope with Jefferson Davis in the 1830s; during the war between the states, Samantha Churchman accompanied her husband and daughter to Valparaiso when Lincoln named Churchman (a former colleague and friend from Illinois) as his consul to Chile.

Rev. Martin Kellogg left Grass Valley's Congregational church to teach Latin at the College of California in Oakland; a few years later he became the first Chairman of the Department of Ancient Languages at the new University of California in Berkeley, and became its president in the 1890s. Edward F. Spence launched banks in San Jose, San Diego and Los Angeles and was elected mayor of Los Angeles. Bailey Gatzert became Seattle's mayor in the 1870s, and probably was the first Jew to hold elective office in Washington state.

Surveyor Charles Marsh became a founding director of the Central Pacific Railroad in 1861, along with the more famous "Big Four" (Crocker, Hopkins, Huntington and Stanford). John R. McConnell, California's attorney general in 1854 and 1855, was defeated for governor by Leland Stanford in 1861. Niles Searls had been offered the Democratic nomination but refused it before McConnell accepted. Searls later served as Chief Justice of the California Supreme Court, a position

Edwin G. Waite, 1826–1894 (California State Library photo).

Alonzo "Old Block" Delano, 1807–1874.

also held by Lorenzo Sawyer, who was tapped later by President Grant to be the first West Coast U. S. Circuit Judge. Others who sat on the California Supreme Court included Addison C. Niles (cousin of Niles Searls), and Thomas B. McFarland. Thomas P. Hawley became Chief Justice of the Nevada State Supreme Court.

One of California's most popular authors was humorist Alonzo "Old Block" Delano of Grass Valley, whose play, *A Live Woman at the Mines*, was performed on the New York stage. Benjamin P. Avery became the editor of the famous *Overland Monthly* magazine, where Bret Harte began his career. Avery was the U.S. Minister to China when he died. Warren B. Ewer, founder of Nevada City's first newspaper, also published the *California Mining Journal*, and for many years edited the *Mining and Scientific Press* at San Francisco. Edwin G. Waite, a political writer for the San Francisco *Times* and the Sacramento *Union*, campaigned vigorously for President Grant, who rewarded him with the post of Naval Officer of San Francisco; Waite was California's secretary of state when he died.

This sampling suggests the variety and quality of the human resources present in the 1850s in this supposedly uncosmopolitan community. In *The World Rushed In*, J. S. Holliday has excellently described the experience of thousands who came to California for a brief time and went home. I decided it was time to reveal the other side of the rush to California, the story of those who stayed. Originally I had thought it could be told in a single volume, but the richness of available material dictated otherwise, and I settled for a trilogy, *The Nevada County Chronicles*.

Nisenan chief Wema (Peter Shearer photo).

Tallman H. Rolfe, 1824–1872.

Polly Cook Niles, 1803–1873 (Frances G. Long photo).

John Niles, 1797–1872 (Frances G. Long photo).

Gold Diggers and Camp Followers, completed in 1982, describes the period from 1845 to 1851. It opens with Chief Wema and the *nisenan* Indians, who were the area's sole inhabitants before the gold discoveries. The book ends with the creation of a new city and a new county in a new state, and the impoverishment and virtual eviction of the Indians. By means of letters, journals, newspaper accounts, and memoirs I was able to recreate the years before and during the Gold Rush, and show how and why certain persons came to be gathered in a particular location between the Yuba and Bear Rivers on the west slope of the Sierra Nevada.

In this second volume I continue the true stories of Tallman Rolfe (a young printer and apostate Mormon who had worked in newspaper offices at Nauvoo, Oregon City, San Francisco, and Sacramento before coming to Nevada City), and Niles Searls and Charles Mulford (who crossed the plains in 1849 and mined California's streams before opening a book and stationery story at Nevada City in 1850). Sharing the limelight are Niles and Charley's cousins—Cornelia, Mary, and Addison Niles—and assorted friends and relatives from Rensselaerville, New York, many of whom emigrated to Nevada City in the 1850s.

As readers of *Gold Diggers and Camp Followers* already know, my preoccupation with the Rensselaerville families stems from the discovery of more than a thousand unpublished letters written by former inhabitants of this tiny village in the nineteenth century, many of which detailed life in Nevada County. But whereas the letters and diaries contained in

Cornelia Niles Allen, 1827–1928
(Frances G. Long photo).

Mary Niles Searls, 1830–1910
(Frances G. Long photo).

Gold Diggers and Camp Followers were written mostly by unmarried men and women, a large number of those in the second volume were composed by young brides. And, as is well known, when couples marry, it is the women who are expected to take over the correspondence along with other household chores.

Thus we are able to view the period from both male and female points of view, which is immensely more interesting and informative. It seems to me that women tend to offer franker opinions—or at least will put them to paper—on a variety of subjects, including politics, economics and crime. For this reason, and also because so many of the changes in Nevada County were the result of the increased presence of women and children, I chose to call this book *Brides of the Gold Rush*. Without their letters and interpretations I could not have fully understood what happened 130 years ago.

Fortunately Nevada City and Grass Valley boasted three newspapers during the 1850s, which for the most part were ably edited (far better in some respects than their modern counterparts). The editors were well educated, well versed in current events and recent history, and they held strong and positive convictions about personal and national destinies. Even when those views are demonstrably wrong in hindsight or intolerably racist and sexist by today's standards, the intellectual content of what they wrote is also by today's standards arresting.

After reading the manuscript my editor, Lorna Price, commented:

I am somewhat overwhelmed to understand the difference in mid 1800s California between their notions of law and lawlessness, and ours. Jeez, it was a violent time! I always "knew" that in an academic sense, but the daily treating with mayhem—not from Indians, but from white Anglo-Saxon Protestants, friends and neighbors—just astounds me, as does their acceptance of it. It bespeaks a level of social disarray, somewhere down there, that shows nothing to astonish a man of the Dark Ages.

She is absolutely correct. But no less impressive is the evidence that there were sensitive and decent people who resisted lawlessness and bigotry and set high standards for themselves and others, despite the level of popular opinion. All of the people in this book are real—they actually did and said the things attributed to them. A few readers may wonder why some favorite anecdotes are absent. My answer is that if their origin was doubtful I left them out unless I could verify the information from reliable sources.

In this regard I was especially disappointed when a large collection of "letters" attributed to Tallman Rolfe proved to be so full of flawed information that I reluctantly concluded (along with some members of the Rolfe family) that they were fabricated in the twentieth century. They

William W. Allen, 1828–1866
(Frances G. Long photo).

Deborah Wickes Mulford, 1828–19--
(Frances G. Long photo).

appeared first in the Grass Valley *Morning Union* in the summer of 1931 under the heading "Golden Fifties," and apparently were compiled by Belle Rolfe Douglass from old files of the *Nevada Democrat*, which the Rolfe brothers published and sometimes edited.

Instead of relying on questionable information in those supposed letters, I have made use of the original newspaper accounts. For those who would like to read the Douglass letters, they were published by Catherine Webb in *History Reconstructed: Stories of Tallman, Ianthus, Horace and Samuel* (listed in my bibliography and available from the author at 843 Washington Avenue, Albany CA 94706).

I have gathered some information about the Rolfe family and other Mormons in an appendix to the book; in the absence of verifiable correspondence connecting Nevada City with San Bernardino it seemed a good idea to separate them from the main story

One more volume remains to be written, covering the years from 1859 to 1876. These include the civil war years, when Californians were faced with difficult choices. Many returned to their places of birth; some fought and even died for the causes in which they believed. Quite a number went to the new territory of Nevada, where rich silver mines had been discovered, and others remained in Nevada County.

After the war the railroads were built—from coast to coast and within the county itself. Then as now, most former Nevada County residents return sooner or later, often to reestablish residence. Perhaps the greatest reunion of all was held in 1876, jointly honoring completion of the Nevada County Narrow Gauge Railroad and observance of the national centennial. The "Grand Reunion of Pioneers" should provide an appropriate conclusion to *The Nevada County Chronicles*.

I am most grateful to Frances Long and William H. Miller, Jr., for their willingness to share this amazing collection of family letters and photos, and to Fred and Doris Searls for their permission to publish. In addition, I am indebted to Janet Haseley, Inez Miller, and Jack Long, for hours spent in sorting, copying, and packaging letters and documents, and for many excellent suggestions in the course of preparing this volume. The warm trust and interested cooperation of these people has never flagged, and has been a necessary ingredient in the accomplishment of this project.

My dependence on libraries is less now that I can read newspaper microfilm at home, but I continue to rely on the excellent librarians at the Nevada City and Grass Valley public libraries, as well as the devoted volunteers at the Searls Historical Library in Nevada City. In Sacramento I have been helped by the experienced staff at the California State Library and the California State Archives.

Nevada City 1851

CHAPTER 1

NEVADA CITY

August–November 1851

I

UNDREDS OF GOLD MINERS thronged into Nevada City every Sunday, arriving from cabins and tents scattered for miles in every direction. They filled the streets, saloons, and dance halls and bought supplies for the coming week. The short holiday ended in the small hours of Monday morning, and all was quiet until the following Sabbath. For the remainder of the week "business was dull," as local merchants put it—much too dull for Mr. Eldridge, whose theatrical troupe appeared nightly in the second story hall over Hamlet Davis's general store.

On Monday morning Eldridge headed for the rustic shed that housed the weekly *Nevada Journal*—he often found it useful to call on the local editor when he had a problem. Aaron Sargent was an imaginative young man who once again came up with a clever solution: a mid-week theatrical benefit for a popular miner who needed help. Sargent thought such an event would attract an audience and help everyone, Eldridge included.

The *Journal* announced the Thursday night performance for Daniel Smith:

Mr. Smith, after passing a critical and painful period, is slowly recovering and gets about on crutches. His long prostration has reduced him to penury and his family at home to want. He's unable to work—a benefit should be taken for his help in the churches.

Daniel Smith's injury was not caused by mining, but resulted from Sandy Brown's rough treatment of a black woman. Alexander "Sandy" Brown was part-owner of the Empire Saloon, one of the city's two largest gambling establishments; the other was Barker's Exchange on the other side of Main Street.

On Friday, August 1, Sandy was standing in front of U. S. Gregory's boarding house when he heard two women quarreling inside. He recognized the voice of Mrs. Susan Gregory, wife of the landlord—the other belonged to Julia, one of five negroes brought from Missouri by the Gregory family in 1850. Although slavery was prohibited by law, and blacks were technically free in the new state of California, they were slaves if taken back to the south.

When Sandy realized Julia was sassing Mrs. Gregory it made him angry. A southerner, he had firm opinions about appropriate behavior. He entered the hotel, knocked Julia to the floor, kicked her a few times (all the while engaging in a fierce diatribe about manners), and then took his leave, making his way to the Empire Saloon. And there the matter might have ended, except Daniel Smith heard the commotion and investigated the cause. His outraged New England conscience told him to follow Sandy at once.

The gambler was astonished when the tall miner came into the saloon and called him names. Sandy Brown was seated at a faro table, and at first he refused to rise when the strapping Yankee insisted he stand up and fight. Brown tried to reason with the man, but that failing, he got to his feet. Smith promptly hit him in the face, and when the gambler backed away, attempted to grab him in a wrestler's bear hug.

Sandy was a small man, but his profession required resourcefulness to stay alive—as the miner came near, Sandy pulled a pistol from his belt and fired point blank. Before the miner hit the floor, Sandy was off and running, headed for Gregory's hotel. Once there, he implored the landlord to bar all doors and send for the sheriff. No love was lost between gold diggers and the camp followers who relieved them of their hard-earned dust.

Already Sandy could hear shouting and hoofbeats in the street, signs that messengers probably were on their way to the streambeds and tunnels outside the city. In a few minutes he knew there would be a mob outside ready to stretch his neck. Sandy shuddered and hoped the sheriff wasn't in Sacramento. Nevada County was three months old and its officers were new at the job.

His luck held—Sheriff Gallagher was in town. When Gallagher heard the news, he told a deputy to find Judge Caswell and bring him to the hotel. This event could result in the first serious challenge to his authority, and Gallagher wanted all the help he could muster. Unfortunately Caswell was ill, but having reached the same conclusion as the sheriff, he shakily got out of bed, dressed, and reached for his Colt's revolver.

By the time the judge reached Gregory House, a small crowd had gathered, and when Caswell and Gallagher came out with Sandy between them, it had swelled in number. For the merest instant they paused—then Gallagher drew and cocked his pistol. The mob drew back and made room. Trailed by the mob, the three men climbed the steep rise of Main Street. Carpenters stopped work on Rev. Warren's church to see what the fuss was about, and watched the crowd move on and finally halt near the courthouse.

A few men laughed when they saw the sheriff intended holding the gambler in the building they all had known as "The Red Store" before the county rented it. Its name came from the crimson canvas walls surrounding its wooden framework. Thanks to a catastrophic fire which destroyed most Nevada City structures in March, carpenters and saw-mills were overwhelmed with work and could not meet the demand for housing. Even at the exorbitant rent of $200 per month, county officials were lucky to have found this makeshift building.

Gallagher ignored the jibes and laughter. After assigning deputies to positions around the building, he summoned the few county and city officers he could find and ordered a teamster to block Main Street with his wagon. When this had been accomplished, Gallagher climbed onto the wagon and motioned other officials to follow. The crowd watched with mingled curiosity, anger, and impatience.

Gallagher said something, but he couldn't be heard for the noise. As the mob quieted, they heard him say he wouldn't stand for lynching. He received an angry response but ignored it and went on to say there was no reason for citizens to interfere with the law—it might have made sense when the nearest jail and court was at Marysville, but such was no longer

3

the case. He urged the crowd to go home and let the law follow its proper course. The prisoner would get a fair trial.

Many agreed, but others would not accept his arguments and continued to demand direct justice; ropes were produced. Then Stanton Buckner addressed the crowd. A middle-aged lawyer, Buckner was a candidate for district judge in the coming election. Buckner asked them to trust the county officers they had elected. Miners had petitioned the legislature to create a new county with its seat at Nevada City to end mob rule—to resort to it now would carry them beyond the bounds of civilized conduct. They could hardly justify such behavior, he said, particularly to their families in the States.

Judge Caswell added his own plea. He said the court of sessions would begin its term in three days. When he promised to convene the grand jury on Monday, someone shouted that Brown would be long gone by then—it was stupid to believe that he, with all his influential friends, would remain long in a canvas jail! Many echoed their agreement, and the mood again shifted. Loud cries demanded Brown be handed over.

A voice with distinctly Germanic accents sounded from the wagon. Valentine Butsch was a blacksmith, not an orator, but his words had more effect because of their obvious sincerity. The powerfully built Butsch told the mob he trusted the men he had voted into office, but if it would ease the situation, he offered to guard the prisoner himself. Were there ten more who would help him? A chorus of voices told the sheriff he had twenty-four volunteer guards. The crisis was over.

On Monday morning Daniel Smith was still alive, but doctors would not speculate on his future. If he died, a knotty legal problem would arise, for the court of sessions could not try the case, and a murder trial could not take place before the November term of the district court, which met in several counties during the year. But Judge Caswell had promised speedy justice, and he took a chance the victim would live. The indictment was for assault with intent to commit murder.

A number of threats were made on the judge's life before the trial commenced on Wednesday. Brown pleaded self-defense, and his lawyers produced witnesses to substantiate the plea. Since no one could be found to contradict their testimony, the jury found him not guilty. After his acquittal, Sandy Brown paid some of Smith's medical bills, but the miner could not work and had no money. Eldridge's theatrical benefit was successful, however, and the money it raised enabled him to go home to his family.

But no restitution was offered for the unprovoked attack on Julia, nor was Brown charged with assaulting her—under California law, the testimony of a negro was worthless. The only person willing to make a public gesture on Julia's behalf had paid dearly for his act.

II

JUSTICE WAS NOT the only responsibility of the Nevada County Court of Sessions: it also was charged with administering county business. Therefore, during its October term, it purchased land for county buildings and signed contracts for construction of a jail and several bridges, including the new crossing over Deer Creek.

Before the session ended, Sheriff Gallagher received news of a riot at Industry Bar on the Yuba River. Undersheriff Endicott and fifteen deputies went to the river, where they were told forty white miners had seized the rich claims of a Chinese company. Eight claim-jumpers were arrested while sleeping at their camp. Only six were brought to Nevada City, two having escaped enroute. Meanwhile, part of the posse remained on the river and struck a bargain with the Chinese: for half the gold, they would work the claims and protect them from future attacks.

Among those arrested was George M. Dibble, a former U. S. Navy midshipman who came to California as a Pacific Mail Steamship officer, but had been discharged for drunkeness. On the day scheduled for his trial the Nevada *Journal* reported:

The men who left this city to assist the Chinamen on the Yuba have been taking out an average of $1200 per day. They have been threatened by the belligerent party and compelled to exercise vigilance night and day. At one time they were told their foes had obtained a four pounder and would blow them to pieces, but matters have subsided and it will take about three more weeks to work out the claims. The Chinamen seem satisfied with the arrangement and have their share of the proceeds.

Dibble and his companions were released and they went back to Industry Bar. Two weeks later, on November 1, 1851, acting on information that a duel there was imminent, Justice John Anderson issued a warrant for the arrest of the combatants—Dibble, Jim Lundy, and their seconds. But the sheriff was late in arriving. On the same day the *Journal* reported:

A duel took place on the Yuba today about eighteen miles from here, on the spot of the disputed Chinese claims.... A trivial dispute had arisen a few evenings previously during a convivial party ... during which Dibble called Lundy a liar, and to which Lundy replied with opprobrious epithets. Dibble challenged Lundy, the challenge was accepted, the second of Lundy being Chas. E. G. Morse of this city.

The preliminaries were arranged by Gen. Morehead, Dibble's second, and Morse—the parties to stand at fifteen paces and use Colt's revolvers. At the signal, Lundy fired, Dibble reserving his fire. He had previously declared his intention to draw Lundy's fire and then shoot him. After Lundy's fire, Dibble called out with an oath, "you have fired too soon." His second asked, "are you satisfied?" At which Dibble opened his coat and showed where a ball had passed in one side and out the other. He pushed aside those who stepped to support him and walked about 150 yards and expired in about twenty minutes.

In a separate article, editor Sargent gave additional details:

We have been convinced that [Lundy] did his best to avert a meeting, so far as the commonly received notion of men of honor will admit, and even more. On the evening previously he fired at the flame of a candle at eighteen paces with a revolver, and out of six shots snuffed the candle four times and twice grazed the flame. He told persons around to report this to Dibble. And he solemnly told Dibble that if he was compelled to take his station as a mark for Dibble to shoot at, he would certainly kill him. At the last moment he expressed his willingness to forgive the insult if Dibble would withdraw the challenge.

Justice Anderson convened a hearing to examine witnesses. Defense lawyers objected to the employment of Aaron Sargent as court clerk, alleging prejudice; in the paper that morning, the editor had condemned the practice of duelling. But after the motion was denied, the defense assured the editor and the court "no personal disrespect" was intended. District Attorney John R. McConnell put Charles Morse on the stand first.

Morse testified that at the time of the quarrel he had prevented Lundy, much the larger of the two men, from assaulting Dibble, and furthermore, he had subsequently urged both to settle their differences amicably, telling Dibble that Lundy bore him no ill will. He claimed Dibble responded that he would die first.

Dibble's second, General Joseph C. Morehead, offered similar testimony: "Last Thursday I went to Industry Bar and was met by Dibble, who stated to me he had had a difficulty with Lundy. Dibble asked me to act as his friend. I stated I was his friend and would do what I could, and would try to arrange the difficulty amicably—but if a duel was on foot, I'd have nothing to do with it."

Morehead had good reasons for wishing to avoid the notoriety a duel would cause: for seven months he had been a fugitive from California authorities. In April 1851 Governor John McDougal charged him with using the office of State Quartermaster-General to appropriate and dispose of 400 muskets and 90,000 cartridges. According to the governor, Morehead intended to equip a filibustering (freebooting) raid on Mexico, and McDougal asked the legislature to authorize the pursuit and arrest of Morehead. The general was nearly caught in San Diego while enroute to Mexico.

E. B. "Jim" Lundy stood no better with the authorities. No stranger to California courts, he declined to make a statement at the hearing. Two years earlier, Lundy had challenged the president of the Sacramento City Council, and only quick action by friends averted a duel. In the same year Lundy had attacked a Sacramento gambler and lost an eye. While out on bail for this offense, he invaded a Marysville courtroom and tried to rescue a prisoner. When the attempt failed, Lundy was whipped, fined, and thrown in jail.

Justice Anderson concluded the Nevada City hearing by ordering the trio to appear before the court of sessions on December 1. Each was released on $1000 bail. Before the trial took place, a pair of editorials appeared in the *Journal* in which Aaron Sargent assailed Mexico, Mexicans, and Spanish-speaking persons. The milder of the articles dealt with Mexico's many current rebellions, some involving French and American adventurers like General Morehead. Sargent attacked what he termed "the peculiar absorption of official palms in Mexico," charging that the "great ignorance of the masses is the reason of the toleration of affairs too disgraceful to exist among any other people in Christendom."

The second article was concerned with the activities of Spanish-speaking scoundrels, about whom the editor said:

Practiced guerrillas, and robbers from Mexico, familiar with all the details of plunder and blood, and remorseless as Moloch, are scattered all over the State, with opportunity, slaying the traveller, firing our cities for plunder, without a particle of restraining principle.

He spoke of "miscreant Mexicans" who "dabble their hands in human gore as a pastime, slaying with fiendish delight." Sargent concluded by arguing that "extermination of such Ishmaelites is the only safeguard of society, and every one of them put out of the way is a public benefit."

Three days later he found a news story to suit his theme. Rather than wait two days for more complete information, Sargent rushed into print with an "Extra" edition on November 18. The tone of the lead article was more hysterical than factual:

SIX MEN FOUND MURDERED.
MOVEMENTS AT GRASS VALLEY.

Below we give the startling intelligence of the reported murder of six men near Auburn, the organization of a Vigilance Committee at a public meeting at Grass Valley, and the arming and mounting of a company to scour the country for the arrest of the murderers, who are undoubtedly Mexicans, so well known for their fatal skill in the use of the lariat, the marks of which instrument were found on the bodies.

We are also informed by private hand that a man was shot at on the outskirts of Grass Valley this morning. We give the intelligence in advance of our regular issue, in order that our citizens may take such measures in cooperation with our neighbors of Grass Valley as they may deem advisable.

Fellow citizens, this is no time for careless security. The circle that limits the operations of the murderous villains who are ravaging the State is every day contracting, and our fellows will be shot down at our very doors if we do not take measures to arrest it. This very day assemble *en masse*, appoint men and provide them with the means to cooperate with the citizens of Grass Valley.... A vigilance committee should be organized at once, by the unanimous voice of our citizens, to deal fearful retribution on the cool blooded pirates who are so remorselessly slaying our brethren.

When the regular edition of the paper appeared two days later, new information suggested that perhaps Mexicans were not to blame, but Sargent continued to urge preparedness:

Whether the report of the discovery of the six bodies is accurate or not, and there is much reason to doubt it, no one can deny that the present state of society in California ... creates the necessity for the assumption of that attitude by the people by which they can act at short warning in their own defence....

A committee of this sort should be composed of cool, determined, conscientious men, not acting on mere excitement, or love of adventure ... When the ordinary process of law fails to secure the end of its adoption, the people by whose consent all law exists, have a right to take measures tending to the same purpose as law.

There was a certain irony in Sargent's reference to "cool, determined, conscientious men, not acting on mere excitement, or love of adventure." Chosen to lead Grass Valley's armed volunteers was none other than Jim

Lundy—presenting the resolutions was his old foe Albert M. Winn, former president of the Sacramento City Council. And at Nevada City, in response to Sargent's cry to arms, a group of citizens meeting at the Empire Saloon was addressed by General Morehead, wanted embezzler, filibuster, and currently charged with participation in the Lundy-Dibble affair.

The matter of the six murders near Auburn became further confused with the information that three Frenchmen (not Mexicans) had been arrested when they were found occupying the cabin of the victims. But, as the *Journal* reported on December 4: "We understand the belief of folks on the Bar is not unanimous as to their guilt, some believing the murder was perpetrated by Indians."

III

NEVADA CITY, then five months old, was nearly bankrupt by midsummer 1851. Although a citizens' meeting at the Empire Saloon elected representatives to assist the city marshal in the collection of back taxes and overdue fees and fines, little progress had been made in resolving the city's problems.

Nevertheless, Alderman Niles Searls, president of the city's Common Council, did not comment upon such matters when writing home. Nor did he refer to such exciting events as the attempt to lynch Sandy Brown, or the duel of Lundy and Dibble, for as he told his favorite cousin, Mary Niles, "I might interest you with the usual news of the day—Accidents, Encounters, Murders, Gossip, Mining News &c., but prefer to recommend you the public prints for such items."

The most common theme in his letters was the lack of news from home and his growing desire to be reunited with his family in Rensselaerville, New York, and Wellington, Canada. After three years of wandering, Niles Searls longed to see the faces of his loved ones. Despite his multiple occupations as bookseller, lawyer, and politician, his life in California lost much of its savor when Charles Mulford, his friend and partner, left the state to return home to Rensselaerville, New York, after their Nevada City bookstore went up in flames in March. In July, sorry not to be sharing the good times described by Charley and his girl cousins, Niles chided Cornelia Niles about the lionization of his former partner:

... of course Charley has reformed since his return. [He] don't *chew tobacco, smoke* or *gamble.* Mary caps the *climax* by saying he is *"more dignified"* than ever—was it not more *Diggerified* that she meant?

9

On September 10, 1851, he reminisced about the three years past:

... it seems but yesterday that I was on the frontier of [Missouri], looking with longing eyes to the sport and novelty of an excursion over the Rocky Mountains—a few eventful months sped [by], and I was in Cal. All the romance of the journey had fully met my expectations, but as ever in life, with joy and pleasure had been intermingled sorrow and pain. Of that little band of six, Charley and I included, who had at starting been buoyant with expectation, three had found graves far from home and friends, and now as I write, I alone of the number remain in Cal.... Take good care of Charley, for I am told Californians all have a relapse after getting home, and are apt to return here again—judging that he will not be exempt from that malady, I caution you against letting him run loose much, or he will be off.

One would think, to hear you talk of Charley, that he had accomplished some wonderful feat by which your lives were saved, when in fact I s'pose he has only culled some choice flowers, or walked and rode with you a few times—for all of which, of course, you are under *immense* obligations.

On September 27, Niles presided over a special meeting of the town council. An audit of the books showed the city owed more than $9000, though it had only $297 in its treasury. The city was owed $4300 in taxes, licenses, and fines, much uncollectable from persons who had left the county. Responding to demands by an outraged citizenry, the council suspended all civic salaries after October 10. Only a few officers were affected because mayor and aldermen served without pay. A day later, in a sentimental letter to Mary, Niles spoke of his loneliness and anxiety about the future:

I might harp upon the old theme of *no letter from you per last mail*, but that is a theme so common as to excite little notice. Were it thus with any other correspondent than you, or did I know *you* less well, I should in all probability send in my valedictory—but with *you* it is different. So long accustomed to look upon *you*, my beloved Mary, as the personification of all that's true, I cannot, *will not*, harbor the thought that you have changed in the least....

Not till in your own hand you say you are changed in sentiment will I harbor a thought of your being different from what you were three years ago, when I used to tell my tale of love and listen to your words of approval.... How I long for the time when I can again take you by the hand, look upon your calm, loving face and be happy....

When I think of it, I almost condemn the stupidity that keeps me here, but again my best reason prompts me yet to tarry for a while. Do not, dear Mary, I pray you, deem me indifferent because I stay so long. Could you know all my feelings and see me in my lonely moods, I *know* you would think me more than desirous to come home. I know I might come at once, but it would be at the sacrifice of the little which I have gained by staying this long. As it is, [Billy] Williams and I are thinking of coming sometime from Jan. to April—more probably the latter. . . .

You ask me for a description of my plans and expectations for the future. I do not think it would be best to describe them all, as they will doubtless be abandoned when I get home. Then, however, I promise you them all, with particulars and reasons. . . . And now, my guardian Angel, I must bid you a "good night."

One morning in mid-November, acting on a sudden impulse, Niles boarded the stage for Sacramento, the first leg of his journey East. With him was Israel Hirst, a well-to-do Nevada City merchant and banker. Niles was grateful for the older man's company, for Billy Williams was unable to leave at this time. Hirst left a large sum of money with the Reverend Mr. Warren to help the sick and needy through the coming winter. Hirst himself was not well, but hoped to recover his health in Ohio and return with his family in the spring.

As the stage rocked over the rough road going out of town, Niles glanced back at the city. It had changed dramatically during his stay, and he was beginning to discover how much of himself was invested in the place. Perhaps, he thought, as the stage jolted around a bend and plunged toward the crossing at Little Deer Creek, only in Rensselaerville could he gauge the true worth of that investment.

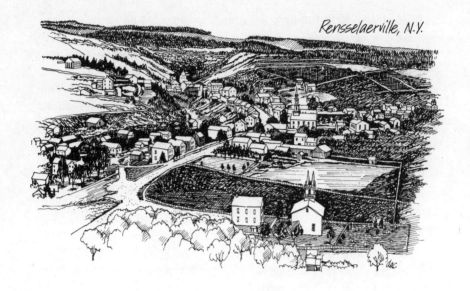

Rensselaerville, N.Y.

CHAPTER 2

GOING HOME

December 1851–April 1852

I

*C*ROSSING THE PLAINS in 1849 took five months. In 1851 Niles
traveled from San Francisco via the Isthmus of Panama to New
York in little more than a month. Having heard endless stories about the
horrors and beauties of the isthmus, he was appropriately curious. The
hazards included such diseases as cholera, typhus, malaria, yellow fever
and dysentery, as well as being robbed or even killed by thieves.

At Panama the passengers disembarked and hired mules and drivers
for the overland trip to Gorgona. It was late when they reached the
midpoint of the trail and found the hotel's dining room closed, but Niles
and others offered a premium to be fed. Beside the table at which they ate
was another over which a large cloth had been spread. At first Niles
assumed it concealed dirty dishes, but when he asked if cholera was
prevalent thereabouts, he was told the shroud covered the deceased hotel
keeper.

Next day they boarded a small steamer for the four-mile trip down
the Chagres River; in earlier years travelers had been transported in

native boats. The sidewheeler took its passengers to a crude port at the new town of Aspinwall, and from there another steamship carried them to New York City, where they arrived in mid-December, almost on the heels of a pair of well-known refugees from Europe: Louis Kossuth, the self-exiled leader of a failed Hungarian revolutionary government, and Lola Montez, professional dancer and former mistress of King Ludwig I of Bavaria.

Despite his own long absence from the Atlantic States, Niles was familiar with both names, for California papers reprinted many stories from the eastern press, items such as this from the Nevada *Journal*:

Lola Montes, the real bona fide Lola, is now under the instruction of a celebrated dancing master, in London, resuscitating the performances on the light fantastic toe, which made her distinguished in her youth, and which brought her to the notice of her old royal lover, in whose palace she soon forgot the art which had before given her her bread. It is said that she will accompany Mr. Barnum in America in the fall, and give a series of flings and twirls, at each of the principal theatres of the Union. The disgraceful celebrity which she has acquired will, doubtless, cause as great a rush to see her as there has been to hear the pure, noble minded Jenny Lind. But so it is with people in general.

Following her exile from Bavaria in 1848, Lola traveled about in Switzerland, England and France. But when she married the young heir to an English fortune, his family interfered. Lola was arrested and charged with bigamy, not having divorced her first husband. Suspecting America would not take to Lola's free and easy ways, Barnum declined to book her.

On the other hand, Jenny Lind's reputation was such that Barnum engaged her for 100 concerts without hearing her sing. From the moment of her arrival in 1850 the Swedish Nightingale was an immediate hit. Addison Niles went to Boston from Williams College to hear Jenny sing in June 1851. Afterwards, he gave this "brief sketch of my adventures" in a letter to his sister Cornelia:

We had a long, dusty and tedious ride for ⅔ of the way, and a heavy rain storm the rest. We arrived in Boston about 5 P.M. . . . . myself and one other student (a Bostonian) went direct to the Old State House to secure tickets for J. Lind's Grand Concert. We found only 2 or 3 left, which had been sent back to be resold on account of the rain, and for which we had to pay $5 apiece.

We then went to the Adams House and took supper, and immediately started for the concert. We found Tremont Temple nearly full, although it was a full hour before the time. At length, after one or two splendid pieces by the greatest orchestra in the world, *Jenny* appeared. I would not undertake to express in words anything about her singing. The first line of the first song would almost have paid for the trip to Europe. She was welcomed with such a burst of spontaneous heartfelt applause as no one else in the world would be by such an audience.... Next to the bird song, the 2 Scotch songs, "Old Robin Grey" and "Comin thro' the Rye" were in my opinion the best, and it needs no critic to judge of her.

Mulford, Niles, Searls, Wickes families to 1859

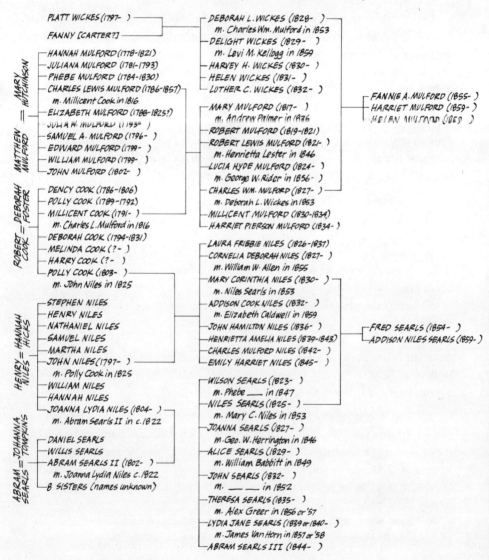

A month later, Addison's sister accompanied Charley Mulford to Albany to hear the singer. Cornelia said she occupied "one of the best seats" in the Third Presbyterian Church, and watched Jenny through "a good opera glass." She was "in a seventh heaven" when she returned home, according to sister Mary.

II

INSTEAD OF GOING directly to his home in Canada, Niles took a steamer to Albany and caught the stage to Rensselaerville. Much as he desired to see his own family, he wanted even more to be reunited with Mary, a moment delayed too long already.

To his vast relief, she and her family greeted him with open arms and no recriminations. They were delighted to see him sooner than expected, and not greatly surprised, having grown accustomed to his manner of making abrupt moves after long periods of indecision. Contributing to their pleasure was the opportunity once again to jointly celebrate the birthdays of Cornelia, twenty-four, and Niles, twenty-six. It was the first time in four years that all the cousins celebrated the holidays under one roof.

For the next several days, Niles entertained family and neighbors with his hilarious and barely credible tales about life in the far west. Eventually Mary complained that she and Niles were being offered few opportunities for privacy—it was also true she was growing weary of the yarns about "fair Señoritas," with which he teased her.

During those infrequent moments when she had him to herself, Mary quizzed Niles about his plans for the future. Despite the pressure of her wishes that he remain in the east and seek opportunities closer at hand, Niles's characteristic ambiguity influenced his thinking. His logical arguments had merit—he wanted to start married life in comfort, wanted to put something by for the future, and the opportunities in California for a young man were extraordinary. But there seemed to be a more complex dimension to his indecision. After all, Niles had gone west, had "seen the elephant," and nothing afterward could look the same.

But there was no way to communicate this to Mary, who remained apprehensive at the prospect of another year's separation, perhaps two. So it can have caused her nothing but pain to understand that whether Niles stayed or went would in fact depend not on her desire to get on with their life together, but rather on whether Charley Mulford decided to return to California. If he did go west again, Niles would surely go with him.

III

WILL ALLEN CAME to the village in 1850, at age twenty-one. Like most young ladies in the Rensselaerville Reading Circle, Cornelia was fascinated by the academy's newest principal, although she was nearly two years older. Even his diminutive size did nothing to lessen Will's popularity. Soon after his arrival Cornelia told Addison he was "gaining esteem and respect day by day. . . . He has a very clear head, good taste, is perfectly upright, and has as kind a heart as ever beat." In February she wrote:

I did not mean to say one word about him, but somehow his name has slipped in once or twice, so I'll tell you that [Will Allen] has the worst fit of 'blues' since you left I ever saw him attacked with. . . . His blues are caused by a want of society of taste and education equal to his own, I am confident, but it cannot be remedied here.

Meanwhile, the subject of her compassion had written of Rensselaer-ville's delights to a former classmate. Henry M. Taylor, himself a teacher in Illinois, replied:

If you find intelligence and refinement in that host of Ladies around you, you are vastly better off in this respect than I am. I am glad to find your merits are becoming appreciated by them—and you must not too modestly attribute all your success to your circumstances—better conclude its owing chiefly to something they discover in *you*, your-self. . . . I am more than half inclined to suspect, my friend, that what you apply to the whole class has a more particular meaning. Isn't there some "bright particular star" in that galaxy of beauty?

In February 1851, Delight Wickes and Cornelia composed a letter on behalf of the reading circle to thank Mr. Allen "for his pleasing and appropriate address, and assure him that no feast of sugar plums and almonds was ever better relished. We admire the taste which, discriminating, distributes toys to children and more rational amusements to the more mature mind."

In July Will Allen wrote Elias Warner, a college friend who was teaching in Virginia, comparing their situations:

... though not favored with the society of superiors, which is highly necessary to a young man, I find equals who sympathise with me, and whose influence is improving and elevating. Not much among my own sex, it is true, but with the fair. The young ladies here are some of them quite superior, and I am on terms of intimate friendship with them.

I never knew before what sincere cordial female friendship was, and I assure you it is one of the loveliest flowers of Life. I am not now speaking of anything warmer, or softer, than friendship. However much you may suspect the existence of such a feeling, it is not that.

A third correspondent, Charles Stowell, recently returned to Chicago from California, chided Will after receiving a similar letter:

It is possible—nay, when I consider your rather susceptible nature, I think it more than probable—that a stronger excitement than that which urges the scholar into the intellectual arena, a passion more intense than the desire of fame, has occupied your time to the exclusion of all objects save one. How ist? has some beautiful Blumine bewitched you? Has she a bosom white as snow?

Soon after the start of his fall term, Cornelia observed that Allen seemed "somewhat discouraged." And in a letter to Warner, Allen confided:

I desire to go South myself, and shall embrace the earliest good offer I have. If you know of any openings in your vicinity, please recommend me, unless Taylor has a prior claim; as he is out of business now, of course I will waive for him. . . . My school here paid pretty well last year, and my prospects are still better this year I think. Still, I desire to enlarge my experience, and would be willing to leave here for any other equally good situation.

Rose King, once a rival for Will's attention, in December conceded the field to Cornelia:

Does Mr. Allen continue to teach, and how does he and my friend Cornelia get along? Between you and me, I wish you would play the agreeable, and he play the part (so natural to him) of an intellectual and interesting gentleman—thus forming an *everlasting friendship*, which happily often ends in love—true and lasting—making two persons mutually happy in each others society—as I know "little Allen" and you would be.

Cornelia was so absorbed in the affairs of Will Allen that she failed to notice the growing attention paid her by Charley Mulford. This oversight was due partly to long familiarity and her fondness for her cousin, whom she assumed still carried a torch for Deborah Wickes. But the Charley who came back from California was not the boy who left the village in 1849. Once he saw Deb had not changed in her devotion to Loyd Copeland, Charley decided to look in other directions. It was natural that his attention should focus on cousin Cornelia, who had been his most faithful correspondent for two years.

Because his hours were flexible and his California fortune permitted him more freedom than most, Charley could spend time escorting Cornelia about, as when he took her to Albany to hear Jenny Lind. Unfortunately Cornelia, not realizing she was being courted, was conscious only that Charley's new maturity made him a more interesting companion. When his partner returned to Rensselaerville, Charley supposed Niles and Mary would become engaged; but when he declared his own intentions toward Cornelia, everything went up in smoke. To his great chagrin, Cornelia reacted with shocked disbelief, and he retreated in anger and mortification.

The longer Charley pondered her refusal, the more he convinced himself she had led him on. His mind was filled with visions of Cornelia pretending to share his feelings while teasing and laughing with her friends behind his back. Considering his earlier rejection by Deborah, he now imagined it would be unbearable to remain at Rensselaerville where everyone shared village gossip. Charley thus resolved to go as far from his home town as possible.

His decision pleased Niles, who had no inkling of what had transpired between his friends; he had frequently remarked that Charley was the finest companion a man could hope to have on a trip to California, and thus their decision to return to Nevada City arose from Charley's anguish.

IV

RENSSELAERVILLE'S MOST ELIGIBLE bachelors were missing when the new year began. Charley and Niles had gone to Canada, and Will Allen was at his parents' home in Canaan, New York. Charley Mulford spent a month in Canada. On the way back he tried to visit Fred Pearks, with whom he and Niles crossed the plains in 1849, but discovered Fred had already gone back to California. On February 3 Charley came home. Niles would follow in a few days, and the two expected to leave for California on February 23. Another cousin, William Tompkins, was departing even sooner, and Billy Williams, who had reached Rensselaerville at last, was also heading back to California as soon as possible.

"Who knows when we will all be here again together?" lamented Cornelia. Mary wrote Addison, now in his senior year at Williams, "I want to tell you how very lonely I have been since you went away. True, your departure was not the *only* cause of my loneliness, but it gave the

finishing touch, and it seemed to me I never missed you so much before."
On March 11 she wrote of the cheerful holiday confusion:

Niles had been here about a week, Aunt Dency a few days, Mrs.
Devereux and Horace had come to spend a day or two, and Joseph
[Murphy] had just arrived in the stage. At the same time, Aunt Dency was
preparing for a tea-party at one place, and all of us young people [went]
to meet Billy Williams and others "in the neighborhood of twenty" at
[Dr. Wickes's house].

We had a glorious time, and I think even you would not have
objected to *such* a *tea-party*. It was rare sport to hear the "three
Californians" spin their yarns, especially when they would bring each
other out by telling the same story in a new way. Niles came the
overland route from Canada with a horse and cutter of his own, which
he used to drive about the country while here, and then sold it to Arthur
Hagadorn for what he gave for it, viz $100.

He and Charlie went to N. York a week ago last Monday, intending to
get tickets to sail immediately if they could do so by paying a high
premium, and we supposed we should not see them again, but Thursday
afternoon they suddenly made their *reappearance*, and now perhaps
you would like to have me come to the point and inform you whether
they are still in the land of Sabbath and civilization, or whether they
have taken their departure for the Land of golden dreams and visions. . . .

Suffice it to say, they started again from here on Monday of this week,
with tickets in their possession for a cabin passage on the steamer that
was to start next day (tickets $330 each). We shall therefore take it for
granted they are gone until we hear to the contrary.

Perhaps you wonder why I am so cheerful about their departure,
when I am so *deeply interested*—so do our people, when they see me
busy as usual, and apparently as thoughtless. They know not the deep
oppressive feelings of loneliness, the *tearless* sorrow which weighs so
heavily upon me. Four long years of silent suffering have given me a self
control which I think few girls of my age possess. Do not think I am going
to be sentimental and pine away because Niles is to be absent a year or
two. I *could* if I would, but I *will not*. I will not only appear, but *be*
cheerful, and wait patiently his return. Is not that right.

Nevertheless, on April 15, Cornelia told Addison of her concern
about Mary's obviously depressed spirits:

It seemed dreary enough after Niles' departure. I would have given very much to have had you here then. Mary seemed so dispirited. I could not get up any kind of smile [from her], and I could not get her out, and if I left her alone a half an hour I found her giving herself up to grief—and my spirits nearly failed too, but gay, hopeful letters from Niles last mail brightened up her face not a little, and seemed to make all more cheerful in sympathy.

Cornelia said nothing of the letter she had received earlier from Charley. It contained nothing gay or hopeful—on the contrary, it was a most unpleasant epistle, in which the disappointed Charley accused her (wrongly, she thought) of the most terrible things. Even now, with the letter in front of her, she found it hard to believe Charley could imagine her capable of such misdeeds.

After the 1852 flood

CHAPTER 3

GROWING PAINS

March–July 1852

I

*I*N A LETTER to Cornelia, written aboard the steamer *Ohio* on March 21, 1852, Niles described the first leg of their journey to Panama:

I came down from the deck a few minutes since, where I had been walking for an hour or more since tea, inhaling the balmy air and watching the twinkling stars, as one by one they became visible in the Heavens. On reaching the cabin I found the tables pretty generally surrounded by *dutiful sons, loving husbands*, and *amorous swains*, all busily engaged in inditing the particulars of their *hairbreadth escapes, imminent perils* and *wondrous achievements* since embarking on the "treacherous deep," for the benefit of their respective friends at home.

Well, thinks I to myself, can't I write to somebody too.... I have a strong inclination to adopt the fellow directly opposite me, with the *short vest*, and *neckcloth* turned under his *ear*, as my model. Then you will be sure of a *loud letter*, and judging from the size of his letters, he either left school immediately after becoming familiar with large hand, [or] else his friends are like the Irishman's mother, *very deaf.*

No doubt too, he will give the full particulars of the voyage from the first day out, up to this date—tell his mother that we have *"more nor"* three hundred passengers—that the wind blew like it would blow down a barn—how the ship rocked like a cradle—how skeezy and sick he felt—how turkey, duck, pudding, fruit and nuts all lost the power to provoke an appetite, and finally that a *crisis* came, when he felt so bad he *had* to *lie down* and his *dinner had* to *come up—*

Then too, he will tell all about Havana—how the people are all tinctured Ethiopian—that they do not take Breakfast 'till after Dinner, and Supper till next morning. The fact that *garlics* are used in preference and to the exclusion of onions, will doubtless prejudice him against the Havanians to an extent too great to remain an impartial historian, consequently I shall leave him to vent his spleen without farther comment.

How do you feel tonight, Cornelia, are you in good health and spirits? Do you feel as tho' you could obey the scriptural injunction to love your neighbor as yourself? Notice, it don't say *neighbors*, so I suppose you can have the privilege of selecting such *one* of *them* as you please. . . .

Seriously, though Cornelia, you asked me once or twice what I thought of Mr. Allen, and by indefinite replies I think I conveyed the idea that I did not admire him particularly. I meant before I left to have told you my candid opinion of the gentleman, but forgot to do so.

Let me briefly say that from the little that I saw of him, I esteem him as a gentleman, and believe him to possess more than ordinary talent. That his intellect is well cultivated is very apparent. I can't say what I would like to here, but remember that in what I do say, I am earnest.

Do you recollect my voyage from Oregon to Cal. on the Sea Gull [with] Capt. Tichner? Rather a poor boat, but the *very best* captain that ever walked a deck. A gentleman—a scholar, and a seaman—were I a captain, he would be my *model.* Well—the news met us at Havana that the Sea Gull was lost at the mouth of the Klamath River, and her noble Capt. drowned. I always feel interested in the fate of every vessel that carries me safe through a voyage, and when I learned of the loss of this one with her commander, I certainly felt *very, very* sorry.

Captain William Tichenor had navigated the treacherous waters between San Francisco and Portland many times in the two years before the sea claimed the 400-ton *Sea Gull.*

Charley and I have a State Room by ourselves and have comfortable times—he gets low spirited sometimes, but being pretty well acquainted with his peculiarities, I know how to cheer him up. No danger but we will get along all right and if spared, be back in due time. At least I shall, unless some unforeseen circumstances should prevent, and of *that* I have no fear.

This will probably be our last night on the "Ohio," as we expect to reach Navy Bay about 2 oclock P.M. on the morrow. I have become quite fond of being at *sea*. The motion of the ship just suits me. It seldom rolls so much that I can't walk the decks—we have about twenty ladies on board, all of them, I think, *married ones*. California forever! When graced with woman's presence, it will be a *Paradise*.

After crossing the Isthmus, Niles and Charley boarded the steamer *Northerner*. The ship was filled nearly to capacity when it steamed out of Panama on the last day of March. Among those on board was a young man whose father, like themselves, was selling books in California's northern mines. It was Hubert Bancroft's first trip west.

About forty or fifty miles south of Acapulco they sighted the wreckage of the steamship *North America*, which had gone aground five weeks earlier. Late on the night of February 27, on a calm sea and under clear moon, the captain had inexplicably turned his ship toward the beach. All 1000 persons on board had come ashore and walked to Acapulco.

The beached passengers expected to be rescued once news of their predicament reached San Francisco. Many were short of funds and could ill afford the added expense of buying meals and lodging at the Mexican port. A few had to rely on the charity of other passengers.

Unfortunately, most steamers heading north were overloaded when they left Panama or Nicaragua. Passengers on the *Tennessee* raised about $700 for their relief, but there was no room for the victims. The *Pacific* and the *Monterey* were equally crowded. Finally, three Mexican sailing vessels were chartered for the trip to San Francisco, and these took off with several hundred passengers aboard.

Thirty-seven persons, including the last of the women and children, bought passage on the *Panama* when it came on March 19. Among their number were Jonas Winchester and his family, enroute to Nevada County. Ten days later, the *Oregon* rescued eighty persons, and after Niles and Charley's ship refueled with coal, eighty men were taken aboard her, too.

So far, only those with money had been rescued. Not until April 24, ten days after Niles and Charley reached San Francisco, would the 350 remaining passengers be picked up by owners of the wrecked ship. On May 15, the first of the chartered Mexican vessels entered San Francisco Bay, followed in a few days by the rescue ship *Northernlight*.

II

A NEW CATASTROPHE had overwhelmed Nevada City in the spring of 1852, and as their stage rolled to a halt alongside the debris-strewn banks of Deer Creek, Niles and Charley saw that the bridges to Main and Broad streets had vanished. Buildings near the creek had been demolished or randomly relocated. A tree had been felled across the stream, and passengers carried their baggage across this makeshift bridge.

Niles and Charley found accommodations at Gregory House, which had burned in February and reopened in March under the management of Dr. William Alban, son-in-law of U. S. Gregory. Dr. Alban also was part-owner of the *Nevada Journal*, and from him they heard about the devastating spring flood.

First there had been snow, he said, and that was followed by three days of rain. On the night of March 5, the Jenny Lind Theatre and several other structures were threatened by the rapidly rising creek. The theater was new and had opened its doors shortly after Niles left the city. It was between the two bridges, and partly overhung the creek's north bank.

During the night a large log swept downstream and collided with the posts supporting the theater. In the morning the Broad Street bridge broke loose and washed away. At noon a log hit the Main Street bridge, lifted it from its foundations, and both log and bridge smashed into the Jenny Lind, tossing it and the Illinois Hotel into the swirling waters.

Dr. Alban described how Patrick Berry's naked corpse turned up on a sandbar three miles downstream from the city. The body had multiple bruises and a stab wound, and because Berry was seen last at her shack, a prostitute known as Harriet was arrested with her pimp. The two were jailed, and by coincidence a second miner fell into the creek the same day. The current carried him off before he could be rescued, and it was three days before the body was found. It, too, was badly bruised, and stripped of clothing. Justice Zeke Dougherty, acting as coroner, ordered Berry disinterred, and a revised verdict of accidental death brought about the quick release of Harriet and her friend.

While Charley looked for a store to rent, Niles called on old friends who told him the city's charter had been revoked. Because Assemblyman Edward Ellis's bill to dissolve the government contained a clause requiring the city's debts to be paid by a special tax, rumor said it was designed to benefit the bill's author and his cronies. Ellis responded indignantly in an open letter to the *Journal*:

I consulted with many of the citizens on this subject before I left, and never heard the idea of repudiation advanced until now ... a rumor is circulated ... that I am the holder of city scrip, and am influenced by interested motives in having the city debts paid. If this were true, I am at a loss to know by what newly discovered rule ... I should be debarred from receiving my just dues, simply because I happen to represent the people.... But it is not true that I hold one cent of city scrip, nor have I ever been interested farther than the amount of eleven dollars, and that I freely forgive them....

No one opposed more than I did the city organization, or was more anxious for its abolition; but I cannot be brought to believe that justice would be consulted by wiping out, with a single dash of the pen, the entire debts of the city.... Having never repudiated my own debts, I cannot persuade myself that a city or a state possess the right to set me or any of its citizens so pernicious an example.

Untrue charges were also made that the bill would pay salaries of city officers to the time of passage. Isaac Williamson was appointed to collect all claims and list all unsold city property. He computed more than $9000 in debts and only $750 in assets. Williamson favored reconveying the city hall and hospital properties to the mortgage holders, for a falling market had reduced their worth. This would bring the total debt to under $8000, supposed to be paid by a special property tax on city residents.

But not all city dwellers owned property, so there was an outcry from those who did, and who persuaded the legislature to pass an "explanatory act" which allowed the county court of sessions to levy a poll or head tax of up to two dollars. Added to the state poll tax of three dollars per adult male, this would amount to about a day's earnings in 1852. So far the court of sessions had failed to levy the special tax.

Niles also discussed the Lundy dueling case with County Prosecutor John R. McConnell, who said all charges had been dropped. The first trial in December found Lundy guilty, but to the prosecutor's disgust, many persons petitioned the outgoing governor to pardon Lundy. It was well known that Governor John McDougal opposed the law against dueling when he was a delegate to the State Constitutional Convention in 1849. At that time he argued that duelists benefited society by eliminating each other. Ironically, when McDougal's term expired in January 1852, one of his first acts had been to challenge a San Francisco editor, whom he wounded but did not kill.

The petition for Lundy proved unnecessary. When the trial of Morse and Morehead began (for seconding Lundy and Dibble), their lawyers claimed the indictments were faulty because too many persons were ⌐

the grand jury. Judge Caswell (who had signed Lundy's petition to the governor) agreed, so Lundy's lawyer successfully argued to arrest judgment in his case also. Both cases were put off until February.

A new grand jury again indicted them, and this time the judge supported defense claims that the witness list was flawed. McConnell, who knew the charge was baseless, angrily wrote the *Journal* to explain. His letter concluded:

I have written this communication in order to set myself right before the people who have selected me ... and because as the prosecuting officer of the county, I am held responsible for the miscarriage of all public prosecutions. In this case, I believe that no rightful blame can attach to me, and I have borne enough already of other people's faults to become somewhat sore under the imposition, and have resolved to bear them no more.

The Lundy affair was resurrected one more time, but McConnell knew when he was licked. Reported the *Journal*:

People vs. E. B. Lundy, Morse and Morehead.—This case came before the court yesterday, and the County Attorney entered a *nolle prosequi*. The reasons, as we understand them, are these: The case has already been twice before the court, and it would now be almost impossible to get a jury who has not already expressed an opinion in the case, and as the pecuniary affairs of the county are somewhat deranged, its further prosecution could have no other effect than to run the county to an additional expense. Moreover, as other men, even high in authority, have been allowed to go out and shoot at each other to their satisfaction, and no attempt made to bring them to justice, the law against duelling is regarded as a dead letter.

III

MAY'S MID-MONTH STEAMER brought news from Cornelia that lowered Niles's spirits. She told him Charley had made some very unpleasant accusations about her, none of them true. She had no intention of replying to Charley, now or ever again. Astonished and dismayed, Niles asked his best friend to explain. Charley, embarrassed but unrepentant, showed him a copy of the letter, which proved every bit as offensive as Cornelia had claimed.

Niles had said little at the time, knowing Charley well enough to realize he would not slander Cornelia intentionally; Charley believed the truth of what he had said. An apology certainly was due Cornelia, but none would come soon. After searching his own conscience, on May 22 Niles decided to write Cornelia and begin the long process of healing the breach:

My first impulse on reading your letter was to brand Charley as an unfeeling wretch unworthy the respect of men. I was more angry than I had been for months. I knew that Charley had left a letter of explanation of some kind with you—for he told me so—told me, too, that it was one of a character "not to be understood in but one sense." But I did not think he would deliberately aim to wound your feelings in the manner he had (I have seen a copy of it) in that note.

Anger has given way to sorrow now on my part, and I only regret that any cause of difference should exist between those whom I esteem as highly as I ever have you and Charley. I have always accustomed myself to think that whatever either of you said or [thought] was about right—Now I am called upon to decide in my own mind which is *wrong*.

Reason would say it is an easy task, but I do not like to blame Charley. My feelings are all averse to it—so I try to excuse him. And Cornelia, I really think there is some excuse for him. In the first place, I believe he was really mistaken in his interpretation of your feelings. When he discovered his mistake, instead of attributing it to his own want of discernment, he very naturally came to the conclusion that *you* had changed.

His pride mortified, and unable to appreciate you in your real character, what has followed is not to me singular. Perhaps under similar circumstances Cornelia, *you* and *I* might act similarly. I do not think we would be as liable to make the like egregious mistakes, but *once perpetrated*, I fear the result would be very nearly the same.

I think I know you *too well* to fear your blaming me for thus defending Charley. That he has wronged you, I admit, but don't, I implore you, Cornelia, infer hence that he is changed in every respect. In some respects he *is* changed, and from being constantly with him I notice it more particularly than others. That this thing will eventually make some slight alteration in the relations existing between Charley and I, there is not much doubt. All I can do is to remember that for years we have been the best of friends—that I have always been treated kindly by Charley, and endeavor to treat *him* in the same manner.

When I began to write, it was in such light spirits that I was almost disposed to treat the whole matter as a kind of joke. But I have concluded to speak of the matter just as I felt. Time, that soother of troubles, will efface the blots of sorrow and grief left upon memory's leaf. I took occasion to learn from Charley that no one had learned from *him* anything of what I have spoken, myself excepted.

Not a month passed without a sentence or two in the *Journal* thanking Mulford and Searls for presenting some magazine or other to the editor. It was an inexpensive method of advertising. They also were agents for Gregory's Atlantic and Pacific Express. An iron safe in the back of their store held gold dust and other valuables for their clients, and there were many who thought what the county needed was an equally secure receptacle for its prisoners.

Ambitious plans for a county jail had been prepared in August 1851, but the lowest construction bid of $1830 cash exceeded the amount in the county treasury. Revised plans called for a smaller structure, less than half the original size, but still made of sturdy, hand hewn twelve by twelve timbers, lined with two inch planks. Nevertheless, on May 3, 1852, the court of sessions again rejected all bids as too high. Judge Caswell proposed that the matter be postponed for three months, but Zeke Dougherty (sitting in for Justice John Anderson) objected to the delay. Dougherty wanted to give bidders a chance to withdraw and resubmit their bids.

At this juncture, County Assessor Wilson and Sheriff Endicott offered to build the jail for $5800 in county scrip, which was $4000 more than the original bid, but less than those submitted on the revised plans. Wilson and Endicott shared an interest in jails, for the assessor had served as the county's first undersheriff. Furthermore, in their roles as tax assessor and tax collector, they were uniquely positioned to see that their scrip was redeemed promptly.

When Justice Dougherty called in the next lowest bidder, B. F. Dickerman, and said he'd have to drop his price to get the job, the contractor refused. When the contract was awarded to Wilson and Endicott, there followed an immediate uproar from other bidders. A letter to the *Journal* from "A Mechanic" queried: "Was the advertisement for proposals to build a jail a mere bait or not? . . . It certainly looks as if there was something 'rotten in Denmark.' " Judge Dougherty said he didn't think the letter was written by a mechanic, but came "from the pen and silly brain of some low pettifogger."

Edwin R. Budd, editing the *Journal* while Sargent was in the East, admitted, "we do not pretend to understand the maneuvering by which it was brought about." Another bidder quoted county statutes to show the contract ought to have gone to the lowest bid received *before* the closing. When county officials refused further comment, Budd wrote:

It seems that the only ground upon which complaint is founded is that the bid of Wilson & Endicott was not given in on the day advertised. . . . We know not when this bid was offered, and so far as the public is concerned, it makes no difference. It is perhaps a hard matter to excuse an officer for violation of official duty. But it is not charitable to censure severely when the act performed was practically right.

But all agreed a jail was needed. On the night of May 22 burglaries occurred at the homes of Rev. James Warren and James Churchman. On June 9 members of San Francisco's Committee of Vigilance arrested a negro at Nevada City; he was alleged to have committed a series of robberies in the bay city. On the following day John Barrett was caught by the night patrol after robbing several cabins on the ridge above Nevada City.

Barrett was known as a "hard case." In 1850, while a soldier at Camp Far West, he was convicted of stealing $1200 in gold. When he refused to confess or reveal the whereabouts of the loot, Alcalde Stephen Field of Marysville ordered him whipped fifty times, and for every twenty-four hours that passed without his revealing his cache, Barrett was to receive fifty additional strokes, until a maximum of 250, "well laid on," had been received. Barrett confessed after twenty strokes, but was given thirty more and branded with the letter "R" (for rogue), and drummed out of the service. Field justified the sentence by saying it was better than hanging.

In April 1852, Barrett was caught immediately after stealing a pistol from a Nevada City store. Because they recovered the gun, store owners declined to prosecute. Barrett next went to Stocking Flat, where he robbed a miner of gold and coins valued at $357. At Newtown he tried to spend it at Hubardis Schardin's store, but was identified as the thief. A miner's jury found him guilty on May 31, gave him fifty lashes and ordered him out of Newtown.

He went directly to Coyoteville, on the ridge above Nevada City, where he committed the thefts which led to his latest arrest. On his person were found a galvanized watch, a gold chain, some thimbles, combs, knitting needles, and religious tracts. He was indicted by the grand jury on June 11, not only for the Coyoteville thefts, but also for the $357 taken at Stocking Flat, for which the miners had punished him.

Many thought Barrett was insane because of his clumsiness and the small worth of objects he sometimes took. Normally the penalty for such crimes would not have been great, but on account of his record and public outrage over increased crime, local attorneys feared a jury would impose the death sentence. California's 1852 laws permitted the hanging of thieves; it was supposed that only a guilty plea would save his life.

After the prisoner had been persuaded to follow this course, attorney Hiram Hodge unexpectedly appeared on behalf of Barrett, and withdrew his plea. A trial followed, with the predicted result. On June 19 the *Journal* reported: "[Barrett] is to be hung on Friday July 16th. He has been taken to Marysville for safe keeping, where we hope he may remain until the allotted time. . . ."

This was to be the county's first legal execution. Five extralegal hangings had taken place a month earlier, and only the prompt arrival at Newtown of the undersheriff and district attorney had saved a pair of accused thieves. Four Indians—Jala, Lono, Kamalok and Hokapa—had been tried June 2 at Wilson's Ranch by a miners' court for the killing of Martin Hopkins. Kamalok alone had been acquitted. The arrow-pierced body of Dwight Comstock was found four days later in a ravine close to the Bridgeport road.

Wema, chief of the Nevada County *nisenan*, had been notified, and on June 9 he delivered two Indians to miners at French Corral, in accordance with the agreement he had signed at Camp Far West. It stipulated that whenever a member of Wema's tribe broke American laws, he was to bring the guilty party before the local justice of the peace. In return, the Americans said they would punish whites who committed crimes against Indians.

On July 15 Barrett was taken from Marysville to Nevada City. Among the escorting party was Father John Shanahan, a Catholic missionary newly arrived in California, where he had been assigned to the northern mining camps. Because Barrett had asked to be executed early in the morning, a volunteer guard composed of Nevada City lawyers gathered outside the jail at 9 o'clock.

At 9:30 the prisoner's irons were removed. He was helped into a shroud and put into a cart, along with his coffin. The guard formed a hollow square around the cart, which they escorted to a flat east of town. A large crowd of citizens followed. At the gallows, Barrett got out and mounted the scaffold, taking a seat next to Father Shanahan. For a few moments he spoke quietly to the priest. When the sheriff asked if he had anything to say to the 600 assembled witnesses, Barrett said no.

After the warrant for execution was read, the cap was drawn over Barrett's face. The sheriff led him to the drop and adjusted the rope. At 10:17 the drop fell. The paper noted that "no unnecessary noise or excitement disturbed the solemnity of the occasion." Forty minutes later, Dr. Charles Cleveland pronounced Barrett dead. His body was cut down, placed in the coffin and buried at the foot of a large pine near the scaffold.

Aaron Sargent house

CHAPTER 4

POLITICAL ADVENTURES

May–December 1852

I

ℳUCH HAD CHANGED in their absence, and for a while Niles and Charley were undecided whether to remain at Nevada City. Merchants complained of slow trade because of spring flooding at the mines. But weather and business had improved, resulting in greater optimism. On May 11 Niles confessed to Cornelia:

I was almost sorry, for a week or two, that I had not concluded to stay at home. Satisfied that I had acted as I deemed best, I concluded there was no use in lamenting. One thing is certain: in coming to Cal. this time, I was impelled by what I conceived *duty*, rather than *inclination*. I like the country, always have and shall continue to. Yet the thought of staying here for any length of time, without a prospect of making this my permanent home, seems wrong. Were I the only one concerned, I should most positively spend my days in California. As it is, if my life is spared for a year or two, I shall as positively leave her.

That evening he and Charley had visitors from Grass Valley, friends who came to discuss politics. Whigs and Democrats were organizing for the first time in California, preparing for the presidential elections. Every county office except that of county judge would be contested, along with four seats in the legislature. In January local Whigs and Democrats had met to select delegates for their state conventions.

William Morris Stewart, chairman of the county Democratic committee was a former Yale student. Like Niles, he had been born twenty-six years earlier in rural New York. But the Stewarts moved soon after to the backwoods of Ohio, where Stewart taught school at seventeen. He was a math teacher at Lyons High School for four years before entering Yale the fall of 1848. There he resisted the lure of California gold until the spring of 1850, when he came to Nevada City by way of Panama.

There he had mined and surveyed ditch routes in the mountains. In 1851 he attended Nevada City's first mining convention. The Gold Flat Quartz Mining District was partly inside the city limits, and one section of the city charter stated:

In actions to determine the right to "mining claims," proof shall be admitted of the customs, usages or regulations established and in force at the bar or diggings embracing such claims; and such customs, usages or regulations, when not in conflict with the constitution and laws of the state, shall govern the decision of the action.

The purpose of the convention was to establish those customs, and Stewart was chairman of the committee which wrote a key provision defining a quartz claim. After being approved by the miners, the results were published in the *Journal*. After that date, November 23, 1851, most other California quartz mining districts copied the language approved at J. S. Porter's store on Gold Flat:

Resolved, That 100 feet on any given quartz ledge, embracing all its dips, angles and variations, shall be the maximum of a quartz claim in this district. *Resolved*, That any person or persons discovering a quartz lead shall be entitled to 100 feet on the lead, with all its dips, angles and variations, by virtue of discovery, provided that he, or they, cause the same to be recorded separate from all other claims, stating that said claim is held by virtue of discovery.

Stewart realized such a definition would result in perpetual litigation over boundaries. As soon as he could wind up his other affairs, Bill Stewart began reading law in the office of McConnell and Churchman.

James Churchman was forty-one years old. His wife Samantha had twice been widowed, and nearly twenty years before had helped Zachary

Taylor's daughter elope with Jefferson Davis, a young army lieutenant under General Taylor's command. The general was furious, especially when Davis resigned his commission and took his bride to his home state of Mississippi. When she died a few months later, Old "Rough and Ready" blamed his son-in-law, not forgiving Davis until they fought together in the Mexican War.

During the years he practiced law at Galena, Illinois, Churchman became a warm friend of Abraham Lincoln, Stephen Douglas, and Edward Baker. After gold was discovered, he came to San Francisco, established a lucrative law practice there, and later came to Nevada City. Recently he had been joined by his wife, but their children remained in the east with relatives.

Churchman's partner, John Randolph McConnell, was only twenty-four, the twelfth of thirteen children born to Scotch-Irish parents in Kentucky. Orphaned at ten, he was raised by an older married sister. For a time he studied law in Kentucky before going to Illinois in 1846. Two years later he went to Natchez, Mississippi, and in 1849 traveled overland to California. He reached Nevada City in 1850 and became the county's first district (or prosecuting) attorney in 1851. He was Master of the Masonic Lodge, a member of the Methodist Episcopal Church South, and a dedicated Democrat.

In the spring of 1852 the office of Churchman and McConnell was the county's unofficial Democratic headquarters. When Niles came by to satisfy his curiosity about the Lundy case, he had been talked into replacing Philip Moore on the county committee; Moore was resigning as secretary to campaign for a seat in the legislature. Bill Stewart also relinquished his office as chairman, for it robbed him of time needed to study for the bar. Hotel owner David Phelps agreed to take his place.

Nevada City Whigs also boasted men with fine credentials. Lorenzo Sawyer, thirty years old, came from New York State, but as a young man had gone with his father to Pennsylvania to clear land for a homestead. Later he studied law, taught school in New York, attended Western Reserve College in Ohio, and read law with several prominent attorneys. In the summer of 1846 he went to Chicago and spent a year in the office of Illinois Attorney General James A. McDougall. Both eventually wound up in California, where McDougall had been the attorney general in 1851.

Sawyer's law partner, Stanton Buckner, was the oldest lawyer in the county—fifty at least—and had been a member of the Kentucky Bar before many of his colleagues were born. From 1828 to 1850 he practiced law in Missouri, and served as that state's supreme court clerk for several years. After coming to Nevada City in 1850 he had narrowly

lost the election for district judge. A solid lawyer, Buckner was nevertheless unsophisticated and lacked a sense of humor. When another attorney
insulted him in court by calling him a "pettifogger," Buckner was well
pleased with his own quick retort: "I emphatically told him I wasn't!"

But the man most important to Whig success was absent from the
county when party conventions were held in January and May. Aaron
Sargent, editor and co-publisher of the *Nevada Journal* since the fall of
1851, had gone home to Newburyport, Massachusetts, where in March
he married his fiancée, Ellen Clark. Sargent returned alone in the early
summer, saying his bride would join him in the fall when their house on
Broad Street was completed.

Edwin R. Budd edited the paper until Sargent returned, and then
purchased Dr. Alban's interest. On July 10, 1852, Sargent and Budd
announced a new policy:

As an independent paper, we have ever claimed the right to discuss
men and measures whenever it please us, yet we have scrupulously kept
aloof from partiality to any party as such. Whatever our political bias, so
long as we edited a paper believed to be neutral in politics, we disdained
to abuse our trust by turning it in any degree into an engine of political
warfare.

Now we DROP THE PLEDGE OF NEUTRALITY and the Nevada Journal
is and henceforth will be, a WHIG PAPER. A great and exciting political
canvas is at hand, and we aim to use our whole influence towards the
success of Whig principles and Whig candidates.

II

CHARLEY WENT FISHING on July 10, taking with him the key to the
iron safe, which caused Niles no end of problems. As he told Cornelia, "I
have no doubt but that I am an especial favorite with Providence, for it is
said, 'whom the Lord *loveth he chasteneth*.' I don't want to be impious,
but my opinion is, the fewer such favors the better." Throughout the
morning depositors had come for their money, only to be informed, "It's
perfectly safe." *Too* safe, Niles thought. Nor was that his only complaint:

Then too, I have lost the beautiful Pin Cushion which Mary sent
me—broke the spring to her miniature and have to open it with a
jack-knife, on the *oyster principle*. These and sundry other mishaps here
swelled the stream of my calamities into a perfect torrent. . . .

I have just been called from writing to wait upon a customer who
purchased a quantity of sealing wafers and then very precisely told me

he had never seen any afore, but thought them mighty fine for paying postage. The fact is, the hombre had heard of *Postage Stamps*, and supposed he was buying them. I could not find it in my heart to disappoint the fellow, so let him put two of them on the North east corner of his letter and start for the P. O. Hope Uncle Sam won't repudiate the currency.

Playfully he noted that a French ship had arrived in San Francisco with a cargo of female passengers which the consignee was offering for sale. "Pretty much on the old Virginia principle, that. As my clothes are sadly deficient in *buttons*, maybe I'll go down and purchase one. I'll think of it and ask Mary, as I have a great deal of confidence in her opinion." Later in July he talked about leaving California:

The "Alleghanians" are singing here at present and are applauded very much. I have not heard them yet. You know I am not over partial to singing anyhow, excepting always Mary's song of *"Home Again."* I need not say that I look forward with more than anxiety to the time when I can hear her sing it again. . . . One short year more, and my rambles will be finished; then for "home again." Then too for a sweet little wife and a "Cottage by the Brook." Aside from my attachment for Mary, there is no inducement for my thinking to live at home again. *That*, however, overbalances all of an opposite character. And why should it not—there are few like her in the world.

In August the post office was moved from Main to Broad Street and the postmaster installed numbered boxes for his customers. At first it had the effect of slowing down the sorting on steamer days. Niles described a mixup that occurred:

I elbowed my way through the dense crowd of anxious expectants, to the great detriment of my coatskirts and *slick hat*, till I reached Box 250 (my number), when O horror! nothing greeted me but a small slip of paper with the inscription "Box rent due 50¢"—

Well, I vamosed for home fully bent upon giving Charley [the dickens] about something, and as to the dog belonging to our Jew neighbor, he was in for a flogging if I caught him, sure. The fire built by the Chinamen in our back yard, too, was classed a *nuisance*, and *must* be abated.

Entering the store, what should I see but a *letter* with my cognomen in a hand there was no mistaking. An acquaintance had seen it and brought it down. Every belligerent feeling vanished in a moment, as with a glow of pleasure I proceeded to peruse the welcome "little joker."

A day later he made a formal request of Mary's parents:

A few months more and the term of my sojourn in Cal. will have expired. Expecting to return east at that time to remain permanently, I wish to know your sentiments more fully, with regard to the attachment existing between Mary and myself. With one of you I have conversed briefly on the subject.

What I wish to know now is whether in case of my return in the Spring we can have your consent to our union at that time? Perhaps in a matter of so much importance we should have consulted you long since. My only answer is that Mary and I thought better not to give publicity to the matter till such time as we were fully convinced of the permanency of our affections. Examples are not wanting, even among our own relatives, of the folly of the opposite course.

It is impossible now to say precisely what time next spring I shall leave here. About the first of May though, in all probability. That is supposing no misfortunes occur in business or otherwise, more than I have anticipated. By that time I hope to accomplish, to a certain extent, my object in coming here a second time.

Please answer at your earliest convenience, and oblige yours truly. . . .

Having taken care of this important business, Niles next did a very strange thing: he accepted the Democratic nomination for district attorney, whose term of office would not begin until May of the following year.

III

BY LATE OCTOBER, Niles seemed to have become disgusted with politics. Already he was sick of the entanglements that went with California elections, but the campaign was not over. Bitter and discouraged, Niles described his growing frustration to Cornelia on October 23:

At the close of a pleasant day in Autumn a solitary individual (not a horseman) might be seen standing at his desk, and apparently engaged in deep thought. Around him, in the utmost confusion, lay books, papers, electioneering documents, letters &c. &c. Judging from the frown resting upon his countenance, we should infer some quiet calamity had occurred to mar his peace and happiness. The furtive glances cast at an open letter by his side would indicate that there was a connexion between his thoughts and the contents of that epistle.

It related, no doubt, to some political strategy, to some new and slanderous charges of incapacity and dishonesty—to some electioneering trick for the success of party, at the expense of truth and honesty. Is it strange then that, in angry mood, he gave vent to his feelings. . .?

You may think this a singular way of beginning a letter, yet for a synopsis of my feelings, the truth is, Nelly, I am pretty extensively mixed up with politics, and am completely disgusted, and I feel too as though, if forgiven this time, I will never more be guilty of a like indiscretion. The turmoil and confusion will soon have passed away, and the sooner the better.

I am wholly indifferent to my election or defeat [but] the idea of being beaten by a man devoid of common sense irritates me. My opponent [C. Wilson Hill] is acknowledged to be deficient in everything that can qualify for the position. Hence, I think his greater chance of success.

But in November, after the ballots were counted, Niles wrote Cornelia in a dramatically changed mood:

The Election is over—the contest is decided—the slain, wounded and missing are enumerated and in common with the Democracy of my county and state, I have to rejoice over a general Democratic Victory from [Presidential candidate] Frank Pierce down, myself included.

I am not certain as it will comport with the dignity of my new position as District Attorney Elect to be corresponding with those of my old acquaintances who have received no distinguished mark of Public consideration to entitle them to attention—yet, in the spirit of a true Democrat, who is ever condescending, I shall still perpetuate the friendship existing between us. . . .

My term of office does not commence till next June, but the present occupant proposes to resign if I will enter on the duties at once. [I] shall determine in a day or two. It is more than probable there will have to be a special election to fill my place in the spring. I hinted this to my friends when nominated, but they enjoined me to keep silent on the subject, as they wanted me to be one of the candidates and help do the electioneering. The task is performed, and I am one of the "Elect." In some points of view the office is preferable to most any other. It brings a man before the public, and his very position is considered prima facie evidence of ability, which he may or may not possess.

Writing to Cornelia, Niles composed an unusually revealing introspective essay on November 30, in which he explored past, present and future:

I have been sitting by the stove, as I am wont to do when alone, thinking of *home*, thinking of the happy days when I used to confide all my troubles to my Mother, fully confident of her power to assuage every grief in life, and to regard every meritorious act.

I have been trying to remember, too, what were my aspirations in those days, but for the life of me, can't remember farther than that as a boy I delighted to climb higher trees, and go on thinner ice than the other boys, and as a man I always expected to have high boots and talk about elections, like Father and Uncle Nathaniel, or to get a pistol and go to War. Well, those days are so far gone. . . .

One thing has for several years afforded me more happiness and more uneasiness than all others combined. It is that of my love for Mary. Not that the least dissension between us has ever given rise to a moments pang, for we have had no quarrels or misunderstandings. The truth is just this: my attachment for her knew no bounds and could only rest satisfied with an equal return. All this was accomplished without premeditation on either side. But then I was by nature wayward and impulsive, and, without experience and the fixed habits which it brings, [and I] feared that instead of promoting her final happiness, Mary was only laying the foundation of future trouble.

One thing was with me reduced to a certainty: unless I could demonstrate, to my own satisfaction, my ability to secure a competence in the world, no consideration would ever induce me to consent to a union of our destinies for life. Distrusting my power to accomplish anything among those of superior advantages in my native state, I went to Missouri.

[I] had concluded to settle in Harrisonville, and was pretty certain of a seat in the next Legislature, when I discovered that the location was too unhealthy for a residence. I need not tell you that Cal. was the next Theatre of my operations—that sickness was for a year my constant companion—that Death stared me in the face, and that for over a year nothing was accomplished. That was the saddest year of my life, and now when I look back, I only wonder that despair and death did not seize me as lawful prey.

With the first return of prosperity came the desire to make Mary my own. With that object steadily in view, I have since labored, till I find myself in the highroad to a position (what it is, I will not now explain) of which I need not be ashamed. But another difficulty now presents itself. I have not accomplished much in the way of a Fortune. . . .

Therefore, admitting there are no objections from other quarters to our matrimonial plans, there are still some difficulties ahead—some serious obstacles to be encountered ere I reach that proper state of bliss which my fancy has pictured. . . . I shall not assume the duties of District Atty till spring, though at one time I nearly agreed to do so immediately.

I have consented to participate in the prosecution of a man who murdered a Spanish woman here a short time since. I can prosecute him with a good will. . . .

I have not yet determined when I shall leave for home. . . . but have had a strong notion within a few days of coming in Feb. By doing so, it will give me an opportunity to seek a location in the spring and get settled for the summer. . . . I can have time to return here again by the middle of May, the period for entering on my official duties.

There is no use concealing the fact, Cornelia, that I would like to return here again; but if I do so, I want Mary to come with me, and unless she is willing to do so, of course I am willing to go elsewhere. I wish simply to state the facts, and leave her and you and her friends to decide the question. Of course, I know well enough what your decision will be in the premises. I have no doubt I could pettifog the case with Mary till she would consent to come, and though you may sneer at the assertion, you would do the same thing under similar circumstances.

When Niles decided against assuming the office, Bill Stewart was appointed district attorney. John McConnell was determined to resign so he could begin campaigning for the office of state attorney general. There was a slight hitch: Stewart had not passed the bar. This turned out to be no obstacle, for one advantage of membership in the majority party lies in having friends in the right places. But Whigs like Aaron Sargent were not pleased, and he vented his annoyance in the *Journal* on December 10:

J. R. McConnell, who for nearly two years past has filled most ably the office of County Attorney in Nevada county, resigned his office before the Court of Sessions on Monday last. The court appointed to fill the vacancy Mr. W. M. Stuart, who was admitted to practise the same day.

Mr. Stuart is undoubtedly a young man of considerable industry, and the office will be a good school for him, but as the design of the office is not to teach beginners, but to furnish an official adviser for the county, and someone able to effectively prosecute criminal cases, we submit it would have been better to have given the office at once to Niles Searles, the newly elected District Attorney. Too much experience cannot be brought to such an office, and this selection of the greenest lawyer of the Nevada Bar, however full of promise, we esteem a decidedly bad move for the public interests.

Rensselaerville
Presbyterian
Church

CHAPTER 5

WEDDING PLANS

August 1852–June 1853

I

ᴀᴅᴅɪsoɴ Nɪʟᴇs received his bachelor's degree from Williams College in August 1852. His parents and sisters proudly watched the ceremonies, together with Will Allen and his Chicago friend Charles Stowell. When Stowell went home he carried some of Will's money, to be invested in the prairie city's booming economy. Once there he reported:

The money is at present in the hands of my father, who is willing to pay the legal interest, 10 pr cent, as long as you choose to let it remain. He also expresses his entire willingness, á la Skinpole, to do anything you may suggest in a business way with pen, ink and paper. At the same time I took the money, I had an eye on two or three places which I felt certain of getting at a reasonable rate, but recent developments with regard to depot grounds for some new [railroads] have carried the proprietors beyond all reasonable bounds. In the winter I think probable that I can purchase much more reasonably than while money is as abundant as at present.

Because Will had hinted at his matrimonial prospects, Stowell offered his own cynical view of that subject:

My observation of wedded life has been that romantic love rapidly loses its sparkle and flavor after marriage; that after a woman has been, so to speak, uncorked, she quickly becomes flat and insipid, with a possibility of subsequent sourness. For a week after marriage we love them; for a month are fond of them; three months afterward, endure.

The next month we differ and quarrel with them, then through the long years that follow, we become accustomed to them, because we cannot get rid of them, and they to us vice versa. If either dies, the other mourns a decent period, and then, like the Bastille prisoner, returns anew to the accustomed bondage on the first opportunity. . . .

Tell Sam I will visit him immediately after your wedding (to which of course you intend to invite me, and which I shall as certainly attend, and pronounce over you a benediction far more fervent than you can purchase from priest or justice), and before that time provided he forestalls you in matrimony.

John and Polly Niles were pleased by Niles's request to marry their daughter, especially as it seemed to promise his early return. But as usual, there were contradictions—a letter to Cornelia spoke of wanting to bring Mary to California—and then they learned Niles was to be his party's candidate for district attorney. But concern in this direction was replaced by a sudden and more immediate calamity: Will Allen had gone mad!

Some mysterious ailment had left Will feverish and incoherent, and he was placed in the asylum at Utica. Under constant care of physicians and nurses he began to show signs of regaining his wits. Dr. Benedict wrote Will's parents in November that he was "hourly improving," but a complete cure would take time.

Cornelia was distraught. Until this unexpected calamity, she and Will had been close to announcing their own wedding plans. And although she supported the decision to remove him from Rensselaerville, it was unbearable to be so far from his side. Will's father said they must all pray to "the Great Giver of all good," the "mysterious providence" who had caused the sickness, and to whom they now must "bow with humble resignation." In the meantime Dr. Benedict promised to do whatever lay within the power of medical science.

II

ON SEPTEMBER 10 Mulford and Searls severed connections with Gregory's Express and became the first Nevada City agency for the new firm of Wells, Fargo and Company. Said Niles:

We are fitting up a new office and store, and shall move in during the coming week, when we expect to be comfortably located for the winter. We are having it papered, and in every respect as well finished as any shop in California. The day of canvas houses has passed away.

After they moved into their new office, Niles declared it was the finest store in town, "clean and neat, and smells like new shoes." At about that time his negro washerwoman Mary had called on him about a matter of extreme urgency. Her owner, Louis M. Best, wished to return to the States, and she was trying to raise the money he demanded as the price of her freedom. Best owned the Washington Hotel on upper Main Street.

In January 1851, when Best and another man had been arrested for the murder of Dr. Lenox, Louis had strutted about the courtroom fully armed but was acquitted after his partner escaped and fled the county. A year later he was formally accused of kidnapping and extortion by Jane Jones, a black woman who had purchased her freedom. She had been seized in her Grass Valley home and taken to John F. Gregory's house at Nevada City. There she had been chained and held prisoner until she agreed to sign a note for $500. Fortunately, she had earlier taken the precaution of having the county clerk record her papers. Unlike so many other free blacks in California, Jane Jones escaped being dragged back into servitude.

Although in his letter Niles appeared to joke about the idea of a company of men buying Mary ("Think I shall take two shares. Female stock is above par in this county. Price $800—two juvenile darkies thrown in"), he and others did precisely that, and gave the woman her freedom.

Mulford and Searls presented the *Journal* with a copy of Harriet Beecher Stowe's best-selling novel, *Uncle Tom's Cabin*. One hundred thousand copies had been printed in the United States and 150,000 in England since its first appearance earlier in the year. Aaron Sargent's opinion was that too much notice was being taken of it:

... it has grown into immense notice, highly praised on one hand, and greatly abused on the other. We believe it merits neither. It is a sprightly written work, filled with graphic and rather too strongly drawn scenes, but its tone is not bitter, and it does not deserve, nor can it be put down by the wholesale denunciations.... We believe the work will do little good, but we do not believe it will do harm, or was designed to do any.

III

CORNELIA PASSED ALONG the California news to Addison, who since graduation had been teaching school at Great Barrington, Massachusetts. The holidays had been a sad time for her, not at all like the year previous. The news from Utica at best was "promising"; Dr. Benedict wrote that Will's health was slowly improving, and they were to hope for his final recovery. Cornelia wanted badly to go to Valatie, where she had been invited by Will's sister and her husband, Charles Tremaine.

Unfortunately, storms had made the roads nearly impassable until at last, on January 24, 1853, the weather improved and Cornelia went with her brother Hamilton to Albany. He was going to Angelica to work in the store of his cousin and namesake, Hamilton Stanton. For nearly a year Ham had been employed at John Huyck's store in Rensselaerville, and the Angelica position was viewed as an advancement.

After Cornelia said goodbye to Ham at the Albany depot, she and other passengers were taken across the frozen surface of the Hudson so they could board southbound cars on the Troy to New York rail line. At Kinderhook she was met by Charles and Lizzie Tremaine and their two daughters. Nelly stayed at Valatie for a week before traveling north to Great Barrington to visit Addison.

In Albany, on her way home, she received the joyful news that Will Allen had recovered and was coming home. Cornelia was so exhilarated that she scarcely noticed or minded when the Rensselaerville stage left without her on Saturday, thus delaying her return till the following Tuesday. In her absence three more letters came from California, one thanking her parents for their consent to Mary's forthcoming marriage.

Niles described a severe snowstorm that had blanketed the county. In Nevada City it was two feet deep, while at the new diggings around Red Dog City and Walloupa it was four feet and more. Houses caved in and roofs collapsed before owners could remove the snow. Deer Creek was a foot higher than when the Jenny Lind washed away in the spring, so planks had been removed from the Main Street bridge and the timbers secured with ropes. No such measures were necessary on the Broad Street bridge, which had been raised two feet during reconstruction. At the county's southern border, the Bear River was thirty feet above the low water mark. Wrote Niles:

I assure you Nelly, it is so cold and disagreeable that even ideas will

43

not vegetate. It is just such weather as you have seen for forty days in succession every January during the last *thirty years*—is snowing just as it did one year ago this day when I was going from Albany to Rensville. . . .

You should hear me talk of going to a warmer climate—Mexico, Chili, Sandwich Islands, yes, these times, are topics frequently discussed. The last foible, however, is a trip home in Feb. or March across Mexico, from Acapulco to Vera Cruz. This plan originated last night at just 1/2 past 11 oclock, and is already pretty well matured. All that is now wanted is a company of ten good men, and fresh caps in my revolver, then the preparations are complete.

He offered condolences for the illness of Will Allen, predicting: "This last great trial, like others, may all vanish in a few weeks and be forgotten." And already it was true, for Will was due to arrive in Rensselaerville in two or three weeks.

But, to everyone's surprise, Niles got there ahead of Will. A delighted Cornelia told Addison:

I am much engaged in these days attending to company, as Niles and W. W. Allen are spending some days with us. The parlor is gaily lighted tonight, and we are all in good spirits. Deborah has just been in to laugh with Niles, and Mr. Allen too is in right good humor, worth twice as much as before he went out on that 'balloon excursion,' as he calls it, and just at this moment he sits opposite me, writing a friend, and I must scribble my news fast, to be finished as soon as he.

Mary is preparing a fire for herself upstairs, I fancy for a tête à tête with a certain coz, who leaves in the morning for Canada. Niles came ten days since—we looked for him in [March's] steamer, but of course he came before, when we did not expect him. He is looking remarkably well—will not return to Cal. if he can find any location at all suitable in the States. Will return [from looking for a spot] in the spring, about the time of your vacation, for Mary, the particulars of which arrangement I leave her to give you.

Two pages right here I could write of the pressure on my spirits, when I think of so soon losing Mary. How we can give her away, I do not know.

Will came here last Saturday, and stays with us, and we are having *fine* times. Often wish for you, and Niles has talked of going to see you.

Mary added more details when she wrote to Addison a few days later, after Niles and Will had left:

Niles has gone to Canada, and after making a short visit there will go

44

west in search of a place of business. He of course prefers returning to Cal. on his own account, as he is in a fair way to wealth and preferment there, but he is willing to be governed by my wishes in the matter, for he will not go back again without me.

After talking it over with our people, they at last concluded that he had better go as soon as possible in pursuit of business, and if he could not find any place where there was a prospect of success, it would not then be too late to return to Cal. in time to enter upon the duties of his office. The latest time for starting in that case would be the 20th of April, but I think there is no doubt that he will find a place somewhere in this country, though it may be very far west.

What say you? Shall I yield to what I know to be his *wish*, though he generously consents to be guided by mine and to make a sacrifice which I know is a very great one for him—or shall I consent to be separated from my friends, perhaps forever, with all the chances and changes of California life before me, without one friend but him to rely upon? It is not an easy question to decide, but if he can only find a place where there is any prospect of success, I think he will be quite willing to remain.

We are quite anxious to arrange our wedding day so that you may be home, and think we will be ready for it in May.... If we wanted you to, would you be willing to act as *groom's man*.... we shall probably be married in the church, with very little parade, and if we have any one stand with us, we would prefer Cornelia and Mr. Allen, yourself, and Niles's sister [Theresa], if she comes with him, as he thinks she will; if not, either Deb [Wickes] or Harriet Rider. Have you any objections to that arrangement? You have never intimated to me whether you were pleased with the idea of my union with Niles, but I take it for granted if you had any serious objections, they would have been made known long ere this....

For six weeks Niles traveled about New York state, visiting villages and talking to friends, relatives, and total strangers. Late in April he seemed to be narrowing his choice to the area around Angelica. Meanwhile, Charley Mulford had sent the betrothed couple a bank draft for $500 to be spent as they wished, although he suggested watches for each. Accordingly, Mary and Niles had gone to Albany and spent $200 for two watches with chains. In addition, Mary had bought a "good crape shawl," and thought she would spend the rest of her share on silver "and other choice articles."

On April 26 Mary gave Addison the most up-to-date information:

Niles starts for N. Y. on Friday of this week and will purchase there a

45

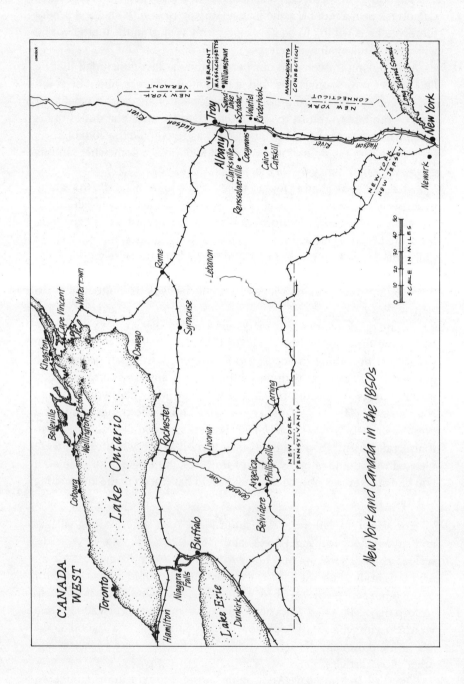

New York and Canada in the 1850s

[law] library, and go on with it to Almond, or Phillipsville, places near Angelica at one of which he thinks of stopping, but has not fully determined which. He is waiting now for a letter from Rufus [Stanton], giving him information with regard to a lawyer in Almond who wishes him to come and form a partnership with him. Niles will remain there, or wherever he concludes to settle, until he returns [for the wedding]. . . .

We are to be married in the church on the 25th of May at 9 or 11 o'clock in the morning. We are to have four couples stand up with us, not in the formal way of dividing off on each side, but in a group about the bride and groom (do you like that?) Mr. Allen and Cornelia, yourself and . . . Harriet Mulford (or Deb if you choose it), Rufus Stanton and Augusta Bellamy, if Ruf will come, and Augustus [Cornell] and Deb (or Harriet if you choose [Deb]). . . .

We shall return home and remain long enough to take refreshments with the few who will be invited to call, and then leave for Canada.

IV

AFTER THE WEDDING the guests went to the Niles residence, where rain had cancelled plans for a garden party. But spirits were scarcely dampened, and Niles worried they never would get away in time to catch the Albany stage. At last Mary managed to slip upstairs and change into her traveling clothes. After packing the last few items, she came down the stairs, and amid hurried embraces, shouted goodbyes, and a flurry of raindrops, the newlyweds walked quickly down to Main Street and caught the stage.

Afterwards, Mary recorded the entire wedding trip to her sister in a pair of letters, the first of which began:

We had a very pleasant ride in to Albany. The rain did not disturb us in the least. I took dinner at Clarksville, because I knew I should be too tired to eat when we got to Albany. We stopped at the City Hotel, had a very nice parlor and room. I had the sick headache all night and till noon the next day, so that I could neither sleep nor eat.

But we took the cars at 1/2 past 10, and I soon got over my headache and had a very pleasant ride. Arrived at Rome just in time to take the cars to Cape Vincent. This road runs through a delightful country, and I was less tired when we took the boat than when we started in the morning. The boat was just starting for Kingston as we arrived, and we went right on.

Fortunately, I remembered that in Canada people are expected to make themselves agreeable in travelling—accordingly, when a young lady whom I had observed all the way from Watertown on the cars addressed me, and seemed inclined to get acquainted, I chatted away with her, and soon found she was a nice girl, who had been attending school at Watertown, and was somewhat acquainted with some of Uncle's family. I of course gave her no clew to who I was, but made some inquiries about them.

She said she believed one of the young men had gone to Cal., had been home this spring &c &c, all of which I assented to. Very soon, however, her father recognized Niles, and they were introduced to me, and we were together until noon the next day, when we started for Picton.

We were very tired and dull, and after dinner on the boat, Niles laid down in the saloon to have a nap, and I went to the cabin for the same purpose. He promised to wake me [in] time enough to point out Aunt Hasy's residence. Pretty soon a lady came into the cabin, a tall handsome lady, with a little baby in her arms. Her face attracted me at once, and as there was no other lady there, we soon got to talking.

She saw that I was an American lady, she said, by my dress. When we came to the landing near Aunt Hasy's, I asked her to point out to me the point that runs out into the lake, which I remembered hearing Niles speak of. She did so, and I remarked I have an aunt living there who is very old, and so on. She looked at me a moment, and then said, "Well, it must be you are some relation of mine then. She is my grandmother." She then asked me my name. I told her it was *Searls* now.

"Oh," she says, "then you are John Niles's daughter, and I am, or was one year ago, Miss Jane Ingersoll." Of course we were acquainted at once; I went and called Niles, with whom she was well acquainted.

The newlyweds spent the next night aboard the Kingston boat. They arrived late the third evening at the home of Niles's sister, Joanna Herrington, and on the following morning, Saturday, the exhausted couple went to the farm of Niles's parents—Mary's Uncle Abram and Aunt Lydia. On Sunday all Niles's brothers and sisters gathered for dinner at the family homestead.

For two days they visited relatives. Then, after tea on Friday, Mary and Niles left Wellington and went by boat to Hamilton by way of Picton and Kingston. From there they took the stage to Lewiston and Niagara Falls. Niles had allowed three hours to see the falls and eat dinner before catching the evening train to Dunkirk, because he was anxious to get back to his business at Phillipsville, where he had finally decided to settle.

Mary's sister had gone to the falls in 1846 with her cousin Joseph Murphy. Then they had stayed the whole day, visiting the most popular tourist attractions—the Battleground, Table Rock, Burning Spring, Goat Island, and the Bower—but although Mary had to be satisfied with less ("We hastened down to the falls, went over onto Goat Island, up into the tower, and took a good long look at the falls from there while we visited—and then went back to the cars"), she was not disappointed:

It far surpassed my expectations. I felt as though I could spend hour after hour in gazing at that mass of water rushing so madly towards the precipice, and then gliding so calmly and majestically over into the sea of foam below.... If I were rich I would go there and stay several weeks. You need not take this for school girl sentiment. Once I should have considered myself bound to go into raptures over Niagara, whether I liked it or not; but I had no such intention when I went there, and the emotions which almost overwhelmed me were entirely unpremeditated and unexpected. I have been several times surprised at myself since I left home. I find that I have an earnest, unfeigned love for Nature in its varied forms, which I was hardly conscious of before.

Their hotel room was not ready when they reached Phillipsville, so Mary had to sit in the parlor for two hours with "some talkative ladies." Niles had sat with her for a time, but he appeared so uncomfortable that Mary sent him out to look up his new friends. Meanwhile, she tried her best to read a novel and ignore the other guests.

Mary had not been pleased when Niles came back with another lawyer—she wasn't anxious to meet anyone until she could freshen up from the trip:

Had [Niles] asked me if he might bring him, I should have said no, but his call did me real good. He is a very pleasant, fine fellow. Our room (we have but one) is a very comfortable one, about the size of Addison's room. The hotel is quiet and orderly, and although rather "country," is clean and comfortable. Could we have two rooms or some closets we could do here, although there is no other lady boarder; but Mr. Ward, the lawyer of whom I spoke, has been kind enough to hunt up a boarding place for us, to which we will go this afternoon. It is with a Baptist Deacon (or "second hand minister" Niles calls him).

We are to have a bedroom and parlor on the first floor, opening upon a piazza. This *sounds* very fine, but though I have not seen it, I am inclined to think our nice room at home would be far preferable. However, it is as good as can be had, and I think I have not overrated my faculty for making the best of every thing, and being contented any-where.

This is a *very* new town, apparently. When we passed through it on the cars it looked very dubious to me, whether I could like it at all, but I already begin to feel an interest in the place, and to imbibe the spirit of a true pioneer. There are some very pleasant residences here, and from *their* appearance, I should judge, some very fine people. Dr. Morris, whose office Niles rents, has a beautiful place within sight of this room, and Niles's office is next door, and a very pretty one.

After supper they went out to meet their landlady, Mrs. Root, whom Mary described as "a pleasant, motherly sort of woman." In their parlor was a lounge, a rocker, an office chair, and a corner stand filled with books, daguerreotypes and trinkets. The floor was covered with a neat carpet, and the three windows were covered with blue drapes and white muslin "overcurtains."

Best of all, there is a door opening right onto the piazza, which runs in front of the house. Our bedroom is very small, there being only room for a bed and washing apparatus. That will be somewhat inconvenient, but I think we will have to get a dressing case and keep it in the parlor (they have none that we can have). Everything about the house is neat and clean, but nothing stylish at all. They do not even keep a girl, but have only four in the family beside us. We have to have our washing done out of the house.

The [daughter] is a very pretty, nice looking girl, something in her manner of speaking like Helen Wickes, but with none of her haughtiness. She plays the piano, and has one, but her brother, a hunchback invalid, has taken it with him to some academy where he is giving music lessons.... Within sight of our door is a most beautiful grove on the bank of the Genesee river, the trees are very high and scattered, so as to shade the soft green sward below; the [railroad] cars pass in full view and cross the river just below the grove.

Two days later, in California, the *Nevada Journal* announced: "Wm. M. Stewart has been appointed to the office of District Attorney for the ensuing year, in place of Niles Searles, elected, but absent in the states."

Council house

CHAPTER 6

WEMA: PART I

1851–1853

I

MUCH HAD CHANGED for the Indian inhabitants in the years since white miners first invaded *nisenan* territory. Indians no longer posed a threat to whites who lived in or near the towns—now they were regarded either as a nuisance or as a form of entertainment. Europeans and Americans were amused by Wema, the nisenan chief, and bestowed such titles on him as "King," "Captain," or "His Highness." Few appreciated the importance of his statesmanship in mediating between the two cultures.

The first whites had merely passed through on their way to the great valley. They came with women, children, and ox-drawn wagons. Wema's tribe feared they might intend to stay, but those fears proved groundless; it was the later invasion by gold seekers that ruined their lives. For a time there had been open warfare. White soldiers had pursued Wema's people from one valley to another, until at last he and his subchiefs went to Camp Far West to sign a treaty of peace with the white soldier-chiefs. Although these agreements brought a measure of peace, the terms favored whites more than Indians. Wema's people watched in angry frustration as the invaders stole land and trees, disrupted food supplies, drugged them with liquor, and molested women and children.

Despite Wema's pleas that violence would cause even greater suffering for their outnumbered people, younger men in his tribe often took revenge for the wrongs and insults. Then, because of the agreements he had signed, Wema was required to hand over the guilty parties. To escape the white man's justice, a nisenan who broke foreign laws had to exile himself and live with outlaws.

A second treaty was signed with the Americans in 1851. This time, in exchange for the white chief's promise to provide them with livestock, supplies, and the white man's tools and clothing, ten chiefs agreed to move their people into a small reservation in the lower foothills. Its northern and southern boundaries were the two rivers that flowed into the great valley, called the Bear and the Yuba by whites.

Soon after the treaty was made, a white youth coming through the reservation with his family was killed by Indians. Some whites went looking for his killers and took several captives from a village on the banks of Yuba River. Only with difficulty were the Indians able to convince them they had come to the wrong village.

The whites then went to Judge Roberts at Rough and Ready, who was charged with enforcing the law for whites and Indians alike. Roberts gave them permission to arrest the guilty parties. But when they tried to take prisoners they were repulsed by Wema's people, who said only their chief could bring in suspects. "Find Wema and he will know who did it," the Indians said. On hearing this, Judge Roberts led a posse to Wema's own village and took him prisoner.

Afraid to retrace their route through Indian territory, the posse elected to go back through Grass Valley. At Boston Ravine they were challenged by miners who knew Wema but not his captors. The miners would have released the chief, but Roberts persuaded them to contact his fellow justice, James Walsh of Grass Valley.

Walsh was able to establish Roberts's identity, but he urged the judge to release his prisoner, explaining that the chief would cooperate. Three days later Wema sent two nisenan youths to Roberts, who questioned them for several hours before releasing one and holding the other for trial.

Many whites gathered at Rough and Ready to witness the trial, and growing impatient, broke into the jail and seized a Spanish-speaking

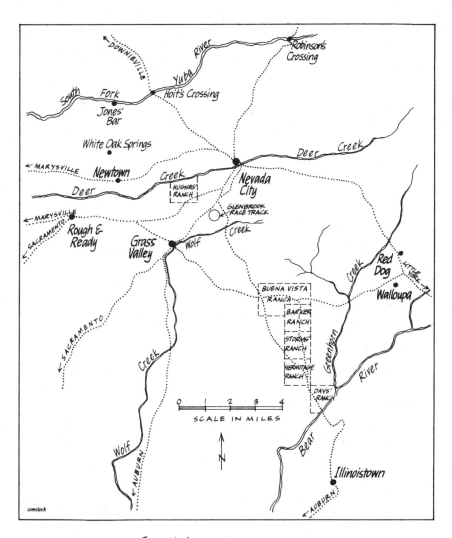

Central Nevada County in the 1850s

prisoner awaiting trial for theft. To pass the time, they tied the Spaniard to a tree and beat him almost to death. At last Roberts brought out the accused man, whose name was Kolo. A jury was chosen and trader David Bovyer, one of the few whites who spoke the nisenan language, interpreted for the Indians.

When the talking was over, they hanged Kolo from a tree. Charles Ferguson remarked afterward, "I would never witness the like again . . . for idle curiosity." Referring to the interpreter, he said:

He was supposed to be some kind of an Indian agent, although I was never able to learn what he did for the Indians or anyone else but himself. This remark is not intended in disparagement of Mr. [Bovyer], but only that I can't see what the government or the Indians wanted of an agent there.

Two months later Aaron Sargent expressed his own disapproval of another incident that he contrasted with the Kolo hanging:

The papers of the States (and indeed throughout California especially) have teemed with accounts of "Indian Outrages" committed upon whites until the caption has become a stereotyped phrase. But we are credibly informed that but a few days ago a white man in the neighborhood of Steep Hollow, whose name is only known as "Charley" forcibly carried off a woman belonging to Wallupi's (Guadaloupe's) branch of Wemeh's tribe in sight of her companions. Complaint was made by the chief to the Government Agent, and to the magistrates of the vicinity who are making efforts to return the woman to her tribe, and punish the depredator.

Unless the whites will respect the rights of the Indians, what reliance can we place upon their good faith in keeping treaties? A few months ago upon a legal demand, an Indian of this same tribe, who was accused of murdering a white man was given up by Wemeh, tried before a magistrate's court and hung in presence of the tribe, by the people. The Indians acquiesced in this decision and consequent punishment, and realized its justice. They are desirous of cultivating friendly relations with the whites—but if we allow abandoned and reckless white men to perpetrate such wanton outrages, we can only hope for a continual series of retaliations, which will end in a bloody war.

After negotiating the July 1851 treaty with Wema and other chiefs at Union Ranch, Indian Commissioner O. M. Wozencraft was interviewed in San Francisco. The *Alta California* reported:

With the exception of [hostile] tribes, all the Indians south of the Pitt river have agreed to the terms proposed by Dr. Wozencraft ... and he has every confidence that they will adhere to the stipulations, and if not molested, give no further trouble to the whites. Dr. W. thinks that before the expiration of the year there will be as many as 80,000 Indians upon the reservations already made, a large number having already commenced their occupation.... Dr. W. is quite confident that the accusation [from white miners and farmers] of reserving lands, rich in mineral and agricultural wealth, cannot be made with reference to these reservations although they are susceptible of producing sufficient to meet the wants of the Indians by such cultivation as they choose to bestow upon them.

Aaron Sargent disagreed, and proposed an alternate plan on December 18, 1851:

Congress should take in consideration some general and effective means for the removal of Indians from California. To leave them on the rich arable lands of Penn Valley, the valleys of the Sacramento and San Joaquin, etc., is but to add additional cause of offence to the whites, and hasten the sacrifice of the Indians....

The only method to quench at once and forever the difficulties with Indians ... is to remove the Indians to the east of [the] Sierra Nevada chain ... [where] on the rivers, in which fish are abundant, the Indians could find as good a subsistence as they here obtain from roots and acorns.... The country of the Gila [River] could maintain many tribes if they removed thither.... The Indians on the Gila and its tributaries are of a superior class to most of their kind, living on agriculture, and raising cattle, etc., and their example would go far towards elevating the character of the Indians that might be removed thither.

The "superior" Indians mentioned by Sargent were the Yumas, who in fact had destroyed two missions and massacred the Spanish inhabitants in 1781, forcing all whites to avoid the country from that time forward. This may nòt have been the example Sargent intended they should set for California's tribes.

In January 1852, Judge Walsh of Grass Valley, now the state senator from Nevada County, announced his personal opposition to the treaty, claiming it was not proper for agricultural lands to be set apart "in large bodies for the use of small parties of Indians, who do not require such bodies of land, and who would never cultivate them."

The report of a special committee in the California Assembly also came out strongly against the treaty:

These reservations ... embrace within their limits, in a large majority of instances, extensive tracts of the most desirable mineral and agricultural lands in California. Many of them include large, permanent, and populous settlements of enterprising American citizens who had located upon and acquired rights and interests in the soil long anterior to the conclusion of these treaties with the Indians.... The character and habits of the Indian and white populations are totally different. They are by nature unsuited for the society of each other.... The Indian is naturally prone to steal and otherwise depredate upon the white population, and the white man in retaliation takes the life of the Indian; and thus there is produced a continual state of hostility between them....

For ages [the Indians] have been in the habit of wandering with unrestricted freedom along the margin of the various streams and over the hunting grounds in this country and subsisting upon the profuse contributions of a beneficent Providence. But now, how changed the scene: The march of mind and the energy of civilization has driven the red man from his wigwam and his hunting grounds, and the farmer has leveled many of his acorn trees to the earth.

The California Senate's Indian Affairs committee produced a similar report, to which Senator J. J. Warner took exception:

To remove the Indians from this State I consider as impracticable: there is no place within the territory of the United States in which to locate them. We cannot suppose that the General Government will remove them to Oregon, to Utah, New Mexico, or to the Indian territory east of the Rocky Mountains.

And where else will you locate them? On the desert and sterile regions east of the Sierra Nevada, that they may die of starvation? Or if, perchance, a few survive, that they may become the Arabs of America? Better, far better, drive them at once into the ocean, or bury them in the land of their birth.

II

IN THE SUMMER OF 1852 the *Nevada Journal* credited David Bovyer for the relative peace and harmony then existing between whites and Indians. True, there had been a few instances where whites had been injured or killed with arrows, or where Indians had been killed by whites, but it was not like the early days:

There are in this county, according to the estimate of the census taken, about four thousand Indians—the number varying at different seasons of the year. This great body, so roving in their habits, with such little presumptive moral principle, with few resources for the supply of their wants, save in labor which they abhor—for the supply of wants increased greatly by the advent of the whites—have nevertheless been in this county controlled so judiciously that few outrages have been committed by them, and they are continually advancing in character and shrewdness.

The Indians, especially females, are generally pretty well clothed, some of them own horses and mules, and the young generation are induced to work upon the ranches, in building fences, houses, and cultivating the ground. If no quarrels occur to excite prejudice against the Indians, thin off their numbers, and drive them to dishonesty and crime, they will become a very different race of people in a few years. They have much natural penetration, are good natured, faithful in paying off debts for goods, and in some qualities are worthy of emulation by those who despise them.

They are yet very filthy in their household affairs, and thus contagious diseases have great effect upon them. But many of them are learning the advantage of cleanliness and appear in clean shirts, etc., in imitation of the whites. These Indians have few of the nobler characteristics of the Atlantic or Sierra tribes. They are unwarlike and unenergetic. But for this reason they are more likely to settle into a useful class in society. With less important elements constituting them a peculiar people, they will more easily subside into a lower stratum of society, and become, if rightly managed, useful.

Among the gentlemen who have been most instrumental in restraining the propensities of Indians in this neighborhood, and elevating their character is Mr. David Bovyer, who has been established on a ranch on the Newtown road for several years past. He first came into this region in August 1849, when no other white man was resident for miles around, and before gold was discovered here. With an idea that hereabouts a populous neighborhood was to spring up, he took up his one hundred and sixty acres of land, and for nearly a year lived alone among the Indians on his ranch....

Mr. Bovyer in his long intercourse with the Indians has obtained a thorough knowledge of their language—speaking it as fluently as a native. They are so accustomed to his control that if they are asked, wherever they may be, whose Indians they are, they will reply "Bovyer's."

Not all this information was true, a letter writer took pains to point out in the next issue of the paper. Presumably, his facts came from Simmon P. Storms:

That David Bovyer would willingly assist in the civilization and improvement of the social condition of the degraded beings we found here when California was first settled by whites, I have no reason to doubt. But that he has been the only one through whose agency the Indians have received benefits, or who can control and influence them— or even that he is foremost in his qualifications—is an error.

And in all probability a sense of his own second rate qualifications and envy for the superior merits of another have been strong inducements with him in wishing to propagate the opinion that he is the sole dictator of the Indians in this region. Contemporary with Mr. Bovyer has been Mr. Simmon P. Storms, who at present is located some eight miles S. E. of Nevada.

Messrs. Bovyer and Storms came to California together—arrived in San Francisco in July 1849. Like other adventurers to the land of gold, they spent a month or two in various pursuits, during which time Mr. Storms had formed an acquaintance with the Indians and their language but rarely attained. Messrs. Kendall and Mosman had located a trading post on the South Yuba, in 1848 or the early part of 1849. On the 3rd day of October '49, Storms and Bovyer, in connection with another who soon retired, bought Kendall and Co.'s establishment and commenced trading, Storms with the Indians and Mr. Bovyer with the whites.

And here let me say, it is a wrong impression that there were no other white men in the vicinity at the time. Successful operations in mining were going on at Grass Valley, on Deer Creek, Woods' Ravine, and on the Yuba in the immediate vicinity. Since that time, the trading post near the White Oak Springs has changed hands several times, sometimes one, and sometimes both having an interest therein; and the rancho now occupied by Bovyer was located and improved by Messrs Storms and Ward in February and March 1851.

This, and his entire interest in that neighborhood being transferred to Mr. Bovyer about the 20th of June 1851, Mr. Storms entered the service of O. M. Wozencraft, Indian Commissioner, as Special Courier and Interpreter. In this capacity Mr. Storms rendered our government agents services which but few if any others could do in collecting together the chiefs and head men of the tribes, on the Yuba and Bear River—and through him they were made to understand the wishes of our government.

On quitting this employment, he entered the service of Mr. Samuel

Norris who had the government contract to supply the Yuba and Bear River, and part of the Feather River Indians with beef. Having the entire control of this business, in connection with the Indian trading establishment of Messrs. Norris and Lavell, his intercourse with the Indians was such as to gain for him the confidence of all those tribes inhabiting the regions above named.

By a strict adherence to justice, and by firmness, prudence, and a steady nerve in any and every case of emergency, he has gained a control over them possessed by no other man in Nevada county, or in California; and without disparaging the pretensions of others, he has unquestionably done more to bring the Indians of this part of California to a fair understanding with the whites than any other man.

The statement that the Indians, wherever you meet them, will refer to Bovyer as chief, is perhaps true to a very limited extent; that is, with a few in the immediate vicinity of his location—no farther. His acquaintance with the Indians has been confined to home—that of Mr. Storms has been with all the tribes and all the head men in the Yuba and Bear River, and a part of the American and Feather River regions.

Simmon was born in Maracaibo, Venezuela, the son of Peter Storms, a sea captain who sailed between that country and New England. When his mother returned to Massachusetts soon after his birth, Simmon was cared for by his godparents, Simon Peña y Parra and María Candelaria Peña. His father died in 1837, and in 1841 a brother took Simmon to Boston.

At the age of eighteen he came to California with Bovyer, a French Canadian carpenter a dozen years older. Because many California Indians had picked up bits and pieces of Spanish, the language of his childhood, Simmon was quick to learn the native tongues. According to James Delavan of Grass Valley, Storms later "married" the daughter of Chief Wema, a customary alliance among traders for cementing relations with an Indian tribe.

In the summer of 1852 he persuaded his father-in-law to host a gathering of Indians on Storms' ranch. Why not, he suggested, show whites what a real nisenan festival was like? Not only would it improve relations between the two peoples, but Storms could profit from those who would patronize his restaurant, bar, and hotel. Wema agreed. Soon Storms had announcement posters printed and distributed throughout the county.

Although they had missed the Indian gathering, Aaron Sargent and some friends visited the ranch a few days afterward. The youthful editor was impressed:

It was nearly a year since we had traversed that portion of the county, and we could not help being struck with the permanent improvements visible on every hand along the road.... Fine ranches, well-stocked, with considerable land under cultivation, and substantial buildings, have been created within the past year. The Illinoistown road is one of the most shaded and otherwise pleasantest road in the county. It runs through a finely timbered region, abounding in bountiful springs of pure water, with much moist low ground, susceptible of great yield with cultivation. We understand application has been made to the Court of Sessions for privilege to construct a bridge at Anderson's Crossing....

Mr. Storms has improved his ranch highly, so that, with its substantial buildings, corrals, &c, it is one of the most valuable in the State. He speaks the Indian language fluently, was formerly Indian agent, and has the full confidence of the tribe. His trade with them is a main feature in his business. He opens regular books with them, giving them credit, and says they always pay up. Upon his account book we saw an hundred such names as Wou ti, &c, and while we were there an Indian, decorated with shirt and pants, came in and squared his account.

The influence of such a man upon the tribe is most beneficial. When aggrieved the Indians resort to him for assistance in peaceable redress. In trouble of every kind they consult him. A runner from Rose's Bar, on the Yuba, came in and informed him that the Indians were very sickly, and that nine had died in three days.

All the *materiel* of a good dinner were forthcoming from the ranch, as vegetables of the finest descriptions, poultry, *beautiful* beef and pork, fine melons, &c, which with adjuncts, all served up by a skillful housekeeper, furnished a repast not to be excelled in the State.

In 1852 there had been reports of smallpox among Nevada County's Indians, but Storms said there were no cases on his ranch. The disease was brought by whites, especially those newly arrived from the Atlantic states. At this very same time an outbreak of smallpox had occurred at Rensselaerville, where Deb's brother Harvey, a medical student, was busy day and night for several weeks helping his father, Dr. Platt Wickes.

A year later, smallpox had become epidemic among Nevada County's Indians. The *Journal* reported on May 27, 1853:

It is computed by those best acquainted with the details of Indian life that not less than 400 of all ages and sexes of the Indians have been destroyed by this disease in this county the past six months—that is, one-tenth the whole number. The Indians are totally helpless when thus attacked, and if anything is resorted to besides groans by the sufferers

EXTRAORDINARY
Attraction!

ONE THOUSAND
INDIANS

With their War Implements, Squaws, Papooses, &c.

WILL ASSEMBLE

At Storms' Rancho,

On the Illinoistown road, six miles from Grass Valley and 6 1-2 from Nevada, on the afternoon and evening of Monday, July 19, 1852, for the purpose of

Celebrating their Annual Feasts and Fancy Dances.

This will be one of the largest Indian collections that has ever taken place in California, and

To those who have never witnessed any thing of the kind,

IT IS WELL WORTH
The Ride.

CAPT. WEYMEH.

Storms' Rancho, July 11, 1852.

or howling of their friends, the supposed remedy generally hastens death.

The most common sufferers are children, which are swept off in numbers. The Indians are very uncleanly, and careless in exposing themselves, and thus easily contract disease in its most deadly shape. The ravages of smallpox have been mostly confined to the Indians, and but very few whites have suffered.

We take this opportunity to pay a merited tribute to David Bovyer, the well known proprietor of Bovyer's ranch, whose influence over the Indians is only equalled by that of Weymeh, their old King. He has prevailed over the Indians in his neighborhood to resort to vaccination, and sends them to Dr. Clark of this city for that purpose. He is thus getting at work the only agency that can save this decimation of the poor beings by whom he is so much loved.

Niagara Falls

CHAPTER 7

SECOND THOUGHTS

June–August 1853

I

ARY'S PHILOSOPHY for living, as expressed to Cornelia in June, was "to enjoy the present to its full extent, without borrowing trouble for the future. . . ." She was happy now, beyond her greatest expectations. Niles and Mary had lived in Phillipsville for two weeks when she assured her sister, "I could be happy·anywhere, and under almost any circumstances with Niles. . . ."

But there had been a bad moment when Niles brought home a letter from California in which Charley proposed to open a new office in Downieville and turn over his Nevada City business to Niles. Mary could be happy anywhere, but she hoped it wouldn't have to be in California. She told her mother about her husband's reaction to Charley's offer:

> Niles says he could have made a *heap* of money in two years, enough to make him independent. It made Niles homesick a little while, and I have not got over it *yet*.

Before continuing, she asked that her next remarks not be repeated at Rensselaerville:

> I do think I ought to have gone with him. . . . The universal opinion here seems to be that we were both very foolish to not go. The best lawyer in the county said he thought Mr. Searls was a man of a good deal

of talent until he heard that a *girl* had induced him to give up such prospects as he had in Cal., and *then* he thought there must be something lacking. I hope Niles has not heard all this talk. I am careful to repeat none (I hear it in Angelica).

He appears to be contented and cheerful, and, if he gets business, *will* be, no doubt. He has some now. One of the old residents, whose business is said to be worth 100$ a year, has had a fuss with the other lawyer, and has already employed Niles once. He will be pretty sure of *his* business.

Because Mary tended to compare local prices with those in her hometown, she was impressed by the hundred dollar promise, but Niles measured worth by a California yardstick. One day when Niles went to Angelica to try a case, Mary came along to visit brother Hamilton at the store of their cousins. She was astonished at how much things cost at the Stanton's store and elsewhere in the western communities. A handsome bureau with a veneered front, three large drawers and two small ones, cost $15 delivered eight miles away. At Phillipsville a year's board, room and laundry for the two of them would cost $260; Mary thought this exhorbitant, but Niles assured her it was cheap by California standards, where his laundry bill was $12 a week. Mary said to her mother:

We could not get a suitable house for less than 80$ or 100$ [per year], and as Niles will not listen to my doing without a girl, I suppose it would not be much cheaper. By the way, Ma, do you think it would be possible to get a girl from R.Ville? I think we would have to pay 8 or 10 [shillings] here.... our work at 1$ a week would be much easier than yours.... Ask Deb if she remembers telling me what a fine thing it would be to *board*, because we would have high living—Delusive *hope*!

Niles says he never saw civilized people live so poorly. We have been here two weeks, and have not seen one bit of fresh meat, and have had fresh fish once. True, there is no beef in market most of the time, and a nice piece that our host says he bought this morning was [stolen from his] basket while he was up town. Still I am sure there are some people here who live better. We have no meat but [pickled pork], codfish, and stewed beef (dried). Our bread I liked very much at first, but it is salt rising, and I have become very sick of it now.

Niles said nothing more about Charley's proposal and appeared to have put it out of his mind. In a letter to Cornelia he was humorous and optimistic:

What a splendid landlord we have, a real genuine, simon pure *Baptist Minister*. Somewhat superannuated, 'tis true, but a very fair specimen of his kind, I mean the kind that flourished long, long ago. Can't really say how we shall like the boarding place on the whole, as we have not had enough to eat as yet, to determine fully. Should the *codfish* crop fail we expect a famine.... Business is only so so, this being the dullest time in the whole year for law business. Still, I am doing something. Tried one cause yesterday, and have one for this afternoon. Rather think I shall do something after a while. Phillipsville is a great town. If you don't believe it, come out and see for yourself. Bring Deb along and we will have a good time....

Mary goes regularly to work at mending my old clothes, like a lineal descendant of the tailor's stock. Buttons are no longer a rarity on my clothes. There is no describing the advantages of a good wife. Rather think my luck has changed and that I am in for good times.... If Phillipsville don't suit, we will go elsewhere—though I don't apprehend any necessity for it at present.

Mary tried hard to understand the attraction California held for her husband, but despite his willingness to discuss the subject at length, nothing she had yet heard served to explain the matter to her satisfaction. She was willing to concede the excitement it offered a young man, the opportunity to play an active role in stirring affairs on the rough frontier. The prospect of sudden wealth was another obvious lure, but everyone knew how those opportunities had been exaggerated.

What she could not accept was the idea of California as a place to build a home and raise a family. Mary believed it could not be considered an acceptable alternative to life at home. But Niles's infatuation with the west caused her to fear that should she go there, he would have no further reason to return to New York.

II

ALTHOUGH NILES had been admitted to the state bar five years before coming to Phillipsville, he had not previously practiced law in New York. In 1848 he had gone to Missouri, and to California in the following year. Thus, each day since his marriage was filled with new discoveries about the differences between east and west. There was much to admire about the old established ways, as Niles was quick to admit, but Phillipsville and Angelica offered little in the way of stimulation to a youth who had spent his formative years on the edges of America's newest and most exciting frontier.

The process of government was undergoing rapid change in California, partly because America's southern states traditionally operated under a set of rules different from those of New England. Many early settlers in the southern states arrived in the New World as representatives of the English Crown, and often belonged to the privileged classes. Because they had no real quarrel with aristocratic forms of government, more offices were appointive than elective, even after the American Revolution. The so-called "better classes" predominated, and elite assemblies made laws and appointed men to enforce them. It did not differ greatly from life in the more liberal English boroughs.

The north, on the other hand, had been settled by malcontents and protesters; radicals who objected to their treatment by British authorities. From the outset they experimented with broader participation in decisions that affected the whole community. Over the years the political base widened as more decisions and more offices were incorporated into the elective process.

New states and territories traditionally adopted the customs of those settlers who were in the majority, but people were coming to California from every part of the union, and from many parts of Europe, Asia and the other Americas. Americans from the north and northeast states, whether poor or rich, expected to have a voice in local affairs. But those from the slave states were divided according to family fortunes. Those from the aristocracy assumed they would be consulted and would hold or control the important offices. The rest supposed they would receive nothing.

The coming-together of these different notions produced interesting and occasionally explosive consequences. When political parties began forming in California, people naturally adopted the labels familiar to them at home, with the result that three major factions were competing for power in the new state: Southern Democrats, Northern Democrats, and Whigs. And although Democrats won most offices in 1852 because of their combined strength, a growing split inside that party provided Whigs with increased hope, despite signs of disarray in their own ranks.

The push and pull of politics in California could be unscrupulous and rough, but it was fluid and full of wonderful surprises, unlike the carefully controlled environment in which Niles's uncle and Charley's father had survived and even prospered. By accepting the rules of Albany County's rigid system of political patronage and remaining generally loyal to the party in power, John Niles and Charles Mulford had been rewarded with offices as justice of the peace and county supervisor. Had they been unwilling to cooperate, each would have met with serious obstacles.

It was not an attractive prospect for a young man with ideas of his own, and as for the law business available to the newest lawyer in town, it was exceedingly dull and unrewarding when compared with the faster pace at Nevada City. In his final trial before coming home, Niles had helped John McConnell and Bill Stewart prosecute a man who had killed a prostitute. Because of the victim's occupation it was not easy to win a conviction, but the trio was determined that the act should not go unpunished.

McConnell had reminded the jury that Californians were acquiring a reputation for "hanging mule thieves and aquitting murderers," which he claimed had resulted in the creation of vigilance committees and the undermining of the social system. After two hours of deliberation the jury found the man guilty of involuntary manslaughter, and he was sentenced to eighteen months in San Quentin.

Although not the murder verdict they had hoped for, Searls, McConnell, and Stewart counted it a victory, given the circumstances. But so far as Mary could see, it was simply one more reason not to live in a town where brothels, drunkenness, and gunfights were part of the normal scheme of things.

III

LIFE AT PHILLIPSVILLE could be downright boring, Mary decided. In Rensselaerville she could always borrow something to read if all else failed, but living among strangers posed problems. Writing to Nelly in mid-July she thanked her for sending old copies of the *Observer*. Niles once had offered to subscribe to it, but as Mary said:

> there are so many things to pay out money for. These three weeks past have been rather trying to my cheerfulness. It has been so dusty as to be uncomfortable. I have been looking all the time in vain for some one from Angelica to come after me, according to promise, to make them a visit.
>
> I had returned the ladies calls and it is not time for them to call again, and to cap the climax, Niles had weak eyes so that he could not read much and but little business, so that he had the blues two or three days. Yet with all these trials I have preserved my cheerfulness nearly all the time, and sing over my work from morning till night.
>
> Niles has taken a great liking to chess and we keep the men out and play almost every time he comes to meals. He has already learned so as he beats me about half the time. It will be more pleasant for me now I think. Niles's eyes have recovered and it bids fair to rain and lay the dust and I shall no doubt go to Angelica soon.

As a way of coping with her boredom, Mary considered going home for a visit. When she heard Charley Mulford was expected at Rensselaerville in late July, she asked Cornelia to find out when and how long he would be there, hoping to time her visit to coincide. But because of Cornelia's long estrangement, she wondered, "Can you be familiar enough with him to talk it over?"

Charley came home on July 29 and went first to see Deborah Wickes, Nelly's closest friend. Charley had found out that Deb's long love affair with Loyd Copeland had come to a bitter end. Two weeks later, On August 17, 1853, Charley and Deb were married at Trinity Episcopal Church. Two days after the wedding they arrived in Phillipsville and spent the next twenty-four hours in excited conversation with Mary and Niles. When the newlyweds boarded the train for Niagara Falls on Saturday night, the two couples had agreed to go to Nevada City as soon as possible.

"My dear sister," began Mary's letter of Monday, August 22. "I have a great many things to say to you and very little time to say them in." She outlined her plans, and managed to sound relieved that the long-dreaded decision had been made at last.

I am glad to learn from Deb that you are not wholly unprepared for the news which I have to communicate. Before Charlie came home, I had fully made up my mind that Niles would not and could not be contented here, and had told him that if he wished to go to Cal. this fall or next spring I would go with him.

Could you have seen the poor fellow's delight at my being *willing* to go, I am sure you would have been touched. He had striven nobly and faithfully to be contented and cheerful for my sake, but I knew him too well to be deceived, and loved him too well to be happy if he was not. He said it was not Cal. that he cared for, but that everything was so high here, and the charges in law so small, that if he had just as much as he could do of the best kind of law business, he could not much more than make a living, and he thought his constitution would not bear many years of toil and study.

He could not bear to think of plodding on, year after year, for a mere competence at most, and obliged to spend his life within the precincts of Alleghany [County] because he could not *afford* to leave his business or to travel.

I began to feel somewhat so myself, and when I heard Charles had come, I felt as though now was the time for us to go. . . . Of course, when I heard Deb was going it was the greatest inducement of all, and now I *want* to go. I should be very much disappointed if I could not. Deb will be more society to me than all my acquaintances in this place are or would be very soon. I do not feel as much at home here now as I did when I first came, and not a single person I see feels at home. There is nothing home-like about the place.

There is but just one objection now to my going, and that is the grief that it will cause you at home. But you *must not* grieve over it. . . . We are to meet Aunt Dencey on the 1st day of Sep. and to go . . . from there to Albany, where Deb and I are to do shopping Sat. morning and go home in the afternoon. I think that I would like to have a dress like her white one, and after talking it all over with her, I wondered if Pa could spare me 40 or 50$ now—it would do me more good than at any other time perhaps in the world. [Niles and Charley] say we may take all the clothes we wish, and it will cost so much less here than there that I think we had better take plenty. . . .

Niles has just been in with the [justice of the peace] to have me sign and acknowledge a deed of his lot, which he has this morning sold to Dr. Morris, and I think without much of any sacrifice, but he has not told me exactly. There is nothing now for him to arrange except to get in some money which he had let for 6 months. . . .

I meant to have written to Pa, but have not time. You may read him this letter, and if he could conveniently send me the money which I spoke of, I wish he would. . . . We leave [here] Thursday morning. I would like to hear from you as soon as possible.

But Cornelia had gone to visit Will's family, so her mother forwarded the letter with this message:

Mary's letter I will send you without note or comment. I have written her this morning to use her own judgment about dress; get the cloth at Mulford's [store]. Pa has arranged the money matter, we are all well, getting on finely. P. Niles.

Stanmer Saloon in the 1850s

CHAPTER 8

CALIFORNIA BOUND

September–October 1853

I

AVING DISCOVERED CORNELIA'S whereabouts, Mary wrote again a week later. She would meet her sister in Albany to shop for clothing. But they would have little time in which to do it—Saturday morning, in fact, for they were to go to Rensselaerville in the afternoon. In the meantime, Mary had paid a final visit to Angelica:

I have promised Cousin [Mary Stanton] that you shall come and make her a visit this winter, and Mr. Allen shall meet you there at his vacation—it is but a little way. One of the [professors] of that college [at Rochester] is preaching at Angelica and is called *very talented*. You would have a delightful time, even if *we are* away off over the sea.

Now Nelly, dont grieve about our going. We should have gone *next spring anyway* and it will be so much better to go now. We will have grand times, and you will find something to make you happy I know. We will talk it all over when I come. We shall be home two or three weeks, and want you and Delight and Addison if possible to go down to N. Y. with us and see the Crystal Palace, and see us "set sail." It will be pleasant for you and for us, and you can see our steamer &c.

As it turned out, they were in Rensselaerville fewer than two weeks, and Cornelia chose not to go with the entourage to New York City. She had expanded her grievance against Charley to include Deborah, whom she held responsible for Mary's decision to go to California. On the eve of departure Mary wrote her mother from Wyckoff's Hotel in New York:

The company have all gone to the Opera at Niblo's tonight, except Niles and I, but we like dutiful children, as we are, will remain in our room and write awhile and then retire. I wanted very much to go to Niblo's, but I have run about a good deal every day since I left, and today have spent nearly all day at the "Palace," and thought prudence would dictate "be quiet this evening and retire early."

I feel perfectly well, and do not ever feel much tired, but you know I never feel it so much at the time. Besides, I felt just like writing home this evening.... The ride into Albany was rather a fitful one. One moment we laughed and the next sobbed, but we were all determined to be as cheerful as possible.

Harriet Backus, a former student at Rensselaerville Academy, was traveling on the same ship. Recently orphaned, she was going to live with relatives in Oregon. More than a year had passed since Mary had seen Hattie, who was about the same age as Addison. Mary thought she had changed in the meantime:

I think she is improved somewhat. She is dressed in deep mourning and looks better than I ever saw her before—she looks perfectly neat, and I think we shall find her a very pleasant companion.

Recalling that Niles's letters to her had not been stored properly, she asked her mother to complete the task:

If you can find the key to the trunk you spoke of, or can contrive any other way to put them where they will be *perfectly* safe from the children or anyone else, I wish you would; if *not* I suppose they had better be destroyed. I should be very sorry to have them destroyed, but rather they would be than have them where they might be read. Charlie [Mulford] says he left some letters in the same way in the corner of a drawer in his room, and that among them were some of mine to Niles which he had brought to deliver to Niles and had forgotten. I want Cornelia to go there and look over the package (Charlie says she may) and select all that are in my handwriting (she will know them) and put them with the others. . . .

Bye and bye, when I dare to think of it, how I shall love to dwell upon that visit home. . . . I had some such good visits with Pa and with you all. Oh, how Pa's calmness sustained me that morning when I left. I don't know what I should have done without it. I do hope it was not all assumed.

Mary's father told Addison, "We of course avoided saying or doing anything to dampen her spirits—as it was decided that they should go, we wished her to go with good courage." But he added, "we hope they may not have cause to regret the move."

II

THE STEAMSHIP *Star of the West* left New York harbor Tuesday, September 20, 1853, and after five days at sea, Mary Searls began her first letter home:

The impression our friends had, or must have had of our steamer was a very unfavorable one. It seemed rather gloomy to us all that first night because it rained so and the decks were all wet, and everything topsy turvy. . . . I have been seasick of course, but have borne it much better than I supposed I should. I went according to Uncle Mulford's rule, "lie on one side awhile and then turn over and vomit."

. . . we have been favored with most excellent weather, showers every night which cool the vessel, and calm seas nearly all the time. Today the ocean is almost like glass and the air like a hot summers day with us, but the motion of the vessel creates a fine breeze on deck. . . . There is a square opening in the deck with a skylight above for admitting air into the main cabin below. Our rooms have windows opening into that space, so that we have a fine breeze nearly all the time drawing through the rooms.

A week later, Mary was less enthusiastic:

The worst place in the world to attempt writing is on a crowded steamer. There are a thousand little things to prevent. One day Deb wrote a long letter, and I wanted to, but there were so many [people] collected in front of my door to enjoy the breeze that I could not write a word, and so it goes. . . .

For instance, this morning just as I took a fancy to lie down and take a nap, not having slept as well as usual last night, a company of Irish women and their children from the 2nd cabin came and seated themselves opposite our door, keeping up a din and clatter of tongues and a catterwauling of babies which put both sleep and patience to flight; and at twilight, when it begins to be cool and pleasant, and the soft southern sky invites [one] to quiet, dreamy fancies, there is a perfect crowd of smoking men, Irish women and dirty children always collected in the coolest places, obstructing our view and offending our olfactory nerves.

I am really afraid my nose will never resume its wonted position, as it is becoming so used to being turned up with an expression of disgust.

Rather than go by way of Panama, they had chosen Vanderbilt's newer Nicaraguan route, shorter by 500 miles and supposed to be easier on passengers.

We congratulate ourselves every day on having come this route. A gentleman on board (Charles Hedges) tells me he has been over the route three times before, and has never known any sickness of consequence among the passengers, not even on the Isthmus. We have a very pleasant party of our own. There are about 100 ladies on board, and some very fine looking ones too.

We are perfectly satisfied with our party, and Deb and I often say we don't believe we could have stood it alone.... Almost every one of our company are reading [Dickens'] Bleak House, which amuses us much. I am reading [Elizabeth Weatherell's] Queechy now, which is just the sort for steamboat reading, as it requires but little attention. As for sewing, I have not yet seen a needle or thimble, and doubt if I do.

We dress in the greatest possible haste in the morning, and with the greatest possible coolness, and gather on deck to get a breath of fresh air before going to the cabin for breakfast. My breakfast usually consists of two cups of tea (coffee is miserable) and a bit of sea biscuit and ham. After breakfast we lounge about in the coolest places, reading, talking, moping and laughing, always choosing, if possible, that method of killing time which requires least exertion.... You cannot form much idea of such weather as we had yesterday and today, yet perspiration is so free that we do not feel as oppressed with it as we do at home with much cooler weather. I have never perspired so much in my life before, I think.

They say we are not liable to have any more such weather as we had yesterday. We were among the Indies and there was scarcely any current of air. Scarcely more of a ripple than on the surface of the Hudson. Cuba was in sight nearly all day, and Jamaica in the afternoon. There was a fine shower over on Cuba Island just at sunset, and all the evening we watched the play of the lightning and the shifting thunder clouds over the terraced table lands of the shore, while over *our* heads the sky was clear and the stars shining.

Another member of their party was the wife of Leopold Chubbuck, Charley's bookkeeper in Nevada City. She was from Boston, and Mary found her quite companionable at first:

Mrs. Chubbuck looks very much as Henrietta Mulford did, and has some such a voice. She is more sociable and less dignified, or haughty, rather. She dresses just about as we do here. I like her very much indeed. . . I have had no opportunity yet to judge of her book knowledge or taste. . . .

Thursday morn. It has been delightfully cool and breezy yesterday afternoon and today. We have all collected on deck and are in fine spirits. Have eaten breakfast with a ravenous appetite and are going at once to arrange our traps for carrying across the Isthmus. It may be that you will not get letters as soon from San Francisco as you might expect, as the mail steamer will be off before we get there. The engineer of the "Cortez," the boat on the other side, is on this vessel now, and says we will have better accommodations on the other side than here—better fare—more room, and the lower cabin passengers kept separate, so that these foreigners will not annoy us so much. We can promenade the hurricane deck there too, which is not allowed here.

Much later, on board the *Cortes*, Mary resumed her narration:

We anchored in San Juan Bay on Friday morning, and it took nearly all day to get the passengers and baggage exchanged onto the small river boats. We . . . amused ourselves somewhat with watching the natives as they came about our vessel with their canoes filled with oranges, lemons, &c., which were twice as large and as fine as anyone ever saw at home. They were so tempting, but Niles and Charlie would not buy one for fear we would get a taste of them and want more.

Just at twilight we started up the San Juan River, and the beauty of the scenery through which the river runs surpasses anything ever dreamed of before. We felt ourselves well repaid for all the fatigue and inconveniences we had endured . . . . We could do nothing but exclaim "Oh, how beautiful, how beautiful." . . . The river is very rapid, and so clear that we drank the water. It is more crooked than the road to Duanesburg, winding about among innumerable islands and dividing off into different streams, so that we could look way off in the distance and see river after river, and island after island, till we were almost bewildered and were fain to believe ourselves in a dream, or gazing at some beautiful picture to which distance lent enchantment.

The beauty of the islands it would be utterly useless to attempt to describe. They were covered with a perfect mass of foliage down to the

waters edge. Trees of dark rich foliage forming a background, and feathery palms quivering in every nook, with their delicate green forming a beautiful contrast to the rest; and over the whole was a drapery of vines, many of them covered with large crimson and purple flowers, sometimes hanging in festoons, and at others forming complete arbors, whose cool shady depths were extremely suggestive of moonlight and fairies.... if I could find words to describe half the exquisite beauty of that river, you would think me quite too sentimental.

The accommodations were no less romantic than the scenery. We were crowded as thick as we could sit on the boat, and had nothing provided for us to eat except such as we had been able to pick up from the other boat. We could get bread and crackers and boxes of sardines, and the gentlemen had procured some cold meats and ale from the other steamer. Of these we made our supper and breakfast, and at night we spread our shawls and over-coats on deck, and with satchels for pillows, we lay as thick together as possible, some even having to sit up against posts.

Of course we did not sleep much, as it was very warm, but with the earliest dawn we were up to enjoy the scenery again, and having made our toilet by taking the corner of a towel and dipping it in the river and wiping our faces and hands, we proceeded to breakfast.

I must not forget to mention our meeting the steamer the evening before, which was taking the passengers from the [Pacific] side to the boat we had left.... Such heartfelt cheerings I am sure were never before heard on that lonely silent river. It was hard to distinguish persons, and only a few hasty questions passed back and forth, before we were again gliding along, alone and quiet.

About noon we came to some rapids, where we had to walk a short distance and take another boat above. We found a very comfortable dinner on shore, and were then packed into a still smaller boat, until towards sundown when we arrived at Lake Nicaragua, where we found quite a large comfortable boat, from the upper deck of which we watched a most glorious sunset, and after the stars came out, we gathered in groups, and with a can of tea and the remains of our provisions made a comfortable supper; slept on the floor again, but were so tired that we scarcely stirred till morning.

In the morning we arrived at Virgin Bay and were rowed to shore in boats.... Took breakfast at the "American House" and fortunately secured good mules and ladies saddles, which was more than some others did. We had a fine opportunity to see the rest start while we were waiting for the boys to get the baggage checks, and we had not a little sport.

The mules were, many of them, perfectly mulish, and would go tearing and pitching into the woods or into the mud, or even into the bamboo houses by the road side, and some utterly refused to go. A good many [persons] were thrown off their mules, but they are so small there is no danger of being injured. The boys [Niles and Charley] were too good judges of the article to get any of that class of beasts for us.

We started at eleven o'clock, and now perhaps you are looking for some terrible experiences to be given of our crossing the long dreaded *Isthmus*. What will you think tho when I tell you that I never enjoyed a horseback ride in my life more than I did every moment of that ride. It was the *rainy season* on the Isthmus, but there had not been a drop of rain for a week, and there was not a drop while we were there. The road was as dry and good for horseback riding as any about R'ville. There is a carriage road finished nearly all the distance, which is only 12½ miles.

There were some places where the mud in the road was very deep, but we had only to let our mules take their own way, and they would go way around into the bushes and pick a dry path, never failing to find the *best* one. We had to take no care about guiding them, all we had to do was to employ one hand with beating them (you can fancy what a beating they got from Deb and me), and we could look about us as much as we pleased at the scenery, some of which was beautiful, and watching for parrots and monkeys.

We stopped at a half way house for dinner, and about that time the sun went behind a cloud and a cool breeze sprung up so that we rode in perfect comfort the rest of the way, and went slowly that we might enjoy to the full....

We came in sight of the Pacific just at sunset and saw the "Cortes" lying in the bay. Of course we had some sentimental feelings about that time, but our mules were determined to stop and eat the damp sand on the shore, and I can assure you that urging mules along with hand and foot is anything but sentimental business. We had miserable accommodations at San Juan del Sur, where we remained until two o'clock next day. From there we had to be carried in the arms of the natives to the small boats, which could not come close to the shore, and were rowed to the steamer. Almost all of them got wet, but we, being so light, the natives succeeded in keeping us "high and dry."

On its first voyage in 1852 the *Cortes* set a speed record of thirteen days and twelve hours from Panama to San Francisco. The ship was not on the Nicaraguan run originally, but after Vanderbilt's line lost four of its six vessels in the Pacific in just over a year, he purchased the *Cortes* for $225,000. One of the ships lost was the *North America*, which Niles and Charley had seen on the beach below Acapulco in the spring of 1852.

We found the Cortes to be a much nicer boat than the "Star of the West." Everything about it is kept perfectly clean, and we have much better fare than we had before. Still, I do not feel as much at home here, because we have rooms with two other ladies, and Charlie and Niles are in a room with 9 [men].

Our room is the pleasantest one on the boat, and if we had it to ourselves we should stay there most of the time with our books and writing, but the room is too small for 4 to stay in, so we stay on deck. We had a pretty high wind one day and night, which sent most of the passengers to their berths; except that, we have not been sick at all.... There have been several cases of fever on board, but this cool weather will restore the sick and prevent others from getting sick.

We have miserable water. We do not pretend to drink it. Tea in the morning and at night, wine at noon we are obliged to drink, and I am tired enough of wines. Sunday at noon we had a fine shower, and after the upper deck had been rinsed a little by it, we caught the water in glasses and drank it with a relish which you at home can hardly imagine. The thought of our cold spring water is perfectly tantalizing, and nothing can provoke us more than to have some one come and ask us if we would like a glass of *ice water*. A glass of clean rain water is as great a luxury as we aspire. We get along very well though, after all, for we have lemonade and claret punch.

By now Mary had changed her opinion of Mrs. Chubbuck:

She is ... clever and sociable, handsome too, but ignorant, vain and weak minded. On the steamer she flirted with the captain (a coarse sailor) and other men at such a rate that Charlie was advised by several to speak to her about it, as she was only thoughtless in the matter.... He did so, and she went and told the captain and others what Charlie had said. They of course said they thought him very foolish, unkind, &c, because she cried over it, but they themselves told Charlie they thought her a very imprudent woman.

One of those who advised Charley was Horace Ferré, who was bringing his bride, the former Lucinda Gage of Staten Island, to Nevada City, where he managed the local office of Adams and Company. The Ferré and Mulford weddings were announced in the September 30 *Journal* with the comment: "By the following it will be seen that the agents of the great rival expresses of this city are united in their action upon one subject."

As their ship steamed up the California coast, Mary wrote one last letter to Addison:

There is no place in the world that will beat a steamship for *gossip*. A country village don't compare.... Mrs. Chubbuck turns out to be a perfect *flirt*, and though pretty and pleasant, is as vain as ever I saw anyone. About the time we arrived at the Isthmus she made the acquaintance of some young gentlemen who flattered her a good deal, and she coolly left our party and joined theirs, and it is really ridiculous the way she conducts herself with them, flirting like a young girl, simpering and putting on airs; and the cream of the joke is that they consider her as intruding upon their party without invitation, and make all sorts of fun of her, even to her face, which her self complacency prevents her seeing....

Harriet Backus has proved a most agreeable companion.... She is really a sweet good girl, and a very intelligent one. I have been taking lessons in Spanish of her.

It is so cold now that the shawls and overcoats are indispensible articles, and one week ago it was so warm that we could scarcely breathe or stir.

III

THE CORTES DROPPED ANCHOR in San Francisco Bay at sundown. For two hours, while they waited to go ashore, the passengers amused themselves by watching those who came to meet the ship. Reported Mary:

We fancied we could tell who were looking for wives and who were idle spectators. There were four ladies of our acquaintance who had come to meet their husbands, but they had the good sense to go to their rooms and wait till they were found, thus avoiding a scene on deck. . . .

We stopped at the Nyantick, a nice quiet house, and never in my life have I enjoyed eating and sleeping as I did there. We had had excellent appetites for some days, but had become so tired of everything on ship board that we could not eat, and here everything was nice and *clean* and the tables filled with every luxury that we have at the best hotels in the States, and we would sit down at table and eat as fast as we dared, and stop only when forced to by a sense of decency.

Then one would eat grapes and pears at intervals, and long for the next meal. We thought such appetites would of course last but a few days, but they stay with us yet, and Deb often says she is in a hurry to get to housekeeping so that we may eat as long and as much as we please without observation. We were weighed yesterday, and Deb weighed 94 lbs. and I but 91½, but I shall gain it again at this rate of eating—I was more seasick than she. . . .

We spent Saturday in San Francisco. Washed and dressed ourselves clean in the morning (a luxury which no one can appreciate till they have been obliged for nearly two weeks to wash in *salt water* and dress in a room about the size of Ma's clothes room, with three berths, a lounge and four women in it, besides one trunk and 4 carpet bags.

We went to Grace Church, and I can assure you, it seemed good to us to be able to listen to the preached word and join in the service, though the clergyman was anything but a man of talent. During the day and evening we received a great number of calls from friends of the boys, and from those who had come with us and were stopping in town. In the evening some gentlemen called on their way to hear a lecture on Home by a Mr. Gray, formerly of Boston, an elderly clergyman, and a popular man. They invited us to go, and we did so. The lecture was very good and the music *very* fine, being a hired choir of band and organ.

We could not go up the river until Monday night, so we spent all of Monday which was not taken up with calls in running about town. I was delighted with the city. I hardly know why, for it is not handsome as we term handsome at home, but there is so much life and spirit, and every one you see looks so happy, and every one you meet seems so cordial. There is none of that careworn anxious look upon the faces of the men you meet hurrying to and fro that we see in our cities at home.

Then there is such an enthusiasm and so much affection, as it were, for the place and the country in all who have been here for years, that it is quite catching. If two persons meet as strangers, who came here in '49, they are friends at once when the coincidence is discovered. There seems a kind of Odd Fellowship about it.

The principal curiosity we saw in the Bay City was the mammoth tree, which completely throws into the shade all the great tree stories which Niles and Charles have been laughed at so much for telling. It was impossible to cut a section of the tree and bring it down from the mountains where it grew, so they have taken off the bark in sections, and have this set up in its original form. The tree was *33 feet* in diameter at the base, but owing to the branching roots, they cut it down 8 feet from the base, where the diameter was 26½ feet. The bark itself is in some places 20 inches *thick*.

There is a muslin roof over it, and it is lined with muslin, to make a nice room of it. Inside the muslin there is a room so large that 6 lounges and a piano are ranged around the sides, and a few days before we were there, a school of 120 scholars with their 6 teachers were in at [one] time, beside the furniture.... To avoid any suspicion of humbug about the bark of the tree, they have cut a slab right across the trunk of the tree 1 ft. in thickness and width, which every one can measure for himself. The base of the tree has been converted into the floor of a ranch [house] which is used as a ball room, and the owners are making a fortune out of it. What say you now to tree stories. If you doubt this, go yourself to see the wonder when it arrives at N. Y., where it is soon to be sent.

At 4 o'clock on Monday evening we went down to the [steamship] *Confidence*, which was to take us to Sacramento, and found there quite a large number of Cortes acquaintances and others to see us off. The Captain of the Cortes and a lady who was with him, and a gentleman who formerly owned the Confidence with his brother, took it into their heads to go with us up to the first landing place and back by the downward boat.

We had a very sociable pleasant evening, it being a most beautiful clear moonlight, and the scenery very fine. When the boys went to engage rooms for us, they found that Hazeltein, the young man referred to as accompanying us, had engaged for us the two *bridal chambers*, which were not often allowed to be occupied by any others than newly married people. He had paid our fare too, but the boys would not permit that to pass at all. They were beautiful little rooms, elegantly furnished with these little tapestried beds, curtained with the richest damask. We were a thousand times obliged. He said he thought if he did us some favor we would remember him enough to call on him, or permit him to call on us when we came to Sacramento, where he lives, I suppose in grand style, as he is very rich.

They had reached Sacramento early the next day and visited Mr. and Mrs. Rich, with whom Niles and Charley usually boarded when in that city. In the morning the couples caught the 5 o'clock stage and rode ten miles to the first stage stop before eating breakfast. The stage paused six more times to change horses, and the passengers ate their noon meal at the half-way point, and had tea in Nevada City. Mary said it was the most exhausting day of her journey.

The road during the first 30 miles was very much like a prairie road, striking off across the country, a good hard road, though unworked. The rest of the way it was very rough and hilly, in some places very rocky, and we were completely tired out when we got here, but slept well all night and nearly all the next day. There was one redeeming quality to the stage route. They have the best horses I ever saw, all the way, changing every 10 miles; some most splendid teams of great white horses such as we seldom see anywhere in the States.

All along, as we stopped at little towns, we had to be introduced to friends of the boys who came to welcome them back, and we were often told that our arrival in Nevada would be an *era*, as there had never come more than one lady at a time, and those not very frequent, and I should think it was an era by the way the people stared and gathered around the stage as we stopped, and by the way they stare now if we step outside the door, or go out on the piazza.

We are stopping at Phelp's Hotel, where we have very good board but poor rooms. There is a new house here where we would like to go, but the boys have always boarded here, and do not like to give offense to the landlord, who is an old friend. They will put up a house as soon as possible (that is if Niles concludes to stay here; he has made no arrangements yet), one large enough for us all to live in and keep house separately. We cannot find board here that will seem at all like home, and Deb thinks she would rather keep house if I do. I am very impatient to commence. We think some of renting a house and taking meals at a restaurant till we get our house built.

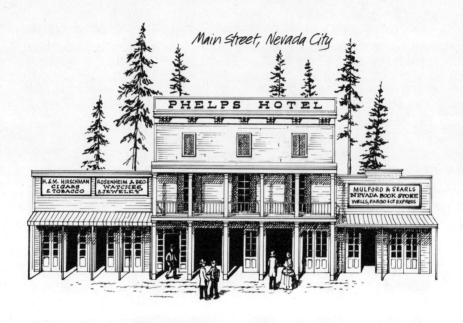

Main Street, Nevada City

PHELPS HOTEL

H.&M. HIRSCHMAN
CIGARS
& TOBACCO

ROSENHEIM & BRO.
WATCHES
& JEWELRY

MULFORD & SEARLS
NEVADA BOOK STORE
WELLS, FARGO & C° EXPRESS

CHAPTER 9

PHELPS HOTEL

November–December 1853

I

$\mathscr{T}$HE PHELPS HOTEL was the former Gregory House, where Niles and Charley had boarded. Located on the west side of Main Street, it was convenient to their bookstore and express office next door. Across the street and facing it were Mr. and Mrs. Frisbie's three popular establishments: a saloon, a restaurant, and the Concert Hall, at the corner of Coyote Street. When his National Hotel on the plaza was gutted by fire, David Phelps took over Gregory House and changed its name. Mary told Addison:

The men stand and gaze at us with mouth and eyes wide open every time we go out. There are quite a number of ladies here; there have [been ten who] called upon us already, and we have not been here a week. . . . most of them the wives of Drs. or lawyers. . . . Mrs. [Ferré], one of the ladies who came with us, [is] very pleasant to those she likes. I laugh almost to kill myself sometimes when she and Deb get to talking

82

together, they are so witty. She is a great acquisition to our society, but woe to the one who offends her and comes under the lash of her sarcasm.

To Cornelia she was more explicit:

I have described [Mrs. Ferré] but have left out her most prominent trait, that of *good taste*. Every article of dress, every piece of furniture and every act is in the most perfect taste, and such a person you know is always agreeable. She has a nice little house, elegantly furnished. Her good taste, or rather sense of propriety, would have led her to furnish it plainly herself, but the gentleman who fitted it up before they came bought the furniture and got a tapestrie carpet, French sofa, bedstead and hair mattress, marble topped bureau and washstand, &c, &c, and it is really pleasant to go and see such nice things once in a while; we run in nearly every day, and a few evenings ago took our work and spent the evening with her, and the boys called for us at 9; and a first rate time too. She has lots of music and has bought a large melodeon, but it is out of order, and she will send it back.

As for Mrs. Chubbuck.... Well Mr. Ferré was one who advised Charlie to [speak to her on the ship], and as she heard of it she was angry at [Mr. Ferré], and she and her husband are not on speaking terms with him, and she will not enter his house. We have passed over all her ill treatment of Charlie, and of us too, on the steamer, because Charlie requested it, as he could not think of losing his bookkeeper, and if Chub got angry he would not stay; besides she is not worth minding anyway.... She is not at all hateful ... but only weak minded and vain.

Writing to her mother, Mary said:

Several very pleasant ladies have called. Mrs. Turner, of whom you have heard Niles speak, is quite a young looking lady, and I think a pleasant one. Three ladies called yesterday, Mrs. [Mary Sampson] and her daughter, and Mrs. Pear. They invited us to attend their *sewing society*, which was to be held at Mrs. Pear's next week Thursday. She is a very sprightly sociable little woman and appears as though used to good society. They brought us the compliments of Mrs. Warren, the minister's wife, with regrets that sickness detained her from calling, but she would call next week.

Now perhaps you would like to know how we like Nevada.... I have been delighted with the country thus far. It far surpasses my ideas of it, and I think I shall like the country and climate very much.... The greatest trouble I have had yet is with the fleas, which are innumerable and very large. I never go out without coming back with 5 or 6, and they keep me awake nights a great deal, but I think when we get into a new clean house and there are none but us, we shall be able to keep them out almost entirely....

There are only cloth partitions between the rooms here, covered with paper, so that every word that is said in one room can be heard in the next, and Deb and I occupy rooms side by side, so that we have many a chat while lying in bed, or writing in our own rooms. Then too, there are hundreds of *rats* here, which are continually racing about over head and down the walls, and moreover, there are little holes, dozens of them, gnawed through the paper where they have made themselves at home and walked into their neighbors rooms. I saw one very cooly walk into my room one evening, but it walked out again and is the only one we have seen, so we do not trouble ourselves much about them.

I find that Deborah and Charlie are more company for me than all the company I had at Phillipsville was. I feel none of that utter loneliness and intense longing for home friends which sometimes seemed so intolerable.

This was small comfort for Cornelia, left alone at Rensselaerville. Deb tried to cheer her and smooth over hurt feelings:

It is Sunday evening, I am seated in a little room beside a round table, covered with a clean spread, on which are piled books of all sorts, including a large Websters Dictionary which Mary and I have been obliged to bring from [Charley's] store to settle disputes about this and that word. A washstand and bed comprise the rest of the furniture. Mary has a room similar to it on the other side of the parlor, these three rooms occupying the whole front part of the second story....

You did not ask me to write when I came away. I noticed it and it pained me.... If I try to think how glad you will be to see me when I come back and how we will enjoy each other's society, I find tears coming in a moment for your distrust of me, and my lasting affection will come to mind. Just write to me Cornelia and tell me you expect we will always be the same as ever, and then I will be satisfied.

II

In mid-November Mary, Deborah and Niles were busily engaged in writing for the outgoing stage, which would connect with the eastbound steamer. Niles was assuring Mary's mother he would not stop writing entirely, but guessed his wife would carry the main burden. The couples intended boarding with the Widow Sampson as soon as her new house, across from the Congregational Church, was completed. Niles wrote:

Mr. McConnell, an old practitioner here, has been elected to the office of Atty General of the State and will leave for San Francisco. His partner, Wm. M. Stewart, our Disct Atty, thinks some of going with him. I have bought him out conditionally, and if he goes I will probably be appointed Disct Atty. If not, he and I will go into the practice in partnership. Law business is good and in that connection I have no fears but we can do well. . . .

We take a walk almost every day, and have such fine times in selecting spots for *our house*. Now we located it on some commanding hill—then in a quiet valley. Once in juxtaposition to my office, where Mary can call me at any time. Again at a considerable distance to afford security from *fire* and a good walk to meals.

We often talk of home and never fail to remember you all kindly, and to hope you will not be uneasy about us. Remember we are among friends, to me quite old friends, and though not equal to those we have left behind, yet they will serve to render our stay more pleasant till we get ready to go back to you all.

Deb paused to consider an uncompleted sentence. She had got as far as the words: "and knowing that you heard"; at that moment Niles leaned across and finished the phrase with "from us all according to statute in such cases made and provided." Indignant, but amused, she explained the interruption to Cornelia:

That pest of a Niles came to my room, pulled my pen out of my hand and finished the sentence. . . . I was going to say that Mary told you all about me. . . . I never saw Mary with so much life and animation and looking so well and hearty; of course she has mentioned the enormity of our appetites; tonight I found myself eating stewed dried apples with a relish I seldom had at home for the best of sweet meats.

I am going to be contented here just two years, learn something of housekeeping, a good deal of the world, and then I shall want to come home to my dear friends. I never would be willing to make a home of Nevada if for no other reason than its non observance of the Sabbath. I cannot be reconciled to the busy hum of business on this day. Whilst I have been writing, the Crier has been through the streets proclaiming a grand exhibition at Concert Hall this evening. . . .

Niles, Mary and I have been to church today, and all three went last Sabbath. I suppose Mary has described the minister and his family to you. His wife is a sweet woman; we are going to be her neighbors, and I think we shall see her often, but if you suppose Mary and I are going to take anyone into our habits to fill your place, you are mistaken. . . . It would please you to hear the remarks made about Mary and me. People think we must be sisters, we look so much alike.... We live in a very sisterly way and I think there is no fear of trouble coming between us....

When we first thought of Thanksgiving day, we had a mind to be a little homesick, but we are now anticipating a great deal of pleasure for the day. We are going to order a dinner at a private room in one of the restaurants and have a RensVille meal. Wont *we* talk of you all, and imagine we see everything that is done that day at home. We have invited Billy Williams and Lucius [Wickes]. Arthur [Hagadorn] will certainly dine with us, but not a single soul that cannot hail from RensVille shall enter the door.

All three men had attended Rensselaerville Academy, and Lucius was Deb's cousin. Mary, also writing to Cornelia, expanded on Niles's version of their plans:

We shall have to stay [at Phelps Hotel] about 3 weeks longer, and before you get this shall be nicely settled at our new boarding place, Mrs [Sampson's]. She is building a new house for a private boarding house, and will take us and Mr. Chubbuck and his wife until we wish to go to housekeeping, at the rate of 28$ a week for each couple. This is pretty high board, but the boys think it will not be much economy to buy a lot, build and furnish a house, and have to hire our washing done after all. Still they intend to go to housekeeping just as soon as they can conveniently, because it will be so much pleasanter. *I* think we could make it more than pay cost.

Still we shall be more confined.... Charlie is building a brick store—fireproof—and is going to build it two stories high and finish the upper story for them to live in if they wish, or to rent if they do not wish it. I have no doubt they will live there, but they cannot go in [for] two months yet, on account of the walls being damp. We have had some grand times making plans for houses and furnishing them on paper.

As for Niles and I, we have scarcely any plans for the future as yet. He has gone into partnership with the District Atty. here, Mr. Stewart. Charles did not need him in the bookstore, although he would make business for him in some way rather than have him leave the place. Stewart has been in partnership with McConnell, who has been elected Attorney General of the State and is about to remove to San Francisco, and Niles takes his place. He thinks he could make more money at [Downieville] a place up higher in the mountains that he has been looking at, but it seemed to me almost as bad as leaving home to go and leave Deb and Charlie and Nevada, where I feel acquainted, and go where I should not see them more than once in 3 or 4 months, and as soon as he found how I felt, he gave up all thought of it.

86

Mary continued to work at healing the breach between Cornelia and Deb. She hoped to have greater success than Niles, who had failed in his earlier attempts to reconcile Cornelia and Charley; cool formality was all that remained of that damaged friendship:

Deb and I have talked over all that occurred while I was gone this Summer, and we talk a great deal about my visit home and all the strange events that have occurred during the past year. She is the same good faithful friend as ever ... and it would hurt her feelings very much to have you think it possible she could be any different from what she has always been to you. As for Charlie, he is just the same as he used to be. Deb is as conscious as I and you are of his disagreeable traits, and she says she means to try to cure him of them, and she manages it so pleasantly and skillfully that I think she will rub off some of the awkward corners.

In the meantime, she appreciates his good qualities and loves him more and more all the time, and seems very happy indeed, and certainly makes him so. I do not think there is the slightest trace of her old flame left, and she says she does not even regret the suffering she has endured, for it has subdued and disciplined her heart as nothing else could. She attends church with me, and last Sabbath, being Communion, she partook of the Communion with us. It is no small gratification to me, I can assure you.

The Church here is Congregational and it seems to be more like Methodist than Presbyterian, but it seems that members of Presbyterian Churches are admitted by letter. Four young men joined the church last Sabbath upon profession of faith. Quite encouraging, isn't it. The clergy-man is a popular man and a very pleasant one; talents not above medium, not equal to Dr. Richards [of Rensselaerville], though a far better speaker. Smarter than the Phillipsville minister. Mrs. Warren, the pastor's wife, is a very pleasant lady indeed and is said to be very intelligent and quite a writer.

She wished they had brought more clothes with them, for prices were outlandish in the west:

[I] will do without rather than pay the price demanded. I am not sure but we shall think it best to send home for some things bye and bye to be sent by express. The ladies here (the western ladies I mean) dress in silks always when they go out, but look like hob at home, and we wear our calicos and travelling dresses in the street every day. I never want to see another large figured brocade again. If you could see such looking ones as I do, you wouldn't wonder. I would not have any more silks if I could.

I wish I had brought a neat hack hat (hack hats of plain straw cost $16 at the Bay) and plenty of collars, shoes, gloves &c, to last me till I went home. It would have been a saving. White shawls are on a par with brocades here. Worsteds are 1/6 a skein, sewing silk 1/8, needles and other little items in proportion.* Enough of this, I have but a few moments more to write and must tell you how strong and hearty I am. I think I was never so well in my life as I am and have been for the last two weeks. I have such an appetite and can walk right up a long hill without getting tired or out of breath. I have no headaches or *anything*, and feel so brisk and lively all the time. I am learning to be spry and to be ready in time. I can dress as quick as Deb can now.

III

THE NEVADA JOURNAL followed the progress of Mulford's new "fireproof" with interest, noting that lintels over its doors and windows had been cut from native granite found along Deer Creek, half a mile above the city. Commenting on Charles Dickens' latest novel, the editor thought *Bleak House* wasn't up to the author's previous standards. But two days after Thanksgiving Niles told Cornelia of one man's utter fascination with the tale of a never-ending lawsuit:

A dark rainy night has succeeded to a dreary rainy day. The outer world assumes a gloomy aspect, but with a comfortable fire in a pleasant office, I am enabled to drive dull care away, and with a cheerful heart sit down to write you. There is no one around to molest me while writing. Not that I am wholly alone, for Mack sits the other side of this stove, but then he is engaged in "Bleak House," and will not of course speak for the next three hours.

Maybe you don't know who Mack is? Why he is our Atty General Elect—formerly plain John R. McConnell, but now the Hon John R. McConnell. Good fellow that—see how complacently he chews his *tobacco* and how utterly unconscious he is that I am watching him. [Jarndyce and Jarndyce] have so completely engrossed his attention that even *fleas* would fail to awaken him to consciousness of the outer world.

*1/6 indicates one shilling, 6 pence; 1/8 is one shilling, 8 pence. The coin Americans called a shilling was in fact the Spanish silver real or "bit." It was the eighth part of a peso or dollar. Pesos were known as pieces of eight because they were stamped with the figure 8 to indicate their value as 8 reales. Because of the purity of these coins they were literally cut in pieces and exchanged as halves (4 bits) or quarters (2 bits), and were legal tender in the United States.

Niles could well understand his friend's desire to lose himself in a book—anything to take his mind off the death of his bride of three months. McConnell had been a bachelor when Niles left California; now he was a widower. The rapid transition caused Niles to ponder changes in his own life:

The clock overhead points to the hour of eight, beyond time for a bachelor to begin a letter, but rather late for the man whose little tribe awaits his coming home for the night. How Matrimony does change our habits, and why should it not? With such a wife as mine a man would be traitorous to his feelings, as well as best interests, not to be domestic in habit.

McConnell had informed Niles that after charges against Lundy were dropped, fate had issued a harsher sentence: when the town of Sonora burned in October, Dibble's killer was found dead in the ruins of Holden's saloon, identifiable only by a pistol he had borrowed.

On December 6, 1853, when most of Nevada City's ladies were sponsoring a dinner and music festival to raise funds for a public school, Niles and Charley asked their wives not to take part in "public affairs." Mary told Addison:

Of course we felt *particularly interested* in the success of the object, but could not make any definite answer just then. The boys did not wish us to identify ourselves with anything of the kind, though the first ladies here were the projectors. So we did not pay any attention to it except to send in some money. They were so kind as to put our names on the general committee, which attention we repayed by going up on Sugar Loaf the day they wanted us to help them, and getting so tired that we could not go to the supper. I rather think they wont trouble us in that way again.

It made Mary uncomfortable to obey, but she did, and later told Cornelia, "I presume the ladies will not like it very well, but we did just as the boys bade us, and of course it makes no difference to them." However, Niles's partner, Bill Stewart, did attend, and during a round of speeches he gallantly toasted the ambition and success of Nevada's ladies:

I responded to your call, not to attempt to discuss the great question of education, but to express what we believe to be the sentiments of all present, by telling the ladies of Nevada, in plain terms, that they have done nobly in this laudable and worthy enterprise. When we first heard of the efforts that were being made by you, we had little confidence in your success. We had not learned to look at the subject in its true light, but still felt something like all felt in '49 and '50, that California was unfit for civilized men—that it might do to amass a fortune in, but that it was necessary to go to the Atlantic States to enjoy it.

In those days no one reflected that California possessed as great, if not greater, national advantages than any other state in the Union, and that it must be the permanent home of a large and enterprising population. The ladies of Nevada have the honor of being the first to take a practical and common sense view of this subject. They have commenced to act as if they believed what all are so willing to proclaim in high sounding words: that California, with her genial climate, her fertile plains, and her hills of gold, will become the homes of themselves and those they love and cherish.

Perhaps Stewart hinted at one reason for the refusal of Niles and Charley to let their wives participate when he said:

We said we did not think you would succeed in this enterprise. We now think that we were very unreasonable in doubting. We ought to have taken into consideration the fact that the ladies of Nevada are California ladies, and have had the enterprise and daring to come to a country supposed in the Atlantic States to be out of the world, or at least to be in the most wild and uncivilized part of it, and that whatever they had attempted must and would succeed. Your present efforts establish the fact that no one has a right to doubt your success in any enterprise that may engage your attention.

Rather than dwell on her disappointment and chagrin at not being able to help, Mary went on to tell of the excursion they had taken on the day of the banquet:

We had a delightful walk to Sugar Loaf. It was just about like a pleasant May day at home, and the fragrance of the sugar pines almost seemed like the fragrance of our orchards in Spring. It was a very hard walk, the hill being very steep, but it was very pleasant on the top, with a fine view on all sides. Some mountains on the other side from here were snow crowned, and all looked beautiful.

On our way home we stopped at some mining claims where they were working under ground, saw the buckets going up and down by horse power, bringing sometimes water, sometimes gold dust, sometimes men, from the dark depths below. The way back through the mines was a crooked one, for we had to wind about over ditches and sluices. We walk almost every pleasant day when the walking is good.

And she revealed surprising information about her husband:

Niles has taken the editorial chair of the "Young America," a Democratic paper of this city. The former editor got into such a quarrel with the editor of the Whig paper that it came near ending in a duel, but finally resulted in the editor leaving town and giving his paper in charge of Niles, whom he pays $100 a month.

He issued one last week, having had only two days to prepare it in, and [lawsuits] on his hands at the same time. He has been very much complimented on his first attempt. A San Francisco paper notices it thus, "Mr. Niles Searls has assumed the editorial chair of the 'Young America.' The number of the paper before us evinces talent and industry.". . . I will send you one of his papers if I can find one. It's nothing wonderful, only a great deal better than it ever was before.

Nevada City 1853-1854

Labels on illustration: DAVIS'S FIREPROOF BRICK · STEWART & SEARLS OFFICE · COUNTY COURT HOUSE · MR. WARREN'S HOUSE · MRS. SAMSON'S BOARDING HOUSE · WARREN'S CHURCH · JOURNAL OFFICE · EMPIRE STABLE & LIVERY · PHELPS HOTEL · BARKER'S EXCHANGE · FRISBIE'S CONCERT HALL EMPIRE · MAIN STREET · MAIN ST. · BROAD STREET · JAIL

CHAPTER 10

YOUNG AMERICA

September 1853–January 1854

I

Young America was meant to speak for the Democratic party in Nevada County. While Niles was in New York, and long after the *Journal* became a Whig paper, Bill Stewart decided to sponsor a rival sheet. Bill preferred to keep his name off the masthead, so when the first issue appeared on September 14, 1853, local postmaster Robert A. Davidge was identified as publisher and editor. Davidge, a native of Kentucky, had family connections high in the party, which secured the post office appointment for him at age twenty-three. Before receiving it in May, he had been a deputy in the county clerk's office.

Democrats lost their exclusive hold on Nevada County in the election held one week before *Young America*'s debut. By hard campaigning and a little help from dissident Democrats, Whigs captured two of the county's five Assembly seats. One of those defeated was Deputy Sheriff William "Billy" Mason, a close friend of Davidge. Mason, a Virginian, blamed his defeat on attorney H. C. Gardiner, also a Democrat, with whom he had differences. Gardiner, who was from Rhode Island, had urged voters to scratch Mason's name from the official Democratic party ticket.

When the ballots were being counted, Mason and Davidge joined other Democrats at Dr. Lark's City Drug Store to await results. When word arrived that he had placed last in a field of ten, Mason was furious. Bill Stewart heard him threaten to whip Gardiner and advised him to watch his step. "Never strike a sleepy-looking fellow like that," Stewart told him. "You'd better know what you're getting into—I wouldn't tackle Gardiner without knowing more about the man."

Mason laughed nastily and beckoned to Davidge to follow. Across the street at Phelps Hotel, Gardiner was standing at the bar when Mason came in with a pistol in one hand and a whip in the other. Mason tried to slash the attorney's face, but his aim was poor, and the rawhide flicked harmlessly across the man's coat. Gardiner drew a small penknife from his pocket and dared Mason to continue.

When Mason struck him a second time, others intervened, but the white-faced and grim Gardiner demanded a meeting in the morning. "If you're not there, I'll find you and shoot you on sight!" he warned.

Shortly before 9 a.m., Gardiner emerged from the Adams Express office and waited until Davidge and Mason came out of the post office next door. When a friend called a warning, the pair glanced quickly in Gardiner's direction and hurried up Broad street to the *Young America* office. Once inside, they immediately ducked out the back door. Gardiner, from in front of the building, inquired for Mason, only to be told he wasn't "in." Moments later the crack of a pistol shot revealed his location: a narrow alley alongside the newspaper shop. Gardiner cried out as the ball pierced his leg.

A crowd of spectators scurried for shelter, calling for Gardiner to follow suit, but the cool New Englander stood his ground. Mason went on firing as Gardiner tried to get a bead on his unseen assailant. At last a yelp from the alley suggested at least one shot had found its mark, but not before both men had emptied their pistols did anyone attempt to investigate. Neither man was capable of reloading his own weapon, especially under such circumstances, and the fight ended.

Both men had received minor leg wounds, and there were other casualties: a dead pig and two calves. Warren Ewer, busily setting type for the first issue of *Young America*, was nearly hit by a stray bullet that buried itself in his hardwood typecase. If Mason's friends were disgusted, his enemies were furious. To save him from the angry crowd, Stewart and others had to hustle Billy inside, lock the door, and claim he was so badly hurt it would be cowardly to beat him.

Not only was Mason forced to leave town, but Davidge's reputation suffered also. The *Journal* claimed 2000 signatures appeared on a petition for Davidge's removal as postmaster. Inevitably the two editors

feuded in print; Sargent began by complaining about unfair competition
for advertising and job printing:

Our prices are the same that they have been the past six months, and
will always conform to the times. But as we do a large share of the work
of our office ourselves . . . we can do work at a profit, where other offices
in the county at the same price would do it at a loss. Therefore, if need
be, we will reduce our prices to the mere cost of material and labor, or
even one half price the latter.

So much for what we will do. What we will not do is to dog the steps
of persons getting work done at any other office and levy black-mail. We
will not threaten to come down on a business unless the proprietor
gives us an advertisement of it as well as to another paper. We will not
querulously complain to persons [who share] our political sentiments
[because] they go to another office to get work done. We will not bribe a
doorkeeper to scatter our imprint in Concert Hall because we don't get
the programmes to print. . . .

If it should happen that, not knowing we were a fishy democrat, we
had a relative in the Senate who got us an office, say the post office, for
which we were not fit, and which we totally neglected, save to make it a
tool for other purposes, we would not earn also the contempt of printers
by compelling expressmen to get all their posters and advertising done
in our office on penalty of being embarrassed in getting their letters. We
don't go to business men and offer to take advertisements at any price,
after pledging ourselves to certain prices. . . .

We don't catch itinerant players and singers in the outskirts of the
town and "compel them to come in" our office for work. And we wont,
after doing all these things, talk of honor and straightforwardness. [But]
if we wont, the *Young America* will and does do one and all of them.

Soon after Mary arrived in Nevada City, the editor of Grass Valley's
new paper, the *Telegraph*, said Warren Ewer claimed to be in "joint
control" at *Young America*. Ewer, who had been the *Journal*'s original
owner, had worked with Tallman Rolfe on the old *Placer Times*, at
Sacramento, and when Ewer started the first paper at Nevada City,
Tallman joined him.

Before that, Tallman had been Yuba City's first justice of the peace
and a member of the Sutter County court of sessions. On his recent
twenty-ninth birthday he had been elected justice of the peace for Nevada
township, and also served as associate justice on the Nevada County
court of sessions. And now, like Ewer, he owned a part of *Young
America*, shares purchased quietly from Davidge. The man on the street
might accept the fiction that Davidge was in full control, but Aaron

Sargent thought otherwise, and on November 25 he published what he knew:

[*Young America*] purports to be edited by R. A. Davidge, but it is well known in this community that R. A. Davidge as editor is a mere figment, put forward to take the curse for a clique, who control the paper, who mistake slang for argument, and who are not acquainted with the first rules of editorial courtesy.... His essays made him a standing jest and laughing stock, and brought most of his own party, and all the rest of the community down upon his paper. He then relapsed into almost total silence, giving up his sheet to an army of doctors, small lawyers, and other tyros, who have completed its infamy.

But even now, when anything particularly soft finds its way into that paper, people say, "that's Davidge." With this harmless individual, in several ways more his own enemy than any one else can be, we desire no controversy. We have tried his metal in that way and found it very poor brass. For the sake of keeping his name in the paper, and before the public, he will play any antics, and receive any amount of kicking from the press, on the principle that similar fops will be cuffed rather than not be noticed by gentlemen.

From the outset Bill Stewart had cautioned Davidge about Sargent, calling him "about the most dangerous man in town to fool with." He warned the hot-blooded Southerner to leave the "mackerel catcher" alone. But Sargent's taunts were too much for Davidge, who launched a verbal attack impugning Sargent's talents, stature, demeanor, and veracity, concluding:

... we should deem that we were derelict in our duty were we to omit calling you in plain, direct, unmistakeable and unequivocal language, *a LIAR*. This perhaps will test your *brass* in another line than that which is purely editorial. Now, sir, if you have any pretensions to the reputation of either a *gentleman* or a man, (both of which we doubt) you are called upon to respond.

Sargent responded with supreme contempt. Even Stewart was astonished, describing the editorial response as the most abusive he'd read— calculated to ruin whatever might be left of Davidge's presumably once-good name. Sargent had said:

Did we wish to win the reputation of a blackguard, by using a blackguard's weapons, we should say [Davidge] is a liar. As it is, we merely deny the assertion [that we are a liar], leaving the legitimate inference to be drawn.... [Davidge says] "It is a matter of *notoriety*" that we will not fight a duel! Indeed. Now mark what follows. After confessing to a knowledge of this fact, we are called upon to "respond," that is, to fight a duel. Nothing will suit R. A. Davidge, he declares, but a duel with a man who he says he knows will not thus meet him. . . .

You [Davidge] offer a "private settlement," on the notorious fact that such a settlement will not be thus accepted. You wish to gain a *cheap* reputation for "chivalry." There might be some merit in your offer had you not so fully first fixed in your mind that it would not be taken up. As it is, you simply prove yourself, as you also did by the manner of your interference between Mason and Gardiner, a *coward*! You are right. We will not fight a duel with you, because we will not disfranchise our-self. . . . And there is another reason, furthermore, why we will not fight thus with you.

We do not hold you to be generally accredited even as a *gentleman*. By the laws of the code you appeal to because you know you will not be taken at your word, a gentleman is required only to meet gentlemen. That you are not a gentleman in public estimation is shown by the unresented insult you received when a gentleman at a recent ball quietly declined to your face to introduce you to his wife. His reasons cover the case.

There is another way we wont settle it, except in self defence. We will not assault you in the street. We pity your shockingly diseased body, caused by association with vile women, as you go pale and almost shadowless through the streets; for all [we care] you shall pass un-molested to your grave. We shall respect your debility even while detesting you. "A private settlement" then is out of the question, unless you choose to avail yourself of the latter method, to which you are entirely welcome.

Bill Stewart judged that unless Davidge responded quickly and positively, he would be excluded from decent society. The lawyer stood in front of the office of Stewart and Searls and watched, bemused, as Aaron Sargent strolled toward the post office. He also watched the postmaster approach from the opposite side of Deer Creek, knowing that because both bridges had washed away and been replaced only by a log with poles for hand rails, it was impossible for two persons to cross without touching shoulders.

The moving figures advanced to the center of the bridge, yet neither man showed signs of pausing or of slowing his pace. For an instant Stewart held his breath. Then, astonished, he saw the moment pass without a word spoken or a blow struck. Scarcely believing his eyes, he entered his office. When Davidge arrived moments later, the district attorney asked if he had read the *Journal*. Davidge replied in the affirmative.

"And you saw what Sargent wrote?"

Davidge flushed. "I'll kill him!" he exploded.

"Sure you will," retorted Stewart, leaving the room in disgust.

Days later, a small notice appeared in *Young America* over Davidge's signature:

> Business calls our attention below for some weeks. In our absence Mr. Niles Searls will take charge of the "Young America." From Mr. Searles' long residence and acquaintance with the people of Nevada county, we are assured the paper could not be left in better hands. When we return we shall again resume our position. Note: Mr. W. B. Ewer is authorized to transact all business pertaining to this office—to receive and contract for work—to collect monies and to receipt therefor in my name, and, in short, to have the control and management of the business of the "Young America Office."

II

THE WEATHER WAS so mild when the new year began that it prompted many complaints. Mary explained this unusual phenomenon to her father on January 10:

> This is the *rainy* season and yesterday was the first cloudy day we have had in several weeks. This morning the sky is as blue as ever, and by afternoon it will be so warm that I can sit in my room with the windows up with perfect comfort. Day after day and week after week it is the same, to the great discomfort of all business men, for without rain the country will soon become bankrupt. People cannot pay their debts because they have no money.
>
> Everything of course depends upon the proceeds of the mines, and there has been but one week of steady rain this winter. Niles frequently charges from $200 to $300 a week in his law business, and with difficulty collects enough to pay our expenses. I was very glad that you gave me some money before we left, as we have to furnish our own room, which cost us nearly $100, and as he has been buying half the law office, and other expenses have been enormous, I should have been sorry to have him obliged to purchase that.
>
> I think the rest you gave me will furnish the rest of our house when we go to housekeeping, for we should get but little furniture, and that of the plainest kind. It is the way most do here. At any rate, when we are as fortunate as to have a week's rain, money will once more be plenty.

There is no danger but we could get all that we need any way, but in Cal. that does not satisfy. We want to be laying up all the time. We pay $14 a week for board, making $112 a month for both, besides our washing, which comes to $3 per week usually. This seems enormous to me, just from the states, but if Niles does $200 or $300 worth of business a week now, in the very dullest season for business in the year, I think he will make a *little something* in the course of a year, over and above expenses.

Of course only half the profits are his, but that is considerable. There was a suit the other day in which the opposing party sent down to [Sacramento] for a lawyer, an ex-senator—to argue the case against Niles. Niles won the suit, and the Judge said they need not send to Sac. or anywhere else for lawyers as long as they had *him* here, and the defeated advocate declared he should know who to send business to after that.

He continues to edit the "Young America" but does not take the pains with it that he would if he thought of continuing to do so. He will give it up as soon as the rain comes and business improves. We like our boarding place very much. We have every delicacy that the country affords, and many that are imported. Radishes, celery, turnips and cabbage, fresh from a ranch below here every few days. Venison, wild game, oysters, pork (fresh of course) and beef alternately, and at tea we have fresh peaches, which come preserved in cans, and look and taste nearly as nice as though just taken from the trees.

Although their landlady wished Mary would agree to sing in the church choir, she demured, citing Niles's reticence: "Niles does not like to have me make myself conspicuous in any way here. . . ." In a postscript she added: "I should not have written what I have about Niles's business to anyone but yourself, because he does not like to have such things talked of by others."

Before 1853 ended, a group of citizens asked Niles to present a petition to the county court for incorporation of Nevada City. Although most persons had welcomed revocation of the first city charter, there had been some unwanted and unforeseen consequences. In September 1853 a less grandiose scheme had been proposed by Justice of the Peace T. W. Colburn, who presented these arguments in its favor:

Nevada, from being for a time governed too much, goes to the other extreme, and for two years past has wholly relied upon the general good character and integrity of its citizens for the preservation of order, and the citizens have done much in this respect; but now the time has come when the voluntary provisional government falls [too] heavily upon the few . . . and such latterly has been the rapid stride and growth of the town ... that an imperative demand is now made upon you to take more active measures for the preservation of the morals, the peace, comfort and safety of the community. ...

[We] know that open and unblushing debauchery of both sexes exists amidst us in the most revolting form, corrupting the morals and offending the common decencies of life in the neighborhoods which they infest. We know that obscenity of conduct and language in these resorts are public as the noonday—

... that the Sabbath is desecrated and religious services frequently disturbed by the shout of the bachanalian—that the hour of sleep is made hideous by the midnight cries and howls and the indiscriminate discharge of fire-arms—sending terror to the heart—that the reckless without remonstrance, may wear concealed weapons with which to deal with on the slightest real or imaginary provocation—that furious driving through our narrow streets may be indulged in to the imminent danger of life and limb of men, women and children.

The petition handed to Niles contained signatures of a majority of city voters, who asked that the city occupy an area of one square mile, with its center at the court house on Broad Street. When Niles presented the document to the county court on January 5, 1854, the request was granted and January 21 fixed as the day to elect city officers.

Next to the courthouse was a new wood frame building occupied by the firm of Stewart and Searls. Because it had been constructed hurriedly, a careless workman installed the chimney with improper clearance, and on January 8 the roof caught fire around the stove pipe. Fortunately, it was seen by a passerby, and several persons helped him climb to the roof and put out the flames. Cautioned the editor of *Young America*:

Gentlemen, look to your stove pipes, and see to it that a few buckets or a barrel of water is always at hand, and accessible at an instant's notice. Nothing but a precaution of this kind could have saved us from a serious conflagration on Sunday last. A barrel of water a few feet distant saved the building. Had the water pipes alone, or the creek been depended on for a supply of water, we should doubtless have been called upon to chronicle a very different result.

With the exception of a hole in the roof and some water damage to volumes of Blackstone and Vattel, there was little loss. Later in the month a like situation caused the Empire Saloon's roof to ignite, and a fire was set at a David Ashmore's Spanish dancehouse. In February these and other recent episodes decided Stewart and Searls to move their office and the newspaper to the upper floor of Hamlet Davis's "fireproof" brick building, completed in December. Most county officers followed their example and moved into the same building.

Niles and Ianthus Rolfe bought Tallman Rolfe's interest in *Young America* and became Stewart's partners in the enterprise, which was renamed the *Nevada Democrat*. At the same time, Aaron Sargent sold his interest in the *Journal* to Edwin R. Budd and John P. Skelton. Budd took over as editor and Sargent began studying for his bar examination.

Deborah and Charley had gone for a buggy ride during the warm spell in January. It was not often that people indulged in such luxuries at Nevada City, where but two or three carriages existed in the whole town. But then a change occurred, and it rained for two days and then snowed from Saturday till Monday, depositing more than two feet on the ground. It was clear and cold on Tuesday, inspiring Grass Valley miner Gil Meredith to fabricate a sled from 3-inch planks with a box on top. He hitched it to a four mule team and took several friends on a sleigh ride to Nevada City. Their outing was reported by the *Journal*, which confused the mules with horses:

The merry ringing of sleigh bells has been heard for several days past in our city. Several temporary sleighs have been fitted up, and the young gentlemen have treated the ladies to dashing turnouts. On Tuesday the Countess of Landsfeldt paid our berg a flying visit per this conveyance and a span of horses, decorated with impromptu cow bells. She flashed like a meteor through the snow flakes and wanton snowballs, and after a thorough tour of the thoroughfares, disappeared in the direction of Grass Valley.

The "Countess" was the notorious Lola Montez, who, having tired of Paris, London, New York, Boston, Washington, and San Francisco, had selected Grass Valley as her residence.

Lola Montez

CHAPTER 11

IRISH VISITORS

February 1854

I

*L*OLA'S MOTHER, a music hall dancer, was thirteen when she gave birth to Marie Dolores Eliza Rosanna Gilbert at Limerick, Ireland, in 1818. Her husband's family hustled the pair off to India, where Edward Gilbert received a commission in the army of Britain's East India Company. When he died of cholera seven years later, Lola's mother married Captain John Craigie.

Young Dolores was in the way and rather wild, so they sent her to Scotland to be educated by Craigie's parents. There she proved a livelier package than they had bargained for. Lola then was passed along to the family of a well-to-do retired army officer who had escorted Dolores on the voyage to England. She became his daughter's companion, and together they enjoyed good times in London, Paris, and Bath—until Lola's eighteenth birthday.

At this point her mother came to England with a scheme to marry her daughter to an elderly judge of the Indian supreme court. Dolores objected, choosing instead to elope with the handsome young Irish lieutenant who came with her mother. Mrs. Craigie refused to consent to their marriage until convinced her underage daughter had been "compromised." Lieutenant Thomas James and his bride and mother-in-law returned to India after the wedding.

Dolores soon regretted her haste. Her stepfather now held an important post, and the estrangement between mother and daughter was noticeable in the narrow confines of the British colony. Furthermore, James resented other men's attentions to his attractive bride. But whereas she at least remained faithful, he did not, and when Dolores confronted him with evidence of an ongoing affair, he eloped with a fellow officer's wife. Dolores received sympathy from most military wives, but not from her mother.

Embittered and humiliated, she at last accepted General Craigie's offer of 2000 pounds sterling and passage to England. At the last minute her husband changed his mind. He boarded her ship at Calcutta and sought a reconciliation. But it was too late, and when he disembarked at Madras, she promptly took up with Captain Lennox, a fellow passenger. Her outraged British companions shunned Mrs. James for the remainder of the voyage, but the American passengers were intrigued by her independent spirit. Watching her waltz with Lennox, they told her she had the makings of a professional dancer.

However, Dolores had dreams of a dramatic career. After she and Lennox moved into London's Imperial Hotel, she began calling on theatrical agents. Again the suggestion was made that she had "possibilities" as a dancer, but not as an actress. For the next four months she studied Spanish dancing, made a brief visit to Spain, and returned to England with a Spanish accent and a new identity: Lola Montez, widow of a mysterious "Don Diego Leon."

Unfortunately, Lt. James chose this precise moment to sue for divorce, and because the case was heard in London, the papers carried spicy details of her adultrous activities with Captain Lennox. Worst of all, instead of a divorce, her husband was awarded permanent separation— each party was forbidden to remarry as long as the other lived. Dolores James shrugged her shoulders and assumed the identity of Lola Montez, who would go anywhere and do anything she pleased. Henceforth, she decided, she would be answerable to no person and no law.

During the next several years she traveled to Brussels, Berlin, Warsaw,

St. Petersburg, Constantinople, Dresden, Vienna, Prague, Leipzig, Carlsbad, Wiesbaden, Baden-Baden, Hamburg, Genoa and Paris. She appeared on the stage, was guest of honor at royal receptions, and conversed with heads of state and their representatives. She also met Europe's great musicians and writers, created scandals, and occasionally set off political fireworks.

In Warsaw she claimed to have rebuffed the advances of Count Paskevich, the Russian general who brutally suppressed the 1830 Polish rebellion. At the time of Lola's visit, he had become the despotic and unpopular governor of that country. Lola thought he was old and ugly, so she refused his offer of romance. According to Lola, Count Paskevich ordered his commander of police to change her mind, but she defied him too. When he refused to leave her hotel room, she clawed his face.

After that, for three nights in a row, her performance was booed and hissed by a noisy claque. On the third night she strode to the footlights and confronted the audience. Ignoring hecklers, she blamed the demonstration on her refusal to submit to Paskevich. Many in the audience who hated the governor rose to her defense, causing a fight between opposing factions. As she was hurried away from the theater, rioting spread to other parts of the city, where many had awaited such a pretext to protest.

An effort was made to arrest Lola, but she barred her door and threatened to shoot at police. At last the French Consul arranged for safe passage out of the country. Her outburst resulted in more than 300 arrests, including that of a banker whose wife had entertained her.

Undaunted, Lola went next to St. Petersburg, saw the czar and czarina, and then proceeded to Dresden for a short and stormy affair with composer Franz Liszt, a notorious womanizer. Richard Wagner encountered Liszt and Montez at the opera, and took an instant dislike to Lola. She was, he said, a "painted and jewelled woman with bold, bad eyes." While in Turkey she persuaded the British Ambassador to arrange a visit to the sultan's harem. After inspecting his wives she called them unattractive.

In Paris she was the lover of journalist Alexandre Dujarier, who introduced her to Dumas, Balzac, Lamartine, Victor Hugo, and George Sand. Lola admired Sand, another of Liszt's lovers, and copied her daring custom of cigar smoking. The friendship with Dujarier was perhaps the happiest in her life thus far, but it ended tragically when he was killed in a duel and died in her arms. The grief-stricken dancer left Paris and traveled to Bavaria, where she became the close friend and confidante of King Ludwig.

That monarch's liberal reforms brought him in conflict with the Catholic church and other conservative factions. Because Lola encouraged him and had well-known ties to French radicals she, too, came under fire. As a result, the king was warned to renounce her unless he wished to lose important political support. In a foolishly defiant gesture, Ludwig gave her citizenship and two titles: Baroness of Rosenthal and Countess of Landsfeld, which entitled her to receive an annuity of 20,000 florins a year, the Landsfeld estates, and feudal rights over 2000 peasants.

Bavaria was the last important conservative stronghold in Europe at this time. Revolutionary movements on the Continent had forced many on the right to flee for their lives to this sanctuary, and everything would be done here to stem the radical tide. Munich University students were encouraged to demonstrate against Lola's presence, and she responded by telling Ludwig to shut down the school. Against his better judgment, the king complied. As his enemies had hoped, the resulting storm of protest was impressive, and in February 1848, Ludwig unhappily put his name on the order which banished Lola forever.

Lola's exit occurred at the same time as John Sutter, another European adventurer, was vainly striving to conceal the discovery of gold at his California sawmill. Six years and two "husbands" later, Lola was in California herself. Her most recent wedding, at San Francisco's Mission Dolores on July 3, 1853, was to Patrick Purdy Hull, publisher of the San Francisco *Whig*. But when he accompanied Lola to Grass Valley two weeks later, for an engagement at the Alta Theatre, there was talk already of a rift between them.

After performing at Grass Valley, she went on to Nevada City and danced each night from July 25 to 30, before returning to Grass Valley. On August 5 the *Journal* gossiped:

The Countess Lola Montez, *de* Lansfeldt, *de* Heald, *de* Hull, had quite a *recherche* performance at the Alta a few evenings since. The attendance at the advertised representation being too thin to justify the Countess in fulfilling the programme, she declined appearing publicly, and the money was returned to the ticket holders. *After which*, a *private* performance was given to about a dozen favorite hombres, when the lovely Lola, "as was said," took the *rag* off the "bush," or in other words, gave the "Spy-dear dance," with extra touches, to the infinite delight of the few admiring friends. All that was *seen* on the occasion has not been divulged.

The leering reference to the "Spy-dear dance" was an allusion to "La Tarantella," a dance for which Lola had become famous in San Francisco and Sacramento. In June the critic for her husband's paper had described her movements in a humorous vein:

She unwittingly gets into one of those huge nests of spiders, found during the spring time in meadows, with a long radius of leading spires and fibres, stretching away into an infinity of space. She commences to dance and the cobwebs entangle her ankles. The myriad spiders, young and old and half grown begin to colonize.... The spiders accumulate and the danseuse stamps.... It is Lola versus the spiders. After a series of examinations and shaking dresses, she succeeds in getting the imaginary intruders away—apparently stamps daylight out of the last ten thousand, and does it with so much naivete that we feel [a] sort of satisfaction at the triumph.

The *Journal* said Lola was a guest at Gil Meredith's cottage on Mill Street:

Madam Lola Montez seems to be quite captivated with the charming village of Grass Valley.... It is a cosy scene, these cool, delicious evenings, to see the charming Countess gracefully swinging in a hammock under the piazza, surrounded by the gallant host and a select circle of worshippers at the shrine of Beauty and Genius. In fact, "Gil" is the envy of the whole town; but he deserves his success with the fair, for he possesses a noble heart, and "winning ways." A lucky dog he is to have a live Countess at his bachelor box.

And there she remained, the "noble Gil" having moved out to accommodate his guest. A month later it was being reported that Lola's marriage to Hull had soured and she would divorce him. Hull did indeed leave her, but had nothing to say to the press. Meanwhile, the men and women of Grass Valley and Nevada City regarded Lola in various ways, each according to previous prejudice and present marital status.

II

NILES SUFFERED a serious loss when the clipper ship *San Francisco*, carrying his valuable but uninsured collection of law books, smashed against rocks on the north shore of the Golden Gate. No lives were lost, but the small amount of its $400,000 cargo that was salvageable was quickly stolen by swarms of armed scavengers. Mary used the unhappy occasion to instruct Addison, who was feeling sorry for himself and had been agonizing over what to make of his life:

I have frequently heard him say they would be worth more than $1,000 to him in Nevada, and his great object in renting a fireproof room was to have a safe place for them.

I do hope for pity's sake you have recovered your cheerfulness before this time, for yours was the bluest letter I ever read. I am sorry enough that it should seem necessary for you to engage in business so distasteful to you, but since you are fairly esconced therein, I see no other way for you than to either learn to like it, or to console yourself with the thought that a year does not last forever. . . . But what business would you like, except studying, and that in itself does not generally prove to be very profitable.

Mary voiced doubts about the wisdom of Addison's coming to California, as well as prospects for Niles's success. She then got down to cases:

. . . between you and I and no one else—it is not a very funny thing to go and buy a pair of $2 shoes and have them charged, because one hasn't the money to pay for them, and at the same time having to pay $28 a week for board, and other things in proportion. True, Niles has on his books charged more than enough to pay all our expenses—and could he get his pay, his business would soon make him rich but he *can't,* and it is very probable will have to give up his business on that account. Now don't you mention a word of this to our folks or any one else. I only tell it to you to show you that people in Cal. have troubles too.

Addison was teaching school at Great Barrington, but had been offered a chance to take another school. John Niles wanted him to study law, something Addison was not eager to do. His father's letter of February 16 was not calculated to lift his spirits:

As to the offer you have received to go South, it appears rather favorable on its face, but . . . it may well be feared that the school may not turn out to be as profitable to you as is represented—and as the expenses of going that distance and establishing yourself in the school would be pretty large—unless you continued it as much as two years. . . .

And if you are fully decided to pursue the study of law as a profession for life, and you feel confident that you will enjoy life best in that business, even though it should not pay very largely, it would not be desirable to put off your studies for two years longer, unless you could make a tolerable fair saving by it, especially if it is likely to injure your eyes, and although you probably could make more money for two or three years by teaching at the south than you would make in the same time after you had been licensed in the profession of law, yet perhaps it may be more desirable to spend the time in laying a firm foundation for future success.

Therefore I think, if you are fully determined to pursue the study of law, and to practise it with the energy necessary to insure success, it will be as well for you to come home when your present term closes, and study in my office during the next spring and summer. . . . But after all I have said, you must exercise your own judgment in the matter to some extent.

Mary began a letter to her mother by recalling Polly's recipe for a happy marriage:

This letter must be finished before Niles comes. I always try to be quite at leisure when he comes in, no matter what is my hurry, for that seems to be the only way in which I can return his constant care and thoughtfulness for me. I have not forgotten your lesson upon meeting him always with a smile, and it has been a valuable one to me, though I seldom *need* to recall it, for the sound of his footstep on the stair brings the smile spontaneously to my lips and the color to my cheek.

Was there ever such a good husband. I suppose there have been a great many, perhaps better, but I doubt if there ever were two persons who *loved* each other more intensely than we do. All my fears about going out into the world and all that were groundless. I am as safe, or feel as safe with his strong arm to support me—his sound sense and good judgment to guide me, as I did under the parental roof in our own quiet village. You know when I was home . . . I always felt a shrinking from new places and new acquaintances, but now I can stay or go, it makes no difference where, if he is with [me], for with him is my home. . . .

We (Deb and I) enjoy very much making plans for keeping house and trying to contrive some place for me to go near her and Niles's office too. His old office [on Broad Street] is empty, contains 4 rooms, is rat proof, new, and a bridge across [Oregon] ravine connects the back yard with that of Charlie's store [and] it is but a few doors below Niles's office. But it cannot be rented for less than $50 a month, so that will not do. . . .

Carry [Sampson] has promised to show me about music, and offered the use of her piano and instruction book if I would learn. I have commenced practicing one or two hours every morning, and get along finely. She hears our French lesson evenings, and when we are interrupted by company evenings, we often take time to read it in the daytime. She is an excellent French and Spanish scholar, and wants us to study Spanish too, but we don't like to undertake more than we can accomplish well. Aunt Mary (as we all call Mrs. Sampson) is full of fun as well as all the rest, and we have some funny times, I can assure you. . . .

Arthur [Hagadorn] was here and spent the evening on Thursday, and we enjoyed it very much, we do not see him very often. He is thought very highly of here, and he deserves it well, for he is a straightforward, upright man.

Thomas F. Meagher lectured here this week and we all went. . . . His lecture was beautiful, as well as his delivery, but he does not compare with Wendell Phillips in my view, though more polished in style and rhetoric. Niles called upon him to see if he wished to give any public notices, as his paper was to come out that morning. Meagher was very affable and pleasant, he said, and last evening called at his office and stayed a long time.

The notice Niles prepared for the *Democrat* read:

Thomas Francis Meagher, the eloquent apostle of Irish liberty, one of the most dazzling stars in the bright galaxy of exiles now on our shores, will deliver a lecture this evening at Dramatic Hall. The world wide renown which this gifted exile has won by his bold and eloquent defence of the principles of liberty so dear to every American heart, is an ample guarantee that our citizens will grasp the present opportunity of listening to the matchless tones of oratory, as they fall in music-like strains from the lips of this illustrious man.

Ireland, her illustrious sons, and her wrongs are the fruitful themes upon which he delights to dwell. The subject of the lecture this evening will be Henry Grattan and the Irish volunteers of 1782.

Because of his part in the radical revolutionary party known as "Young Ireland," Meagher had been found guilty of high treason and condemned to death. Through the intervention of friends his sentence was commuted to life imprisonment in the penal colony at Tasmania. He arrived there in 1849, escaped in 1852, and came to New York to begin a lecture tour of American cities to stir up support for the Irish cause. Meagher was thirty years old.

Less enthusiastic was the *Journal*'s editor, whose dislike of the Irish reflected his party's belief that the Democratic Party encouraged immigrants, whether aliens or citizens, to vote against Whig candidates. After listening to Meagher he concluded:

Mr. Meagher is a fluent speaker; his construction of sentences is beautiful, rather than forcible. The only peculiarity we saw to mar the harmony of his oratory was a slight Irish accent, but not sufficient to be really disagreeable. His allusions to the American government, and the brilliant triumph of the revolution gained over the English not only [were] happily expressed, but extremely pleasant to every American ear. But the parallel which he strove to carry out between that and the Irish

struggle about the same time, we regarded as anything but complimentary to the Irish nation.

He described the Irish forces in the most glowing colors, giving them
the appearance of invincibility; yet *without a struggle*, even when the
British were so much reduced and engaged by other wars that a single
brigade could not be mustered on Irish ground—when their financial
condition was so deranged that a loan of a few thousand pounds sterling
was out of their reach—when, in fact, the Irish had no opposition, they
tamely put their necks under the yoke—and licked the hand of the
tyrant while he was fettering them.

Predictably, there was an angry outcry from Nevada County's Irish
population, a few of whom denounced the *Journal* in letters to the
Democrat. Editor Searls published the letters and offered his own quite
different reaction:

In the smooth flowing elegance of his diction as he narrates his
dreams of California, when confined in a far distant land, we have never
heard his superior. His description of the Irish Volunteers, arrayed in the
streets of Dublin, places the scene before our eyes more graphically
than could the pencil of the artist. While we are convulsed with laughter
by his spicy jokes and comical descriptions, we also feel a chill of
sadness as he thrillingly describes the misfortunes and struggles of his
beloved country.

The *Journal* editor replied with condescension to the protesting
letters:

A people unaccustomed to free thought and discussion find it
extremely difficult to understand how American journalists DARE to
examine and criticise—even rebuke—men who aim to be better than
common clay. We willingly forgive this narrow view where it encroaches
upon ourself, even if, as in the Irish effusions of the last "Democrat," it
takes the form of low abuse....

Mr. Meagher lectured on Wednesday evening last on "Young Ireland."
We say of this lecture also that it was violently abusive of all classes in
Ireland who were not members of that party. It denounced O'Connell
and the moderate Catholic party as toadies to office and to patronage. It
denounced the Protestant party as devoted to their tea kettle and
church. All but the men with whom Meagher acted were treacherous to
Ireland.

Now if we accused Mr. M. of partiality to his own partisans, and
prejudice to the rest of his nation, we probably should be called British
tories. Nevertheless, in spite of such a terror, and that other (in a free

country) contemptible threat of Irish voters' opposition, we do say that
Mr. M.'s tirades against the majority of his fellow-citizens is not recom-
pensed by his eulogies on the rest—that he does an injury to the good
fame of Ireland. And thus he proves one of two things—that the action of
the "Young Ireland" party was ill-timed and premature, or that all the
rest of his country was treacherous.

The schoolhouse for which Nevada City's ladies had raised money
had been built next door to the Congregational Church. It had two
rooms, each 20 feet square. The county treasurer said the district was
entitled to $1075.90 in state funds for the coming term, enough to
provide about $5 per child between the ages of four and eleven. Should
every eligible child attend, the sum would pay about half the tuition for
six months. To make up the difference, each scholar was to be assessed
$1.50 per month, still a bargain compared to the $6 charged by private
schools.

Because the school board had been criticized for some of its actions,
Editor Budd (himself a school commissioner) reprinted a *Democrat*
editorial, which Budd claimed, "cannot be supposed to have any partiality towards the commissioners." On visiting the school, Niles reported
on the boys' schoolmaster, Mr. McCain, who had thirty-five pupils, none
older than twelve years. Acknowledging the general difficulty of disci-
plining boys, he voiced confidence in McCain and proceeded to the
"female department" and Miss Mather:

We could see on our entrance that this lady is an accomplished
teacher, and well understands her business. The school was quiet and
orderly, and its management unexceptionable. Miss Mather more than
sustains the high reputation as a teacher with which she came in our
midst. We understand that the number of scholars in her school is 33.

We understand that Mr. McCain receives $150 per month for his
services and Miss Mather $100. We can not see why the Commissioners
should make this difference. The duties of one are as arduous as those of
the other, and they therefore should receive equal remuneration. The
time is past when a difference of sex should make a difference in the
salaries of teachers. It is not only ungallant but unjust.

The [partition] between the two schools is so loosely put together
that what is said in one room is heard in the other, which must cause
great annoyance in both departments. We also notice that a building is
in process of erection within a few feet of the school house. It would
have been much better we think, had the whole lot been purchased and
retained for school purposes. The scholars need some place for a play
ground.

But Commissioner Budd ridiculed the suggestion of "equal pay for equal work," reminding his readers that

It is the universal custom for female teachers to work cheaper than males. A good female teacher will work cheaper than a good male teacher can be had, and the commissioners have no right to throw away the additional amount of the school money. Secondly, it is not correct, as premised in the above, that the labor in each department is equal, as is shown in the above extract in reference to the undisciplined condition of scholars in the male department; and further, the salary of the male teacher is $140 per month—not $150.

Mary informed Cornelia, who was looking ahead to her own marriage to a clergyman, that Rev. Warren was taking a great interest in Niles and the paper:

He comes in every time the paper comes out, or an extra, which they get out if any news of importance is telegraphed, and talks over the paper with me. He is a democrat himself, and thinks Niles is just about the right kind of an editor. The other paper here is noted for its unjust fault finding and personalities, and if it says anything against Niles paper, it makes him much more angry than it does Niles. . . .

I wish you friends at home could look into Charlie's store some evening when it is lighted. I can assure you it is a finer store than any other in Nevada—a large high room, with one side filled with handsome books and stationary which look really imposing here, and the seals and other things connected with the express business at one end and fitted up in a style really elegant, while from the roof, or rather floor above, hangs a beautiful chandelier, with 4 solar lamps. The upper story too will be far nicer and better for a residence than any other in Nevada, having high hard finished walls. . . .

I must boast a little on my skill in firing a pistol. I fired three times. The second time hit a mark about the size of a half dollar. I am going to practise again the first pleasant day. At first I started and trembled when *Niles* fired it, and now I can fire [it] myself without being frightened at all.

CHAPTER 12

MARRIED LIFE

March–June 1854

I

*E*DWIN BUDD POKED FUN at his rival on March 17, pleased to have caught the *Democrat* editor in an embarrassing situation. It came about when C. Wilson Hill asked Niles to assist in defending three Nevada City men accused of stealing and butchering Marshall Miller's hogs. In court there had been confrontations between Niles and Miller that went beyond the merely verbal:

The above affair was intensified by some collisions between Mr. Miller, the complainant, and our grave contemporary, Mr. Searls, of the "Democrat," who was counsel for the defence. On Monday evening Mr. Searls used some expressions in the trial not suiting Mr. Miller, when the latter "pitched in." He had mistaken the arena for his chivalry, for the court took the demonstration as contempt, and put Mr. M in jail for twenty four hours, but properly released him in an hour. On Tuesday evening the champions met opposite Felt's bookstore on Broad street, and disregarding father Watt's "Let dogs delight," &c. came again to a tussle.

"They fought and hit, and scratched and bit, And struggled in the mud," &c. but were happily parted without injury, although both were armed. We presume neither wished to do the other serious injury. At any rate we know both to be "good fellows," and doubt not that they will shake hands and laugh at the whole matter after this special introduction to acquaintance.

Deb's cousin James Carter was going home with messages and gifts to all the friends in Rensselaerville, Mary told Cornelia in April:

Oh, those [gold quartz] specimens that I sent by James are some that were sent to the "Editor of the Democrat," and he gave them to me to send home (wasn't that good in him). I send them for you to do what you please with them. . . . The jewellers cut and polish those specimens it is said, and make very handsome jewelry. If the boys would like to have the smaller specimens set into rings or pins they can, and the largest one must be for Pa, the next for Addison, the third for Hammie. . . . I have some handsome specimens of petrified oak, almost as well polished as the natural wood. If you had it home, you could have it made into beautiful boxes, but it will never pay to be taken there. . . .

Deb had a horseback ride the other day, but Niles is so busy now, I do not expect to ride till Dist. Court is adjourned. The flowers are very plentiful and very beautiful about a mile from here, and will be with us in a week or two. We keep three or four boquets in the parlor all the time, some of the boarders or callers keep bringing them to us. Charlie brought some of the handsomest ones the other day that I ever saw, without any exception, and some were very fragrant. We shall try to go this week and get some ourselves.

There was an advertisement or something of the kind in the paper last week signed by [Will] Allen's brothers name, but is dated at a place about a day's ride from here. Niles did not see him when he bought it, but thinks he will be in town soon on similar business, when he shall try to see him. . . . Niles was much gratified by [Ma's] letter, and I presume will write again when Dist. Court adjourns. Till then he has scarcely time to be civil to any one *but* his wife—he never neglects her. . . .

We attended Madam Anna Bishops concert on Tuesday evening. . . . We were of course delighted to hear such music as that evening afforded us—away in the mountains here. Madam Thillon will be here too you see.... The "Editor and his lady" have complimentary tickets to all such places. Madam Anna's singing was the best I ever heard, but that you know is not saying much, as my hearing has been very limited.

San Francisco critics had not been thrilled by Madam Anna Thillon's voice—according to one, "She is a *beautiful* singer—but as an *artiste*, compared with 'the Nightingale,' Madame Anna Bishop, Parodi, Kate Hayes, or Biscaccianti, she is 'no whar.' She has, however, more expression of face and manner than any of this set. She has a good parlor voice, and is capable of making a good deal of music in a quiet way." Another called her a "charming creature" who "makes up in *naivete* what she lacks in *spizerinktum*." However, she was received enthusiastically at Nevada City, where she appeared with an Irish comedian. The *Journal's* favorites were "I Dreamt I Dwelt in Marble Halls," and "Comin' Thro' the Rye."

Praise for Anna Bishop was unanimous, despite a scandalous history that made even Lola Montez appear virtuous. Born in London in 1810 of French parents, Anna Rivière studied piano at the Royal Academy of Music and then took vocal lessons from Sir Henry Bishop, the composer of *Home, Sweet Home.* Four weeks after Bishop's invalid wife died in 1831, he married Anna, twenty-three years his junior. But after eight years of marriage, Anna Bishop deserted husband, children, and "Home, Sweet Home" to roam the world with harpist Signor Bochsa.

Bochsa was the greatest—and most infamous—harp player of the day. He was a favorite of Emperor Napoleon and Louis XVIII when a French court sentenced him to twelve years in prison for musical forgeries. Fortunately, Bochsa had not stayed for the trial. By fleeing to England, he remained free to go where he pleased, so long as it was not on French soil. For ten years he taught at England's Royal Academy, but criticism of his moral character eventually forced his resignation. He then became Madam Bishop's musical advisor, accompanist, and lover.

After their elopement the pair traveled widely, and she won universal acclaim as a prima donna. In the 1840s Anna Bishop appeared 327 times at the San Carlo Opera in Naples, with Bochsa conducting every performance. When Madame Bishop (still using her husband's name) came to California in 1854, she was considered to possess one of the world's finest operatic voices.

At Frisbie's Concert Hall, where Bishop and Thillon performed in April, the walls had been newly plastered and most seats were cushioned. Lyman Frisbie spoke of adding a stage to accommodate dramatic performances. Next door, between the hall and Frisbie's Saloon, was wife Caroline Frisbie's restaurant, where Aaron Sargent hosted a magnificent supper on the night after Madam Thillon had come and gone. In a grand gesture, Sargent had invited the county's lawyers to celebrate his admission to the bar.

II

IN APRIL THE Right Reverend Bishop William Ingraham Kip and his lady were the guests of Jonas Winchester at Grass Valley. On Friday, April 21, the newly appointed Episcopal missionary bishop of California came to Nevada City for the first Episcopal services held in that place. Because of short notice, not more than fifty attended his evening service at Reverend Warren's church, but Kip assured his audience that number was forty-five more than he expected.

Many wanted to form an Episcopal congregation at Nevada City, among them Charles and Deborah. At Rensselaerville the Mulford family belonged to Trinity Church, and Bishop Kip for many years had been rector of St. Paul's at Albany, New York. Kip commented that Nevada City was unlike any other American town. He described it as "crowded into a defile of the mountain," and thought if its wooden houses were changed to stone and surrounded by a wall, it would be "exactly like some towns perched up in the recesses of the Apennines."

In 1853 Rev. Warren's church had played host to a joint session of California's Congregational Association and the Presbytery of the New School Presbyterian Church. Of those attending, six were young missionaries fresh from the States. Four were Presbyterians, and of the two Congregationalists, Rev. William C. Pond had been assigned to North San Francisco, and Rev. J. G. Hale was to form a congregation at Grass Valley. Also present was Rev. Henry Durant, a Congregational minister and former head of Dummer Academy at Byfield, Massachusetts.

Durant was in California to establish an academy that might one day become a college. The idea appealed to the missionaries, who agreed to create a committee of four, two from each denomination, to work with Durant. After the Nevada City conference, the committee rented a thirteen-room boarding house and dancehall in Oakland at the corner of Fifth and Broadway for the new academy, and less than a month later the College School was operating with an enrollment of three. Now, in 1854, land had been acquired, a schoolhouse built, and plans were afoot to request a state charter for the College of California.

When Bishop Kip held morning services at Grass Valley on Sunday morning, about fifty persons turned out, and a second service at Grass Valley's Congregational Church that evening attracted more than a hundred. Between services he visited Melville Attwood, the British

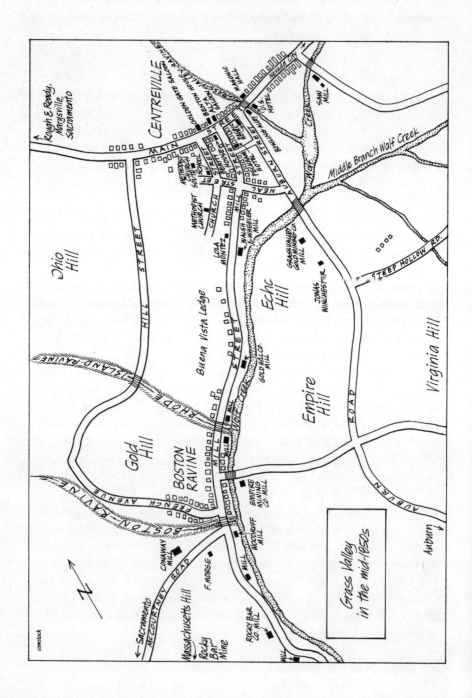

Grass Valley
in the mid-1850s

chemist who managed local mining operations for the English Quartz Company. Attwood's brother-in-law was Edward Forbes, the great British scientist and professor of natural history at Edinburgh.

Atwood took the Kips for a stroll past the Mill Street cottage of Lola Montez, and the bishop noted in his diary:

It has a conservatory behind it, and flowers and bird cages about it, giving it an air of taste and refinement. She is said to have a pension from the King of Bavaria, who, when she was his *chère amie*, gave her the title of countess of Landsfeldt. Among her pets—and we were told she has a number—is a young grizzly bear which was chained to the stump of a tree just outside her front court-yard. We stopped for a moment to look at it, and while so engaged, Lola came out on the porch to arrange her flowers. She has a rather fine countenance, as well as we could judge at this distance. We cannot imagine what induced her to select this retired village for her residence, after the kind of life she has led in Europe.

The bear was available to a new owner, according to an advertisement in the Grass Valley *Telegraph*:

GRIZZLY FOR SALE—We are authorized to inform the public that any persons or family desirous of obtaining an animal of the above mentioned species, either for public or family uses, they can gratify their desires by applying at the residence of Madam Lola Montez, on Mill Street, Grass Valley.

By the way, like his present mistress, Mr. Grizzly is *amiably inclined*, and was never known to interfere with the rights of others unprovoked. This animal would be a great acquisition to the *amusements* of families and children, to say nothing about his other good qualities.

Given this good character, the bear was eventually purchased by Simmon Storms, and for a time became something of a feature of Nevada County festivities.

III

MARY SENT HER FAMILY a new view of Nevada City published by A. W. Potter, proprietor of the Miners' Bookstore. George Kilbourn, son-in-law of hotelman U. S. Gregory, had opened a daguerreotype studio on Commercial Street, and one day he climbed Prospect Hill to capture a modern likeness of the town. From his daguerreotype, a San Francisco artist made a crayon drawing on lithographic stone, from which many copies could be printed.

Mary marked the locations of Mrs. Sampson's boarding house, the Phelps Hotel, Reverend Warren's church and parsonage, Mrs. Ferré's residence, her husband's former office, and his current one in Davis's fireproof building. Charley's brick store was hidden by the larger Phelps Hotel. Charley and Deb had decided to stay a while longer at Mrs. Sampson's. The upper floor of the store was finished, but Aaron Sargent was renting one room for a law office, and the *Journal* had occupied the other. Deb explained the changed plans to Cornelia:

Our walls dried very slowly and we found that it would be midsummer almost before they would be any ways agreeable for lodgers. . . . The warm weather had already wilted down some of my ambition in regard to being considered a great housekeeper, and the last and greatest reason of all, Charlie was offered $130 per month rent for the rooms, which was more than sufficient to pay our board. We all counselled together a long time and at last resolved to . . . be content to stay at Mrs Sampsons and be waited upon till cooler weather came.

Mrs. Sampson has promised to take down the partition between my bedroom and the one Mrs. Chubbuck occupied, so I shall have a large airy front room fixed up nicely with the furniture I had bought for my parlor, and I am already congratulating myself upon that, which would have brought sore disappointment two weeks ago—so easy is it for human nature to adapt itself to circumstances.

The Chubbucks had moved to Sonora, where he would be the agent for Wells, Fargo and Company. Charley was not sorry, for he said his bookkeeper had not been worth much after his marriage. Niles teased Deb when the *Journal*'s printing press was being installed over Charley's store. "So Deborah, you are to keep a dairy are you? I see your cheese press is already set up in your parlor." Charley worried that not having their own apartment would "fairly end up the honeymoon," but Deb pooh-poohed the notion, telling Cornelia:

It has not caused me a desponding thought, and if the termination of the honeymoon means a decrease in the love and tenderness I feel for him, I think there is little danger of that, for Nellie, he grows dearer to me every day, his heart is so good and his kindness so unceasing, that it wins me more fully than I had expected.

As "your Will" told you, there *is* a deeper and more thrilling enjoyment for you and him, yet if [Charlie and I] cannot drink at that fount, though it is a bitter thing to turn away, is it not better than to waste life in vain regret and hopeless yearnings? Those beautiful words in Hyperion, how much they say to me: "The setting of a great hope is like the setting of the sun. The brightness of our life is gone. Shadows of evening fall around us and the world seems but a dim reflection—itself a broader shadow. We look forward into the coming night. The soul withdraws into itself. *Then stars arise and the night is holy*."

Stars have risen on my darkened sky and made the night *indeed* holy, and if through my efforts Charlies pathway can be made a bright one, then may we bless God together. I have just finished Hyperion and it seems to me to contain more real poetry than anything else I have ever read of Longfellows.

Mary, writing at the same time, told her mother:

Charles is growing *young* every day, and Deb sustains well her reputation for wit by keeping us all in a giggle or a roar nearly all the time. She is a dear good sister to me. We are together constantly, and share every thought almost. We feel perfectly at home here. Aunt Mary [Sampson] is the best *mother* I have found except my own *mothers*, and she seems to love us all as much as we do her. . . . if they can contrive to have a larger room for me . . . I think we will stay [here] till fall. . . .

Two weeks ago we went to Gold Run, a mining claim owned by some acquaintances of ours. They invited us over to spend the day and get some gold. We had a delightful walk, found plenty of flowers, and a beautiful valley at Gold Run. We spent the morning in the mines, dug each of us two pans of earth with our own hands, and with a little help *washed* them. Deb dug the first pan, I the next, and Aunt Mary the third in the same place.

They got not a shilling and I got nearly 10 dollars, which was more than any others got at two pans. So much for *luck*. I took $12.50 from two pans, Deb had $8, Aunt Mary $2 or 3, and Carrie (being a young lady) had four pans, from which she took $16. The gentlemen were quite displeased because Charlie offered to pay for the gold, but miners generally expect it. Mr. [Levi] Kellog and Mr [Lewis] Sheets are the friends who entertained us so finely, and fine young men they are too. We took dinner in their log cabin and enjoyed it finely. I believe I could live very comfortably in a log cabin. We have not spent a pleasanter day in the country than that.

I have spent *two* afternoons in writing for Niles, tell Cornelia, and shall soon acquire quite a business hand, and then I shall be like "the dearest girl in the world," in Copperfield. . . . Niles had rather a sick turn after District Court closed, as I feared he would from being out so late and working so hard, but he was at the office every day, and only had to live about a week on pills and toast. I made all his toast for him except when he came in season to *help*, when of course we had plenty of fun.

He has got a grand hobby now. We have our water brought in pipes, and some times the water stops running from some cause, and then we have to bring it from the neighbors. So when it runs freely they put it in barrels and tubs. He has taken a great fancy to seeing the water run in such a clear cold stream, and his first question on coming in is "does the water run?" and if it does, no matter if it is midnight, he will insist on filling all the empty tubs.... one night, having filled everything else, he tried to make me get the *tea cups* for him.

He has been and had his hair cut close to his head and looks so odd we call him the *convict*, but he has got a new hat and a new brown coat and looks as spruced as you could wish. He is full of fun as ever, and we have just as good times as we could wish, all the time.

At the end of May Mary told Cornelia she had a great craving for "sweet" bread like her mother used to make. "We have the best bread here I have eaten in the country, but it is not like Ma's bread." She wondered if brewer's yeast (available locally) could be used in place of the "hop emptings" they used at home—or were they the same? She wanted the recipe at once, as she was about to "go to housekeeping."

Niles has at last bought a lot, one of the pleasantest building spots in town, a little back from Main Street, and only a few steps from here. There were three small lots and Charlie and Niles bought the three, which will make two nice large ones with garden room plenty. There is a fine view and a fine breeze up there, and Niles has made a contract with the best carpenter here to have a house built well, and finished in four weeks, ready for us to go into it.

There was a particular reason for the move which Mary chose not to reveal: she was expecting a child in October. Rather than add to her parents' anxiety, she wanted to wait for the baby's arrival before telling them.

One year ago this week I left home, and for the first time was thrown among strangers with new ties and new duties devolving upon me. The year has been a short and happy one to me. One thing only has cast a shadow upon its happy hours, that was parting with my dear family and home. I dared not hope when I left you all one year ago that I should be so happy as I have been. Had I then thought I should be *here* when the anniversary came around, I should have feared for the future, but I *am* here and am very happy and contented. Much more than I was at Phillipsville, for we are prospering here, and have Deb and Charlie, besides better society in general than there.

I worked some slippers for Niles as a memento of that memorable day. They are beautiful, being worked on canvas, with a ground work of maroon, and a wreath of roses and blue flowers running all around the shoe. He gave me a handsome gold thimble, which is to be marked with my name, "May," which is also the name of the month when we were married, you know. We talked over the events of "one year ago today" and of the past year, and we concluded that we were "glad we were married," wasn't that a singular conclusion to arrive at?

One year also had elapsed since Niles relinquished the office of district attorney to Bill Stewart. In September 1853 Stewart was elected for a full term, but now he was resigning because Governor Bigler had appointed him to replace John McConnell as attorney general. McConnell was taking a leave of absence to go home to Kentucky. Niles had been appointed district attorney in place of Stewart. Searls and Stewart sold their interest in the *Democrat* to Warren Ewer, John Boardman and George Russell, all practical printers. Niles happily turned over the editorial tasks to Tallman Rolfe, and devoted his full time to the practice of law.

For the first time, Mary began to consider what the passage of time meant to her aging parents. On June 27, she wrote her mother:

How kind it was of you to write those few lines when so tired and busy. You speak in that and several other letters of your growing old and childish &c. Do not, my dear mother, make yourself believe that you are growing old any faster than the rest of us. You seem to me almost like a sister, so much do you retain the fresh feelings of youth, and enter into all the emotions of younger days, which people are generally supposed to forget at your age; and I cannot bear to have you talk thus of yourself, for you are neither old nor childish in the least degree. I only wonder that with the cares and trials which have been yours ever since my remembrance, you can retain so perfectly the vigour and elasticity of youthful days.

There had been delays in the building of their house—Mary expected it would be finished now—but the builder promised it would be ready in a few more days.

I shall not attempt a description of my house till I am settled, as it would be an imperfect one. They are now painting the last coat of the inside and putting up the piazza. When the paint is dry we shall put down our carpets and get our furniture all in before we stop boarding here.

It would please you, I am sure, to see how much interest Niles takes in having everything nice.... I find I have to keep a check upon him, rather than otherwise, to keep him from having things more expensive and nicer than we need. He goes up to the house five or six times a day, and when he has time often takes hold and puts things to rights.

This morning he was out long before breakfast and came home with a handsome carpet for the parlor, and almost every time he comes in he brings something that he has happened to think of, until Aunt Mary has had to veto his bringing any more furniture, without he puts it in his own room, which is so filled we can scarcely turn around. Don't be alarmed at his extravagance—they are only *necessaries*, but rather too much for a house already full.

[Deb] and Charles attended a wedding last Sat. evening of [Miss Statira Tomlinson to Mr. William Maltman]. The bride lived in a very small house and could only invite a very few, so her father selected, as he said, his banker (Charlie), his lawyer, his merchant, and minister, who with their wives formed the select few.... I went with Charlie and Deb yesterday to call on the bride, who is about 15 years old, and looks and appears like Lucia Bellamy....

Niles spends most of his leisure time about our house. Deb says he has just gone up now, and I suppose will have the shavings swept out ready to make the carpet tomorrow, before he comes to tea. I think he will be more likely to write when we get settled. We hear now and then from his friends [in Canada], but not very often.... Joanna has a little boy baby and is very well.

I had a letter from Martha Niles last mail. She hears with a kind of virtuous horror that I am *happy* in Cal. and glad I came. She supposes people *differ* but *nothing* would ever tempt her to do so unfilial a thing as to go so far from her dear Mother that she could not come to her at any time, &c, &c. Do you believe, my dear Mother, that she loves her Mother better than I do you, or would sacrifice more for her happiness? I do not, but when she expresses her surprise that *I* should be *willing* to leave *all that is dear to me* and come to this far off country just for *gold*, I just conclude that people *do differ* and that *we* differ so much that she can never understand or appreciate my feelings and motives in coming here. I have not answered her letter, but shall soon, and pretty plainly too.

Grass Valley in the early 1850s

CHAPTER 13

WEMA: PART II

1853–1854

I

GRASS VALLEY AUTHOR Alonzo Delano, better known as "Old Block," was an ardent admirer of Lola Montez. In his latest book he spoke of her "little white cottage, with a piazza lemonading around it, with the bright green mansinietas blooming before it, the yard laid out for a flower garden, in delicate beds and good taste." When Lola's pet bear allegedly bit her hand, Old Block versified:

> When Lola came to feed her bear,
> With comfits sweets and sugar rare,
> Bruin ran out in haste to meet her,
> Seized her hand because 'twas sweeter

Old Block was born in 1807, the tenth of eleven children of Dr Frederick Delano of Aurora, New York. He married in 1830 and was living with his wife and two children at Ottawa, Illinois, when gold was discovered. In 1849 he crossed the plains to California, leaving his family behind. He came to Grass Valley in 1851, established the Massachusetts Hill Mine, and sold it to James Delavan, who represented a group of

New York capitalists with investments in the Rocky Bar Gold Mining Company.

Delavan had written *Notes on California and the Placers*, a work based on his first visit to California, which encouraged Delano to submit his own manuscript to a New York publisher It was published in 1854 as *Life on the Plains and Among the Diggings*. But before it came out, he wrote another, *Pen-knife Sketches, or Chips of the Old Block*, published at Sacramento in 1853. Composed during his idle moments as the Wells, Fargo agent, it was an immediate success, and a second printing was issued in a few months.

Another of Delano's friends was Simmon Storms. In the summer of 1853, Old Block accompanied Storms, Chief Wema and a Cherokee called Charlie on a pack trip to the Sierra Nevada summit. Starting at Illinoistown, across the Bear River from Storms' Ranch, they went upstream past a mining camp known as Dutch Charlie's Flat, rested at Bear Valley, climbed the Emigrant Gap, and finally reached a place where they could see the beautiful lake beside which the Donner Party camped one terrible winter

Along the way Wema demonstrated his culinary skills. At one meal he showed them how to cook a squirrel. He inserted the undressed rodent between split ends of a green stick, then held it over an open fire. When he had singed off the hair, he scraped aside the hot ashes, scooped out a hole in the ground, and buried the squirrel under a layer of green leaves. Over this he placed a layer of hot ashes, followed by another of live coals and left it to bake.

When Delano and Storms protested his failure to remove the entrails, Wema looked puzzled. According to Old Block, this conversation followed:

"Storms," said his Majesty gravely, "you like 'em beef liber?"

"Yes."

"You like 'em heart bake 'em?"

"Yes."

"Well, you like 'em tripe cook?"

"Yes, you old fool, they are all the best part; everybody knows they are good."

"Topee, topee Storms. You like 'em pig, hog, string—what-you-call-'em, stuff?"

"Oh! Sausages! Of course I do, you dirty wretch."

"Yes—sackagy. Well, squirrel hab liber, hab heart, hab tripe, hab sackagy, all stuff. Me like 'em, too. You no like 'em now, when me cook 'em all togedder?"

"Storms, he's got you on a swinging limb!" I shouted, with a laugh; "Your Majesty is a logician."

He smiled, *faintly*. "It's a fact," replied Storms, goodnaturedly. "The old fellow is no fool."

Later the Cherokee shot a large horned owl, and Wema gave it the same treatment. He told them it was like eating chicken. "Chicken!" echoed Storms, in disgust. "Why owls eat mice, moles and lizards—faugh!"

Once again, Wema patiently explained, "Chicken hab liber, heart, gizzy, head and tail, and mucha neck; chicken eat worms, grubs and grasshoppers. Mucha bueno, chicken! Mucha bueno owl! American mahala eat 'em chicken salad, smackee lips for chicken liber, lickee finger for chicken egg, and chicken eat worms and flies. Owl hab berry good egg."

"Got you again, Storms," laughed Delano. "There are worse things than owls—turkey buzzards, for instance. I tried owls when crossing the Plains. They were Northern owls, and they were rather strong. This being a Southern owl, it may be more palatable."

One mouthful settled the question. "Give me chicken, worms, grasshoppers and all, before either a Northern or Southern owl," Old Block declared. But Wema and Charlie happily shared the owl, and licked their fingers clean.

While many of Old Block's stories were colored to suit his white readers, in one letter to a San Francisco paper he presented a straightforward account of Wema's views of the Americans. The candid exchange was interpreted by Storms and recorded by Delano, who spelled the chief's name "Weimar":

[WEMA]: The Americans, like the Indians, some are good—very good, and some are bad. I like the good ones, who are kind to the Indians, but the bad ones are *mucho malo*.

[DELANO]: Are you as happy now as you were before the Americans came?"

[WEMA]: No—no; before they came we had enough to eat; we could gather acorns enough for winter; our women could gather grass and seeds in the valleys; there was plenty of game on the hills; Indians no go hungry then ... but the Americans come, they take our women, they kill all the deer and hares, all the game, and none is left for us; they cut down the oaks and destroy our acorns, and they first fence-in our valleys, then dig up the ground and destroy the grass that gives us seeds for flour; they take our good land and nothing grows for us.

[DELANO]: Yes, Weimar, but Indians can work—they can dig gold, and with it buy provisions.

[WEMA]: No, Americans have got the land, and claim the gold. If an Indian is digging gold, some white man comes along and says, 'Get off of my claim, you damned Indian,' and points his rifle and drives him off, so that we have nothing left, and the white man will not let us dig for gold. Once we were very strong, I had many warriors. Seventy braves two years ago were in my councils. Now there are but ten left—all [the others] dead. We cannot get enough to eat—get sick and die. What shall we do?

[DELANO]: Lieutenant Beale [Superintendent of California Indians] will come soon and provide for you. Our great Captain at home has sent him to take care of the Indians and he will furnish you with good food and enough, if you will do as he desires.

[WEMA]: Ah! the Americans promised us before, made long speeches, and told us fine stories, that they would give us beef, but they did not do it and now we have no confidence. They talk much and do nothing We don't know what to believe. If the Indians, driven by hunger, steal an ox or a mule, or anything to eat, the whites hunt them down and kill them, and sometimes they burn our towns and kill those who are not guilty. We cannot fight now, the Americans are too many and have rifles, what can we do?

Delano went on to offer his own conclusions:

As for Weimar, he feels sad, his looks constantly show the troubles of his mind. Since his visit to San Francisco he is still more satisfied of the hopelessness of his case, and he tells the Indians that the Americans are numerous and strong, and for himself, he thinks it best for them to remove to [the reservation at] Tulare Valley. Yet he dislikes to leave his old mountain home, and many of his tribe will not consent.

Then again there are whites, who for some selfish purpose probably, are endeavoring to persuade the Indians not to remove. They tell them that they will get sick, that they never can return, that the climate and water is bad, that their women and children will be carried off in waggons, making a bug-a-boo story out of nothing. I can scarcely conceive why any reasonable man should try to dissuade them from being placed under the protection of the Government, where their wants will be amply supplied, and desire them to stay here, where they must drag out a wretched existence, in starvation and misery.

Certainly this class of men cannot feel for the actual comfort of this poor, degraded race. But the Indians are dwindling off, and a few years more will see the race extinct, unless they can be placed where they can obtain the means of subsistence. There are many who do not get a full meal oftener than once a week, and notwithstanding their suffering they do not know what to do, because so many contrary stories are told them. Alas! the poor Indian. .

II

A SPRING FESTIVAL, the *Journal* called it. Nevada County's dwindling Indian population had gathered two miles east of Nevada City on March 1, 1854, to celebrate the arrival of spring. To reach the site, hundreds of the *nisenan* had to pass through the town, and, according to the paper, many whites went to see the show, for which the Indians charged a $1 admission:

They found the Indians encamped to the number of about four hundred, having erected a large conical house, 60 feet in diameter constructed of pine branches and bark, covered over with earth.

The dancing was in the house, entirely by the warriors—the women sitting about on the ground. The dances were varied from rude cotillon sets to hybrid polkas. The music was made by striking sticks together, and blowing melancholy reeds. The dancers were in primitive costume—that is, with a breech cloth instead of fig leaves and a head decoration of feathers. The dancing was kept up till about ten o'clock. This was the second "assembly" of the season, and one more takes place in a day or two.

Some of the "boys" attended on the information that the Digger ladies would dance *a la mode l'artistes*—but that part of the programme, though announced by his majesty the King himself, did not transpire. It is peculiar to notice the Indian processions that pass through this city. The women carry large wicker baskets, in the shape of an inverted cone, containing utensils, food, clothes, &c. and often a picaninny on top of all, making a load from thirty to a hundred weight—while the lord of the family, with feathers in his hair, and bow and arrows in his hand, marches in dignified gravity at the head.

Some of the Americanos, not seeing the justice of this distribution of labor, sometimes interfere to tell the male to take the burden. Such an idea is totally disgusting to the Indian husband, who emphatically dissents from such interference with his family discipline. We are informed by those best acquainted with the habits of the Indians that the squaws are scrupulously faithful to their lords, and save in making them do all the work, the husbands are kind in return.

Mary observed the procession and described it to her youngest brother, Charlie Niles:

One thing I think you would like to see, that is the Indians. We see a great many every day. Yesterday when I was visiting at Mr Harrison's there were some passing and stopped to talk to us. One was dressed in mourning. The way they do that, they burn the body of the one that dies and mix the ashes with tar and plaster it all over their heads and faces, except their eyes and mouth and a little place on each cheek. It makes them look dreadfully.

The woman said her picaninny was dead, she meant her baby. We asked her how long since, and she held up two fingers which meant two days ago. . . . It makes me sick to watch them they are so dirty. You ought to see them once with their papooses tied to a board and fastened by a strip of cloth which they just slip onto their heads and so carry them without any trouble. The women or squaws will carry great weights suspended from their heads in that way. The men will never carry anything but their bows and arrows.

On May 25, 1854, the Grass Valley *Telegraph* reported a serious battle between two groups of Indians a mile and a half south of Nevada City. They were identified as "Yuba" and "Nevada" tribes, and it was said the Nevadans won. Three men were killed and several wounded. After the battle, the paper said "the streets of Nevada were filled with the victorious warriors, many of whom were in a perfect state of nudity."

Another story in the same edition told of an Indian Festival at Storms Ranch on May 21, with foot races, shooting, and games. But Wema complained to the *Telegraph* editor:

We have been waited upon by Capt. Weimar, the high chief of the Indian tribes in this section of the country, for the purpose of getting our influence in endeavoring to prevent the sale of ardent spirits to his Indians. He represents that it makes the Indians quarrelsome and bad, that it makes them act foolish, and keeps them poor.

He desires that his friends, the Americans, give them food and clothes—instead of whiskey for their gold. He says they are willing to dig and to work—and trade their gold to the Americans for bread, meat, shirts, coats and pantaloons, but it is his express desire that no liquor be given or sold to them on any occasion.

Lola's bear was advertised as a prime attraction at the coming Fourth of July celebration at Storms Ranch. It would fight six of the best dogs in the country, two at a time, until bear or dogs where whipped. The owner of a 45-pound dog offered to match it against others of equal weight for side bets of $100 to $500. Up to a thousand spectators could watch the events from a newly built amphitheater; featured would be the grand Indian "War Dance" and a one mile footrace between an Englishman and a nisenan runner.

Americans were discovering the surprising fact that the lowly "Diggers" could be extraordinary athletes. One such contest was reported by the *Journal* that summer:

One of the Indians was large, athletic, and handsomely formed. The other two were less in stature, but with strong limbs, and apparently confident. In the race they displayed a skill perfectly astonishing, and the first named would have made no mean figure at the Olympiads. They started off slowly and steadily, slightly moving the arms, bent at right angles at the elbow, and preserved their relative positions, and slight speed till over three-fourths of a mile of the track.

They then seemed to strain every nerve on the "home stretch," when the larger Indian gained rapidly on his fellows, and came in much ahead; and thus in two "heats." The average speed round the [one mile] track was about the ordinary "lope" of a horse. The winning Indian received from one of the judges the pile of about $50.

One day in 1854, Wema's people were called upon to execute a member of their own tribe. The *Journal* learned the details from Simmon Storms:

Some six weeks ago a fine looking young squaw on Bear River suddenly disappeared from among her associates, and on her absence exciting some enquiry, a young Indian of her acquaintance reported that a white man had taken her off.

Thus matters remained, though not without exciting some suspicion, until last Sunday, [when] some men, being in the woods near Storms ranch, found the remains of human bones, partly consumed. It was also remembered that a fire was seen exactly in that locality on the night she was last seen.

These circumstances immediately aroused suspicion among the Indians and others in the vicinity, and Mr. Storms began making enquiry, upon which it was soon ascertained that the Indian who reported she had been carried off by a white man, [had] in company with another Indian ... taken her out there, murdered her, and burned her up. The suspicion rested upon these two as she was last seen with them.

As Mr. Storms has an extensive knowledge of this whole tribe, he immediately set about to capture him, in which he succeeded on Sunday night. [The Indian] confessed murdering the squaw, and also that he, with the assistance of the [other] Indian (whose name is Jack and who is now at large on Bear River) and two others, had murdered a Mexican last spring.

The Mexican had been at work for Mr. Storms, [and] was paid off at Grass Valley, from whence he was going down to the Valley to drive cattle, and until this confession, the contrary was not known. He also confessed that they had killed four Chinamen within the last six months, one of them last week.

He was delivered over to the tribe, headed by Wemeh, and was hung on Monday morning, in presence of over a hundred of the tribe. He was a most desperate fellow, and it was not without some difficulty he was taken. After being hung until he was supposed to be dead, he was taken down, and according to their custom his body was given to the squaws, who carried him off a short distance to give a respectable burial.

But they found he was not dead, whereupon they were struck with the greatest terror; but as sentence of death was passed upon him, it was necessary he should die; owing however, to their superstition, it was difficult to get any one to take hold of him.

Wemeh alone performed this task unaided, not being able to bring any one of his men to his assistance, [and] carried him some ten rods to a convenient tree, tied the rope around his neck and hung him up. He hung an hour longer, during which time they had prepared his funeral pile, and the instant he was taken down, he was thrown upon the burning pile and consumed.

The sentence of death has also been passed upon his accomplice, Jack, who will be shot down by any of the tribe who may find and recognise him. It is also supposed these same fellows have murdered white men, but to this he would not confess—making no answers to questions touching this point. He however informed Mr. Storms that a great many white men and Chinamen were killed [by Indians] of which nothing was said. He also confessed to having contemplated the death of Storms, but had been deterred with the fear of immediate detection, and by Mr. Storms knowledge of the Indian peculiarities, which always kept him on his guard when they were about.

CHAPTER 14

SUMMER PLEASURES

July–August 1854

I

O N INDEPENDENCE DAY, as Lola's bear and Wema's Indians were thrilling crowds at Storms' Ranch, Mary and Niles moved into their new house. Mary was overjoyed, and promptly dubbed it "Durden Cottage" in honor of the heroine of Dickens' *Bleak House*. Ten days after the move began, Niles and Charley took part in the county Democratic convention at Frisbie's Concert Hall.

Niles made sure he didn't receive the nomination for district attorney, not wishing to campaign for office in the last months of Mary's pregnancy. There would be two contests to succeed him: one for the remainder of Bill Stewart's term, and another for the period beginning in May, 1855. Engineer and surveyor Charles Marsh, also a delegate, told his friends of a mountain excursion being organized by Grass Valley people. He suggested forming a similar expedition, which he would guide. Wives were to be included, and Niles thought it prudent to consult Mary's physician, who was a delegate at the same convention.

Dr. William J. Knox, a small blond southerner, had crossed the plains from Missouri with his wife. He had a successful Nevada City practice, owned much real estate, was a stockholder in ditch companies and mining ventures, and was a town trustee. His purpose at the Democratic meeting was to win nomination to the state assembly.

Dr. Knox gave his approval to the outing, noting it would provide Mary with welcome relief from the oppressive summer heat. Mary loved the idea; soon she would be tied to her home and this might be her only chance to visit the summit and see the cabins used by the ill-fated Donner Party. Deb, whose health always had been delicate, was equally enthusiastic. Marsh announced a departure date of July 20.

The Grass Valley party left on July 13. The group consisted of Old Block, Simmon Storms, James and Lewis Delavan, John E. Southwick, Lola Montez, and Miss Richmer. Southwick was part owner of the newly incorporated Empire Mining Company, and James Delavan was agent for the Helvetia and Lafayette Gold Mining Company, having been dismissed as superintendent of the disappointing Massachusetts Hill Mine. Lewis, James's brother, had been given charge of the party's provisions. Miss Richmer was Lola's companion and private secretary.

Storms and Delano had proposed the trip, based on their earlier excursion with Wema. Although the pair would have preferred to limit the company to themselves and Lola, this was impossible, for her admirers were numerous and persistent. Storms then extended an invitation to *Journal* editor Edwin Budd, who ruefully declined, pleading prior engagements.

Lola and Miss Richmer arrived wearing bloomers, a daring touch that added further spice to the outing. Lola prettily displayed her full figure and tiny waist, though her face was her most striking feature, with high cheekbones, long black lashes, and unusually large and flashing blue eyes. The sight of Lola and the scent of her perfume wafting through clean mountain air was a heady mixture for her male companions.

They made their first camp at Bear Valley. James Delavan had pressing business in Grass Valley which did not permit him to remain with the party; in the morning he turned back reluctantly, and the others began the long climb out of the valley. Later in the day they reached the summit and descended to the lake beside which the Donner Party had wintered. Here Lola quarreled with Miss Richmer, and because Old Block by then had wearied of Lola's "eccentricities," he offered to escort the unhappy secretary back to civilization. He anticipated no difficulty, having been over the trail three times, and no one was in a mood to dispute him.

Lola's three remaining gallants—Southwick, Storms, and Lewis Delavan—continued with her for two days more along the Truckee River, until they reached a trading post on the desert rim. They stayed three days before setting out on the return journey. On the second morning Lewis Delavan left earlier than the others, driving the single pack horse ahead. It was a pleasant morning, and as he rode contentedly beside the sparkling river, he failed to notice when the main road turned away from the stream. He continued to follow the Truckee for several miles before realizing his error.

Delavan dismounted and tried to turn the pack horse around, but the animal broke away and plunged into the river. Leading his own horse, Lewis coaxed the other from the stream and seized the lead rope. Once again the animal headed for the water, dragging the frightened youth, who could not swim. Fearing he would drown, Lewis let go of the rope and waded to shore. Meanwhile, the runaway had crossed the river and was grazing happily on the other side.

He tried swimming his horse across the stream, but once more lost his nerve and slid off into the swift current, which fortunately carried him to shore. Minus coat and hat, he scrambled out, soaking wet and frightened. Now both animals were grazing on the opposite side, and he could see no solution but to find his companions. It was too late to retrace his steps, for the others would long ago have passed the fork in the trail. His best chance was to keep going, for he suspected the main road would rejoin the river.

His guess was right. He found the main trail near the lake, but tracks indicated his friends had gone by already. Adding to his troubles, a summer thunderstorm pelted the coatless Delavan with hailstones as he attempted the long and difficult climb to the summit. At last, cold and miserable, he sought shelter under a projecting ledge on the mountain.

Hours before, Lola and her companions had been alternately puzzled and annoyed by his mysterious disappearance. With the passage of time and miles their annoyance turned to anger at Delavan, whose prolonged absence threatened to deprive them of needed food and comfort. By day's end, having reached the summit, they were forced to retire hungry, tired, and confused.

In the morning, after a poor night's rest, Lola's party awoke to a chorus of gay shouts from the slopes below. To their immense relief, they could see Charley Marsh's expedition approaching on horseback.

Deb and Mary impolitely stared at Lola as their men unpacked food for the hungry trio. It was their first close look at the notorious dancer, and the two young women were both pleased and disappointed by Lola's lack of glamour at that early hour.

After breakfast, with Lola's spirits partially restored, the young people waved goodbye and resumed their journey to Truckee Lake. While descending the steep and rugged east face of the mountain they encountered a miserable and very hungry Lewis Delavan. When he had finished eating, he was given the spare horse they had borrowed at Bear Valley in case of trouble.

Once again they camped overnight at Bear Valley. Delavan's horse had to be returned, but the youth assured them he could walk the remaining distance. Nevertheless, Charles Marsh left the party and rode ahead to notify Delavan's brother of the situation.

When Marsh arrived at Grass Valley, James Delavan was in the process of engaging a dozen experienced mountain men to search for his brother, having been informed of his disappearance by Lola's companions. Two and a half days later, Lewis Delavan arrived home, with feet so tender it had taken him a day and a half to walk the thirteen miles from Red Dog to Grass Valley.

James Delavan advertised his appreciation in the *Telegraph* on August 3:

A Card. The subscriber would respectfully tender his thanks to Messrs. Haskell, Marsh, Mulford, Searls, Hurlburt and others of the party from Nevada, who so kindly relieved his brother from his critical situation in the Sierra Nevada mountains, administered to his comfort and assisted him in returning to his anxious friends.

II

NEVADA CITY was an overheated oven. Ice cream saloons and soda fountains suddenly appeared all over town. Caroline Frisbie opened one for "ladies and gentlemen" next door to her Coyote Street restaurant, and around the corner on Main Street Jacobs and Copp were making ice cream in their Nevada Bakery. Two doors away was the Confectionery Manufactory of John Foster, who specialized in frozen creams and had installed one of Swan's Superior Soda Fountains to supply the public with "pure sparkling Soda Water, iced."

The Fountain Restaurant on Broad Street served soda water, ice creams, and "various fancy drinks," as well as oysters, and strawberries and cream. But George Jacobs went them one better: his ice cream saloon on the hill east of town was enhanced by the presence of a giant revolving wheel on which as many as eight persons could ride at one time. In August, before Jacobs dismantled the swing and moved it to San Francisco, a new sport was invented. Reported the *Journal*:

New mode of shower bathing. Some eight of our high blooded youths a few days since made a visit to Jacobs' swing. All got in, two in each car, each one taking with him a bucket of water, and madam rumor says, a half dozen bottles of soda beside, and on reaching the top of the circle, those in the opposite carriage being immediately beneath them, commenced pouring the water down, a distance of over a hundred feet. Thus in turn, each one would administer and receive the shower until their supply of water was exhausted; where there was no alternative but to resort to soda. This being exhausted also, it became necessary to retire for the purpose of completing their comforts by applications from the wardrobe.

But the heat did not impede those whose sporting instincts were strong. Two race tracks were built in 1854, one at Hughes' Ranch on the ridge between Deer and Wolf creeks. Called the Union Race Course, it opened in May and was a straight half-mile track. The course offered a commanding view of the surrounding countryside, and caught breezes from every direction. The Glenbrook track was located in the basin between Grass Valley and Nevada City.

On July 4 Mr. T. L. Hughes competed with Storms for holiday crowds, advertising a program of horse and foot races, and bull and bear fights. Three Spanish bulls and three grizzly bears were promised. Unfortunately, the day was marred by a fatal accident which the *Journal* described in detail:

One of the bears which had been provided for the sports in the ring, refused to come out of the cage, when some one ... suggested that a pistol be fired near him.... a brother of Mr. Hughes ... discharged his pistol. Mr. Hughes was behind the cage (outside the ring), when the first shot was fired, and seeing the ball pass through the timber, requested them to shoot no more.... [The pistol] did not revolve in cocking it, and he placed his thumb on the cock ... [and] revolved it with his left hand; but at that moment some one struck his elbow, by which means the pistol was discharged, passing through the cage (made of inch boards), and entering the right breast of a man standing on the outside.

He died almost instantly.... His name was Frank Schmerbauch, was a native of Germany, and about 33 years of age.

The Glenbrook Race Course belonged to Adam Smith, who had been James O. Barker's partner at Barker's Exchange until the latter died in the winter of 1852–1853. For years the Exchange had been one of Nevada City's two largest gambling saloons. After Smith married his partner's widow in January 1854, business declined, and Smith sold the building in order to build a circular track halfway between the two cities.

The *Journal* approved the change, which it saw as part of an encouraging trend:

Within the last few days, one of the principal gambling houses has been finally closed, and is now being remodeled, and turned into a livery stable. Much to the gratification of the lovers of good order, the business of gambling has been gradually, but steadily decreasing among us for the past year.... A few years ago, too, it was a common thing to find a deck of cards lying on the table of miner's cabins, stores and shops. But now one may walk round the country and town all day, visiting stores and cabins, and not see anything of the kind.

Prostitution was another form of "moral depravity" which disturbed Nevada's better citizens. Sporadic efforts to abate or control this nuisance had resulted in no long term gains, much to the distress of local clergymen and wives. Spanish saloons were most suspect, but lately the Chinese houses were undergoing greater criticism. In May the *Telegraph* editorialized:

These worthless beings seem to have called forth the general opinion of the press that some measures should be taken to prohibit them from emigrating to this country. Many persons are ready to cry out against the demoralizing effects of slave labor, who are content to see these filthy mortals come here by the thousand. We believe the effect of the [Chinese] is more pernicious and prejudicial to society as well as more degrading to white labor than [black slaves].

In June the court of sessions fined the owners of a Chinese brothel $100 for running a disorderly house, and ordered the proprietor of a Mexican house to pay $50 for the same offense. But the severest blow was dealt in August, when a mob made up of nearly 100 members of the "Society of Nary Reds" made the rounds of Chinese brothels in Nevada City, ejected the occupants and vandalized buildings and contents. Editor Budd slyly approved in the August 25 *Journal*:

We are no advocates of mob law. But notwithstanding all this, as they have cleared our town of the greatest curse that ever visited us, and as our courts have either winked at them, or were too weak to do anything with them, every good citizen will and does rejoice at the result.

It is now generally understood that the Mexican houses of similar character may be visited soon in the same way. Of course it would be a desperate thing for a mob to cleanse our streets of all the filth the law allows to remain among us in spite of the public wish. These Chinese and Mexican filth holes are such an ornament to the town! But then, to have them driven out by an unauthorized mob! Oh! aint it horrible?

On the other hand, some citizens argued that black children were entitled to attend public school if their parents paid taxes. School Commissioner Edwin Budd asked and answered the question of how and where:

Shall Negroes go to School?—The above question has somewhat agitated our village for a few days past, owing to a mulatto girl's having applied to our district school for admission. The law under which this school is organized includes ALL CHILDREN between the ages of four and eighteen years of age without making any exceptions.

But very many of our citizens object, in the most bitter terms to this mixing the two colors in such close contact and direct equality. The plain and more generous interpretation of the enigma would be that a separate school room should be occupied by them, as nearly all admit the propriety of having them educated.

In August the "*elite* of the colored population of Nevada" assembled at Abbott's Hall at the corner of Pine and Commercial, where they had a "most delightful cotillion party." And when the African Methodist Episcopal Church building at Grass Valley was dedicated, two of that town's white clergy assisted at the ceremony. Rev. T. M. D. Ward was the black presiding elder and Rev. Emory Waters was first minister at the church, which had cost $1400 to build.

As for misbehaving whites, Nevada City had its share of wild spirits. In June the *Journal* reported one such example:

A young "gentleman," or some other kind of an animal, dressed in a boy's suit, named Minerva Fountain, was arrested and brought before Justice Rolfe on Wednesday last, for furiously driving through the streets with a horse and buggy, and for violation of the ordinance prohibiting females from appearing in the streets in male attire. She was fined $25 and costs. An eye witness to her furious, but awkward driving through the streets thinks she deserved a few days entertainment in the county jail beside.

Women were not discriminated against, for the same ordinance contained a provision forbidding males to wear female clothing. Under the leadership of local ministers, a concerted effort was made to persuade merchants to observe the Sabbath. Nine months earlier Deborah Mulford had complained, "I never would be willing to make a home of Nevada if for no other reason than its non observance of the Sabbath." In August she could claim a small but significant victory when this notice appeared:

On and after September 1, 1854, the Express and Banking House of Wells, Fargo & Co., will be closed on Sundays. The Office will be opened after the arrival of the Sacramento stage for the delivery of Letters and Packages, but no Banking Business will be done on Sunday's. Express Matter will come and go as usual—on each and every day of the week. A Letter Box will be found at the door. Also, a List of Letters remaining in the Office on Saturday.

Nevada, August 4, 1854.   Chas. W. Mulford, Agent.

Deborah still hoped to persuade Charley to attend church, but it seemed unlikely he would unless an Episcopal society was organized. Deb usually went to the Congregational services with Mary and Niles, but however much she liked Mr. Warren and his wife, she preferred not to be preached at with such vigor.

Chinese miners

CHAPTER 15

CHINESE INDIANS

September–October 1854

I

*L*IFE WAS HECTIC in California—at least it seemed so to Mary as the time drew near for her delivery. On September 12, she explained to Cornelia the difference between Nevada City and Rensselaerville: it was the absence of time for "quiet thought" in this new place:

Action—Action is the motto and the watchword with all. It is impossible to do otherwise than join in the busy hurrying scenes with both mind and strength. There is no room for complaint *here* that there is not material enough for the most active nature to work upon. I think you had better *come* here, don't you? I have no doubt Cal. would just suit [you]. There is no time or place for dreaming here, and I find that many, indeed all, with whom I have talked on the subject complain that they cannot *read* even such books as they used to at home: books of sentiment and poetry, or metaphysics, anything that requires abstract thought or a dreamy state of mind to appreciate. . . .

I fear we shall not be able to keep our promise to be home at [your] wedding, we have all concluded that it is more sensible to remain until two years from last spring, as the winter is altogether the best season for business; more can be made in one winter than in two or three summers, and then summer is the best time to go home.... Charlie is already independent in money matters, so that they can reasonably feel they can go when they take a fancy, but with us it is somewhat different, and they would wait 6 months I think, for the sake of all going together....

The news of Loyd's marriage was a great shock to Deb, much greater than I thought it would be, and she has not recovered from it yet, but she is a noble girl and has kept every trace of her feelings from Charlie, who is glad enough that Loyd is married. So is *she glad* and thankful she is *Charlie's* wife, and in Cal. Still the shock was a great one—it is the last cord broken, that bound her to the passion and the happy dreams of her early life. She wants you to write to him at once if you have not—she would write to you but dare not attempt it lest her feelings should get the better of her control. She says she loves Charlie better than ever, and he is as happy as ever he need be.

Deb did not mention the subject to Cornelia for two months, at which time she confessed:

I had a great deal of feeling when I heard of Loyd's marriage—though I should have had very little had he married any other person, still "all is well" and I am very glad he is married. I never have seen one moment when I would wish to exchange Charlie for him. I am *fully* and *perfectly* satisfied.

According to Mary, the election had gone to suit Niles:

It would make considerable difference with his business which men were elected. I am glad he did not run for office, though he could easily have been elected judge or state senator, but the election was rather *small* business this year. Many of the candidates acted so like fools that I was glad Niles had no part with them.

Once again the results had been mixed. Democrats won most contests, but Whigs made a respectable showing. A Whig assemblyman replaced the incumbent Democrat in the state senate, and in the lower house the existing balance of two Whigs and three Democrats was preserved. A Democrat would succeed Niles and fill out the remaining months of Bill Stewart's term, but Aaron Sargent, a Whig, had been elected district attorney for the following two years. Charles Marsh had declined renomination as county surveyor, and Tallman Rolfe gave up his justice court to devote full time to the *Democrat*.

After the election the San Francisco *News* editorially proposed the adoption of voter registration to reduce voter fraud, which the *Journal* seconded, noting "It would be the best check to illegal voting that could be devised." When the election was over, Sargent again bought into the *Journal*, replacing Edwin Budd, whose forceful rhetoric had fueled the political wars while Sargent advanced his legal career.

Early in the year Edwin Budd had begun a series of editorial attacks against Democrat Thomas Caswell, whose term as county judge would expire in 1855. The vendetta began after Caswell denied payment of a bill for county advertising, but Budd's wrath was especially aroused when the court of sessions looked askance at bills presented by Budd and other school commissioners. Informed that "economy should be observed," Budd retaliated with an angry blast on February 24, 1854:

Judge Caswell recently absented himself for six months from the state [and] . . . his place was filled by another man, who was . . . paid out of the county treasury for his services. On [Caswell's] return he . . . received, by order of the court over which he presided, some $1,500; for what? Not for honest labor . . . not even for imaginary services done the county, for he laid no claim to having done such; but it was wholly gratuitous—for his own gratification—money filched from the treasury, without any equivalent, real or imaginary.

Again, in August [1853], the Court of Sessions over which *he* presided, paid him over $1750 . . . in increase of his past salary. . . . he has thus received thousands of dollars out of the treasury, above what was due by actual service, or by law, and thus the public have a fair rule by which to judge of his "economy."

When Niles took exception to his accusations, Budd retorted:

The last number of the *Democrat* goes a good deal out of its way, to take up the defence of the court of sessions. . . . It says it dislikes to see a public journalist resort to the "pages of a newspaper to vent private malice;" and yet the editor [commits the sin] . . . of taking upon his own shoulders the responsibility of another person's controversy.

In answer to our charge against Judge Caswell, they say . . . only $1100 accrued to him during his absence . . . together with the [1750] as back pay, which raised his salary to $4000 per year. . . . But they say he was granted the privilege to leave the state, and therefore, he had a right to his pay. . . .

Judge Heydenfeldt and Judge Caswell were granted leave of absence by the legislature of 1852. When the question was before the Assembly, Mr. Brush of Tuolumne objected . . . on the ground that these men . . . would present bills for the time of their absence, and duplicate judges would be paid. Mr. Peachy ... said ... Mr. Heydenfeldt was "a man of too high honor to take something for nothing." Mr. E. F. W. Ellis then said *his* friend, Judge Caswell, was also "a man of too much honor to receive any such money—to take something for nothing." ... The people now see what such "principle" and "honor" are worth.

Budd speculated whether Niles, who also had gone east to marry, might have similar intentions, although there was no similarity in the cases, Niles having resigned his office before the term began. Budd also attacked Tallman Rolfe, who had participated in the decision to deny payment to Budd:

But let it be remembered that the *Democrat* is governed by a clique composed partly of county officials, to whose mandates it must bow with implicit obedience.... as Judge Rolfe, one of [the] associates in the Court of Sessions, is part proprietor of that concern he probably expects soon to have some enormous bills to be paid by them....

The law fixes the pay of associates at $8 per day. [Recently] ... the court was to meet on Wednesday; but the Presiding Judge being indisposed, [Rolfe] goes to the court house and adjourns court, a work of about three minutes, and charges the county $8, and the court of sessions allows it.... Who ever heard of so ridiculous a bill?.... And yet this same Rolfe made himself rather conspicuous in setting aside bills in which others charged eight dollars for an honest ten hours work.

Rolfe claimed that when Mary Sampson's daughter Carrie had applied for the position of schoolteacher, Budd refused to examine her qualifications. The charge was angrily denied by Budd, who said:

... the Judge's honesty dont prevent him from saying ... that the commissioners declined examining a certain candidate "in English Grammar because they had no grammar book." At the time alluded to, this same *judge*, who was called in to act in place of an absent member of the Board, proposed to give the lady a certificate without an examination, and on approaching the branch of grammar, he assured us that "for his part he had been raised in the back country in Illinois, where he had no opportunity of getting an education, and that he knew nothing about grammar." This is probably where he got the expression "grammar book."

Niles had replied: "Know all men by these presents that said Rolfe has no interest whatever in our 'concern,' neither has he had any such interest since the date of our purchase." Little more was said until Tallman Rolfe replaced Niles as editor of the *Democrat*. As the election grew near, Budd renewed his attack on Caswell:

Our friends have several times within a month complained to us that the County Judge has taken their legal notices from them and given them to the *Democrat*, when they wished to publish them in the *Journal*, representing that he had the authority to control the matter. . . .

Judge Caswell is a candidate for re-election, and a most forlorn one. He has not the confidence of any portion of his own party. . . . The people will hardly re-elect a man of such narrow prejudices for others, but such unbounded liberality for himself. . . .

Despite Budd's efforts, Caswell won easily, and once Sargent resumed control of the *Journal*, he began mending fences. As a novice lawyer and district attorney-elect, Sargent knew better than to perpetuate a quarrel with the county judge. The *Journal* diplomatically observed:

[Caswell's] course as judge has suited the people, and we doubt not will continue to do so, for if anything would lead a man to desire to be worthy of an office, it is such a cordial re-endorsement.

Budd's last words were, "I fear I have in some instances come short of the expectations of the community," but declared it had been his ambition to make the paper "a valuable sheet, rather than a profitable one."

II

THE CHINESE ARE INDIANS, declared the California Supreme Court on October 1, 1854. The announcement surprised most scientists, for they had not participated in the historic debate. Even those persons who favored the result had trouble following the court's reasoning. The decision said:

Section 394 of the Civil Practice Act provides, "No Indian or Negro shall be allowed to testify as a witness in any action in which a white man is a party." Section 14 of the Criminal Act provides, "No black, or mulatto person, or Indian shall be allowed to give evidence in favor of, or against a white man." Held, that the words, Indian, Negro, Black and White, are generic terms, designating race. That, therefore, Chinese and all other people [that] are not white, are included in the prohibition from being witnesses against whites.

The first (and intended) result was to release George W. Hall from the jail at Nevada City. He had been held for more than a year after the slaying of Ling Sing near the junction of Greenhorn Creek and Bear River on August 9, 1853. District Attorney William Stewart had prosecuted George and John Hall and a third person. Assisting in the prosecution were James Churchman and H. C. Gardiner. The defense team included Attorney General-elect John McConnell, Stanton Buckner, James S. Carpenter, and John C. Palmer.

Both Stewart and District Judge William T. Barbour worried about the fact that all material witnesses were Chinese. Stewart asked for and received an extra appropriation from the county so he could lock up the Chinese witnesses and keep them separated until the trial. At San Francisco he interviewed Rev. William Speer, a Presbyterian who had served four years in Canton before coming to San Francisco to open a mission in the Chinese quarter. Stewart wanted to know what form of oath was binding on the Chinese—he'd heard that cutting off a chicken's head or burning paper, or something of the kind would "swear" them. According to Stewart, Speers told him that "burning paper is just as good as anything." The missionary agreed to come to Nevada City and interpret for the court.

The trial was in October 1853, and while in the city Speer gave two lectures on his China experiences at Rev. Warren's church. He told of having gone to Canton in 1846 with his wife and infant daughter, both of whom had died within six months. He had been there when the British threatened to bombard Canton with naval guns unless it was opened to trade. Despite the intense anti-white feeling and the loss of his wife and child, Speer persisted and started his mission school. His recurring lung problems finally caused his sponsors to declare him physically unfit for overseas duty. He returned to the U.S. at the same time some of his former pupils were leaving for California to seek their fortunes.

Before the trial Speer questioned all witnesses, eliciting the same story from each. Speer summarized their testimony in a letter to a friend:

Two brothers named Hall (from Illinois or Indiana) and a person named Wiseman were "prospecting" on Bear River. Near sundown, on the 9th of August, they came upon a Chinese camp. The Halls, with little or no provocation, fell upon and cruelly beat one of the Chinese whom they met alone, and as he says, searched him for gold, though without obtaining any. The man, as soon as released, fled crying for help "to save his life."

The Americans started upon his track, carrying their baggage and rifles. As they passed by some tents at a little distance, the cousin of the man, hearing his cries, ran out, and was immediately shot down by the elder Hall.

Judge Barbour decided to swear the witnesses using a ceremony already in use by courts at Hong Kong and San Francisco: A piece of yellow paper bearing Chinese characters was burned in front of the witness. The Chinese writing was said to spell out a pledge before Imperial Heaven to speak the truth. As each witness testified, the similarity of the statements so impressed the jury that it acquitted two of the defendants and convicted George Hall.

Judge Barbour asked if Hall had any statement to make before sentence was passed, and the prisoner responded:

I do not think I have had a fair chance. I do not complain of the trial, for I think the jury did what they thought was right. But I ask for a new hearing. I have more evidence I can now produce that will put the matter in another light. It never entered my head to kill a man. . . . It seems hard that because I was so unlucky as to be there when that Chinaman was killed, I should be put down as his murderer. Those Chinamen, because I had a difficulty with one of them, swore my life away. I must now leave my wife and friends and all I hold dear because I was so unlucky as to have trouble with them. I have other witnesses I can produce if I am allowed a new hearing.

Judge Barbour denied the request, saying:

There is but little doubt from the character of the testimony that the verdict of the jury was just, and in strict conformity to the evidence. The firm belief of your guilt was impressed on the minds of the jury and the Court. Indeed, the clear and positive proof of the Chinese witnesses, corroborated by American testimony, together with the strong circumstantial evidence attending the whole affair, would not have permitted the most incredulous to form any other conclusion. . . .

You most unfortunately have participated in a delusion which has prevailed to an alarming extent in California. Many persons here have supposed that it is less heinous to kill a Negro, an Indian or a Chinaman than a white person. This is a gross error. The law of our country throws the aegis of its protection upon all within its jurisdiction, it knows no race, color or distinction.

Barbour sentenced Hall to hang on December 30, 1853. The *Journal* guessed a movement would be made to obtain a commutation of the sentence. Instead, an appeal was made to the supreme court, which agreed to hear John McConnell's arguments in the spring of 1854, by which time McConnell had assumed the office of attorney general and was about to leave the state—he intended to ask the governor to appoint Bill Stewart in his place.

Stewart was puzzled. No exceptions had been taken during the trial, so he assumed there was no basis for an appeal and expected it would be dismissed. To his surprise, the court listened to McConnell's argument with apparent interest, and was receptive to the peculiar logic that Chinese were Indians and therefore could not testify against whites. Stewart insisted that Chinese were *not* Indians, but even supposing they were, no one had claimed so during the trial.

Jobs were scarce in 1853 and many who were unemployed blamed competition from Asians and free blacks, who were said to accept wages and conditions no white man could abide. McConnell's novel argument was what many Californians wanted to hear, especially those from southern and border states. A majority of the court, with one eye on the electorate, embraced the curious logic that because Columbus thought he was in Asia all subsequent lawmakers were equally confused.

A long and strange discussion of race, archeology, geology, and the history of legal and scientific thinking followed, leading inevitably to the conclusion that 'Indian' meant 'Chinese.' It was necessary, in fact, for such terms as 'black,' 'mulatto,' and 'Indian' to embrace every known class or shade of color in order

... to protect the White person from the influence of all testimony other than that of persons of the same caste. The use of these terms must, by every sound rule of construction, exclude every one who is not of white blood.... We have carefully considered all the consequences resulting from a different rule of construction, and are satisfied that even in a doubtful case we would be impelled to this decision on grounds of public policy.

The same rule which would admit them to testify, would admit them to all the equal rights of citizenship, and we might soon see them at the polls, in the jury box, upon the bench, and in our legislative halls.... The anomalous spectacle of a distinct people, living in our community, recognizing no laws of this State except through necessity, bringing with them their prejudices and national feuds, in which they indulge in open violation of the law; whose mendacity is proverbial; a race of people whom nature has marked as inferior, and who are incapable of progress or intellectual development beyond a certain point, as their history has shown ... is now presented, and for them is claimed, not only the right to swear away the life of a citizen, but the further privilege of participating with us in administering the affairs of our Government.

The *Journal* wasted no words on constitutional questions but concerned itself solely with the effect on George Hall and the local budget:

Thus after being in jail over a year, since his trial, waiting for the action of the supreme court, at an expense of thousands of dollars to the county, Hall is virtually set at liberty. One of the principal white witnesses is dead; another cannot be found, and the testimony of Chinese is ruled from the case. Mr. Fletcher, the District Attorney, informs us that a *nolle prosequi* will probably be entered in the case.

Hall has had a severe lesson, and we trust it will be a profitable one to him. He is suddenly raised as if to life again, and has opportunity to wipe out, by a life of good conduct, the single yet deep stain of his former one.

Stewart visited Rev. Speer once more after arguing the case before the supreme court in April. He wondered why Speer had been doubtful about the method used to swear a Chinese witness. Speer then confessed he had withheld information, afraid it would prejudice Americans against the Cantonese. According to Stewart, Speer told him it was the custom in China to arrest various community leaders when a crime was committed, and torture sometimes was used to ascertain the facts. To avoid being tortured, witnesses to crimes tried, when possible, to agree on their stories in advance. Hence, the testimony might or might not be accurate.

Speer invited the young lawyer to dine with him and two important Chinese visitors who were passing through San Francisco. The dinner was hosted by the Six Chinese Companies, and the overseas guests had degrees from European universities, spoke numerous languages fluently and seemed well acquainted with American customs, religion and form of government.

When Stewart expressed the hope that someday relations between the races might be improved by better acquaintance, his dinner partners thought it unlikely. Why so, asked Stewart?

"There never can be friendly social intercourse between the Chinese and American people" said one. "There may be among the higher classes who understand the situation, but not among the common people."

"Because of color?"

"No. Because of religion. The Chinese are strongly wedded to their religion and to their gods, and they have no faith in your religion or your god. After all, your American god was killed by a man. Therefore, in the Chinese mind, your Jesus does not count for much."

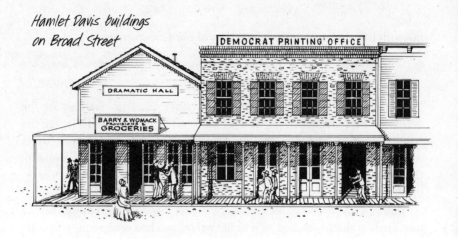

Hamlet Davis buildings on Broad Street

CHAPTER 16
NEW ARRIVALS
October–November 1854

I

ILES RELINQUISHED the office of district attorney to Sherman Fletcher with a vast sense of relief. He was especially happy to avoid prosecuting the case of William H. Wood, accused of the attempted rape of his landlady, Mrs. Hinckley. Niles had been upset when the victim fainted during questioning at the preliminary hearing, and he became increasingly reluctant to probe further, despite promptings from his professional conscience.

Examining such delicate matters was not a gentleman's business. Worse yet, the trial appeared likely to coincide with the arrival of Mary's first child, and Niles's new partner, Charles Tweed, was defending the accused man. Tweed, a distinguished lawyer in his fifties, had served on the Sacramento City Council in 1850. The trial was set for October 16, and Fred Searls was born on October 14. His astonished grandparents learned of his arrival when Fred's mother wrote two weeks later:

What can I say—where can I begin—to tell you of all that has taken place in our little house within the last two weeks. I wish I had written by the last steamer, as I might just as well have done, for I was quite well and busy sewing, but I could not bear to write again till I could tell you *all*. I was tired of keeping anything back in my letters.

But the time has come at last when I need keep nothing from you any longer. I am sitting in my large rocking chair in the parlor by the stove, and on the sofa beside me lies the sweetest, tiniest little *boy* that ever you saw, and every little while I go and uncover his little face and try to realize that it is indeed *my* little one—mine and Niles's. . . .

I meant to have had a *girl*, for Niles said he did not care, and I would rather have one, but I find he is very glad it is a boy after all, and so of course *I* am glad. Had it been a girl we should have named it "Nellie," and I was so sure of a girl that I came near working that name on a little blue merino cushion that I made for little pins, but concluded to work *Baby* instead.

We have thought over all the family names and do not seem quite satisfied with any, as names merely, and do not find it easy to choose one friend to name it after. . . . Niles has proposed to call him Fred, and seems to like the name very much. It is short, and pleasant to speak, and "Freddie" is such a pretty pet name.

I had from the first set Sunday the 15th as the day for my confinement—that was just one year from the day of my landing in San Francisco. But Thursday night at 12 o'clock I was taken with so much pain that I sent for "Aunt Mary" [Sampson] as I had promised to do at the first symptoms. I grew worse till near morning when the pains left me, and at breakfast time I felt well enough to sit up and eat some breakfast, and I can assure you I got nicely *teazed* that day for "putting it off a day or two" as Niles said, and for being so *slow*.

I lay on the sofa in the parlor all day and Aunt Mary staid with me. I had pains from noon that day until my baby was born next morning, but they were not so severe but that I could eat my *rations*, as Niles says—until 5 o'clock A.M. Then we called the Dr. and for 3 hours Aunt Mary stood by me aiding—and encouraging me—and I think I endured the trial with pretty good fortitude. . . .

I had a good physician, an elderly man of much experience: Dr. Knox. I would not let Deb be here, I thought it was enough to have poor dear Niles in the next room. I suppose he suffered almost as much as I did, but Deb was here before the baby was 10 minutes old, and while Aunt Mary dressed it was a great relief to me to hear her exclaim, "What a pretty baby—how perfect—every feature good, not a spot or blemish," &c. &c. Deb was almost beside herself with joyful excitement, and Niles could not speak.

The "elderly" physician was only thirty-four, but at least he was older than Niles and Mary. Deb described her reaction when she heard the news:

I felt some sympathy for Aunt Betsey Trotwood, I can assure you, as I met the breathless messenger (Laura) at Mrs. Sampson's door, who had come to tell me that a *man* child was born into the world.... Mary has told you of course, that we expected to have the child christened "Nellie" whatever it might be, still all human expectations are liable to fail, and the little fellow proved such a decided case of the masculine gender that we were forced to give up all our fondly cherished fancies.... I was not many moments in flying to the house, and I *would* say, "Aint *she* pretty?" though Niles stood by to correct me. Mary was the same calm Mary as ever, laughed at our disappointment, and in a few moments called for her breakfast.

Mary upset neighbors by her unwillingness to follow local customs. People from the border states in particular expected to have access to the new baby at once, but Mary firmly drew the line:

... they take it as quite an unheard of thing to be refused admittance to the mother, but I took the liberty to refuse all company for *one* day, and *offended* all whom I refused. Aunt Mary has very poor health now, and could not stay with me the first two nights as she had intended, so Deb and Niles took care of me and baby, and Aunt Mary came up and dressed us during the first week.

Since then my girl [Laura] has dressed us. She is very handy and very willing—can dress baby as well as any one. Deb was going to nurse us day times, and did stay here nearly all the time the first week, but the excitement made her feel stronger than she was, and when I got so as to help myself a little, she gave out and has been quite ill for a few days—slight fever—and some old troubles of hers—

Deb was brokenhearted that she could not care for Mary and the child, telling Cornelia:

I had just obtained Mrs. Browning's poems and was to read them to her. I had a rose bush loaded with white roses for her room, but I could do *nothing*, and did not see her again in a fortnight. We could write notes to each other and I could look out my window and see her walking sometimes on her verandah and sometimes on mine. Don't you believe I was sore tried then?

My "new house" was finished and stood right beside hers waiting patiently (I hope) for its new mistress. Niles brought the baby down to see me, carrying it through the street with all the pride of a new made father. You would laugh, Nellie, and be very much gratified too, if you could see Niles in his home with his arm around Mary and kissing Fred every other moment. He seems perfectly happy.

Mary credited this "great country" for her easy pregnancy and quick recovery—a viewpoint echoed by Deb, who insisted her friend had never spent a more pleasant summer. "You could not know until you had had some proofs what a difference California climate made in such matters," Deb told Cornelia, to explain their silence before the birth. Less than two weeks after the delivery, Mary could get around almost as well as before:

[I] can walk all around the house, dress myself, and one day dressed baby. I sit up nearly all day, lying on the sofa when tired. I have not had a bit of fever, or headache, no trouble with my breasts, except a little in drawing them the first time, and no drawbacks—anyway as yet. I mean to be very careful to not have any. I have plenty of milk, and the baby grows like every thing. . . .

Mary found the baby resembled Niles, herself, and Emmie and Charley, her youngest siblings. After describing Fred's limbs, hands, height, and amiable expression, she went on to assure Cornelia:

You need not fear that this little stranger will prevent our returning home or detain us here much longer. It will detain us *some*, I suppose, as our expenses have been much increased by it. It costs something to have children where the fee for the one visit is $50, and $8 for every other visit. Fortunately, I had no occasion for a second visit, have taken nothing but one portion of oil. We shall be so anxious to display our boy, that you may be assured we shall hasten home as soon as possible. Besides, we shall not want him to have his *bringing up* in Cal. It is no place for children, or rather a very *bad* place. . . .

I am quite in hopes Niles will write soon too. I had no idea he would be so delighted as he is. I can already see that he is going to be more domestic in his tastes, and I am glad of it, for it will be easier to make his home pleasant for him. I have filled my sheets with myself and Fred— and I could easily fill another about my dear Niles, for every new trial seems to call forth some new phase in his character, something to awaken still deeper and more devoted love. He has been a patient, faithful, devoted husband to me during all my trials, and has made them seem almost nothing, and my cares have seemed pleasures, because by enduring them cheerfully I could prove my love to him and make him happy.

Niles did write, adding his version to those already given:

First in order of news is the advent of a little stranger in our midst who if able to speak at all would be apt from his looks to call me *Pa*. Or, in other words, Nelly, we have a *baby*, a real living baby of the full age of two weeks. Not a little wry faced squalling brat, but one of the most quiet orderly little blue eyed boys you ever saw, just the kind of a child that would be stolen every night if not well guarded, *at least it seems so to me.* . . .

I must say that small children have risen in my estimation vastly within two weeks, and instead of the nuisances I had before deemed them, I find them the most attractive little beings in the world. Only think, Nelly, I took *Fred* today after dinner and brought him down in my arms through the street to Mrs Sampsons for Deb to see him, and was proud to do it too. Do you think I could have been induced to do such a thing three months ago? No, nothing like it. . . .

My old partner Bill Stewart is at present acting Atty General of the State, by appointment from the Governor. A fool for luck is Bill's motto, and mine too, so I expect to have a share after awhile somewhere, provided always I stay in California long enough. Not that I need anything in particular the more than I have at present—a good business, the best wife in the world and the prettiest baby, and a neat quiet home for them, should satisfy the ambition of a more deserving man than myself. . . . The sea of Kamchatka, the islands of the Ocean, the far off places of the Earth have fewer attractions by far than in former years, and ere long I expect to be as domestic and fond of home as my more civilized neighbors. In short, I am changing very fast, feel a deep interest in the cause of *common schools* and expect ere long to return to the Atlantic States to educate my family.

II

SPECTATORS PACKED the courtroom for William Wood's trial, eager to hear spicy details of his alleged attack on Mrs. Hinckley. Except during recesses, no one left the court until the case went to the jury late that night. Judge Caswell appointed Aaron Sargent to assist the new district attorney, and F. W. Thayer joined Col. Tweed for the defense.

Mrs. Hinckley testified her husband had gone from Nevada City to Steep Hollow overnight, leaving her alone with their boarder, Mr. Wood. She asked a friend, Mr. Snyder, to keep her company in the early evening, and about nine o'clock they both went to her bedroom to look at her watch and check the time. Afterwards they returned to the dining room, found Wood at the table, and Snyder announced he was going home. Mrs. Hinckley said she wished to retire and asked Mr. Wood to take his light and go to his room.

Wood seemed to comply, throwing a leg over the bench as if to rise. But once the door closed behind Snyder, he settled back and made no further move to leave. Mrs. Hinckley was uneasy, but went to her room. A few minutes later, she came out and again asked Wood to go to his room, saying she was tired. When he refused, she told him in that case she would go to Mrs. Ludwig's house and stay the night. She described to the court what happened next:

I started to the door, got hold of the door, still talking. I caught the handle of the door with my right hand. He then wrenched my right hand from the door with his right hand. I then caught the handle of the door with my left hand. He then wrenched my left hand from the door and whirled me round.

As he whirled me round, I caught a flat iron that was standing near the door with my right hand. He then took it from me, and I caught hold of the casing of the door with both hands. He attempted to get me into the bedroom. He then got me onto my knees three times. He tried to trip me over, endeavoring each time to raise my clothes ... he pulled my clothes to my waist three times, and I pushed them back. I begged and entreated of him if he had a spark of manhood to let me be. He did not say a word.

At that moment I heard somebody speak, and Mr. Crouch was standing in the door. Mr. Wood then let go of me, and I should have fallen had not Mr. Crouch caught me. What passed after that, I have no recollections. I was insensible for twelve hours after that.

When asked if she had cried out, she said, "When I tried to halloo, he put his hand over my mouth." Tweed asked if it was true she had neglected to tell Mr. Searls about Wood pulling up her clothes. Mrs. Hinckley replied she hadn't told him because she did not see Mr. Searls "personally."

"Did you tell him about Mr. Wood pulling you onto your knees?"

"I don't recollect."

"Did you tell him Mr. Wood tried to get you into your bedroom?"

"I think so."

"Did you tell Mr. Searls the only force used was to prevent your leaving the room?"

"No."

"Had Mr. Wood ever been in your bedroom before that night?"

"I suppose. Many boarders go in there."

"You say 'many boarders go in there.' By that you mean they entered your bedroom?"

"Well, yes—you see, the house is small and—"

"I see. Had Mr. Wood ever lain on your bed?"

"I don't know—it's possible."

"Please excuse me for what I am about to ask, but it is important to my client's case. Did you ever allow the defendant to kiss your breast?"

"No! Never! That's a nasty lie!"

"Did you and he ever discuss a book called *Paul the Profligate*?"

"No."

"You never told him you had looked at the frontispiece engraving?"

"No!"

After Tweed had finished his cross examination, the district attorney asked her to explain why boarders sometimes entered her bedroom. She replied that because they had no proper sitting room, her bedroom doubled as such.

Mr. Crouch, a former boarder at the Hinckley house, testified he had gone by the house and heard a cry—a low noise like someone saying "Let me go!" He went to the front door and found it partly open:

I saw Wood and Mrs. Hinckley. Wood appeared to be restraining her from going out. He had hold of her left arm—she had hold of the casing with her right hand. I went into the house and pushed Wood back. He stepped back and let her go as soon as he saw me. Mrs. Hinckley, as soon as he let go of her, seemed to be falling. I put my arm out and steadied her, and she turned round and walked into the bedroom.

He said Mrs. Hinckley fainted about ten or fifteen minutes later, so he sent Mr. Wood to get Mrs. Ludwig. Tweed asked Crouch if the landlady permitted men to speak to her in a "familiar way." He replied that, to his knowledge, she did not.

Tallman Rolfe, justice of the peace, was next on the stand. He had presided over the original examination and said both Searls and Tweed had exhibited some "reluctance" to ask questions of Mrs. Hinckley. Rolfe replied in the negative when asked if anything was said at the time about a flat iron, or the raising of Mrs. Hinckley's garments.

Mr. Leach testified he had once heard Wood boast "he intended to have connection" with Mrs. Hinckley, but didn't think Wood had said "he'd have her if it killed him." Nor had anyone except Wood talked that way about her. She had a reputation for "sport and fun," but not for having "wanton desires."

The final witness was Niles Searls, who said of his inquiry at the Hinckley residence, "I did not examine her as fully as I should have done in such a trial as this. I did not question her as to the liberties taken with her person."

The jury retired at 11 p.m., deliberated all night, and brought in a guilty verdict in the morning. Wood was sentenced to six months in jail and fined $500.

III

ACCORDING TO THE *Journal*, Commodore Matthew C. Perry had persuaded Japan to sign a treaty of "amity and intercourse" guaranteeing Americans free access to the port cities of Simoda and Hakodate. In the same issue the editor commented on relations with local Asians:

Notwithstanding the summary cleansing of the Chinese houses of ill fame a few weeks ago, the vermin have crawled back to their nests, and hold out as aforetime. On Wednesday night last, a deputation of smart young men visited the houses and told the occupants that they must leave town before next Saturday night, or they would "clean them out." *Verbum sap*. The Chinese had better leave—the dirty nuisances.

A few days later, Nevada City hosted the Old Settlers' Ball, celebrating four years of local history. Aaron Sargent nostalgically recalled the "old days":

Many of us remember when the flourishing berg of Nevada was a motley collection of cabins, tents, and shingle shanties, and small at that. How the rush of events has carried it onward! Handsome structures of wood and brick occupy the sites of buildings where tall hats could touch the roofs, and the shins of the customer could just escape the Scylla of pork barrels by rubbing the Charybdis of bean bags. Ah, the days of lang syne. We'll remember the times of hickory and red and gray shirts in standing collars and cassimeres, as we tread to the measures that never grow old.

Already the rush of events had destroyed two of California's best-known landmarks, Sutter's Fort and Sutter's Mill. In the six and a half years since the gold discovery, vandals had razed the fort; its adobe bricks were used to pave a road through the slough. At Coloma, the sawmill frame was being converted into walking sticks.

Tallman Rolfe, who had been in San Francisco when news of Marshall's discovery reached that place in 1848, now was celebrating the arrival of brother Ianthus and his new wife from the east. Another brother, Horace, was also in Nevada City now, having come north the year before from the new Mormon colony at San Bernardino. Horace had accompanied his parents on the long Mormon emigration to Salt Lake City in 1846 and 1847, as well as on the later equally hazardous trek across the southern desert to San Bernardino Ranch in 1851. He attended school part of the time, and during the rest was a carpenter. At the age of nineteen, he came to Nevada County to visit his older brothers.

Neither Tallman nor Ianthus had taken part in the Mormon exodus from Nauvoo. Instead, Tallman had joined a wagon train to Oregon in 1845, and Ianthus traveled to Massachusetts, where he went to school at Brighton. There he met his future wife, Emily Lindsey, newly arrived from Maine, his own birthplace. After rejoining his family briefly at Salt Lake City in 1850, Ianthus continued west to live with Tallman at Nevada City.*

For a time Ianthus mined for gold, and both brothers owned claims at the Walloupa diggings between Little York and Red Dog. When Horace arrived, he was put to work on the claim. In the winter of 1853–1854 Ianthus purchased an interest in the *Democrat* with Searls and Stewart. He then borrowed money to go east and marry Emily. In October 1854, he arrived back in California with his bride, and the wife and teenage son of another newspaperman, Warren Ewer. In the same party were Nevada City businessman and banker Jesse Wall and his bride from Tennessee.

Ewer, who now owned the Grass Valley *Telegraph*, invited Emily to stay with his family until Ianthus found a place at Nevada City. Two weeks later, in mid-November, Emily viewed her new home on the north side of Spring Street, half a block below Pine. Her house, which faced that of gunsmith Zeno Philosopher Davis, was unlike any she had seen:

It was battened, which is wide boards with narrow strips nailed over the cracks. Some of the boards and strips just reached to the sills, some covered them, and others of all lengths below, making the house at the back look like an old broken tooth comb. It had two front doors, each leading into the front rooms and the strips run across the boards, just boards for steps with no backs to them.

As we drove to the house I could see under the house through to the back yard.... The view was not artistic. The house had five rooms, two front rooms and two bedrooms and a small work room. In the work-room, or sink room, was a slide window [over] the sink. I washed the window, which made the room so light I threw a pan of water against it, thinking it open.

The house had been papered and painted inside and looked clean, but after a fire had been built in the cook stove, the paper soon showed grease spots and I noticed two little pyramids shaped like blocks on top of the paste boards below the grease spots on the paper. I investigated and found the cold grease that had piled up from fry pans that had evidently been hung up by the miners without being washed. The grease had drained from the pans and the painter had painted over them.

*For more about the Rolfe family in San Bernardino, see appendix at end of book.

On the sides of the front doors I noticed a great deal of sticky stuff where the miners had cleaned their knives after scraping the remains of the table to the pigs who run the streets. The first night in my new home I slept little, owing to the pigs and fleas. The pigs slept under the house, and "where there is pigs there are fleas," I was told, never having seen a flea till I came to California. I caught a few to send to a friend in the East as [a] curiosity.

In the morning I told Mr. Rolfe that the house and the lot must be enclosed to keep out the pigs, and he told me that the pigs were healthy, as they ate the refuse that was thrown from the house, and that also the refuse under the house must be cleaned out. He sent a colored man the next day and the miscellaneous things that came to light were astonishing to a person just from civilization. There were gum boots, old coats, pants, and vests, red shirts, blue shirts, and white ones, any number of old socks, bottles of all sizes and description, tin cans of every shape and size, bones that the dogs had carried under there, and I cannot describe the odor or now remember the number of wheel barrow loads that were dumped into Deer Creek. . . .

Our house was lined with cloth and when a gust of wind came and it would sail up and down, I imagined myself on ship board and felt sea sick. The view at the back of our house included the backs of all the houses of Broad Street ... and the buildings were used mostly for saloons. Many saloons had small pines grouped at the back to cover the drunks that were hauled out after they could sit no longer in their chairs.

Yankee
Sullivan

CHAPTER 17

CHIVALRY MISFIRES

November 1854

I

ROSE COTTAGE was Deb's name for her new house alongide Mary's Durden Cottage. On November 11 she described it to Cornelia:

I could not have a pleasanter little home anywhere. All the trimmings in my parlor are green, making a pretty contrast with the white papered walls. I have a pretty set of bookshelves hanging on the side where there are no curtains; they are suspended by green cords and tassels and filled with books from Charlie's store.

My bedroom is all white, instead of pink as we agreed. I have at the head of my bed precisely such a little square stand as you and I used to sit by in your grandmother's room, where you so often tried to whisper sweet words of consolation to me and heal the wounds of my ever bleeding heart—bitter, bitter days—but they are past—never more to return. I got the stand of Mrs. Sampson. I told her I wanted it because it reminded me so much of a friend. I have it spread with a white towel. My bureau is painted white, white plaid muslin curtains and a white chamber set of course. My dining room is buff—buff and crimson carpet, buff and crimson bordering buff paper and buff curtains.

I commenced with a girl but she was taken sick and Charlie and I took her home (a little distance from town) day before yesterday She will probably return in a few days, though I get along nicely without her; still Charlie thinks the washing, ironing and cleaning would cost nearly as much as to keep her all the time. We have but two meals a day, breakfast at 8½, dinner at 4 o'clock. Charlie *will* broil the steak and grind the coffee, I prepare the vegetables and set the table, and to tell the truth [Mary's] Laura generally steps in and washes my dishes; they are all so careful of me, I cannot get a chance to bring out my latent powers.

I wish you *could* step in to dinner with me. I have scarlet radishes, new onions, celery and lettuce in my cellar. It seems strange to have such vegetables at all seasons as we do here. I shall have baked sweet potatoes, broiled fresh pork and coffee; wouldn't that tempt you now, if I could only be within visiting distance? Now that we are all housekeeping we realize more than ever the distance that separates us. If our brothers should come here, they may rest assured of a most hearty welcome. We shall be able to accommodate them without the least inconvenience, and I do not feel like saying a discouraging word, for if they do not succeed in business, they will have homes.

Deborah was referring to hints that more of Rensselaerville's young people might be coming to California. Her own brother Harvey and Mary's brother Addison were known to be interested, as was Jerome Moore, brother-in-law to Deb's cousins, the Carter boys, whose mine was near Nevada City. Deb went on to say:

They will not be strangers in a strange land; without any doubt they can earn enough to take them home again, and a year lost at home would not be a great deal, taking into consideration what they might learn from a trip here; then too, they may do well, none can tell, still I would set forth no inducements on that score. It will be a great trial for you all to part with them, but is it not a sore one to keep them when they are so discontented?

Addison had so far confided his hopes to go west only to Cornelia. She wrote him in care of Rufus King's office at Catskill, where her brother was reading law:

... for your sake, [I] cannot help wishing you success in your plans. I trust in a Divinity which guides us all, and hope for your happiness. I do not think any person here suspects your intentions, unless it be Dr. Wickes' family I guessed from some hint Delight [Wickes] gave me the other day when here at tea with Mrs. Carter and James that she did. But she was very cautious, and I dare not ask her what she knew.

James [Carter] is still here, and will be here again, before he leaves for Cal. He stays a week or two longer now. It *is* noised about that Jerome goes, but I hear nothing said of Harvey. Pa and Ma of course are ignorant of all—although Ma thinks you would go if you could. I do not think they will oppose any practicable scheme.

Cornelia wrote him again on November 28:

The time is approaching when some decision will be arrived at, I presume, as to your farther course this winter. I feel a kind of uneasiness about it this week, and presume you are quite as impatient as I to know how to plan for yourself. Our people are still in profound ignorance of your intentions, though it is well known everywhere that Harvey and Jerome are going. They were forced to tell in order to *collect* [bills] promptly But nothing has been said about you. . . .

Ma has said once or twice, "If Addison were through his studies he would be for going, I think." I *think* they will not object *strongly* but cannot tell. . . .

7 o'clock—Letters have arrived—and one from Mary and one from Niles, dated *Oct 28th*, but you cant guess the news. You're an *Uncle* and I'm "Aunt Nellie." Oh! Oh! Oh! They have taken us by surprise entirely! . . . And *Mary*—you should hear her talk. A perfect little goose she is. . . . She wrote Ma a long letter, when after filling six pages with stories of her new experiences and baby, she hastens with apologies "to say something about Baby" I laughed and cried together for an hour or more with Delight, who came to hear the news. . . .

I envy you the anticipation you have of seeing [Mary]. I would *go* clear there in one moment if I had the means and were not otherwise "engaged."

At some point before the year's end, Addison made the decision to join Mary and Niles. He began his westward voyage in the first week of January 1855.

II

WHEN FRED WAS a month old and had changed her life entirely, Mary told Cornelia:

It is now Sunday, and this morning I washed and dressed myself . . .

which with the care little Fred requires was a pretty good mornings work for me, and now I have been over to Deb's for a few minutes, and with Fred grunting on the sofa—trying to wake up—and Niles by my side writing to his mother about our little new boy, I will write as fast and as much as I can. . . . I am interrupted once in 5 minutes on an average. . . .

Deb and Charles have a beautiful place, and have things on a more expensive as well as more extensive scale than we do, but they have no *baby* to provide for, and beside had our house &c to improve upon, while ours was an innovation upon the ways of *this* part of the country at least, in point of convenience and comfort. . . . [Fred] grows very fast indeed. We did not weigh him till he was three weeks old, and then he weighed 7 *lbs* and Aunt Mary thinks he could not have weighed over 4½ when born, but he is not *poor* and scrawny He is as fat and plump as though he were a *big* boy . . .

[Niles] says that Freddie talks to *him* a great deal when they are alone, but he is *bashful* before me, and he has all sorts of funny stories to tell that Fred has told him. I suppose he told you, didn't he, of the wonderful feats baby performed the first day, counting the chairs, learning the multiplication table, &c. He [Niles] has established [Fred's] politics and taken him through Daboll's Arithmetic, and talks of sending him soon to San Francisco to learn Chinese, Spanish &c. . . .

My girl does all the [house] work and finds some time to sew. I have a great deal to do. I have scarcely a dress that I can nurse baby in, and am entirely at a loss to know how to make them so as to be convenient. . . . I might wear open fronts, but they are so much trouble and expense, and I fear I should take cold. I have a cheap delaine for every day, and a dark French blue merino for nice, and think of making my merino with a bertha cape embroidered a little with silk the same color. Do you think it would be pretty? It makes no difference here about the *fashion*, if things are only pretty and becoming.

Later in the month Mary referred to Addison's contemplated trip; she had no way of knowing if her sister had heard of the plan, but guessed it was too late to matter:

I feel as though I must write about it even if it should be a secret still, for [the news] will reach you before he leaves if he comes, and if he does not you can keep this letter to yourself. As for the wisdom of the step, I have nothing to say . . . He is young enough so that if he does not succeed well here after a year or two he will have seen something of the world, and can return and try the States with perhaps as good—perhaps a better start than now.

If he is coming *at all* I hope he will come now without fail for I should think James's company worth everything on the voyage. Harvey too, being a physician, will be an advantage. He will of course come right to us and stay with us till he gets into business. I am so bewildered when I think of his coming.... I think of the joy it will bring to our hearts to have them come.... I am almost beside myself with excitement, but then comes always the thought of the sorrow it will cause you at home, that I cannot even *hope* he *will* come.

Mary ended with a note about her husband's affairs:

Niles is as busy as ever, has just as much business as he can do, but owing to the drunken judge who fools away nearly half the time at each session of the court, he loses hundreds of dollars every season, suits are withdrawn or postponed till it takes nearly all the profits of his business at some sessions. I am almost afraid he will have to relinquish the business unless they can get rid of Judge Barbour.

III

THERE WERE MANY who shared Mary's outrage toward William T. Barbour. It was certain he would be opposed for reelection, but that time was rather distant. The only chance for his quick removal lay in convincing the legislators to redraw district boundaries.

Barbour was in his early thirties and came from Missouri. He was elected district judge the first time in 1851, but was prevented from presiding when incumbent Judge Gordon Mott claimed the election was invalid. Mott filed suit, retaining Stephen J. Field for counsel, but California's supreme court ruled in favor of Barbour. When the district was enlarged in 1852 to include the counties of Yuba, Sutter, Nevada, and Sierra, Barbour was reelected despite vigorous opposition.

In 1853, the judge and Field nearly met on the field of honor. Gordon Mott was Field's second, and Assemblyman Charles Fairfax agreed to stand for Judge Barbour. After some angry words over who issued the first challenge, Field waived the point. Then, according to Field, the affair took a bizarre turn:

Fairfax then stated that Barbour, being the challenged party, had the right to choose the weapons and the time and place of meeting; to all of which Mott assented. Fairfax then said ... [Barbour] had fixed the time for that evening; the place, a room twenty feet square, describing it; the weapons, Colt's revolvers and Bowie knives; that the two principals so armed were to be placed at opposite sides of the room with their faces to the wall; that they were to turn and fire at the word, then advance and finish the conflict with their knives.

Mott answered that the terms were unusual, unprecedented, and barbarous, and that he could not consent to them. Fairfax admitted that they were so; but replied that they were those Barbour had prescribed. He would, however, see Barbour and endeavor to obtain a modification of them. Soon afterwards he reported that Barbour still insisted upon the terms first named and would not agree to any other.

When Mott reported the result of his conference with Fairfax, I at once said that Barbour was a coward and would not fight at all.... So I told Mott to accept them by all means.... Fairfax soon afterwards made his appearance with a message that his. principal would waive the Bowie-knives; and not long afterwards he came a second time with another message that it would not do to have the fight in the room designated, because the firing would be heard outside and attract a crowd.... it was finally agreed that the meeting should take place the next morning in Sutter County.... accordingly, I took a carriage, and with my friend Judge Mott drove down to the appointed place.

After we had been there some time the first stage appeared and stopped. Soon after the second stage appeared and stopped, and Judge Barbour and Mr. Fairfax got out. But instead of proceeding to the designated place, Barbour declared that he was a judicial officer, and as such could not engage in a duel. At the same time he would take occasion to say that he would protect himself, and, if assaulted, would kill the assailant.

With these words, leaving Fairfax standing where he was, he walked over to the first stage, and mounting rode on to Sacramento. Seeing Fairfax standing alone on the ground I sent word to him that I would be happy to give him a place in my carriage—an invitation which he accepted, and we then drove to Nicolaus, where we breakfasted, and thence returned to Marysville.

One member of Yuba County's court of sessions, referring to Barbour, spoke contemptuously of a "hell-concocted junta, headed by the judge of the 10th district, and tailed by a noted gambler of Marysville." On October 14, 1854, Oliver P. Stidger was assaulted by Barbour and a companion. The judge threatened to cut Stidger's heart out for critical remarks made by him in a letter to the Marysville *Herald*. After the grand jury indicted Barbour for assault with a deadly weapon his lawyers had asked the court of sessions for a change of venue to Nevada County.

While members of the bar schemed how best to rid themselves of Barbour, they also wondered who might be appointed to the supreme court vacancy created by the recent death of Alexander Wells. The Nevada *Democrat* urged the appointment of Nevada City's own James Churchman, but the Placerville *Democrat* and the *Daily California Chronicle* objected, the latter paper saying Churchman's "meagre intellect, little learning, less law, and still less moral integrity, would disgrace the Governor, and be a misfortune to the Bench, Bar and people."

Aaron Sargent, though a Whig, defended the local attorney in the *Journal*:

Mr. Churchman and ourself are not political friends, and in any affairs of his with his own party we have no concern.... But Mr. Churchman is our friend, and one esteemed for noble characteristics of mind and heart.... As a lawyer he stands pre-eminent in this State, practising successfully in the highest courts.... In private life he is beloved and respected. No man or thing ever before breathed a word against his "moral integrity."...

Mr. C. has one fault, which is shared by many generous spirits. He loves a social glass, and is not always temperate in its use. But no Washingtonian ever made mightier efforts to free himself of this single fault. Sometimes for months not a drop of liquor passes his lips. But he is a kind husband and parent, an upright citizen, and every inch a man.

It was not the only time Sargent had commented in print about the use of intoxicants by public figures; two weeks earlier he had written:

It is published in the papers of the week that [Congressman Joseph W.] McCorkle and [ex-governor] McDougall have joined the Sons of Temperance. It is an excellent feature in public men, and paves the way to a Maine Liquor Law for this state. McCorkle visited Nevada the past week, and illustrated his new professions by refusing to comply with the silly custom of drinking at a bar.

By the way, the postscript of a note from our friend Shipley of the Grass Valley *Telegraph* informs us that he has joined the Sons of Temperance. We know it is improper, unbearable, to state anything of a man's "private" affairs, but we know the victim of these remarks will excuse this liberty on the ground of "oversight." Seriously, we are greatly pleased with the intelligence. Henry Shipley is a gentleman of true native talent, extensive practical and classic acquirements, a vigorous and polished writer, and goes into whatever he undertakes, whether a spree or an oration, with all the zest of an active brain and sanguine temperament.

IV

SHIPLEY'S ZEST was not admired by Mill Street's resident celebrity, Lola Montez, whose run-in with him drew wide notice in November. The affair began when Lola summoned the editor to her cottage and requested a favorable review for friends who were about to perform in Grass Valley. She thought they reached an understanding, but the resulting article demonstrated otherwise.

In his next issue Shipley borrowed an item from the New York *Times* which credited the Queen of Spain with possessing "Lola Montez-like insolence and affrontry." The countess reacted with predictable fury:

I recollected the Woman's Rights Convention, took the benefit of Miss Lucy Stone's principles, bonnet on head and whip in hand; that whip which never was used but on a horse was this time to be disgraced by falling on the back of an ASS.

I went forth [to the Golden Gate saloon] . . . and as quick as a flash of lightning, laid the said whip on [Shipley's] shoulder and head. . . . After having given him four good whippings he got up and squared himself on the most approved Yankee Sullivan principles, and was preparing to give me a stunner in the eye.

The spirit of my Irish ancestors (I being a kind of ¾ breed of Irish, Spanish and Scotch) took possession of my left hand, and on the most approved Tom Hyer principles, before he could attain my eye I took his, on which, thanks to some rings I had on at the time, I made a cutting impression. As usual, this would-be-great shoulder-striker ended the combat with certain abuse, of which, to do him justice, he is perfect master of.

Shipley's somewhat different version appeared in an "Extra" edition of the *Telegraph* under the headline, "Grass Valley Ring: First Fight of the Season":

TIME: 11 A.M., Tuesday, November 21st. PLACE: Golden Gate Saloon, Grass Valley. Weapons: horsewhips, nails and tongue.

1ST ROUND: Countess pitching in, strikes blow with whip; Ship catches it—both close. Countess's second takes her off. Ship falls back with whip in his possession.

2D ROUND: Countess returns to attack—with her tongue. Ship, provokingly cool, smokes his pipe and laughs at her.

3D ROUND: Countess urged to desperation, strikes at Ship and spits in his face. Ship magnanimously advises her not to go too far.

4TH ROUND: Countess tries on her old tactics—appeals to crowd as "Miners," etc. Crowd sensibly laughs at her.

4½ ROUND: A "green" chap in the crowd said something [and] the Countess informed him it was not his "put in."

5TH ROUND: Crowd greatly amused.

6TH ROUND: Cries of "Speech from Shipley." Ship offers the stump to Lola. Countess informed Ship her name is "Mad Lola."

7TH ROUND: Countess reads extracts from *Grass Valley Telegraph*, counts number of words, and informs Ship there are twenty words to be accounted for.

8TH ROUND: Ship remarks that crowd has been sufficiently amused and concludes to retire in disgust.

9TH ROUND: Countess springs forward and demands the whip—"her father's whip." Article in dispute placed in hands of disinterested party.

10TH ROUND: Countess asks all hands in to drink—crowd laughs and refuses.

Lola's and Shipley's use of prize fight metaphors and slang reflected the atmosphere created by a recent well-publicized raid at Hughes' Race Track. Among those arrested was James "Yankee" Sullivan, a famous boxer. At the time of the Lola's assault on Shipley, Sullivan was locked up at Nevada City.

The "principles of Sullivan and Tom Hyer" referred to English boxing rules governing a fight for the American heavyweight title in 1849. Before that, Tom's father Jacob Hyer, a New Yorker of Dutch ancestry, won America's first public prize fight in 1816, by defeating Tom Beasley. Whereas popularity of the illegal sport grew rapidly in England, it languished in the U. S. until the 1849 battle between Jake's son and Yankee Sullivan, an Irishman of many names. Known sometimes as James Ambrose, and at others as F. Murray, Sullivan had escaped from the British penal colony at Sydney and fled to America in 1841. He was called "Yankee" because in one fight the sash tied round his waist was decorated with an American flag.

London rules permitted bare-knuckle punching and wrestling holds above the waist, with each round lasting until one man was thrown or knocked to the ground. His seconds had half a minute to revive him before the next round started. The loser was the man who, at the beginning of a new round, could not "come to the mark" scratched on the ground inside the fenced circle. The title fight between Hyer and Sullivan on February 7, 1849, lasted sixteen rounds, with Hyer the eventual winner.

Hyer retired as champion and joined the California gold rush, but

Sullivan continued in the ring and gave boxing lessons. Most of those he trained were young toughs from the city, but occasionally he demonstrated the "art of self defense" to college students like Addison Niles and his fraternity friends at Williams College. On October 12, 1853, after losing a thirty-seven round fight at Boston Corners, New York, Sullivan followed Hyer to California.

On November 17, 1854, the *Journal* reported the event that placed Sullivan and his associates behind bars:

Disgraceful Scenes. On Friday, this place was inundated by a gang of despicable rowdies, assembled to witness the most revolting of all exhibitions—a prize fight.... and was attended by a large crowd from the neighboring places, besides blacklegs, villains, pickpockets and pimps, from Marysville and Sacramento. The brutal contest continued nearly an hour, but we shall not defile our columns with its nauseating details. Kelly, one of the combatants, was severely, perhaps fatally injured, and now he is in a deranged state of mind at the Union hotel.

Previous to the fight, Mr. Hughes obtained a license from the deputy county treasurer, for a "sparring match without gloves," although it was [well known] to ... the officer granting it, and to the public, that no sparring match was intended, but a bloody fight between the combatants, that could only end in severe injury to one or both, and a public disturbance.... After the fight the combatants were arrested and brought to town, and Fitzgerald was put under bonds for $5,000. He took French leave immediately, but was arrested at Sacramento, and again brought back.

The discreditable crowd, drawn together like foul birds to carrion, gave their blessing to this place for many hours after the occasion ... by discharging pistols in the streets, riding furiously about, getting drunk and disorderly generally.... From such another visitation, "good Lord deliver us."

An anonymous reader wondered if a similar piece in the *Nevada Democrat* entitled "Sparring Exhibition without Gloves" had come "from the hip or the shoulder." Two months later, the Sacramento *Union* had this to say concerning Kelly's injuries:

Kelly broke his arm in the third round, thereby disabling him during the remainder of the contest. On medical examination in [Sacramento] thirty-six days after the accident, both bones of the fore arm were found to be dislocated at the wrist, leaving the hand in such a twisted and unnatural position that the patient could only get the back of the little finger to the mouth....

Dr. F. M. Morton, assisted by Drs. Barry and Pierson, undertook the case at this stage, and by the aid of pullies were enabled to break up the adhesion, adjust the dislocated bones, and bring the hand to its natural position.

The patient suffered great agony during the operation, and for twenty-four hours afterwards labored under tetanic and convulsive spasms. Chloroform was administered ... but the patient could not be brought wholly under its influence. This case is very interesting, from the fact that it was two weeks beyond the stated period at which so successful a result ought to be anticipated.

The Gate of Panama

CHAPTER 18

FAMILY REUNIONS

December 1854–February 1855

I

REDDIE'S FIRST CHRISTMAS was celebrated at home. Mary Samp-son and widower Sidney Herbert, with their respective families, had dinner with the Mulfords. Because Laura had gone home to Stockton for the holidays, Niles helped Mary serve dinner next door at Durden Cottage. Mary described the result to Cornelia:

> A friend of ours was out in the country, and, seeing some turkeys fattening for Christmas, ordered one sent to us, and so we invited him and some friends of his to take dinner with us.... The turkey was the best one I ever saw. Indeed, I never saw any fowl that would compare with it. Our cold winters home [in New York] make fowls tough they say is the reason we have so much finer ones here....

Last week, we had a goose one day and [the Mulfords] came here; next day they all came again to meet ... Mr and Mrs Young from up in the mountains—we had *roast* ducks that day. A few days before, we took dinner with the same company [at Deb's]; but ... our really *fine* dinner was hardly appreciated, as it was nearly the same that we had had before ... Well, our [Christmas] company most of them disappointed us again, but the one I cared for, Charlie Marsh, our companion and guide in the mountain trip was here.

On January 1, the Searls and Mulford families were visited by Will Allen's brother Uriah, who lived in Sierra County. His arrival coincided with the first big storm of the season. The day began to the accompaniment of boisterous winds and heavy rain, and by late evening snow was falling. Mary and Niles invited Uriah to stay with them during his entire two week holiday in the city, but, as Uriah later told his parents, he felt it would be "coming it a little too strong for a short acquaintance." Nevertheless, he agreed to stay four or five nights. Uriah said of his future in-laws: "[I] was very much pleased with them, in fact they seemed like our own Folks at Home and as though I had known them for years."

The storm lasted five days, blanketing the city with a foot of snow. Then the sky cleared, the temperature rose, and for the remainder of the month residents basked in springlike weather. Back at his mining claim, Uriah struggled through four feet of new snow on the ridges, but said the weather felt like September in New York:

We have a little Frost nights, but hardly enough to make Ice in a bucket of Water out door—In fact I do believe there is no country under the sun more healthy than the Northern part of *California*. I doubt whether the deaths will exceed *five* out of *One thousand*, from actual *disease*. The night is advancing and I must close for I have a hard days work to perform on the morrow, if my health is spared. I like to have forgotten to mention, that I attended church while in Nevada with Mr & Mrs Searls it being the first church I have entered if I mistake not in over Four Years—I have heard preaching a number of times during that time, but have not been to church before the good-old-Fashioned-way, since '51 in Sacramento.

Mary feared Laura might not return after the holidays, "as she dreads so much the ride here." She told Cornelia Laura was the best girl she ever saw:

She takes just as much interest in my work as though it were my own, and will go to market and get all the requisites and get up as nice a dinner as need be without the least assist or directions. Then too, she is so good with baby, so careful, and understands much better than I do how to care for him.

Mary thought $50 a month quite a lot to pay her, but Niles was satisfied and offered to extend her contract another six months. Mary agreed with Niles that "*good* girls cannot be had for less here . . . she is cheaper at $50 than most girls at $40." Laura promised if she did not come to send another to take her place. During her absence a "little girl" was helping Mary in return for board and schooling, the latter amounting to $2 a month.

Fortunately, Laura did return, because Niles had to go to Sacramento for the opening of the legislature in mid-January. During his five-day absence, Mary's Grass Valley friend Mrs. Deane was bringing her baby boy for a visit. The Deanes would sleep nights at Deb's house where there was an extra bed, but days would be spent with both families.

Niles was part of a delegation of Nevada County attorneys and politicians going to Sacramento to lobby new bills. Among other things, they hoped to amend the incorporation measure to enable Nevada City to levy special taxes such as dog and poll taxes. Whereas the 1851 charter government had been given too much latitude, the 1854 incorporation act was proving too restrictive. Other lobbyists, like Niles, hoped to create a new judicial district in Nevada County to rid themselves of Judge Barbour.

For some a few nights in the big city proved too much to handle. The *Journal*'s capitol correspondent reported that Robert Davidge, Nevada City's postmaster and onetime editor of *Young America* had been arrested by Sacramento authorities for brutally attacking James Churchman:

I did not see the occurrence, but am informed that Davidge struck Churchman several times in the face with a heavy cane, when they clinched. In the melee, which occurred in the Orleans, a pistol was discharged, by whom I am not informed, the ball from which, as usual in such cases, struck a spectator, Hon. D. Mahony, Senator from San Francisco, inflicting a severe but not dangerous wound in his mouth. I met [Sheriff] Endicott a few moments after the occurrence, and advised him to take your lobby delegates home if he could not compel them to be more quiet when they got down here "among folks."

The *Journal* correspondent, himself a Whig, was prepared for a display of rowdiness when an acquaintance insisted on his meeting Democratic boss David C. Broderick. In a tongue-in-cheek account, he wrote:

You know what my opinion has been of him.... I approached Broderick with a great deal of caution—looked out for a "soft place to fall" in case I shouldn't be able to dodge his blows. I went through the formula of an introduction as hastily as possible and threw myself "on guard."...

Broderick gazed inquiringly for a moment, turned to D. and remarked "your friend is excited." Thinking this a *professional* ruse to throw me off my guard, I sprang back after the most approved "Fitzgerald style" and determined to "go down" on his first motion towards me. Broderick, bursting into a laugh, quietly remarked "this gent must be a careful reader of the *Times and Transcript*" and walked away.

This remark was true.... Since then I have seen much of him and had my mind disabused of many impressions concerning him. He is a quiet, dignified, *commanding* man. I believe he has been traduced and villified to a point bordering on criminality. 'Tis a convenient but diabolical way to crush a laudable ambition.

Editor Sargent also gave Democrat John Bigler generous credit for his message to the legislature:

The Governor's Message, though altogether too long for our columns, is an able document, and deserves careful perusal. It treats with singular clearness many matters of vital interest to the State, and for ability and practical wisdom, will, we doubt not, be excelled by not one other of the thirty-one such messages sent in by the governors of the States to the various legislatures. It is incomparably better in style and matter than the President's Message.

II

BETWEEN CUBA AND ASPINWALL, aboard the steamer *George Law*, Addison Niles wrote his mother on Saturday, January 13, 1855. More than a week had elapsed since his departure from New York with Harvey and Delight Wickes, Jerome Moore, and James Carter.

The voyage was similar in many respects to earlier reports sent by Mary. He described a reasonably pleasant passage, without the crowding Mary and Deb had experienced ("very few passengers, only 250 in the whole and . . . half of those in the steerage"). Comfortable double-berth accommodations and decent cuisine offset a moderate bout of seasickness; the rolling movement of the boat in heavy seas was inconvenient:

. . . a great many passengers were on deck, and every once in a while a sudden lurch would bring down a dozen or so, to their great discomfiture and of course the great amusement of the rest. I fell but once and then I made a strike, for I brought down a man and a boy and came near upsetting the Captain.

But the night was the worst. It required a skillful balance to keep in bed at all, at least it seemed so while we were awake, but we were not rolled out at all when we were asleep. I suppose we kept on bracing ourselves unconsciously. The first mate told me this was the roughest trip they had ever made.

Thursday we passed Cuba within two miles of the land. We do not stop there, or anywhere as we supposed. The steamer takes out coal for the whole trip. We got a very fine view of the island, for it was a pleasant day, but it was a hilly point, the extreme eastern end, and we saw no signs of life. . . .

We shall reach Aspinwall they tell us sometime tomorrow, and I write you now because the mails will probably be made up today. We shall probably sleep in Aspinwall Sunday [tomorrow] night, and start out by the cars at 8 o'clock Mon. morning; we shall then have about 13 miles they say, to ride mule. Those who know say that this is the best time of all the year for crossing the isthmus, and that we are to have on the other side the best steamer of any on the line. . . .

We are in good health all of us. . . . Delight has been very sick, that is, sea sick, but not near as much as many other passengers. . . . We eat all day nearly. Our fare is middling good, and our appetites voracious. There are so few passengers that we all eat at once and do not fill the tables at that. I have wanted nothing, besides what I took with me.

On the *Golden Age*, heading north to San Francisco, Addison continued his account:

We arrived [at Aspinwall] on Sunday the 14th about 4 o.c. P.M. and found it beyond my worst imagination the most dirty, swampy, sickly hole I ever saw or dreamed of. A few houses, stores, 2 or 3 very passable hotels, and swarms of dirty half naked natives made up all that is describable of the place. We slept there and started the next morning at about 9 in the cars for the summit.

I wish I could give you even a faint idea of the beauty that we saw during the first part of that ride on a rail. I can safely aver that there is one thing (and it's one of a few) that the description of travellers has not overrated, and that is the luxuriance and beauty of tropical scenery.

Addison's enthusiastic description of the country and the muleback passage across the isthmus was also by now familiar to his relatives. Delight fared less well than her sister and Mary, as her mule bolted and she fell, but was unhurt. Addison described their arrival in Panama City:

We were accommodated with most miserable supper and lodgings at the American Hotel, and spent the next forenoon in viewing the wonders of the town. It is an old walled town, the walls and most of the town in vines. The houses are of stone, queer shaped things with balconies everywhere. We visited the Cathedral and the fort where they [have] a few of the finest guns in the world, brass 32 and 59 pounders but all dismantled and filled with gravel.

About 4 P.M. we took a boat and went off to the steamer and sailed at 6. Our trip on this side is a repetition of the other except that we have a much finer vessel, a much finer set of officers, better fare, and a smooth sea. It is now afternoon and if nothing happens we shall be at S. Francisco tomorrow at 10 or 11 A.M. . . . Not a person has been sea sick since we left Panama and what is better still there has been no other sickness that I know of.

On Monday the 22d we touched at Acapulco for coal, stayed four hrs and most of the passengers went ashore. We saw a little of Mexico there, quite enough. I am willing to be personally ignorant of the rest. The first thing I saw was a beggar of course, the next, a party of long knived, murderous looking rascals, playing cards, and the entire rest of the population to all appearances were orange and banana women and here and there a soldier, a dirty, cowardly looking dog with an old flint lock musket and long knife.

I went up to the fort, I couldn't enter, but warlike preparations were going on outside, mounting cannon and casting bullets. This fort and town you know is the stronghold of the Rebel Alvarez. He is in the mountains a few miles below, fighting constantly and they say getting the best of Santa Anna. We arrived too early by a day, for 2000 deserters from the Army of Santa Anna were expected at Acapulco on the 23d to join the army of Alvarez. . . .

We shall be all bustle and confusion in the morning, and I shall only write you a few lines then to tell you of our safe arrival within the Golden Gate. My next will probably be from Nevada. By the way, I must mention that Captain or rather Commodore Watkins of the Golden Age was the commander of the ill fated San Francisco that was wrecked not long ago in the Atlantic while transporting troops, and a better Captain I am sure never walked a deck.

San Francisco
Monday Morning.

We came up to the dock at 9.20 this morning and are safely domiciled at "our inn." We shall dine here and start for Sacramento in the St. Boat at 4 P.M. Have just been to the Telegraph office to inform Nevada friends of our arrival. Hope to see them all tomorrow. I spect Freddy is all anxiety to see me. My love to all.

III

MARY SAT IN HER PARLOR, Fred asleep by her side, contentedly writing to her mother. From the Mulford piazza next door she could hear the voices of Addison, Harvey, Delight, Jerome, Charley, Niles, and Deb. Through the window she could see them walk about, talk, laugh, and smoke, and she told Polly how grateful she was to the kind Providence that brought them safely to California:

I wish you could have seen us the few days before their arrival, as well as on that evening. We ... were so excited we could hardly accomplish anything. Addison telegraphed immediately on their arrival, so we knew just when to expect them. . . .

[Before they came] Niles was at Sacramento, and while he was there Freddie was taken quite sick. He and I had both taken a violent cold (how I do not know) and when Niles came home [Fred] was quite sick, had some fever, and bowels quite disordered. We called a physician, who gave him some small powders &c, but for nearly two weeks he was quite unwell. I cannot tell you how anxious I was, for Mrs [Sampson] was sick, and *our* physician was absent. At last I sent for Mrs Tweed, wife of Niles' partner, and she came and spent half a day with me, assured me he was *not* very sick and told me of some little light medicines to give. . . .

The day before Addison came, Niles met with a misfortune; while brushing and shaking his coat, a button came loose and flew against his eyeball with such force as to knock him down, and cut the eyeball. It pained him severely for a number of days so that he had to have the rooms darkened and his eyes bandaged. By great care [we] prevented inflammation from setting in and his eye is nearly well now, though it looks red yet. By reason of his being in the house all the time, I had all the visit with Addison.

Expressing concern that the family would think hard of her and Niles for saying nothing about Addison's intentions to come to California, Mary went on to offer assurances about his future. She revealed, as well, her own changing attitudes about the merits and virtues of life in the west:

I have always thought of Addison's talents as I presume you all have—that his turn of mind and finished scholarship would be better appreciated in the States than here, but I think now that he needs, perhaps as *I* did, a more stirring, active community to develop his powers fully.... If he does no *better* here than in the states he will accomplish what he does do with much more ease and pleasure, and I have no doubt he *will* do *better*. I am confident that any young man whose principles are sufficiently firm to keep him in the right path can do better in Cal. than elsewhere, though the time for sudden fortune making is past....

I need not say that Niles will do all he can for him. You know he always did think a great deal of Addison, and I have no doubt would share his last dollar with him if necessary. Of course they have had little to say about business yet, we want a good long visit first, and besides there is no business in the country at present, for want of rain.... I think Niles will think it best for A. to stop with us a while and study the statutes of Cal. and then go wherever there seems the best opening for a lawyer.

A. is afraid of being a burden but we want him to feel that this is his *home*, and that he is as free and welcome here as he would be at the old homestead.... He has grown since I saw him and appears much more manly and mature. I can assure you it is with no small feeling of pride that I introduce him as my brother, Mr Niles.... Freddie likes his new uncles very much. He gets tossed about and played with so much....

Mr Allen's brother is in town again, and has been here to dinner once. He is a very fine man I think, easy, goodnatured, and sociable, a great talker and with good principles. Not by any means as intellectual as Will, not as smart in any way, but we like him because he seems a little like him besides being very agreeable himself. He has no intention of returning to the States to *live*, thinks there is no country like Cal.

Mary began a letter to her sister, and hoped she would finish in time for the steamer. Harvey and Jerome had left Nevada City and moved to Auburn, where they had purchased a drug store. Mary wrote:

The boys all took dinner here one day while James was here. My [dining] room was too small to accommodate the girls too. Last week I had to get up a dinner for some *big bugs* again; Mr [William W.] Stowe, the Speaker of the Assembly and one of the members were in town and Niles invited them to dinner. Would you like to know the bill of fare? First some oysters, then a fine piece of roast pork, cabbage cooked with milk and nutmeg, onions, pickled beets, ditto tomatoes, (potatoes of course) &c. After removing the meats and vegetables, which Laura does with a great deal of skill, she brought the coffee tray, and while I poured coffee, she brought the dessert, consisting of cranberry and squash pies.

I tell the particulars because it is the common course when we have company, and differs a little from home customs. I believe I have not told you my more recent arrangement about dress. I sent by Niles for ladies cloth and other materials for a mantilla, thinking it would be the cheapest and best way (I could get no materials here at all), but he could not find what suited him, so he bought one ready made, a dun colored satin, lined with quilted silk a little darker, and trimmed with silk plush very deep, which looks just like martin's fur at a little distance. It cost $18 dollars.

I could not have got the material that I sent for for less than $10 and they would not have been near as nice. Those who had prized such mantillas below thought this must have cost $40. The baby has spoiled my merino dress, at least for the present, by spitting on it (he beats all the spitting babies I ever saw or heard of), so I concluded I need not make up my blue merino, and let Laura have it, bought me a cheap black silk priced $1.50 per yd, the cheapest I ever saw in the country. I made it with a full waist top and bottom, a belt, and no point. It is the best sitting dress I ever had I think.

I have made a pointed cape of the same with two ruffles to match my old black silk, which was nearly worn out, and that I wear afternoons. . . . My merino I shall wash and make over when Fred is done spitting. Few as are my dresses, I feel as though I had been extravagant, for the one suit that I have been obliged to get cost over $50. I shall have to spend considerable this summer, too, but *then* it cant be helped. . . . Addison is doing finely, made $35 one day in the office and is engaged in one or two suits with Niles & Tweed. He is the happiest I ever saw him, and is glad every day that he is in Cal.

Addison wrote Cornelia that he was "in the land of Gold, in Nevada that far famed city, chiefly famed as the birthplace of Fred the 1st." He continued:

Since I have been here I have been running about the country some, among the diggings, and trying to make up my mind about the country generally. It is a strange place and strange people but I can see very well how people become attached to it and I fancy I shall like it well, but I can tell you that better a year or 2 hence. . . . Niles wishes me to stay with him and busy myself in the office learning the practice &c and be ready to take advantage of changes that are very likely to occur before long, to get into business here. I dont like to do this exactly, but as I know he would like to have me and as I can be of some use to him I may stay for a month or so, in case I find no other employment in the meantime.

I think, from what I see, that this is an excellent place for Law business. There is a great deal of litigation and large fees, and the profession is not crowded.... I have had one application for legal services already. The Dist. Attorney, Fletcher, applied to me yesterday to assist in the trial of Yankee Sullivan (an old friend of mine) which comes off tomorrow in the court of sessions. He is up for aiding and abetting at a prize fight here lately. I think I shall decline, because he is pretty certain to be acquitted and I dont wish to commence practice here with a hopeless case.

Nevada City Baptist
Church before 1856 fire

CHAPTER 19

TROUBLED TIMES

February–April 1855

I

ON SATURDAY, FEBRUARY 17, San Franciscans learned of the failure of the St. Louis bank of Page and Bacon, caused in part by the collapse of two private banks in New York. This news resulted in an immediate run on its San Francisco branch; depositors afraid of losing their funds withdrew about $300,000 before nightfall and forced the closure of Page and Bacon in a few days. The run spread to other local banks, some of which closed the following day.

Lucas, Turner and Company, however, remained open in a heroic effort to ride out the storm. The bank's manager, William Tecumseh Sherman, was a West Point graduate who had been in California during the Mexican War. Since then he had resigned his commission and become a San Francisco banker. With steely nerve, Sherman faced lines of panicked customers day after day, paying every demand. The bank's assets dropped disastrously, but the strategy finally stopped the run, and those who had withdrawn their money returned with renewed confidence.

When Adams and Company closed its doors, Sherman privately expressed contempt for its owners, calling them "dishonest, craven, cowardly. . . . Nothing but air and impudence to stand on." His opinion of Wells, Fargo and Company was that they were "better, but . . . unable to pay." Though not badly hurt, Charles Mulford resolved to sever his relationship with Wells, Fargo as soon as possible. However, the Adams agent at Nevada City was nearly ruined. Undaunted, Horace Ferré began an uphill struggle to establish his own banking firm at the same location.

In February Rodman Backus was tried for murder at San Francisco. Rodman was the brother of Harriet, the young woman who had accompanied Mary and Deb to California in 1853 and gone from there to Oregon City. Rodman and Harriet were orphans who were related to a respected and well-to-do Philadelphia family.

At the time of the 1854 killing Rodman was twenty-four, employed as a teamster by Wells, Fargo's San Francisco office, where his uncle was manager. Some said it was the best work the young man could obtain because of his dissolute habits. Rodman shared quarters in the red light district north of Washington Street with Jennie French, a prostitute, and as he staggered home one night in 1854, Jennie pointed to a man she said had robbed her. Backus pursued the man down Stout Lane and shot him in the back. The victim, Frederick Simon, was discovered to be a newly arrived and unarmed German immigrant, and his killing aroused a furious reaction in the city's German colony.

To defend Backus, his uncle retained San Francisco's finest legal talent, including Abraham Lincoln's close friend Edward D. Baker. The first trial had resulted in a divided jury. The second began on February 20 and produced a verdict of manslaughter. The judge sentenced him to three years in prison and a $3000 fine. Because a member of the jury had absented himself without permission during the proceedings, and because of a disagreement with the judge about jury selection, the case was appealed to the supreme court.

II

ON THE NIGHT of February 20, fire broke out in Nevada City in the Virginia House on Broad Street. It spread quickly to buildings on both sides, and nearly every structure between the two Methodist churches was burned or else demolished to stop the fire. The losses totaled $36,600, including the Hotel de Paris, the Virginia House, and the three adjacent hospitals of Dr. Hillerscheidt, Dr. Von Poellnitz, and Mrs. Holdridge. Also burned were a bakery, three Spanish brothels, a billiard saloon, a Chinese wash house, a stable, a carpenter shop, and some private dwellings.

The fact that the Virginia House well rope had been severed suggested the fire was deliberately set, but no suspects were discovered. Rev. R. W. Bigham thanked a number of citizens who worked successfully to save the Methodist Episcopal Church South. District Attorney Sherman Fletcher had escaped serious injury when he fell from the church roof. Among those commended for their efforts included Charles Mulford and Rev. James Warren, whose own church was safely out of the fire's path.

The latter minister was himself the victim of a conflagration on March 9, which Mary described to her sister:

Mr Warren's house was burned to the ground, and scarcely a thing saved. It is quite out of town . . . and having taken on the roof, was all in flames before discovered. Mrs Warren seized her children, who were in bed, and after placing them in safety, went back and got the bonnet Deb made for her, a few of her best dresses . . . and some one saved a book case containing daguerreotypes, relics, presents &c.

Mr Warren was down town and . . . was almost distracted before he got near enough to learn whether his family were safe, and when he found them, he sobbed like a child. . . . at least a dozen offers of homes sent to them and early next morning a subscription was taken up at once to get funds for another house, and in less than half a day $500 had been raised towards it. They went to Mrs Sampsons, and will make it their home there for the present. All their clothing except the dresses I spoke of is burned, but next day there were packages sent in from every direction . . . and at 1 o'clock a large number of ladies met at Mrs [Sampson's] to sew and take home work to make up for them.

One of the merchants sent word they were welcome to anything he had in his store, another has promised to furnish all needed crockery for them, some one gave Mrs W. $50. for sundries, and she says she has already a better wardrobe of underclothes than before the fire. So you see Nellie what it is to be a *ministers wife*, especially if one can be so much beloved as Mrs W. No one else in Nevada would have had half the sympathy, and certainly not half the assistance. . . . I have a dress to make for Anna [Warren] and some other things, and I gave Mrs W. a pair of sheets, two of pillow cases, one pair of drawers and my white quilt which I never have worn because I like my merino better.

"Aunt Mary," with whom the minister and his family would stay, was no longer Mrs. Sampson, for she had married Sidney Herbert two weeks earlier. Mary reported:

Rumor has had her engaged and married to him a great many times since we came here, but about two weeks ago they went to Mr Warren's study privately and were married, and not even Deb or I knew of it. . . . I hope she has done well, he is a very kind gentlemanly man, but not very good in business matters, loves to *spend* a good deal better than to pay his *debts*. Still, she will have a good home and a kind husband.

Sidney Herbert was a town trustee and had been a deputy county clerk since 1852. He also speculated in real estate, and shortly after the Warrens occupied his wife's house, the Herberts moved to a rural homestead and offered their town residences for sale.

Not all church troubles concerned earthly fires. The devil's hand might have been in evidence at the Baptist Church. Addison spoke of the matter in a letter:

I am not in business exactly yet, though I have done considerable in the legal way and am counted among the Nevada Bar. I have tried four suits in Justice Court and won two and was not disappointed in losing the others. Have two suits in the Dist. Court this term, both important, which will be tried if the Judge gets sober. Tweed is with me in both, but I shall have the leading part. One is a quarrel between members of the Bapt. Church here, in which the Minister and two members are sued by the trustees for the possession of the Church. We defend the Minister.

The first public notice of the dispute came near the end of December, when the *Democrat* spoke of some members having "a difficulty with their Pastor." One faction, which included several women, wished to remove the minister, but failed because women could not vote. Then the *Journal* published a list of resolutions said to have been adopted "unanimously," one of which accused two unnamed persons of responsibility for the controversy. Rev. Stone's supporters said the two persons who had been excluded from the congregation already were in a "serious difficulty with each other" before Stone came to Nevada City.

Dissidents had charged Rev. O. B. Stone with refusing to allow an examination of church accounts pertaining to construction of the new brick sanctuary at Spring and Pine streets, but five members said they had looked at the accounts and found them in order. It was untrue, according to another resolution, that female rights had been infringed upon, for it was "contrary to scripture, to the principles of civil law and the teachings of nature" for women to take part in business matters or in the discipline of the male members of the church.

Fourteen Baptists disagreed with this statement, arguing it conflicted with customary Baptist usage. This group, which had met in the Congregational church when they were refused admission to their own building, demanded the resignation of Mr. Stone, and claimed his six male adherents were a minority of the total church membership of twenty-five. The ousted faction hired Frank Dunn and F. W. Thayer to sue the minister, while Stone retained Col. Tweed and Addison Niles, and urged the community to disregard false reports made by Baptist "pretenders."

When the case was heard in Justice Van Hagan's court, several attorneys had been drinking, Frank Dunn more than the others. The judge was seated at a flimsy pine table, and every time Dunn emphasized a point, he hit the table with a law book. The table would dance and the judge would flinch, until Van Hagan protested, "Please don't pound my table, Mr. Dunn."

"May it please your honor, I *will* pound your table!" Dunn replied, striking the table another blow. A few days earlier, Van Hagan had ruled against Dunn in a case involving a dog, and now the tipsy lawyer peered at the justice through bloodshot eyes and said, "I dreamed a dream the other night about an old fool of a justice who decided a *dog* is *property*!" and Dunn struck the table with his book harder still.

"Don't pound my table, Mr. Dunn!" the judge ordered.

"May it please your honor" (Whack!) "I will pound your table!" (Whack!)

At this juncture a disgusted juryman demanded an end to the nonsense, saying "We've had enough of this sort of thing—I've got better things to do than listen to this drunken gabble."

"Yes, you have, have you?" sneered Dunn. "Who are you? Know it all, don't you!"

This was too much for the other lawyers, who until now had sat back and enjoyed the show. Concealing their grins, they succeeded in quieting Dunn until it came time for him to address the jury.

"Gentlemen of the jury," he began. "When I say 'gentlemen' I include eleven of you, for one of you is very far from being one—" Before Dunn could speak another word, the juror leaped to his feet and took off his coat, ready to attack the attorney.

When order was restored the jury retired. Their verdict was for Addison's client, causing Dunn and Thayer to appeal the case to the supreme court.

III

A NEW COURT DISTRICT had been created to serve Nevada, Sierra, and Plumas counties. A judge was to be appointed by the governor, and the *Journal* thought Niles Searls was the most likely candidate, saying "a

better man could not be selected—one more capable, popular, or acceptable."

In Yuba County, where Barbour would continue to sit on the bench,
the Marysville *Express* claimed there was widespread support in the new
district for F. J. McCann. The *Journal* disagreed:

The Petition of Niles Searls, Esq., was signed by every member but
one of the bar in this county, by every member of the Legislature from
this county, and part of those of Sierra and Plumas. A voluminous
petition of the *people* was also sent to the Governor for the appointment
of Mr. Searls.... The new district asks for and expects the appointment
of Mr. Searls.

Looking to the future, Niles and Addison joined the Sons of Temperance, an organization with rising influence in the gold towns. Addison
said it was a necessary step, because "it is about the only [acceptable]
excuse a man, especially a lawyer, can give in California for not drinking
with those who ask them." But the well-laid plans went awry, as Addison
explained to his father on May 9:

... by the provisions of the original bill, as passed by the Legislature, a
Judge was to be appointed by the Governor to fill the Bench of the new
Dist. until the election in Sept. next. It was confidently expected that
Niles Searls would be the appointee. There was but one other applicant,
McCann of Sierra County, and his only chance was that he was recom-
mended by one or two persons whom Gov. Bigler would not like to
offend. Niles was recommended by all the members of the Bar of Nevada
Co., by several of Sierra (McCanns own Co.), by the whole of the
members of Legislature from this Dist., Senate and Assembly; by
Broderick, one of the prominent candidates for U. S. Senator and the
man to whom Gov. Bigler owes his election—and by an enormous
petition of the citizens generally.
    ... the Gov. had declared to some of Niles friends that no application
for any position in his gift had ever come before him so warmly and
unanimously seconded by the expressed wish of the whole people, and
that he should appoint him—when all of a sudden he took a new freak
into his head, viz: that the Constitution only gave him the power to fill
vacancies, and that this was not a vacancy but a new office—therefore
he couldnt appoint, and refused to sign the bill unless the Legislature
would pass a supplemental act empowering the old Judge (Barbour) to
hold court until Sept. election. The whole secret of the matter was that
his excellency would like to be his excellency again next year, and is

very afraid of making enemies, which he thought he must do by an appointment.

So the matter stands until election. Niles will probably be a candidate for Dist. Judge this fall, and if he is, will be elected, for he is the most popular man in the District today. I have not explained yet what connection all this has with me. I have made arrangements with Col. Tweed, Niles' partner, to go into partnership with him in case Niles goes out of the firm. . . .

It will be an excellent arrangement for me, for the business of the firm is large, and Col. Tweed is a gentleman and a good lawyer. The offer came from him of his own accord, and he is anxious I should go in with him. He and Searls own the best library in town, which will of course remain with us if Niles goes out. The arrangement will be an excellent thing all around, for if Niles is Judge he must be absent in the other two counties for some portion of his time, and as I should board with Niles, Mary would not be alone at all.

But this is all for the future. During the months that intervene till election, I have nothing to busy myself very extensively here, and I have been looking about to find some profitable employment for that time. This was the object of my visit to Iowa Hill, but I found nothing there to suit me. I have about concluded to take Niles' advice and remain here during the summer. I do business enough to pay expenses—make grub, as the miners say—tho that does not quite satisfy me. Yet, Law business is so dull everywhere now that I could not probably do much better.

I do the [errands] riding about the hills, pettifogging &c. besides reading, and posting myself in business generally. I rode to Cherokee yesterday, 12 miles, and ride to the South Yuba today, on business for the firm. I argued the case of [William J.] Knox vs. Mrs. Beard at the last term of Dist. Court and won it.

Rachel Beard had sued the estate of her husband after he died at Nevada City and left her only $500 out of an estate valued at $12,000. Before he died William Beard accumulated a modest fortune in real estate, ditch property, and mining shares, the bulk of which he left to his infant daughter. Dr. Knox was executor of the estate and was represented by Searls, Dunn and Smith, who argued that Rachel had no rights under California's common property law because she had remained in Illinois when Beard came to California in 1849.

The widow retained Tweed, who invited Addison to research the case. Both were convinced she was entitled to half the property in addition to the $500 he had willed her, which they thought should come from his share. Addison told his father, "I shall have Dunn and Searls, two of the best lawyers in the county to contend against, and if I win, as I mean to do if the Judge happens to be sober, it will be a feather in my cap sure."

They had won the case, but it was being appealed to the supreme court by the executor of the estate. Addison expected to win again, at which time he would receive $150 for his services. The case had been his first in district court, and Addison was "rather proud of my first success." He added a precautionary postscript to his father:

I would not like to have anything said about Niles affairs out of the family. I suppose if he knew it, he would not like any thing to be known of it even there. So you need not mention it in any of your letters to us. He is very sensitive you know, and politics are always uncertain.

Niles called the governor "a good honest old soul (I liked to have said fool)" in a letter to Nellie, and said he wasn't ready to announce his candidacy. In other years he would not doubt his chances to win, with such widespread Democratic support, but this year was different:

With the Know Nothing element which has suddenly sprung up in our midst at work, everything politically is uncertain. . . . I stand at present in a condition (as I think) to get a nomination from either the K. N. or Anti's, but of course can't get it from both, and for the life of me cant tell which is going to win. . . . The salary is $5000 per annum and the office lasts for 6 years.

Perhaps you will ask if I am expecting to remain in Cal. for 6 long years more. I answer probably not. Should I by any chance be elected to an office of this kind, I should expect to have May and Fred come home for a visit next summer with Charley and Deb, and if I could get leave of absence, come with them; if not, let them come and I come after them the season after, and then either all come back here, or stay at home, as we might think best. . . . I have only one favor to ask, and that is that you do not extend the information beyond the family limits.

Despite his hesitation, Niles acted very much the candidate:

Addison and I have joined the Sons of Temperance and are figuring largely, he as Secretary and I as Associate to the Worthy Patriarch. I have also become a Member of a Masonic Lodge, and Fred joined the Church last week, i.e. he was christened. Aint we getting morally temperate &c &c.

Mary's description of the baptism was more elegant:

On communion Sabbath the congregation is dismissed before communion, and Laura brought [Fred] down to me just after the people were dismissed, and Niles stood with me during the ceremony. Fred behaved admirably, laughed and jumped, and wanted to put his hands in the bowl of water, but was not at all noisy. I made over his prettiest white dress into a short one for him to wear, and tied it on the shoulder with knots of white ribbons.

Niles did not object to his being baptized, but thought it was mere ceremony. Still I think when it came to the time he was glad, for he seemed quite impressed with the service. I never saw any one so fond and *proud* of a baby as he is of Fred. [Judge] Caswell makes a greater fuss about his, and is the laughing stock of the town for it. Niles says but little, but thinks the more. . . .

I cannot tell you how I long to be with you. I do not dare to think about it much, for I get homesick when I do, and that does no good. I am really promising myself a visit home next summer. . . .

I have been twice to hear Madame Anna Bishop this week and once to hear Mr. Speer lecture upon the Chinese, hence my letter writing has again been neglected. . . . I dont know what I am writing now, for Niles is singing to Fred, and such singing is incompatible with anything like *thinking.*

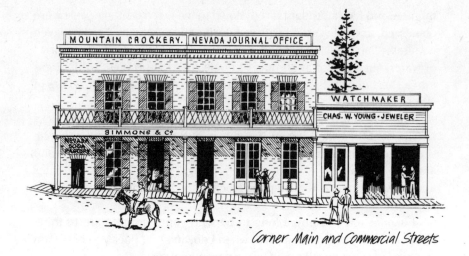

Corner Main and Commercial Streets

CHAPTER 20

KNOW NOTHING

April–July 1855

I

THE KNOW NOTHING party was changing politics not only in California, but all across the nation. It made its first appearance in New York State, where it began as a secret society: the Order of the Star Spangled Banner. Early in 1852 it had forty-three members, but this increased to nearly a thousand in four months, after organizers from the Order of United Americans took it over for use as a tool for political action.

The Order of the Star Spangled Banner charged no membership dues, which made it easy to sign up members, who then were persuaded it was in their best interest to keep Catholics and foreigners out of public office. The new leadership altered the by-laws to permit the O.S.S.B. to operate outside New York state. Organizers were hired, and by the end of 1854 they had enrolled a million and a half voters in various states. Because members were instructed to answer outside queries with the words, "I know nothing about it," newspapers started calling them "Know Nothings."

In the eastern states membership was limited to non-Catholic native-born Americans without close relatives who were Catholics. Candidates were picked in secret sessions and members voted for them in solid blocks. Existing laws allowed persons to run for office without prior notification to authorities or voters, so identification of the Know Nothing candidates was withheld until the last minute.

Because voters were not registered and there were no official ballots, each party or faction printed and distributed its own "ticket" listing candidates and the offices for which they were running. On election day a voter simply presented the ticket of his party, unmarked if he supported the entire slate, or with names "scratched" off if he wished to exclude a particular candidate. In place of the deleted name he could write in another or leave it blank. In some cases Know Nothing choices were kept secret from non-members until the results were announced and the candidates had won. The new party defeated many experienced candidates and made a shambles of traditional politics. It appeared the Know Nothings had devised a nearly invincible machine.

The new party had to adapt to local conditions when it came to California in 1854. There it took on a slightly different coloration, for in a state so full of foreign-born and Catholic voters it would have been difficult to win elections by stressing nationalism and religious bigotry. Instead, the party focused on corruption and reform, issues of universal appeal. The first test occurred in San Francisco. The *Alta California* of August 24, 1854, commented:

> It is stated ... and very generally believed, that there is in this city a large body of men made up of all classes of society, parties and factions, who, under the euphonius appelation of "Know Nothings," are united for the purpose of placing good men in office, and who will either nominate a ticket of their own, or give their support to that which they believe will, if elected, be for the best interests of the city.... Their operations, however, are of such a mysterious nature that it is impossible to form any idea of how they influence the election.

The Know Nothings swept the election, having left nothing to chance. Not only did they turn out in force, but they policed the polls, preventing fraud by force when necessary. There were fights between their adherents and opposition hoodlums and "shoulder-strikers" throughout the city. In one ward an attempt was made to seize the ballot box, but the watchers interfered. Shots were fired, one man was killed and three injured.

The new party had defeated California's toughest political machine after only three months of organizing, an impressive feat. Within a few weeks Know Nothing councils appeared throughout the state. In a desperate effort to stem the tide, Democrats created an opposition group, mentioned by the *Journal* on April 6, 1855:

A secret organization, called Freedom's Phalanx, has been organized in this place, among naturalized citizens and others who are associated with them. The objects of the order are not stated, but we presume it is designed to act in opposition to the Know Nothings. Secret organizations seem to be taking the place of the old parties, and the terms Whig and Democrat fall flat on may ears that a short time since deemed them law and religion.

The administration of California's counties was being changed at the same time. A board of supervisors took over the executive powers formerly exercised by the court of sessions, which became a purely judicial body. On April 9 voters were to select three men to run Nevada County, each representing two or more townships. Before the election the *Journal* warned voters:

It is of great importance to the interests of the county that careful, prudent, honest men be elected, whether Whig or Democrat, Know Nothing or Freedom's Phalanx. All the business of the county heretofore transacted by the Court of Sessions is transferred to them—they will have charge of finance and expenditures—the control of property—levying of taxes—management of bridges, roads and ferries—the division of the county into townships—establishing of precincts and officers of election—to erect county buildings &c....

There is time enough between the organization of the Board on the first Monday in May next and the September election following to ruin the affairs of the county, and depreciate scrip to the rate it had a couple of years ago....

The pay is no consideration whatever, being not more than $8 per day and not to exceed $500 per year.... But the station is honorable, influential and responsible—not to be sought for, but accepted. Party politics should enter as little as possible into the contest, so that the Board may have no friends to reward, or enemies to punish.

Charles Marsh was elected in the first district, which contained the central portion of the county. All the southern townships were in the second district, and what remained was in the third.

Grass Valley became a city in March, and officers were elected to serve until regular city elections in May. Grass Valley enthusiasts immediately announced a campaign to capture the county seat, a plan Sargent ridiculed:

In order to have an election as to the removal or location of a county seat ... a *majority* of the legal voters of the previous election [must] petition for such election to the supervisors.... To show the brilliant prospect they have, and how much good sense there is in all this absurd action, on their part, I here give the result of my investigation in the statistics of the last election.

We will give to our ambitious neighbor the following townships ... Grass Valley, which cast 809 [votes]; Little York, 290; Rough & Ready, 662; Bear River, 19. Total: 1780. Nevada would *unquestionably* get the following townships: Nevada, 1322; Bridgeport, 691; Eureka, 647; Washington, 436. Total: 3096.

II

GRASS VALLEY lost two of its better known citizens in the spring and early summer of 1855. Lola Montez packed her bags in May and resumed her westward journey, this time to tour the gold fields of Australia. Augustus Noel Follin, who had helped her organize a company of players for the tour, was the new man in her life. Follin left a wife and children in Cincinnati when he came to San Francisco in search of adventure. But until he met Lola he had found nothing more thrilling than a job as theater cashier. He told his half-sister, Miriam:

Madam the Countess of Landsfeldt thinks *your* daguerreotype the most beautiful one she ever saw. She says, "una cara tan *intelegente* tan *linda*." She is in love with you, and actually kept it for two days. . . . there is all the *remnants* of a lovely woman about her, her nose appears chiseled out of marble and her conversational powers are fascinating to a degree: I talked with her in English, French and Spanish, she speaks German Italian Portuguese and Russian in addition.

On February 27, 1855, Noel announced:

In 3 days I leave California. I am going to ... Australia—China—Calcutta—Bombay. . . . I shall be gone two years or over: I go with the Countess Landsfeldt "Lola Montes" as agent. . . . I have nothing to lose and all to gain.

The second of Grass Valley's celebrities to quit the city was Lola's adversary Henry Shipley, who left in June. But his tour took him only as far as Nevada City, where he replaced Tallman Rolfe as editor of the *Democrat*. Rolfe was willing enough to retire to the back room and set type, for the 1855 general election would be a tough one for his party. A more volatile spirit was needed to keep pace with sharp-tongued critics at the *Journal*, and Shipley had proved his ability to scrap with the best of them.

Warren Ewer, at one time or another on the staff of every county paper, now was editor of the Grass Valley *Telegraph*, and Assemblyman Edwin G. Waite had bought Aaron Sargent's interest in the *Journal*. When Sargent took office as district attorney he announced his retirement from the field of journalism:

We have entered upon other duties that are ... inconsistent with the cares of a newspaper. But ... we do not design to retire from an interest in public affairs, or any the less labor for what we may deem correct principles in politics.... We have chosen our position ... and frankly given our adhesion to the American [Know Nothing] party ... and so far as we know the opinions of our successor coincide with ours.

The new editor, like Niles Searls, was a young New York lawyer who had come west in 1849. But Edwin Waite's former allegiance had been to the Whig party, under whose banner he was elected to the state assembly in 1854. In his first editorial Waite said:

No intolerance shall characterize our sheet. We war against no religion, or creed or any church.... Among the citizens of Nevada County, there are many born on a foreign soil, whom it has been our pleasure and pride to number among our friends.... We advocate the divestiture of none of the civil or religious rights which they now enjoy, nor any privileges, but such as they if true American citizens, would not willingly surrender for the national weal.

Two better-known citizens returned to Nevada City with new brides that summer. John R. McConnell's second wife was the former Ann Eliza Moore of Kentucky. Bill Stewart had married another Ann, daughter of Mississippi's Henry Stuart Foote, formerly the governor and senator of that state. Bill and Annie gave a party at Nevada City four days after their wedding. Mary described the occasion to Cornelia:

It was very pleasant, the bride was very plain looking but agreeable. Stewart was as happy as ever a man was, and all seemed to have a good time. I wore my flowered silk ... some geranium leaves and a beautiful blossom in my hair, and a similar boquet at the corsage.... Deb gave me the flowers. Deb and Delight were invited but did not care to go. The boys do so hate to go to parties, and there is not much pleasure to us. We would not have gone if Stewart had not been a particular friend of Niles's.

Mary's second anniversary occurred exactly one week before the Stewart wedding, and she shared her thoughts with her sister on that day:

There is a deep and satisfying happiness in the love of such a husband as *I* have got which I do not think can be found in any other love. His *heart* is my *home*, and I dont think I can ever be very lonely or unhappy while I am with him. He used to say I would not love him as well when I had a *little* pet to take up my attention, but I know that I do love him *better*, and he admits it now too, though he would not at first.

He grows more considerate of my happiness and more *lover* like in his attentions, instead of indifferent, as many husbands of 2 years standing do, and I try to return his thoughtful kindness, though I find Freddie often prevents my doing many things for [Niles] that I would like to do.

He gave me a beautiful little patent lever clock, with a porcelain face, as a memento of our wedding day, and I made for him a handsome satin cravat which a neighbor showed me how to make. I could think of nothing else that I *could* make, and feel real sorry I could not have done something better for him, though he is quite satisfied. . . . I am sure you will not think it strange when I assure you that these have been the two happiest years of my life.

III

SUCCESS BRINGS its own problems, as Know Nothings learned at Philadelphia in June. A serious split over the slavery plank resulted in many northern delegates walking out of the National Council meeting. The majority of delegates approved a "Union" position that favored pro-slavery forces, and said the issue was not sufficiently important to endanger the union of states.

The same convention ended the secrecy rule, which had been opposed by many who otherwise supported the organization's aims. Henceforth all political action would be taken openly in the name of the American party. Among those in the leadership of the reorganized party was Bill Stewart's father-in-law, who had moved his family from Mississippi to California. In June Senator Foote began stumping the state to build support.

Most California editors favored the Union plank and opposed anything that smacked of "abolitionism." But they played down the anti-Catholic and anti-foreign sentiments of the national platform. At Nevada City Edwin Waite defended the party's stance, referring to the controversial Kansas-Nebraska bill introduced by Senator Stephen A. Douglas, which allowed the people of the territory to decide for themselves whether it should be free or slave:

The rapid growth of the party, and the intense agitation growing out of the foolish and reckless Kansas bill commenced about the same time. Every one knows how greatly the north was agitated—how party lines were dropped, and overwhelming majorities rebuked the administration.... The wave of popular feeling against the south was ... leading men to ask if the Union was of sufficient value to be bought at the price of pusillanimous submission to political gamesters....

Trouble of the worst aspect was just ahead, and there seemed good reason to believe that Pierce would be the last President that would rule over the present Union. At this time the American party came boldly into the field. It presented a new issue, and one adequate to draw off much of the public attention from the slavery issue.... in a few months the storm calmed down, and the north as a whole now ask only that an armed mob be restrained in the territories, and that the people in each fairly decide its institutions. There is now no talk of dividing the Union....

All the prominent abolitionists of the north denounce the American order ... because it has quelled that mighty storm that was raised in opposition to slavery extension.... the [American] party is gradually weaning the north and south from violence in reference to slavery, and the fraternity of feeling between the north and south is daily increasing by means of the Order.

Waite then enumerated several planks in the national platform that stood at the heart of the division between the Democratic and Know Nothing parties:

Hostility to the assumptions of the Pope through the bishops, priests, and prelates of the Roman Catholic church, here in a republic sanctified by Protestant blood.... Thorough reform in the naturalization laws.... Free and liberal educational institutions for all sects and classes, with the [Protestant] Bible, God's holy word, as a universal text book.

When Nevada City Democrats held a primary meeting in July, Waite ridiculed the affair:

PHALANX PRIMARY MEETING—On Saturday, the 21st, the last sad relics of the loco foco party met at the court house to condole over misfortunes and sorrows, and ordain somebody to administer the rites of extreme unction to a few office seekers.... [A committee will] meet on Saturday next and nominate pall bearers to carry the putrid carcass of Democracy in this county to the tomb in September.

Notably absent from the meeting were such former party stalwarts as

John McConnell, Bill Stewart, Niles Searls and James Churchman. The latter, who had been practicing law in San Francisco for several months, was back in Nevada City with a new partner David Belden, formerly of Marysville; while in the bay city Churchman had renewed acquaintance with his Illinois friend Edward Baker, for whom Abraham Lincoln had named his own son in 1846. Colonel Baker had recently defended Rodman Backus, whose appeal was being opposed by Attorney General McConnell on behalf of the people of California. At its July term the supreme court reversed judgment and ordered a new trial for Backus.

Harriet Backus had moved from Oregon City to San Francisco soon after her brother's second trial, and the Searls and Mulford families had asked her to visit them soon. Not a word was said about Rodman in letters to Rensselaerville.

Brick Courthouse 1856

CHAPTER 21

JUSTICE TRIUMPHS

July–September 1855

I

*N*EVADA CITY, soon to be California's third largest city, was about to have the state's newest and most modern court-house—the low bid of $41,500 for the new building having been submitted by Sacramento contractor Charles H. Shaw. It was to be fireproof, with brick walls on a granite foundation. Interior walls were to be lath and plaster, and all windows and doors would have iron shutters able to be closed in the event of fire. Heavy roof rafters were to be covered with sound 1¼ inch rough planks, over which two thicknesses of brick would be laid in sand and lime mortar, covered with painted metal (either copper, zinc or tin).

The plans that first went out to bid in the fall of 1854 did not include a jail, but afterwards the grand jury came in with a report that demanded inclusion of a jail in the basement. The jury was shocked by the condition of the existing jail, rented by the sheriff at exorbitant rates. The revised drawings called for a jail under the first floor county offices. The courtroom would occupy the second story, along with smaller rooms for the grand and petty juries. The lot on which it would be built had been donated to the county by local businessmen, who contributed $4000 to purchase "Court House Square," bounded by Church and Pine streets.

Some citizens were objecting to the high cost of the new county facility, saying it would impair the value of current county scrip, but the *Journal* thought the reverse would be true:

The debt of the county is now but about $16,000—less than ever before, and the Board of Supervisors are cutting off every possible expense and strictly scrutinizing all accounts brought before them. At least one thousand dollars were saved at the late session of the Supervisors by cutting off illegal charges. Scrip should now be worth in the market ninety cents on the dollar, and then it would pay better than any other investment. Taxes are fast pouring into the treasury, and the foreign miners tax especially is paying a large revenue. We predict the county will be out of debt except the liabilities upon account of the county buildings, in six months from this date.

When John Williams resigned as justice of the peace, Addison Niles was named to succeed him. On July 27 he wrote Cornelia about this stroke of good fortune:

I formed a partnership about a month and a half ago with A. A. Sargent, the present District Attorney, which was intended to last till fall, when I had a prospect of a rather better situation, as Sargent was young in the law. We remained together but about three weeks, when I had the offer of an appointment to fill the office of Justice of the Peace.... and here I am ... doing a better business I presume than any lawyer who practices in the county.

Its quite a different thing from the same rank at home, as a justice here has jurisdiction over mining disputes to any amount, and that forms a large portion of the business. My term of office lasts till 1st October. My good friends say they are going to elect me again.... it is a very respectable position, and *pays* well. $4000 per year is a small estimate. In regard to this matter however, say nothing. If I should be nominated by my party I should probably be elected, but if I should not I have several strings to my bow....

I am boarding with Mary yet, but I have a very neat little bedroom back of my office, which I shall begin to occupy next week, but shall continue to board with Mary. I rent the whole of a building on Broad

Street, with a good sized court room and 5 smaller rooms, for which I pay $60 per month. You would think that rather steep if you could see the old building. The two constables occupy 3 of the vacant rooms, so that my real rent is small. I average about 2 suits a day, which keeps me pretty busy. I wish you could look in and see the dignity with which I lay down the law to all and sundry, the suitors in my court.

Niles is well and full of business. The time for election draws near, and the general opinion is that he will be elected Dist. Judge.... if he is elected you may be certain it will be the fair choice of the people, and if he is not, it will be by the maneuvering of politicians.

We, that is the great *Know Nothing Party* (the cat is out) have a grand meeting in the plaza to night when Gov. Foote, of Mississippi (Pa will know him) will address us.

It was Bill Stewart who confidentially advised Niles not to go with the Democratic ticket that year. Niles was less sure, but eventually agreed to accept the Know Nothing nomination. It bothered him to ally himself with former foes, knowing their convictions hadn't changed, but as Stewart said, the important thing was to get elected. Then Niles hoped he could avoid further involvement with political campaigns.

In August he attended the American convention at Sacramento with Will Allen's brother, who was a delegate from Sierra County. Uriah liked being included with Niles's friends—James Churchman and Bill Stewart were well known throughout the mining country, and Alfred Dibble and Sam Boring had played key roles in Grass Valley's recent incorporation. At Sacramento, three Nevada County men—Stewart, Dibble and Henry Meredith—competed for the Know Nothing nomination for attorney general, but lost to a San Francisco lawyer. In special caucus the Nevada, Sierra and Plumas delegates selected Niles to run for district judge.

To avoid pitfalls created by the national organization, the state convention wrote its own platform. The *Alta California* said it contained nothing but "words to which every member . . . could subscribe, no one dared to prejudice his chances . . . by introducing such a thing as a 'living issue'." As for the slavery issue, the *Alta* said:

The twelfth section . . . merely deprecates agitation, without saying whether it is agitation or not to oppose the invasion of armed bullies into a territory (Kansas) for the avowed purpose of establishing their favorite institution (slavery).

The candidate for governor was J. Neely Johnson, thirty years old and the son of a prominent Indiana politician. Since his arrival in California in 1849, Johnson had been the Sacramento city attorney in 1850 and

1851, and was President Fillmore's choice to oversee the 1850 California census. He participated in an expedition to quell Indian uprisings at Mariposa, a venture which incidentally led to the discovery of Yosemite. In the same year (1851), when the *Sacramento Times and Transcript* published a defamatory article about him, Johnson seized its editor by the nose, and in return was nearly shot to death.

Theodore Judah, a young surveyor who had worked on the Niagara Gorge railroad and the Erie Canal before coming to California, tried unsuccessfully for the surveyor-general nomination. Judah was superintending construction of California's first rail line. Banker William Tecumseh Sherman, a vice president of the Sacramento Valley Railroad, described the venture as "a direct line towards Nevada [City] and the best populated part of the mining region. . . ."

Aaron Sargent, who four years earlier had called for the building of such a link, was attending a political convention of settlers and miners in Sacramento at the same time. This gathering fielded no candidates of its own, but resolved to support only those who backed their call for new laws to protect settlers and miners from being removed from Mexican land grants. A recent U.S. Supreme Court decision held that such grants were valid even though the owners had failed to occupy or survey the land, a position Sargent's fellow delegates found inappropriate.

II

JOURNAL EDITOR Edwin Waite, also the Know Nothing candidate for state senate, enthusiastically endorsed Niles Searls, calling his former political foe "a man of irreproachable character, an accomplished lawyer, with a large and successful practice," and said Niles's opponent was a man with "no qualifications for the position." Addison Niles, the party's candidate for justice of the peace, was "a very efficient officer, possessed of a thorough legal education and a perfect gentleman."

Running for district judge on the Democratic side was State Senator John T. Crenshaw, whom Waite described as "a man that could not get enough business as a lawyer to find his whiskey." The *State Tribune* had called Niles's opponent a "professional politician of the old fogy school." In April Senators Crenshaw and Norman wrote a minority report on the Chinese problem which the *Journal* said had proposed

... to pass laws prohibiting future immigration, and to let those "Celestials" who are now in the country alone—believing, as the authors of the report do, that they will gradually work their way back to their own country, and thus rid the State of their presence. The number of these people in California is variously estimated between thirty-eight and fifty-five thousand.

The campaign moved swiftly, for only thirty days separated convention and election. On August 31 the American candidates for governor and supreme court justice held a street rally at the intersection of Main, Commercial and Coyote streets. Niles and other local candidates were present, fresh from a fast tour of the outlying camps. They had entertained a crowd of miners at Orleans Flat until two o'clock one Sunday morning. Alfred Dibble, though not a candidate, orated for two hours to the miners, many of whom had walked there from Moore's Flat, Woolsey's Flat, or Snow Point.

As soon as the votes were counted, Niles passed on the result to his father-in-law:

The battle is fought, the victory is won, and I am elected by from ten to fifteen hundred majority. Of course my pride is gratified. The position is one well worthy of the aspirations of any man, and to which no man of my age has been before elected in the state.

Our courts are organized as follows: 1st Justice Courts, 2d Courts of Sessions, 3d County Courts, 4th [District] Courts, 5th Supreme Court. . . . The Supreme Court, consisting of three judges, is held at the capital of the state and has only appellate jurisdiction; like your Courts of Appeal it is one of dernier [last] resort.

The [District] Court answers to your Superior Court except that there is but one judge for each [District] and that appeals lie from his court directly to the Superior Court, there being no general terms as with you. In this [District] there are eleven terms annually: 4 in this [county], 4 in Sierra, and 3 in Plumas. The office lasts for six years and the salary, which is paid by the state, is $5000 per annum. I shall enter on the duties of the office as soon as the returns are certified, which will take only 20 days.

Addison too, is elected justice of the peace for this township for the ensuing year. Office worth say $3000 per year in the way of fees. So you see we are pretty well fixed so far as offices are concerned. We have now only to regret that we did not run *Fred* for constable. Mary avows her intention of keeping up with the times by becoming a candidate for Presidentess of the sewing society.

Addison is, as you are aware, filling the office of justice by appointment. He attends to his business carefully and succeeds admirably, and unless I am mistaken looks more dignified than will the new [District] Judge of the 14th. My law practice has been good for the last year, better probably than that of any other lawyer in the county, yet many men with half the business would have collected about as much money as I have. The fact is I have no faculty for dunning up clients. Still I have taken in some $5000, have the 1/2 of a good [law] library, have a pleasant living, a house and lot purchased for an office, have expended $500 in electioneering, owe no man and have money in my pocket.

Under the new arrangement we shall doubtless be compelled to remain in California longer than we had expected. I think now that we will manage for May and Fred to come home next year, either with Charley and Deb or with Addison, and then I can probably get leave of absence to come and visit you and bring her back.

Thus far my plans in California have, since our return, succeeded well as I ever wished, and with all my love for *Phillipsville* I do not regret having left there. I appreciate the pleasure of a residence near our friends, and were I able to do so, would willingly forgo all ambitious projects here, for a house in New York state, but while I feel capable of doing well here, I must say that I have ever felt incompetent and insignificant whenever I have thought of trying to do anything at home. It may be only a fancy of mine, but it has taken deep root.

My business will keep me from home about one half of the time, but Addison will be with Mary and act as the head of the family except when they accompany me.

Mary, writing to Ham Niles, provided additional details:

We thought it would be a very close contest, and though we expected Niles would—as was the case—run far ahead of his ticket, yet *he* thought the party would be defeated, but to the surprise of all parties, the Know Nothings had an overwhelming majority.... Dont you feel proud now to think that you have a brother who is a *Squire* (or *Judge*, they call them here)—and a brother-in-law with a title of *Hon.* ... Niles is the youngest man who has ever been elected to that office in this state, and this state is remarkable too for youthful public officers. But then the Gov. Elect is one year younger than Niles.

Mary was wrong about this; Niles would not be thirty until December, whereas Johnson had passed that mark already.

People cant accuse us of putting on *airs*, I imagine, for Niles has got our breakfast for us half the time since he was elected. I let Laura go to Mrs Shermans one week when [Mrs Sherman] was sick. You would have laughed tonight (it is evening now) to have seen the "Hon. Judge Searls" in the kitchen with a long apron on, cooking meat, frying eggs, making coffee &c &c while Fred and I sat and laughed at him.

Tell Cornelia that he does not "wear the same *clothes* that he *always* wore." They used it as an argument against his opponent that he was too dirty and ragged to be fit for a Judge, which would a few years ago have been a strange objection to raise against a man in Cal., but those days have passed, and it is now expected that gentlemen will dress *as* gentlemen, with neatness and propriety. So you see, since election Niles wears his *best clothes every day* and we teaze him a good deal about it, though being a plain fine suit of black, with sometimes a white vest, it of course would not be noticed by any but the family.

He is quite at liberty now till the Oct. term commences there, and is in the house a great deal. Fred is perfectly crazy after him when he is in the house. He was gone so long before election that I thought Fred would forget him, but he did not, and ever since he has seemed to think more of him than ever. The moment he hears [Niles's] voice or step he begins to jump and call pa-pa, pa-pa, and when Niles does any thing he watches every motion with intense interest.

For Addison the election had been a great adventure; he told his father:

You can have no idea in the sober quiet State of New York how exciting the game of politics becomes here in California. My friendships and associations in Nevada being chiefly with the men who are especially interested in politics, I had become drawn into it myself, and could hardly think of anything else till the election decided the matter and nothing more remained to be done.

The result has proved excellent far beyond my expectations, for our whole ticket, state, county, District and township is elected by large majorities, and the whole set of Professional politicians, who have mismanaged California ever since it was a state, are removed from office to make way for newer, and it is to be hoped, better men.

III

MARY'S MOTHER had suffered a mild heart attack the previous winter, and her slow recovery since that time was chief cause for the delay of Cornelia's marriage. Cornelia had assumed responsibility for the entire household and looked after her younger brother and sister, as well as her mother, for most of the year. When Mary received the first news of her mother's illness she had told Cornelia:

I have felt very anxious about Ma's difficulty with her heart, and have often thought I would write her expressly to urge her to consult the Dr. about it, but I had so often urged her when I was home, that I thought it would be useless. . . .

How thankful I am that *you* were with her, and we all feel grateful to you for your devotion to *our* dear mother. I know, dear Nellie, that you missed us all then, and our absence caused your burden to be very heavy. You felt all the care and anxiety and love which we *all would* have had, had we been with you, and that your duty to the absent ones, as well as those at home, required almost superhuman efforts at your hands.

Addison blamed himself for his mother's attack. He told Cornelia he suspected it was linked to his going to California:

Whenever I think so I am sorry I left you at all. I know you have had a sorrowful time and I feel almost guilty that I am thousands of miles away and you all alone in your care and anxiety for her. But I know that Ma or you wont think that we love you any the less because we have gone so far from you. Indeed, I dont know that I could have remained at home, though I might have been where I could have come to you if you wanted me.

In July Mary told her sister how grateful she was to Will Allen "for his love and kindness to you and to Ma. I trust his kindness will meet with its reward, and it certainly will if he ever gets you for a wife, which I hope he will very soon." In the same letter she said, "I am disheartened at your stories about R.Ville, what a terribly dull place it is. Those who remain are truly to be pitied."

But by mid-summer Polly Niles had recovered sufficiently for the date of September 12 to be set for Cornelia's wedding. Her Nevada City friends celebrated the day with appropriate festivities at the Searls residence. Mary wrote Ham:

We take it for granted that the proposed wedding came off on the 12 of this month. We did not fail to celebrate it I assure you. Our *pigs* were not large enough to roast so we killed some chickens and Charlies folks all came over and we had a grand dinner. They were the first *fresh chickens* we have tasted since we left home, and with roast-beef, sweet potatoes, onions &c, followed by custard pie, *wedding cake*, nuts, raisins, and a splendid watermelon that Charlie brought over, we thought we had a dinner which would have been good enough to eat before the bride and groom. The cake I made on purpose and put *lots* of raisins in it. It was *beautiful*, and the first really *good* that I ever did make.

Uriah Allen, while mining at Mohawk Flat in Sierra County, read a notice of the wedding in his hometown newspaper, and told his family he would "claim relationship" on his next trip to Nevada City. He said Niles, Mary and Addison seemed like "Young folks at Home . . . to say I am much pleased with them would not express *half I feel.*" As for himself, having worked hard for Niles's nomination and subsequent election, he was about to settle down "to spend another *old bachelor's* winter in California."

Addison told his father, "[Cornelia] has had a hard spell of confinement, and I know some relief will do her much good—I wish we could hear that Ma was entirely well, but we know that is impossible, and try to be content with her gradual recovery."

Nisenan Indians and others at Nome Cult

CHAPTER 22

WEMA: PART III

1854–1856

I

*I*N SEPTEMBER 1854 Col. Thomas J. Henley ordered Simmon Storms to summon local Indians to Storms Ranch for a meeting with government agents in the first week of October. Henley was California's new Superintendent of Indian Affairs, and Storms had been hired as Special Agent of Nevada County Indians at a salary of $100 a month. Henley told Storms important politicians would be attending, and he wanted a good turnout.

Henley explained his intention to move all tribes out of the mining country and onto the Nome Lackee Reservation in Colusa County. Storms was to supervise the relocation of Nevada and Yuba County Indians, and they would be his special charges at the reservation. Henley suggested that Storms dispose of his Nevada County holdings—better land was available near the reservation. He could become a rich man in the process, Henley said, strongly hinting he had every intention of doing likewise.

On September 30 a stage overturned between Grass Valley and Nevada City, severely injuring one passenger and breaking the driver's collarbone. The other passengers included four women and a group of

U.S. Army officers, all of them going to Storms Ranch. The injured man was Colonel J. B. Starr, aide to General John E. Wool. General Wool, seventy years old, commanded all American troops on the Pacific coast. His long military career had begun with the War of 1812 and reached its pinnacle in the Mexican War.

Wool and his companions were joined at the ranch by California's two senators, William Gwin and John Weller; Secretary of State James F. Denver, millionaire businessman Samuel Brannan, and various agents and subagents of the Indian Affairs Department. Denver, a southern Democrat, had killed California's first congressman, Edward Gilbert, in a duel. Gilbert had been a friend of Brannan and Tallman Rolfe at Yerba Buena before the gold discovery. Now Denver himself was a congressman, and would accompany Gwin and Weller to Washington.

Editors of all three Nevada County papers were on hand when the "pow wow" (as they called it) began on October 2. However, of the 500 or more expected, only a few Indians had appeared. Aaron Sargent gave his version of the event in the *Journal* four days later:

The trifling circumstance of many Indians not being present was overlooked, and about a dozen, for whom was claimed sovereign authority among the tribes, were called together, and seated on boards in a bull ring, while the [white] spectators took seats in the amphitheatre.

After the ceremony of introducing the sachems by Mr. Storms had taken place, Mr. Henley made a talk to them to the purport that the Indians once owned all the land hereabouts—that they could fish in the streams and hunt in the woods; but that the discovery of gold had brought the white men here, and they had taken possession, as they were in the habit of doing, of all new countries. That the government had taken in consideration their condition and had made provision for them on the reservation, where they could live unmolested by the white man, and raise crops, &c.

This was interpreted by Mr. Storms. The Indians listened patiently, and then, through Wemier and another chief, stated their objections: They had been lied to for three years by government agents—Wozencraft had lied to them, Beale had lied to them—so had McKee, and so had all the officials, and they did not believe Henley more than the others. They were contented as they were, and did not wish to leave.

Having little effect with the Indians, Mr. Henley addressed the whites, stating he would obey public sentiment, and requested an expression. [Editor Henry] Shipley of [the] Grass Valley [*Telegraph*] then read a formidable list of names for an organization to the meeting, which was [accepted] by a few ayes. The president [of the organization] then read another list of names, which he called a committee on resolutions, and put a motion that the Indians be removed. A few ayes responded.

The committee retired, and [Senator] Gwin was called for, and stated he had favored the appropriations for the removal of the Indians, and shared the service with his colleague. His "colleague," Weller, was then called, and made some remarks about ancestral graves, and the love of the Indian for his home, and that if removed, their destiny was sure destruction—nevertheless, he wanted them removed to avoid their destruction. This logical speech elicited some applause.

Gen. Wool made a few sensible remarks, the result of his experience among the fiercer tribes, whose contact with the whites is dangerous to both. About two thirds of the audience had retired, when the committee brought in their report, signed by four of the members, three bringing in a minority report. The majority report was an approval of Mr. Henley and his supporters, and in favor of the removal of the Indians.

The minority report expressed confidence in the Indians, stated their harmlessness, and called upon the government to spend among them here the money to be expended for their removal and maintenance in a strange place.

The question on the majority report was taken, and declared carried.... Thus ended for the present this grand scheme to find an outlet for the government appropriation. We learn that some of the Indians are willing to try the new location, to report on it in the spring. There is considerable division in public sentiment ... the majority however are indifferent as to the result.

Several days later Superintendent Henley submitted his official version to Washington:

The meeting with the Indians of Nevada County of which I advised you by last mail came off at Storms Ranch on the 6th inst., and resulted in an agreement with the chiefs present to send to the Nomelackee Reservation a deputation of three from each tribe, about thirty in all, to remain there during the winter and assist in planting the crop, preparatory to the removal of their respective Tribes next summer.

At this place I found what I have not encountered anywhere else, some opposition to the removal of the Indians; but the force of public sentiment which is very strong on the other side will soon silence all opposition in this quarter. I was strongly solicited at Nevada [City] and other places to furnish temporary subsistence to the Indians in their present locations, but I have given it as my decided opinion that the appropriation is intended only for the benefit of those who will submit to

the policy of removal, and have uniformly refused all such applications—a policy which I shall continue except in extreme cases, unless
otherwise instructed.

Mr. S. P. Storms, who speaks their language well and has resided
among them since 1849, has been appointed special agent and will
accompany the delegation above alluded to, to the Reserve.

Meanwhile, Storms' former partner David Bovyer was inviting Ne-
vada County residents to attend the great annual Indian festival at his
Newtown road ranch. As many as 1500 Indians were expected on
Sunday, October 15. The *Journal* reported:

They are making extensive preparations to enjoy a grand
"Yomashee," [*yomuse*] or Fandango, and to excel in the various sports
and pastimes peculiar to the aborigines of California. This will be a rare
treat to the curious. . . .

II

OLD BLOCK received a letter from Storms in December 1854. It was
written at Nome Lackee Reservation, and his friend told him Chief
Wema and more than seventy of his Grass Valley tribe were there with
him. Already the Indians had plowed more than 200 acres for the spring
planting.

Storms and Wema came back to Grass Valley in March, and the
Telegraph said they would conduct another march to Nome Lackee:

One of our citizens who has recently returned from the Reservation,
represents all things there as being in a most prosperous and favorable
condition. An immense deal of labor has been accomplished by the
Indians during the season, and all the different tribes are all contented,
well cared for, and happy. King Weimah is intending to return thither
from this place, with all his squaws, and a large party, so soon as the
travelling will permit.

But Storms was finding the Indians not so easy to recruit, even with
Wema's help. In May he reported to Col. Henley:

I arrived here yesterday with between sixty and seventy Indians—
men, women and children. I had more trouble than I expected in
collecting the Indians. If it were not for a few bad white men, the Indians
would all come out of the mountains willingly. The better class of
citizens of Yuba and Nevada counties have wished for the removal of the

Indians . . . for their present condition is, indeed, pitiful. . . .

First I had a lot of Indians at Empire Ranch all willing to come to the reserve—but during my temporary absence, some trader sold whiskey to them causing among them riots, so that nearly all left. . . .

Storms made another trip in October with about 150 *nisenan*, the largest conscription yet—but the *Journal* observed that "a score of tar heads" were on Nevada City streets, and surmised that "Nome Lackee has no charms when acorns are plenty in their old homes."

A month later, when the state was full of rumors and tales of Indian uprisings, north and south, the *Journal* said:

Day by day the danger of a general Indian war grows more imminent. The mail from the south brings the startling intelligence that the aborigines in the lower part of the state are beginning to show unmistakeable signs of hostility. It is feared that a secret understanding exists between the Indians now committing atrocities in Northern California and Oregon, and the race generally on the Pacific coast.

Indeed, if reports are true, there is a preconcerted movement on the part of the Indians to rise simultaneously in arms and by one sudden and bold stroke endeavor to regain their power which has of late so rapidly paled before the march of the Anglo Saxon. . . .

They see themselves dying by disease, their lands stolen and themselves driven gradually back into the worthless recesses of the mountains, and even the effeminate, unreasoning tribes of California see that they are destined ere long to disappear ingloriously and by piecemeal, and more in consonance with an Indians spirit is it to die as a brave, in regaining rights of which he is as tenacious as the whites, than tamely to submit to slow extermination. . . . but the seal is set, and the irrevocable fiat has gone forth that the land that now knows him, shall know him no more forever.

Meanwhile, rumors from Washington indicated that even Col. Henley was not immune from efforts at extinction of the political variety. According to some sources, Senator Weller wished to remove Henley, who many perceived as a liability to the Democratic party. Henley's first California job as postmaster of San Francisco had been a gift of President Pierce. The *Journal* said:

While he held that office it was ascertained that letters and newspapers, directed to various parts of the State, used to be deposited occasionally in the Bay, through a hole in Long wharf, and when at last this was discovered the indignation of the people of that politically-doomed city knew no bounds. Mr. Henley undertook to explain the matter—said it was an accident—an unavoidable occurrence. But it was proved that the same thing had occurred before....

So on he goes to Washington and reveals to the President the astounding fact that Lieut. Beale—the most successful and humane Indian Agent the government ever had—was not a Democrat. Of course the Pres. removed him. He would remove his Savior and appoint a Democrat in his place if he had the power and·doubted his democracy....

Personally we have nothing against Henley. But we believe him totally unqualified to discharge the duties of Indian Supt. He is possessed of such an insane desire to be making stump speeches that, were he elected our next President, he could not forego the pleasure of spouting bad grammar and fustian every autumn.

A federal appropriation was voted in 1853 to be used to educate the reservation Indians. When J. Ross Browne was hired by a later administration to investigate conditions at Nome Lackee and other California reservations, he was not impressed by the quality of the instruction—nor did he think much of those employed for that purpose. With heavy sarcasm, he criticized the habit of rewarding political hacks by giving them jobs in the Indian department:

... the Executive Department adopted the policy of selecting officers experienced in the art of public speaking, and thoroughly acquainted with the prevailing systems of primary elections. A similar policy had been found to operate beneficially in the case of Collectors of Customs, and there was no reason why it should not in other branches of the public service.

Gentlemen skilled in the tactics of state Legislatures, and capable of influencing those refractory bodies by the exercise of moral suasion, could be relied upon to deal with the Indians, who are not so far advanced in the arts of civilization, and whose necessities, in a pecuniary point of view, are not usually so urgent. Besides, it was known that the Digger tribes were exceedingly ignorant of our political institutions, and required more instruction, perhaps, in this branch of knowledge than in any other....

The California delegation made it a point never to endorse any person for office in the service who was not considered peculiarly deserving of patronage. They knew exactly the kind of men that were wanted, because they lived in the state and had read about the Indians in the newspapers. Some of them had even visited a few of the wigwams.

Having the public welfare at heart ... they saw where the greatest difficulty lay, and did all in their power to aid the executive. They endorsed the very best friends they had—gentlemen who had contributed to their election, and fought for them through thick and thin.

The capacity of such persons for conducting the affairs of a reservation could not be doubted. If they ... could control half a dozen members of the Legislature in a senatorial contest, why not be able to control Indians, who were not near so difficult to manage? If they could swallow obnoxious measures of the administration, were they not qualified to teach savages how to swallow government provisions?

III

As GENUINE NISENAN became fewer in the county, ersatz Indians were created to take their places. Along with their lands, the Americans began taking their names. In February 1856, when the Order of Redmen established its first California lodge at the mining camp of Red Dog, the charter members called their chapter "Wemeh No. 1." The neighboring camp of Walloupa already had taken the name of Wema's subchief, Walupa.

The Odd Fellows at Nevada City thought Oustomah would be an appropriate title for their lodge, because they were told it was the Indian name for their city. Others argued that it meant only "town" or "town people," but it was also possible the word described the location—long before foreigners came to Nevada City, it had been a nisenan summer resort. The words ʔosí tamas or ʔosí tamashi have a sound like "oustomah" to European ears, and they can be understood to mean "bad winter." Wema's people were in the habit of moving below the snow line when the harvest ended and the air turned cold.

In May 1856 an office clerk at Nome Lackee wondered why no report was received from Simmon Storms at the Nevada Indian camp. Upon investigation he learned that "Mr. Storms (overseer) was taken with a bleeding at the lungs, and has been absent at Tehama, in charge of a physician until Saturday evening. . . . During the week, Bourne, Pollard, Weimah and Antonio, with an average of 18 Indians per day, have been employed in cutting, hauling and stacking hay."

Charles H. Bourne came to California with Storms and David Bovyer, and was the owner of the Hermitage Ranch, which adjoined Storms Ranch in Nevada County. The Hermitage had been for sale for some time, and Storms had turned his ranch over to Samuel Norris, an Indian trader for whom he had worked in 1851. Antonio was the name Americans had bestowed upon a member of Wema's village near Grass Valley.

Several hunting parties had informed Storms of the existence of an idyllic valley in the mountains west of Nome Lackee. It sounded like an ideal location for a reservation, and Simmon mentioned it to Col. Henley on more than one occasion. Eventually the superintendent gave him instructions to investigate and report. On June 12, 1856, Storms led a party into the country between Nome Lackee and Cape Mendocino. Among other things, he hoped to learn as much as he could about Indians already occupying the region.

Eight days later he reported his findings to Henley:

I did not get started until late in the morning of the 12th. I then travelled as far as the foot of the mountains, when we rested until the cool of the evening, when we continued up the mountains about ten miles and camped in a fine valley. We kept [to the] divide between Tom's and Stony Creek, found the mountains heavily timbered and game in abundance.

On the 13th we made an early start; travelling up the divide to the summit, we had a fine view of the Sacramento Valley to our East, and a large valley to the West, beyond which as far as the eye could reach nothing was to be seen but mountains, which appeared to be rugged and broken, the same to the North and South, found but little snow on the summit and but little timber.

About 1 p.m. we started for the valley in our West, which appeared to be about 20 miles distant. We kept down a divide between two small streams—on getting down to the forks, found the river much larger than I expected, in fact quite a large one.

Storms had reached the Middle Fork of the Eel River, where it is joined by the Black Butte River. On the way down to the river they met one Indian who was acquainted with some of the Indians in Storms' party, and the meeting was friendly for that reason. The men camped alongside the river, and on the following day reached the valley a little after sunrise. They stayed there for three days, exploring and acquiring information about the Indians who lived there.

On the first day of my arrival I was satisfied in my mind, that of all the places I have ever seen, this was the place for an Indian Reservation. And accordingly, I laid claim to the valley in the name of the government for that purpose. In the afternoon I called my party around me and christened it "Nome Cult" Valley.

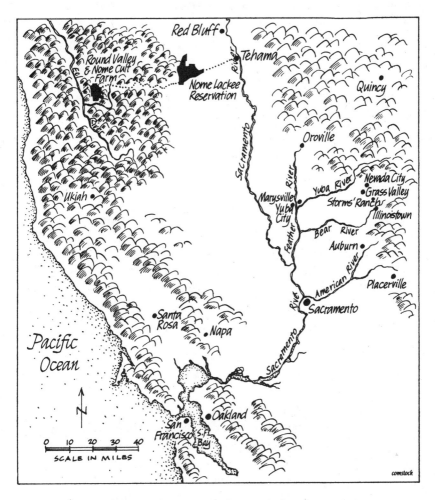

Northern California Indian Reservations

Nome Cult was an approximation of *wintun* words that could be said to mean "west place." Storms judged it was about half way between Nome Lackee Reservation and the coast; about fifty miles in either direction.

There are several small streams running through the valley, all of which empty into the river south of it, in these streams or creeks there is an abundance of timber, and the finest I have ever seen, oak, cottonwood and willows. I found oak trees that were from 60 to 70 feet without a limb and 4 to 6 feet through—the principle grasses in the valley are timothy and clover, there are also a great variety of these the names of which are unknown to me.

On riding through the valley the grass was up even with our horses backs and it was often difficult to get through it.... The land there does not bake and there is but little clay in the soil. While we remained we had many dews which would wet our blankets about through.... I found any amount of Currants, Blackberries, Strawberries, Grapes, with a plenty of Manzanita berries and acorns. The mountains which extend down to the valley are covered with the best of grass and timber, and within one fourth of a mile from the valley there is as fine Sugar pine as I have ever seen and no trouble to get at them.

Storms thought they would have little trouble with local Indians, who seemed friendly:

I think in less than a half hour after our arrival, there was collected on a small knoll north of us two hundred Indians—I sent my interpreter to tell them to come over where I was. When they saw him approaching, many of them ran off, but soon as he commenced talking with them, they came back; in a few minutes he returned with six Indians, one of whom I afterwards learned was their head chief. When he came up he offered me his Bow and Arrows. I told him to keep them. I then told him I was sent over by the great Captain to see them and have a talk with them and to settle among them and teach them how to work, &c.

He appeared much pleased. I told him that I wanted him to get his head men together and meet me the next day—that I might talk with them. During the day the Indians were coming and going all the time, as soon as they found we did not wish to molest them. I found these Indians about the same as all the California Indians which I have seen. The most of them have deer skins—but no other clothing.

I find there has been a number of squaws and children taken away by white men, which is the principle reason of their being so much afraid of the whites. When we first went in the valley some of the Indians stole our knives and cups. I told them it was very wrong to do so and the old chief made them return all. After that they never attempted to take anything again.

I saw among them a number of shells which they said came from the coast, and that they could get there in two sleeps, and that white men were living there. The next morning a band of about two hundred came into camp, but few had their bows and arrows. I then explained to them the object of my visit, with which they appeared much pleased, and when the interpreter told them how the Indians on Nome Lackee Reservation lived, they seemed delighted and said they would all work at anything I wanted them to, if I would only protect their squaws and children.

I told them that hereafter no one should molest them, that I intended to leave men to look out for them while I went back for tools, &c, to work with, and if any men came into the valley to trouble them to let my men know it and they would stop them. The old chief told me he would like to go to Nome Lackee with me and see the place, he and one other came over with me. I then gave them the presents I had for them. I was careful not to make any promises but such as I knew I could carry out.

I think that in the valley and in the low mountains around there are at least five thousand Indians, and that the valley can be made to support twenty thousand or more, it is the best place for Indians I ever saw.

Storms left three of his men at the valley when he departed. He would have liked to stay longer, but his provisions gave out and he had nothing to eat on the way back but venison and wild onions. The men he left behind would have to live on deer meat and whatever the Indians could give them until Storms could return with supplies and tools.

On August 8 the *Journal* noted: "The Nevada and Yuba Indians have been taken to a small valley fifty miles west of the Nome Lackee reservation, where they are colonized with about 1500 others."

The daily reports from Nome Cult in July and August told of Indians mowing and putting up hay, cutting timber, digging ditches and hauling supplies. On July 21 Storms said the Nevada Indians were "very tired and not doing much." Some were digging a well, others were erecting fences and corrals, and two Indians hunted full time, killing two or three deer most days to provide a supply of meat for the camp. A dozen Indian women were put to work gathering berries. Logs were hewed and split, hay was cut and hauled from more distant meadows.

Three days after one Indian died from an undiagnosed illness, Storms had to go to Nome Lackee. No sooner was he out of sight than twenty Indians deserted. To keep the others under control, the two whites left in the valley had to abandon most work for the six days Storms was away. The escaped Indians were not located, and it was assumed they had returned to where they came from.

In later reports, Storms summarized the summer and fall activities of 1856:

No planting was done the first year as the season was so far advanced—we erected a few cabins within an inclosure of pickets for the occupancy of the whites and a few Nevada Indians that I brought with me. We began to pack farming tools, seeds and provisions from Nome Lackee, but the winter set in sooner than we anticipated and we did not accomplish much.

On several occasions I nearly lost my life in the mountains. One Indian was frozen to death, two men drowned in Eel river and several mules lost in the snow. Some of the [native] Nome Cult Indians twice surrounded our quarters, threatening our lives, and killing some stock. In resisting them we were forced to kill many of them, which stopped their proceedings.

In October Storms had gone back to Nevada County again, perhaps to look for the escaped Indians. The *Journal* reported:

Friend Storms gives a glowing description of the beautiful valley in which he resides. The hostile Indians about him are numerous, but by the assistance of a well constructed fort he is able to hold them in check and give security to the Nevada Indians, who are with him.

Preparations are being made to sow a great many acres of wheat at Nomecult. Plows and other farming implements have lately been obtained for the purpose. The Indians at Nome Lackee are in a prosperous condition. They have on hand at the Reservation 20,000 bushels of wheat. Nomecult is not yet established as an Indian Reserve, but is rather a squatter branch or colony from Nome Lackee.

Squatter was the appropriate word, for no survey had been made, no legal description written, no title taken to the land at Nome Cult.

Downieville in the 1850s

CHAPTER 23

COURT CALENDARS

September–November 1855

I

ꞬRASS VALLEY'S GOOD FORTUNE ended abruptly in late summer. Until then it had escaped major disaster, but on the night of September 13 nearly 300 buildings went up in flames. Total losses were estimated at from $250,000 to $400,000, and according to the Grass Valley *Telegraph*, whose press and materials were somehow saved, individual losses ranged between $200 and $20,000. Aaron Sargent passed the ruins en route to Sacramento and lamented, "Poor Grass Valley . . . at last rubbed out in a night, like an old account from a slate." At the same time, he predicted she would rebuild better than ever, "like all California towns."

In the days following the original blaze, four smaller fires broke out, all thought to be the work of arsonists. To make matters worse, Grass Valley police reported thieves were "thick about the scene." Among the lost structures was Grass Valley's Masonic Hall, owned by Col. S.

Conway Richardson, a town trustee and officer of Emmanuel Episcopal Church, which before the fire met in his building.

Emmanuel was Grass Valley's newest congregation, and included many prominent citizens: mining executives such as Melville Attwood and James Delavan, attorneys Alfred Dibble and C. J. Lansing, and County Board Chairman James Walsh. Emmanuel's rector, the Reverend Mr. William H. Hill, also served Nevada City's Trinity Episcopal Church, whose members included Charles and Deb Mulford. On October 2, Mary wrote her mother:

The Rev. Mr. Hill is going home for his family, and has promised to go to R.Ville and see you all, and takes with him another daguerreotype of Freddie, which we had taken yesterday for that purpose. We think it some better than the other one, but he will not sit still until he is so sleepy that he looks dull . . . and he *would* have his thumb in his mouth. I did not feel well enough to go down in the hot sun, so Niles took him alone, and he got very hungry and tired before he got a good one. . . . Do not be frightened at Niles looking so old, and think that the weight of his new honors are going to bring premature old age. He does not look but very little older than when we left home. He only happened to look so in the picture. I suppose anxiety to keep Fred still made him frown. . . .

You must ask Mr. Hill all kinds of questions about us, he is a pleasant sociable man—easy and fond of talking. We think very much of him and shall be glad to see [him] back again with his family.

Tweed and Searls dissolved their partnership in September, and Sherman Fletcher took Niles's place in the firm. Although Charley Mulford was about to resign the agency of Wells, Fargo and Company, more important was the fact of the birth of his daughter on September 20. Mary said of the event:

Deb has got a baby, a sweet little girl, fat and healthy and hearty, a little "Fanny Augusta," and Deb is as smart and thriving as can be expected, much smarter than we had reason to expect she would be, she is so slender.

She has every good symptom—plenty of milk, scarcely any fever, once in while a little, but no more than she used to have before. She is going to be *very very* careful about sitting up and all that, so as to try and get well of her old troubles that have affected her so much, particularly this summer. I have no doubt that with proper care she will be healthier than ever before. . . .

She has been very feeble, and much of the time not able to walk over here, has not been able even to ride but a few times, but she has been cheerful and patient as any one could be all the time, and was willing to endure all for even the chance of having a living healthy baby. . . . The most trying of all was that she had to wait almost a month after the time, and expecting every day to be confined.

Mary's own physician, Dr. Knox, had gone to the east with his family, and would not return for a month or two. Fortunately, Dr. Harvey Wickes understood the delicate nature of his sister's health better than anyone:

Harvey came [from Auburn] once and staid a week or more waiting, and then went back and just *chanced* to be down again when she was taken. . . . He was such a comfort to her and to us all, for there was no physician here—that we know much about any way. She had *no trouble* more than *ordinary*, but we feared she might have some with her heart.

Charlie has had a daguerreotype of our houses taken for [his sister] Lucia, and we should have had another taken for Nellie or some of you, but thought it would be much cheaper and more convenient for you to have one taken from that, which would in reality be a better one, as it is now all *inverted*, and we can hardly ourselves tell which is which house.

In this case the mirror-image reversal typical of the daguerreotype process was confused even more by the photographer's retouching:

They have put Charlies *dahlia blossoms* on our *peach trees* in finishing up the picture, and Niles makes quite a fuss about it—he says it will surely *kill* our trees to blossom so much the first year.

We . . . are considering an offer from a man to rent our house and board us, counting the rent for my board and Fred's, and Niles paying his when here. It will not be as pleasant on many accounts as to have a home of our own, but it will seem like home to us, being in our own house (we shall have a room built on for ourselves) and so near Charlies.

II

ADDISON BEGAN HIS LETTER "Dear Sister," claiming not to know how to address her—whether as Nellie Niles or Cornelia Allen, "girl or wife":

I know you were to be the latter by this [time], but there are so many slips between the cup and lip—but I hope the thing is gone and done and I congratulate you accordingly, and wish you, not as a form, but with all my heart, very many years of happiness—and I can assure you that I have that confidence in Allen that I know they will be yours if he can effect it. . . .

I have been in very tolerable luck, and my situation in the present and my prospects for the future are very satisfactory to me. When I come to look back to what I expected when I left the states I feel very particularly contented. Only 8½ months in the state and I am, in the first place, Justice of Peace—not high in rank very, its true, but respectable, and promises to be (when the rains come on, like all good things here), fairly lucrative. Then, though my practice has of course not been large, I believe I stand well at the bar of our county, better at all events than with my age and experience I had any right to expect in so short a time.

Then, for I suppose I may as well give a schedule of my hours, I am a very reverend and most Worthy Patriarch of a Division of the Sons of Temperance—and finally Brethren, the Grand Hia-Muck-a Muck, Sachem, president, Noble Grand Humbug, or by whatever name benighted outsiders may choose to call it, the presiding officer of (tell it not in Goth) the order of Know Nothings in Nevada City—"Some are born great, some become great, and some have greatness thrust upon them"—Which am I, judge ye—I try to bear my blushing honors meekly.

Niles has donned the ermine and is now holding his first term at Nevada. He is well liked on the bench, as off, and I predict a high station for him among the judges of Cal. . . .

I'm full of criminal business for the last 3 weeks—the City Recorder has been otherwise employed and I have done all the Police Court business. You should see me clear the calaboose of a Monday morning—I dont believe John O. Cole himself could dispose of a set of thieves, drunkards and vagrants more summarily than I do—I am rather afraid I begin to like it and shall grow bloodthirsty. Tell Pa I enclose for him the decision of the Supreme Court in the case of Beard v. Knox— The judges have done me the honor to quote sentiments and almost language from my brief—probably to save time—much obliged nevertheless—

In a postscript Addison teased, "I'll direct to Miss C. D. Niles—for if it shouldn't have come off, how mortified you would be to have it to Mrs. Allen."

Criminal matters in California were handled by three levels of courts: Addison's justice court tried cases with penalties not exceeding $500 or one year in prison. Niles's district court had jurisdiction in cases of murder, manslaughter, and arson, and also heard appeals from the court of sessions, which tried all other crimes. In 1855, civil disputes were divided between Justice Courts ($500 or less) and District Courts (more than $500).

Having inherited a large backlog of cases from Judge Barbour, Niles quickly impressed lawyers and litigants by his willingness to work night and day. On, October 8, 1855, his first day in court, he scheduled 150 cases for later trial. On the second he received an "information against the people of Nevada City for the usurpation of incorporate privilege," in which John McConnell, the outgoing state attorney general, claimed the city's incorporation in 1854 was invalid. After ordering the city to respond, Niles heard a bankruptcy case and processed a divorce application.

On the third day he granted naturalization to five men, dismissed a civil case and tried a case of arson. The jury returned a guilty verdict; Niles said he would pronounce sentence on Saturday. His late opponent for the bench, John T. Crenshaw, was admitted to practice in district court on Thursday, a second divorce action was heard, and a murder case was continued to the next term at the district attorney's request.

Erastus Keeler was tried and found guilty of manslaughter on the fifth day, and two more naturalizations were granted. On Saturday, the sixth day, Judge Searls approved a divorce, a foreclosure, several naturalizations, dismissed two civil cases, rendered several judgements, confirmed a referee's report, and rescheduled two cases for later in the month.

Court resumed after the Sabbath with a two-day trial. The suit of Daniel Rich versus the Estate of Israel T. Hirst had plagued the court for three years. The *Journal* compared it to "Jarndyce versus Jarndyce":

> The interminable case of Rich vs. Hirst bids fair to rival the celebrated one in *Bleak House*. Monday and Tuesday were occupied by the District Court in the investigation of the case for the less than one hundredth time. The case has been bandied about between the District Court and the Supreme Court of the State, until the brains of everybody who has had anything to do with it, are said to be in a state of confusion worse confounded.

Israel Hirst was Hamlet Davis's partner in 1850 and 1851 before he returned to Ohio, where he died, leaving considerable assets and liabilities in California. On October 1, 1852, Daniel Rich sued Hirst's estate for $11,301, which he claimed was owed him. Since then he had initiated others, one of which included Hamlet Davis as co-defendant.

The trial on Tuesday produced a temporary victory for Hirst's heirs, but Rich won a $1400 verdict against the defunct firm of Davis and Hirst a week later. A motion for a new trial in the first case was taken under advisement. Even Judge Searls seemed powerless to bring an end to the "interminable case," but the legal community was impressed nevertheless. As his first court term neared its end the *Journal* said:

The court will hardly be able to clear the calendar this term, although Judge Searls has labored intently, day and night to this end and dispatched more business than was ever before disposed of in *two* terms of the District Court in this County. The District has reason to be proud of its new Judge, and we predict he will not have a superior on the California bench before the close of his term.

For the first time, the *Journal* was publishing weekly summaries of all court business, including a calendar of upcoming cases. To improve efficiency and decorum, Judge Searls appointed veteran attorneys Dunn, Churchman, Buckner, McConnell, and Tweed to compile a set of rules for the District Court.

The professionalism and competency displayed in Niles's court made it the most interesting show in town, but placed a heavy strain on his family. At the end of two weeks, Mary wrote her mother:

Niles often wishes we were home now and could spend the winter with you. He will have to be absent two months now in a few weeks, and he doesnt know what to do with us in the meantime. If we could find board in a private family we would break up housekeeping. It is such a care to him to provide everything, and when Fred is troublesome [Niles] often has to help me or wait for his dinner &c, and then [even] if we *keep no girl* our expenses are as great as they would be if we boarded, and we have all the care and work beside.

Niles never liked keeping house very well. He does not like to have to think about bringing home meat and potatoes and all the items which are requisite and necessary, and in this country he has to do it *all*. . . . He is just as busy as he can be now all the time, and I enclose the "opinion of the press" upon his success, which I just happened to see in a paper lying here on the table. Addison too is very busy. I have dinner ready at 5 oclock and it is almost always 6 before either of them come and everything is over done or cold or something else, and Fred is sleepy and cross, and they have to compare notes and talk law &c, and it requires a good deal of good nature all around to keep things straight, but they are very patient generally and lay all failures and troubles to my being *slow* which they seem to take as a matter of course—a necessary evil—

On another day, in a more cheerful mood, she referred to the compliments Niles was receiving:

He deserves it *all* for he works incessantly and has a business capacity which enables him to work to advantage. I wish you could

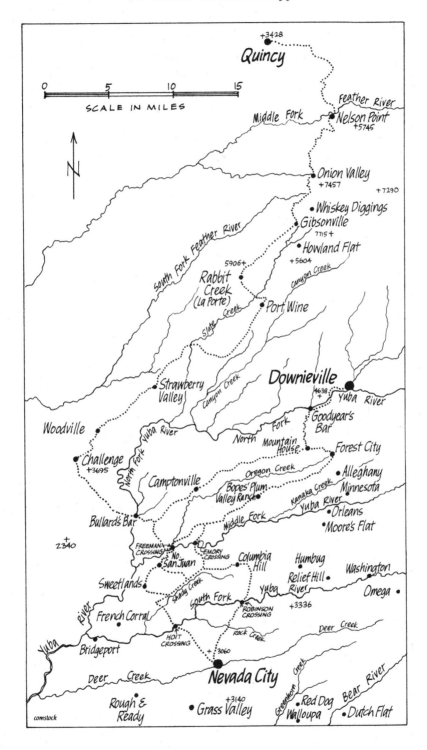

know, but it is useless to try to tell you, how kind and patient and thoughtful he is to us with all the pressure of business on his mind too. If it were quite *natural* to him I would not perhaps appreciate it so much, but I often see that it costs him a great effort to be patient and not speak cross when he has to see to household matters, and his mind is weary and over tasked.

Before Niles left for Quincy, high in the mountains of Plumas County, Mary wrote:

I would not put off my letters till the last day so much if I wasnt so constantly hurried. I think while Niles is gone I shall write more. He leaves day after tomorrow to be gone 6 weeks.... Hattie Backus has at last found her way up here, and is staying at Charlies. Perhaps she will stay with me while Niles is gone. It will make me some more trouble, but not much, and she is a dear good girl, first rate company, very thoughtful of others, and in several respects wonderfully improved. Is neat and tidy here. Addison is delighted to see "a girl as *is* a girl," and if she can stay from home so long, I think she will stay with me.

She plays the guitar beautifully, and—what do you think—the night after [Addison] borrowed one for her, Niles went down town and bought *me* one, and Hattie is giving me lessons. I think I can learn pretty easily, but it will take a good deal of time.

III

NILES WAS ABSENT only two weeks, having quickly cleared the smaller Plumas County docket, and received much praise from the Quincy weekly *Old Mountaineer* for his efforts.

On November 17 Addison wrote his father:

Niles is setting in my office ... next week he goes to Sierra Co. (Downieville) to remain about 3 weeks—He has won good opinions from all parties since he took his place in the bench.

In answer to his father's queries about the California judicial system, Addison commented that the "practice act" was quite similar to the New York Code:

In fact, it was drafted by [Stephen] Field of Sacramento, a brother of David Dudly Field of New York, one of the N.Y. codifiers—we have almost exactly the code of '48, with all its defects.... I enclose a decision of the Supreme Court in a case of mine—I meant to have sent it before—it is going to be a leading case in Cal.

From Downieville, Niles wrote to Cornelia suggesting she come to California, where "there is plenty of room for ministers."

It is Thanksgiving day and I have adjourned court over till tomorrow and find myself at leisure for the first time in two months, and as no visions of slaughtered fowl and all of the et cetera accompanying them arise in my mind as the dinner hour approaches, I feel perfectly at liberty as on other days to write, walk, talk, or attend to such other business as may offer. Were I at home we should no doubt have a nice dinner and a nice little family party, but "alas for poor Yorick" I have been here almost two weeks and have ten days more to remain before the close of my Term.

Of course I dont allow myself to become homesick, yet I would like *dreadful* well to see May and Fred. I fear however that they are getting along well, and although to me it seems impossible, May reports that Fred is growing more cunning every day.

The only objection to my office is that it takes me from home so much. I hope however by next summer the conveniences for travelling will be such that May can travel with me a portion of the time, which will obviate every difficulty.

Dont suppose that I am by any means dissatisfied with my present position, for be assured, it suits me first rate, even better than *Phillips-Ville*, with all its attractions and inducements for *industrious young men of economical habits*. Oh ye Gads, was not there an escape when we left that delectable portion of creation!

Once again the matter of visiting Rensselaerville was broached:

I would like for May and Fred to come home on a visit next summer if a good opportunity offers, but would not consent unless I could find just the right kind of company, for you know May could not get along as well on such a trip as you could. We will see when spring comes. She would like very much to come, but when I talk about it she seems sometimes to feel as though going without me would be unpleasant.

Much litigation reflected current economic problems in the state. Many persons who had experienced early successes had borrowed to expand, thus overextending themselves. Bank failures, poorly managed enterprises, and uninsured fire losses contributed to the malaise. A case in point was Hamlet Davis, once Nevada City's leading merchant-banker. He had owned hotels, office buildings, a theater, and a bank, but the demise of larger banks and prolonged litigation with Daniel Rich and others led to his own failure. Davis was denying reports of his insolvency in July, but any doubts were laid to rest with the success of George Kidd's suit against him in October. Judge Searls ordered the sheriff to sell Davis's United States Hotel, across Broad Street from his pioneer "fireproof."

Simon Rosenthal, whose two-story brick adjoined Mulford's, was also suing Davis. Rosenthal was naturalized during the October term of court, along with numerous other European emigrants. The recent successes of the Know Nothing party had made it prudent for foreigners to acquire citizenship; none wanted to repeat the horrors of persecution that had caused so many to leave their homes in Poland, Germany, France and Ireland.

Into Niles's court came merchants suing for overdue bills run up by lawyers; miners sued water companies. Surveyors sued miners, ranchers, and land speculators. Lawyers won or lost suits—and then sued for their fees. Miners sued over rights and boundaries, and partners sued each other. B. B. Laton, of Grass Valley's Empire Mining Company won a judgment against fellow shareholder John E. Southwick. From his elevated role as Lola's escort in the mountains, Southwick was reduced to selling his most valuable possession, the Empire Mine stock.

Lola Montez coincidentally was beset by bill collectors in Australia. The San Francisco *Daily American* said she had removed her clothes and gone to bed after daring police to come to her hotel room and seize her if they wished. It was a plausible story.

Another casualty of the times was Nevada City's pioneer gambler Adam Smith, once a partner in Barker's Exchange and now the proprietor of Glenbrook Race Course. The man who built Smith's new house at the race track foreclosed when his invoices went unpaid because S. S. Green, who had purchased Barker's Exchange, failed to make his payments to Smith—Green was the owner of the Empire Saloon, and it was being foreclosed as well. Passage of laws against gambling had made both properties unprofitable.

Nevertheless, the general mood was one of cautious optimism, and one of the surest indications was the county's willingness to erect a new courthouse, however slow the pace. The *Journal* wondered why there was so little activity at the site:

What is the matter with our new Court House? We hear no noise of laborers at work in that quarter. Perhaps it is to be built like Solomon's temple, without the sound of tools disturbing the solemn stillness of Court House Square. Had Nevada architects been awarded the contract to erect our temple of justice, there would have been as much noise of workmen in a certain locality as at Babel....

Some Nevada City builders objected to the selection of Grass Valley architect William Bettis to design the structure, a Sacramento firm to build it, and a San Francisco architect to oversee construction. The latter person had impressive credentials, for C. C. Ordemann had designed the much-admired court houses at Mobile, Montgomery, Tuskegee, and Eufaula.

Specifications called for foundations to be dug five feet below grade, but County Supervisor J. B. Johnson thought the ground "wasn't firm enough" when he saw the excavation. After some informal discussion with Supervisor Charles Marsh, who was inclined to agree, Johnson ordered the contractor to go deeper. Later, when the bill for six additional feet of granite walls was presented for payment, Johnson balked at paying, claiming he hadn't acted in an "official" capacity. The *Journal* was incredulous:

He, as a member of the Board, did not feel authorized to sanction an order given by himself while not acting in his official capacity! . . . Some two thousand dollars have been spent by the contractors in extra work, done by order of the agents of the county, and one of the agents, who was most officious in making the expense, refuses to pay it. Mr. Heritage [the third supervisor] is opposed to the payment for the extra work, because he considered it useless, and not having been consulted . . . he can very properly dissent from the action of the other two members of the Board.

Eventually a compromise was negotiated and work resumed. Of the three original supervisors, only Marsh was reelected in September. When the new board met on October 1, with James Walsh as chairman, it awarded $8000 worth of bonds to the contractor, who promptly sold them to Charles Mulford's bank at 20 per cent discount.

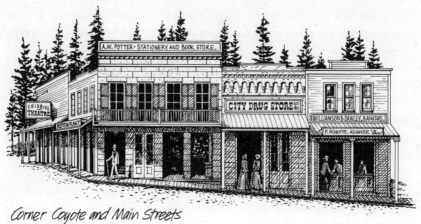

Corner Coyote and Main Streets

CHAPTER 24

JOURNAL EDITOR

December 1855—January 1856

I

$\mathscr{A}$ LETTER FOR MARY arrived on the last day of November. It was nearly midnight when Addison brought the first communication from Cornelia since her wedding. Mary was in bed, but not asleep when he came in; by the time she finished reading she was wide awake. She thought of home and what her sister had said, and hours passed before she drifted into sleep.

Next day she wrote about what had gone through her mind:

Dear sister Allen ... I might almost as well have written all day, for I have been thinking of you so much that I could do nothing else. I cannot bear to think that you are a bride and passing through those blissful days which never *can come* but once ... and I should be so far away. It is too bad Nellie. When any such event occurs ... we regret ... the separation that at other times we learn to think of as a matter of course....

After the honeymoon Cornelia had gone home to Rensselaerville, while Will investigated a vacant pastorate at Sand Lake, across the Hudson River in Rensselaer County. It was an ideal location, near to

228

Albany and close to Will's parents and sister. Mary hoped he would get the position, for it would permit Cornelia to visit their parents easily.

Cornelia's letter informed her that John Niles had refused nomination and probable election as judge of Albany County. It was a shame he had to forego the honor, but Mary understood and approved his reasons, noting:

> Isnt it amusing how the title of *Judge* runs in our family. I am much gratified at the compliment paid Pa by the nomination, but am also glad that he did not accept it, for it would have been too much care and anxiety for him in his present state of health, and I am sure that all the honors or proffits or pleasures of the office would not compensate to him and to Ma for the great pleasures and home comforts which surround them where they now are. How thankful I am for Ma's recovery.

Niles and Mary were agreed she ought to go home, but had not decided how or when:

> If Charlies folks go home next summer do you think I had better come with them? If I do not ... I probably cannot till Niles's term expires—6 years—It would seem to suit *our* convenience better to wait another year, as Niles would like to lay by some of his salary and invest it proffitably, but if I remain [at Rensselaerville] 6 months or so ... the difference in [my] expense there will almost equal the cost of our trip. . . .
> Niles cannot come for me, and Addison will hardly be ready to go as soon, and Niles would not trust us to return with any one else, he thinks. Then too, it would be very *hard* for Niles to *have* me take Fred and myself too, away from him so long, and if any thing should happen to any of us we might always regret it.

Matters were nearly as undecided about where she should live in the meantime, although there was a possibility she might stay with Mr. and Mrs. Jesse Wall:

> There is a very pleasant young married couple who would like us to board with them and will give us their parlor—a very nice, plastered room, with French windows opening on a piazza. We have also several other proposals now and I only await a letter from Niles before making a decision. You see, Nellie, our honors are dearly bought, to *me* at least, for Niles is absent so much. He has now been absent 4 weeks, with only one day's unexpected visit, and will not be home till 8 days more are passed, and then enters next morning into business here, so that I cannot expect him to take any care from me, and the worst of it is, I can

hardly expect to see him long enough to talk any with him when he *is* home.

We hear flattering reports of his popularity in the upper counties. They say up there that he will be *Gov.* next, but "a new broom sweeps clean," and the tune may change in a short time. Not that I think it is any more than he *deserves* (of course I don't), but popular favor is an uncertain thing and the best way is to be neither puffed up by its flattery or depressed by its abuse. I am glad to know that Niles *is* what he *seems,* and does not cater to public opinion. . . .

His mind is constantly over tasked, and I fear he will be sick if he does not relax his labors a little. Sometimes for days when he is home I cannot speak to him of the least thing, and have to wait till he speaks first, lest I may disturb his thoughts. He is determined to push through the business which has been lagging for 4 years, and he will succeed admirably I think, if he can endure it. . . .

Addison is jogging on in the usual way—went down to San Fran. last week with Hattie [Backus]. Charlie was to have gone [with her], but was detained and Addison took it into his head to go.

Mary neglected to add that the reason for Hattie's trip to the bay city was her brother's retrial, ordered by the supreme court. Mary enclosed a note to Will with a "sisterly kiss," and told him his brother Uriah had been to see them again:

I delivered the card you sent him, and read your letter to him. He makes us a call now and then, and we have many talks about you all. He seems very happy and contented, and likes the country exceedingly. I think he has some idea of going home next summer on a visit.

Deb Mulford began her next letter to Cornelia with an outrageous pun:

My will is good enough to write you the dearest kind of a love letter, but would your "Will" be *good* enough if I should? . . . If you could only see my precious little darling with one of her sweet smiles when I speak her name. She knows it well and always responds with a smile. I never before was so happy or saw so much to live for or justly appreciated a mothers love.

I knew it was something deep, earnest and all abiding, but it is something beyond these all—indescribable. . . . I know you will laugh and say, "Oh, the foolishness of these young mothers," but wait till a little pair of blue eyes look you in the face, belonging to you and Will wholly. . . . Do you remember of drawing a woeful picture to me of a woman about my size sitting upright in bed on a cold night patting a crying baby on the back? I don't know as it ever recurred to me until the first time I assumed that position with Fannie, then I laughed outright and told Charlie I wished Cornelia could see me.

When Niles returned two weeks later he moved his family to the Jesse Wall residence at the top of Broad Street. The Walls had been married a year and a half, and Mrs. Wall was expecting a child shortly. On December 18, Mary told Cornelia:

Mrs. Wall is a very pleasant young woman, her husband a very pleasant man, and they have a very fine new house a little out of town. She is one of the best housekeepers in the country, and he is *not* one of the most correct business men, but like most such easy men, *lives* on the *fat of the land* which makes it very agreeable for us, if not for his customers.

We have their parlor, which is a very nice room with French windows and blinds opening on a piazza. The house is plastered, which is a rare thing here—the room is rather small—12 ft. by 18 ft., and it is not easy to keep all the rubbish that we have to use in place. We bought some beautiful drugget for the floor, and a sink wash stand, a pretty piece of furniture that shuts up all the washing apparatus, and with our bed, bureau, rocking chairs, table, trunks, &c, with Freds chairs, bath-tub &c &c, we have a well filled room, but a very prettily furnished one withal.

There is a nice closet out of it, and I have my white curtains from the parlor, and am going to cover a wood-box and stools with worsted damask and have my stove blackened a little, and then we shall be nicely fixed. . . .

They are very fond of Fred here, and he has the range of the whole house, and seems happier than he was when we were alone so much. The only trouble I have is that it is quite a walk from here to Deb's, but we are in plain sight of each other, and I can leave Fred here when I want to run over, and can have Niles take him over any morning, if I want to stay a few hours. . . .

Niles . . . will be [home] for two or three months, after which he will be absent most of the time for 6 months. . . . He doesnt work so hard as he did last term, but is pretty busy yet. Addison boards at a restaurant, and I miss him very much. He doesnt come up very often. By the way, I must not forget this time to write you about some poetry of his which came out in the "Pioneer" of August, and another piece in the [December number]. I have been trying to get another copy of the August [issue], as I did not like to part with mine, but can get more, so will send you that. . . . they are very pretty indeed. . . .

For a while after that Mary found little time to write; first there were the holidays, and then Mrs. Wall was delivered of a daughter. Her next letter to Cornelia was dated January 15, and she was less sure than ever about coming home:

I don't think Charlies folks will go home next summer. . . . I suppose it will be more convenient on some accounts for me to wait another season, but I do want very much to come home for a visit. . . . you *can't* know how I long to see [my dear mother]. I dare not think about it when I sit down to write—if I do I cannot write at all.

I made a dress for Fred last week—spent one day at Mr. Warren's, one at Deb's, fitted a cloak for Fred—*and weaned* him. You will be surprised at that, I know, but I had a bad cold and my milk was not good. He seemed to be growing thin and pale, and I thought I had better wean him while Niles is home, and before spring, so that he might get used to eating before warm weather. He was the best little fellow you ever saw. He has never cried but once about it, and then only a little.

I was going to put on [my breasts] something bitter, but Niles kept forgetting to bring it, so I just gave him something else to eat or drink when he asked for it, and the novelty of getting up in the night to eat amused him at first, and now I give him some sage tea with plenty of milk and sugar when he wakes—without lighting any candle—and he lies down and goes right to sleep. It is not a week yet since I commenced. I drew a quart of milk, or nearly that, a day, the first two days.

Fred does not seem very well now, but I suppose it is change of diet. He lives mostly on rice, and cracker scalded in milk and water, sweetened—is fond of meat, but it does not agree with him. He talks, or rather says a great many words. The last new ones are "thank you" "scissors" "water" "gone" "what" &c.

II

IN HER MID-JANUARY letter Mary spoke of her brother's newest undertaking:

Addison has promised to write this week. He has bought a share in the "Journal," and is editor while Waite, the former editor is in the Assembly. He said he dont often have any thing to write [home] about, and is going to write this week to tell you about *that*, so I will leave it for him, though I doubt if he will keep his promise.

Addison provided further details, but not until February 2, when he told his father:

Waite, the editor of the "Journal," was elected State Senator last fall, and I have taken his place during his absence. I made a bargain for purchasing 1/4 of the establishment [from John P. Skelton], but money has been so extremely scarce here for a few weeks past that I doubted if I could fulfil the terms of the bargain easily, and therfore retransferred and am now simply editor, until the close of the Session of Legislature, on a salary. The little money I had was out on mortgage, and although perfectly secure, it was impossible to raise it now without forclosure.

The editing does not interfere materially with my official business [as Justice of the Peace], I make something by it, though not very much. I have moved my office into the upper part of Charlie Mulfords brick building; I get it for less rent and much more comfortable and convenient. Have a large room for a court room, and a small bedroom.

The adjoining room was occupied by the law firm of Charles F. Smith and William F. Anderson. Besides being Addison's friend, Anderson also edited the rival *Democrat*. Their friendship notwithstanding, each authored fierce editorials disapproving the foolishness of the other party.

In his letters, Addison did not mention a frightening encounter which resulted from his new occupation. In January Senator Waite sent an editorial to Addison with instructions to include it in the next issue. The story was about an effort to recover estates claimed by the state. The article, while factually correct, amounted to a political attack on several Nevada City Democrats, and said in part:

The committee ... placed $30,000 at the disposal of the Attorney General [McConnell], an officer elected and endorsed by the people as honest and efficient, to be used in securing to the school fund, estates alleged to have been escheated. Sanguine hopes were entertained that several millions of dollars might ... be turned to the benefit of the children of the state. ...

The Atty Gen put forth all the energies of his great intellect, but knowing that his efforts would be vain and futile without the aid of eminent counsel ... called upon Wm. M. Stewart, who ... received, as shown by the books of the controller of State, the beggarly pittance of $10,000. But the Atty Gen, as the legal adviser of the State, was bound to leave no stone unturned which might contribute to success.

Accordingly, Senator Foote and Judge Aldrich, both gentlemen standing in intimate relations to the Atty Gen and his assistant, were implored to lend a helping hand ... and received for their valuable services $10,000 more. That no legal ability might be wanting, the pair of Atty Gens, one U.S. Senator, and a Judge, were reinforced by Louis

Blanding and H. I. Thornton, Jr., who received, the one the sum of $2,500 and the other $1000.

Dr. Coryell was judiciously employed as physician to the corps, receiving for his professional services the sum of $1,500. Having seen the most desperate diseases cured with like remedies in the State Marine Hospital, he was a fit man to be employed in a case where quick consumption was preying upon the vitals of the State. . . .

The enormous sum of $598.25 still remains in the treasury, a convincing proof that the balance has been honestly expended, or the whole would have been taken.

The loudest outcry issued from the least important target. Harry I. Thornton, Jr. bought space in the *Democrat*, to denounce Waite as a "vulgar scribling blackguard," and the *Journal* responded in belittling terms:

Poor little boy Thornton! Like "Bottom" in *Mid-Summer Night's Dreams*, he is "such a marvelous tender ass that if a hair do but tickle him, he must scratch."

That evening, when Addison entered Frisbie's saloon across the street from his office, he was accosted by "little boy" Thornton, who at age twenty-two was a year younger than Addison. He came from an old and respected southern family—President Fillmore had sent Thornton's father to California in the early 1850s to sit on the Land Commission—and Thornton demanded to know the author of this slur on the family name.

Addison refused to tell him, angry words followed, and suddenly Thornton was aiming a loaded pistol at the youthful editor. As it fired someone deflected the barrel, and the ball hit the ceiling. Addison immediately reached for his own weapon, but a quick-thinking friend had already removed it from his belt. Thornton, too, was disarmed, arrested, then released on bail. Addison made no public comment until April, when he wrote his farewell from the paper:

One little fight we have had—a very small one of the kind—and we are happy to be able to state that it has not proved particularly fatal. The main object, however, of all editorial "scrimages" was accomplished, for the circulation of the *Journal* increased six copies in a single week.

III

IN AN ANXIOUSLY awaited decision, Judge Searls ruled in January that Nevada City's incorporation was legal. The case had its origins during

McConnell and Stewart's dual occupation of the attorney general's office. The law which delegated power to county courts of sessions to incorporate cities was suspect, they thought, for it seemed to violate the historical division of powers between legislative and judicial bodies. It occurred to them that this knowledge might one day prove useful.

One day a man came to Stewart and said he had broken a Nevada City ordinance, but thought the statute was unfair. Stewart took the case and warned city officials that unless charges were dropped he would break the city. When they laughed, Stewart played his trump card, calculated to void every ordinance on the books: Attorney General McConnell challenged the city's legal status on behalf of the people of California.

Judge Searls ruled that the legislature had the power to incorporate cities; had the right to delegate authority; and that the action required of the court of sessions was "judicial," because it only had to determine if requirements specified by the legislature had been met. Nevertheless, Niles added a partial disclaimer to his opinion:

I will not say that in the investigation of this cause doubts have not arisen as to the constitutionality of some portions of the statute; but the plain letter of the law, the evident intent of the legislature, should not, I hold, be disregarded and set at naught without graver cause than to my mind has been offered.

When McConnell appealed the ruling, worried city trustees persuaded Senator Waite to introduce a bill that would re-incorporate Nevada City under new authority and continue its present laws and officers. Should McConnell and Stewart succeed in breaking the city, at least it would be a temporary suspension.

At San Francisco Charles Cora had been charged with the murder of a federal marshal in November. Middle-class white Protestants, already frightened by evidence of widespread corruption in the city, which they blamed on foreigners and Catholics, viewed this assault with alarm. Edward Baker, who had defended Rodman Backus, now agreed to represent Cora, an Italian gambler who claimed to have fired in self-defense. Baker's willingness to defend such "scum" was roundly condemned. Much bitterness was expressed when the Cora trial resulted in a hung jury—six for manslaughter and two for acquittal.

At Nevada City Addison applauded a crusading editor who had launched a campaign aimed at exposing vice and corruption in the bay city:

What private wrongs or personal enmities may have moved James

King of William to his ferocious onslaught upon vice, we know little and care less. . . . but we do admire very heartily the spirit and vigor with which he has attacked rascality in all places, high and low, without fear or favor.

San Francisco is undoubtedly the most corrupt civilized city on earth. This is no mere matter of opinion, but a plain simple fact. . . . In whatever other thing our metropolis may be inferior to the sisterhood of cities, in all that relates to vice and corruption it stands pre-eminent and unapproachable. . . .

Then James King of William came out with the *Evening Bulletin*. He bores the public with no honied discourses upon sin, but steps boldly up to the sinner, and tears from his face the mask that concealed his deformity. He stands before the public and points his finger at the knaves themselves, and calls them by name . . . till every eye is turned upon them, and every citizen knows who . . . have betrayed trust, broken their words of honor, and by their crimes, given the city that is so unfortunate as to be the theatre of their knavery, its pre-eminence of disgrace.

God speed to him in his efforts. May he hit heavier blows and faster, till the miracle is wrought, and honesty becomes popular even in San Francisco.

Meanwhile ambitious men were scheming to bring that sinful place closer to the rest of the state; a proposition to bridge the bay was to be introduced at Sacramento:

The distance is computed at about seven miles. The object of the work is to connect the city and [Alameda County] with a carriage road at first, which is shortly to assist in the construction of a rail track by its side. The same structure is intended also to convey water from the fine and never failing streams of the opposite coast to the city of San Francisco. The Bay is reported as not to exceed forty feet in depth at any place between Rincon and the shore opposite. A wagon road might easily be constructed on piles, eventually to be succeeded by a structure of more durable foundation.

The cost of such an enterprise must of course be immense, but in the event of a railroad being built connecting San Francisco with Sacramento, Stockton, and other interior towns, upwards of thirty miles in distance will be saved by this route, instead of a circuit by the way of San Jose.

Nevada City Methodist Church 1851-1856

CHAPTER 25

NEW DECISIONS

January–April 1856

I

*T*HE DARKNESS OF WINTER is sometimes more than a person can bear. So it seemed to William Bullington, a respected gentleman and native of Georgia. He had lost his right arm in an accident soon after arriving at Nevada City, and was put in charge of the 1852 census for the county. After serving as county treasurer for two years, he and Dr. Alban had built a two story brick building at the southwest corner of Pine and Broad. He also was a partner of bookseller H. R. Stiles, whose store was in the Bullington-Alban building.

In January 1856, he and Stiles dissolved their partnership and Stiles sold the business. Bullington, who lived with his wife on Broad Street, two doors below the Methodist Church, killed himself six days after the transaction was completed. The *Journal* offered the usual explanation for suicide, that he died in "a fit of temporary insanity." But whatever the cause, the deceased was remembered with affection and buried with full Masonic honors. His widow chose to remain in Nevada City among her new friends rather than return to Georgia.

On the other hand, the gloom of winter could suddenly disappear in a blaze of sunshine—or in the brilliance of such thrilling feats as those of Charles Blondin, the French tightrope walker who had crossed Niagara Falls the summer before. Blondin and Dubouchet, celebrated acrobats and tightrope performers, arrived with Gabriel Ravel's Ballet Troupe, which included dancers and mimes. And when they had gone, a company of actors appeared at Frisbie's Theatre.

On February 6 Edwin, a talented son of the legendary Booth family, joined Mrs. Sinclair and Henry Sedley in a four day run of "Marble Heart, or the Sculptor's Dream." Addison's review said:

From the favor with which the play and the company have been received below, we were prepared for something more than usually excellent, and we were not disappointed. Mrs. Sinclair sustains the character of the heroine, Marble Heart, excellently well. The conflict of the passions of love and avarice, can hardly be better expressed by voice and look.

Mr. Booth, as the morbidly sensitive Artist, and Mr. Sedley as the Parisian Editor, gay, shrewd, kind, true hearted, seem to us in our "mind's eye" the models of the characters they represent.

As Mary had feared, Niles became ill in mid-January and was confined to his bed for nearly two weeks. During the convalescence he received many visitors, Fred observed with interest the rituals they performed. Mary explained his reaction:

He has learned to say "good-day" and make at the same time a very polite bow, half way to the ground—just from seeing the gentlemen who called to see Niles when he was sick. He would stand with his eyes fixed upon them till they were gone and then go through the same ceremony precisely, and now says it whenever any one goes out.

He is quite jealous of Niles, and if he sees Niles pet *me* he comes running with his thumb in his mouth and is *so tired* that he must have me take him, and the moment Niles wakes in the morning, he turns over and puts his little hand on my face for fear I will talk to Niles instead of to him. Niles is gone so much that he thinks he can have me all to himself.

Niles has quite recovered his health, and will be better I hope, for the *rest* [he had] of two weeks, though he was too sick to *enjoy* it much. He has been to [Sacramento] a few days since I wrote, and yesterday morning [February 11] started for Downieville for an absence of 2½ months, which will bring his return about the middle of April.

A week later, Mary resumed her writing:

Mrs. Wall is "*mistress* in her own house" and just as far *out* of it as her *husband* dares to go, but she is generally pretty good natured for all that, and I have no fear that she will interfere with me, unless it be through jealousy. She does not like to have any thing said that she don't hear and so wants to be invited in whenever I have company, in which she is often disappointed—poor woman. Though, as she is very kind and accommodating to me thus far, I try to please her when I can consistently.

Two days last week we spent in making calls, and made over 30—a good years task done in that line, for I can't think of going the *rounds* oftener than once a year. Now I am at liberty to go where I *like* to go, and mean to visit a few ladies here often. I am going this week to spend the day with [Mrs. Sarah Bostwick] ... she is delicate in health, gentle, modest, sensible, affectionate &c.—has a fine little girl and a beautiful house, *and* a kind of a Muggins for a husband, who is County Clerk.

I went last week and took dinner with a young married couple living about 1/2 a mile out of town. Fred enjoyed it much and so did I. The lady was a sweet little girl of 16 when she was married ... and is handsome as a doll, and it seems like playing at housekeeping to see her preside with such *wonderful* dignity over her household.

III

THE MURDER TRIAL of Mordecai Harlow was one of five tried in Niles's court at Downieville. Harlow's crime dated back to 1854, but he had evaded arrest until caught in San Francisco recently. Thirty-four years old, born in Kentucky, he had lived in Ohio, Missouri and Mexico before coming west in 1851.

By his own admission Harlow had been a thief since childhood. In California he made a precarious living by robbing miners, which forced him to move constantly to escape detection and arrest. For a short time he earned his living honestly at a Yuba County sawmill. Given the chance to buy half the mill, he accepted, and then offered a job to a man he had met at Marysville. Henry Smith accepted, and because Harlow liked the look of Mrs. Smith he hired her as well.

At the end of three or four months Harlow lost his enthusiasm for work and sold his share in the business. He helped the Smiths relocate to another camp, and they exchanged letters occasionally. Once Harlow helped smooth over a misunderstanding between Smith and another man, mostly to help Mrs. Smith, he said.

In the summer of 1854 the Smiths came to Rabbit Creek in Plumas County, where Harlow was back in his old line of business robbing sluices. Henry wanted Mordecai for a partner. At first Harlow refused, but after a while he could see some profit in the arrangement. He moved in with the Smiths, and this pleased Mrs. Smith as much as her husband.

In October, with the first snow of winter already on the ground, the two men went into the forest to cut firewood. Later on, a neighbor happened along and saw Harlow sitting on a log alongside a pile of brush. But when he saw a bloody axe in Harlow's hand and what looked like a man's body poorly concealed beneath a pile of brush he pretended not to notice and hurried down the trail to tell others what he had seen.

Several men, well-armed and long suspicious of Harlow, went out to investigate. They found Smith's corpse, his skull split; Harlow was gone. Next day he was spotted. Although pursuers wounded him in both thighs, Harlow escaped by hiding in thick chaparral. When the searchers left, he made his way painfully out of the mountains, and for nearly a year hid out in Placer and Tuolumne counties using the alias 'Tilford Monroe.' In the fall of 1855, intending to go either to Oregon or Missouri, he arrived at San Francisco so drunk that a policeman investigated and uncovered his identity.

Harlow's defense was temporary insanity. Defending him was William S. Spear, a figure of some notoriety whose 1852 duel with a fiddler still brought chuckles at Downieville, for the weapons of both men had been unloaded before the event. To persuade jurors of Harlow's insanity, Spear called two experts from the Downieville medical profession, Drs. C. D. Aiken and Wilson Carr. In 1851 they had been involved with the infamous 1851 hanging of a Spanish woman at Downieville. Aiken tried to save her by claiming she was pregnant; Dr. Carr was one of three chivalrous practitioners who swore she was not, thus clearing the way for her execution.

In 1855 Aiken and Carr were the designated surgeons at the duel near Brandy City, in which Charles Lippincott killed the younger brother of Lloyd Tevis, a wealthy San Franciscan. Despite such forensic expertise, the jury ignored their opinions and found the defendant guilty. On February 27, for the first time, Judge Searls sentenced a man to be hanged by the neck until dead.

The Downieville *Sierra Citizen* applauded the new decorum in Judge Searls's courtroom:

> The District Court is a most industrious institution, keeping in session day and night. We have never known a judicial functionary so popular as Judge Searls is. The fact that he is a Know Nothing judge seems to have been lost sight of, and he is looked to with confidence by everybody. This remark we heard of from a very prominent Democrat.

During sundry, but brief, visits to the Court room, we observed but little bickering among the attorneys, no waste of time or boring of jurymen; the decision of the bench is prompt, and apparently satisfactory to all parties.

In Nevada City, District Attorney Sargent was making a concerted effort to harness vice. The problem with getting convictions was the difficulty of persuading witnesses to testify in court. Though he doubted his ability to eradicate it entirely, he was determined at least to push it off the main streets. Fourteen women, American, Chinese and Spanish, were convicted of keeping houses of ill fame. Liz Applegate's bawdyhouse on the corner of Pine and Commercial had been shut down, and the building was sold at auction by the sheriff to collect her $300 fine.

The Sacramento *Union* described the legal definition of a house of ill fame, brothel, or bawdyhouse as being a place for the common habitation of prostitutes, kept for the resort and convenience of lewd persons of both sexes. It could not be applied to the habitation of only one woman, no matter how lewd, nor could a woman be prosecuted for living in a house of ill fame for purposes of prostitution. A woman who is "unchaste, lives by herself, and admits one or many to illicit intercourse with her" is subject only to "Ecclesiastical Courts," advised the *Union*.

Others caught in Sargent's vice net included Thomas Rogers, sentenced to twenty-one years at hard labor for raping a child of four, and John Gardiner, who received ten years for "the infamous crime against nature." Two local saloon keepers were fined for gaming.

Three prisoners cut their way out of the old log jail using an auger and a knife but were foiled by deputies who entertained themselves watching the long process. Everyone hoped the new jail, with walls of solid granite, would be more secure. However, work was progressing rather slowly on the courthouse. A new view of Nevada City, published in March, showed the courthouse as it would appear, but in fact only the basement and half the outer walls were in place. The contractor promised completion in three months if fair weather continued.

Mining was at a standstill in many parts of the county, thanks to miners' strikes against the water suppliers. Ditch companies were charging fifty cents an inch for water, which most miners refused to pay. Meetings had been held in many districts, and it was reported they would not work the diggings until the price was cut in half. In a normal season there should have been ample water in streams and creeks to satisfy most needs, but this was an unusually dry and cold winter. Explained the *Journal*:

In this vicinity and further north, the nights are so excessively cold as to prevent mining [from] being carried on only on the smallest scale. The water and gravel that are left in sluiceboxes over night are found too much frozen the next morning to go to washing, with any hope of saving the gold, and so nothing is done until the sluice-boxes thaw out. This prevents the hiring of extra men, and so the large class that are dependent on wages for support are obliged to shift for themselves as best they can.

On the other hand, prospects for hard rock mining appeared better than ever. The *Journal* boasted on February 29:

We believe this to be the only gold-mining in which capitalists can engage without risks; and in quartz mining there need be no greater risks run than the mere prospecting of leads. When it is fully ascertained that a lead will pay, machinery can be erected and the work of making money can commence at once.

In the early days of quartz mining the richest company which could be formed would be made to fail from the excess and extravagance of its expenditures. Mills then cost $50,000 to $100,000. Now, we undertake to say that a mill better than any of those which cost such princely sums can be erected for $7,500, including a steam engine for the propelling power. And if waterpower can be obtained where the mill is wanted, then a much smaller sum will suffice.... Men of experience have come to the conclusion that the simplest machinery is the best. Hence it is that [stampmills] are now almost exclusively used.

The Chalk Bluff Ditch Company capitulated to demands in March, lowering water rates to twenty-five cents; miners eagerly returned to claims at Red Dog and Walloupa. Other suppliers soon followed their example, but San Francisco bankers continued to worry about the lack of rain; William Tecumseh Sherman feared it could bring on "another hard year," and warned his parent company in St. Louis that gold receipts from the interior towns had fallen off and gold bars were practically non-existent. His March shipment would consist mostly of coins and exchange notes.

At the opening of California's first railroad, the 22½ mile Sacramento Valley line, Sherman gave a short speech. The *Journal* printed a train schedule in its issue of February 8, and observed:

Little did the projector of the *Journal* think, at the time the first number was issued, that in 1856 it would advertise a California railroad. Yet such is the fact. And we are glad to learn, as we have done, from the Superintendent, that the road is now paying much better than was anticipated.

IV

JESSE WALL'S BUSINESS had failed, wrote Mary on April 2. Mrs. Wall dismissed her girl servant, and both women stopped sending ironing out. This saved each family $2 a week, and the women found it rather pleasant to work together. And although Mary still thought $70 rather steep for board and room for her and Fred, she realized how badly Mrs. Wall needed the money.

We shall decide [what to do] for the summer when Niles gets home [from Quincy], which will be in three days more. He has been absent but 10 days, and after his *long* absence in the winter it seems quite short, yet I am impatient for him to come. It is raining, so that I cant get over to Debs, and I am very lonely.

Cornelia had expressed concern in her last letter over Addison's sudden interest in Hattie Backus. She wondered what connection there was (if any) between Addison's published poetry and the young lady in question. Addison was rather young, and besides, wasn't there some understanding between Hattie and Harvey Wickes? Mary hastened to clarify:

Oh, about that poetry, and the young lady who played the guitar— you need not be at all *afraid*. In the first place, she is one of the sweetest, most winning girls I ever knew, and would be a good wife—*I think* for *any* one—*but* that poetry Add wrote before ever she came up here at all, and so of course it had no reference to her. I suspect there is someone in *the "Jerseys"* who would preclude all the other loves from her mind— even Harvey's—and I dont think Harvey had ever thought of *any* girl as a wife—so he will not be heart broken on her account, though he says she is just such a girl as he would choose for a wife *if* he wanted one.

Didnt I tell you how large Add has grown? He is a great broad shouldered stout looking *man*, and a fine looking one too. He comes up to wait on me when Niles is gone—true, he almost always forgets half a dozen times what I want, but I can most always wait a week or so. I laugh at him about it, he *ought* to be an old bachelor, hadnt he—but perhaps if he had a little "merry hearted Nellie" to wait on, he would be more thoughtful. He is a dear good brother, and a great comfort to me.

A third trial of Rodman Backus had resulted in a verdict of murder, but the supreme court agreed with his attorneys that the lower court had erred in allowing him to be tried for murder after he had been convicted of a lesser crime. Once again it ordered a new trial, this time on a charge of manslaughter only. Meanwhile Rodman resided in the San Francisco jail.

I think of going to Downieville with Niles next time, if I can get my sewing done. I have bought a summer silk, of which I will send a scrap. I wish you could tell me how to make it—it only cost $12, which is very cheap here. I think of making it plain waist with [bretelles] of ribbon, with a bow behind and before. Do you think it will be pretty. Deb has one similar, only green and black instead of blue—it is prettier than mine. You see, Nellie, I cannot help dressing more expensively than I would at home. Every one dresses extravagantly here, and I try to dress as plainly as I can without being odd. You know the "Judge's wife" is very much criticised, and every one knows what our salary is—I ought not to care, I suppose, what others say—I dont much.

The supreme court reversed Judge Searls on the question of incorporation of towns and colleges, calling it a ministerial act that could not be delegated to a judicial body. The consequences might have been disastrous for many cities, including Grass Valley, which had been incorporated in the same manner; but Senator Waite's bill had passed both houses and awaited only the governor's signature to become law. Then the town trustees could petition the board of supervisors for reincorporation.

But until that happened there could be serious problems, as Addison noted in the April 11 *Journal*:

The authority of the town Marshal and his assistants is taken from them, the town ordinances are null and void, and rioters and drunkards can have as good a time as they wish in Nevada. . . . Every good citizen will . . . be indignant that the quiet and good order of our town and the safety of our citizens should be offered as a sacrifice to test the soundness of a legal quibble.

Addison's prophecy may have inspired local hoodlums, to judge by subsequent events reported in the *Journal*:

The night following the news of the dissolution of the government of Nevada, hell broke loose. A large party of men came into town for the purpose of getting drunk, and having a row. fights were going on in several places at once. Pistol shooting, outrageous bellowings, discord infernal, kept many citizens awake, while an alarm of fire was momentarily expected.

On Sunday night the rows reached a climax. One man was stabbed nearly in front of our office, a lager bier saloon on Commercial street was the scene of a fight that drew a large crowd, and a pistol fired across the street struck a man on the corner of the eye, but luckily did no damage. Confusion was supreme. Every night since, there have been rows of greater or less magnitude.... Many of our citizens who doubted the value of the old organization, now look anxiously for its successor. It will probably be a fortnight before the bill can be received here, and the new officers elected.

Another recent decision of the supreme court limiting justice court jurisdiction over mining disputes to cases of $200 or less transferred the most profitable litigation to district courts. Because it would be nearly impossible to make a decent living from justice court fees, and his stint as editor of the *Journal* was nearing its end, Addison resigned as justice of the peace and became David Belden's law partner.

Belden and Niles opened an office in Bicknell's Block, the city's newest and most prestigious office building on Broad Street, between the United States and Union hotels. In his "valedictory" editorial on April 25, Addison summed up his journalistic career:

The call at this present moment being for "copy," and there being no copy, we take this opportunity of bidding ... an affectionate farewell.... We have been connected with the press just three months and twenty— five days neither more nor less.

Casting an admiring glance backward over our brief but brilliant career, we regret to say that we see many errors ... that we might have shunned. Once, in a moment of inspiration, we conceived a brilliant pun, which we totally forgot to insert until it was too late. On another occasion we copied a San Francisco advertisement as an item of news. We shall never hear the last of it....

Several times we have injudiciously puffed clothing stores and other institutions, confidently expecting to be arrayed in gorgeous apparel free of expense, because of these delicate little flatteries, as we have been informed was usually the case. It is needless to add, our expectations have never been realized. We are the victim of misplaced confidence. We give it as an astounding fact that the sum total of substantial favors, which we have received ... amounts to one copy of "Phoenixiana" and one Jack-knife.

In this estimate we leave out sundry bottles of champaigne and chunks of indigestible cake, the votive offerings of happy pairs ("the currents of whose lives have mingled into one"), and also the proffered loan, upon one occasion, of six revolvers, one sword, a derringer, two bowie knives and a blunderbuss, all of which (the revolvers we mean, not the cake and wine) we thankfully but firmly declined. Some wretch

. . . has feloniously taken and carried away our "Phoenixiana." That that unprincipled individual may laugh himself into an apoplexy over the humors of "Squibob," is our fervent prayer.

We have had some experiences. We have received any quantity of good advice, in the conduct of the *Journal*, all and sundry of which, we are happy to say, we never followed in the slightest particular. One very curious aesthetical fact has come to our notice, viz: that when the *Journal* for any cause has come down on any person, or institution, the particular enemies of that person or institution always pronounce that article the very best that has yet appeared.

Several times we have been patted on the shoulder and kindly advised to "hit 'em again," when in reality, owing to the fact that we seldom read the *Journal*, we were in total ignorance of who or what we had been hitting. . . . If any person should ask us if we like the business of newspaper-making, our answer [is] . . . emphatically, no! We can't stand the *press*. To write is well enough, but to write *to order* is a bore. "The voice of the people is the voice of God," but the cry for *copy* is the voice of the *Devil*.

Panama Train Wreck

CHAPTER 26

VIGILANCE COMMITTEE

May–June 1856

I

*J*UDGE SEARLS had a conflict of interest. Because of his earlier connection with several cases to be heard in his court between April 21 and May 17, he traded benches with District Judge Howell of Placer County. It was hard on Mary, who had counted on his being home, but there was a chance she might accompany him on a coming trip, she told her mother on May 2:

In a few weeks [Niles] goes to Marysville and *perhaps* I shall go with him. That is one reason I am hurrying so much with my sewing. I shall be pretty well fitted to go this summer. I have the prettiest bonnet I have seen in *ever* so long—a plain straw—fine—trimmed with white ribbon, and small white rosebuds in a full cap—and such a sweet shape, and a mantilla which is elegant. It is scarf-shape, embroidered and trimmed

247

with quillings of ribbon at top and bottom, and a deep rich fringe at the lower edge. It is black—cost a good deal—but Hattie said she couldnt suit herself with any other and so she got this.... We (that is, Deb, Delight and I) have been sending to Hattie [in San Francisco] for bonnets, mantillas &c, as we could not suit ourselves here....

Luther Wickes, the younger brother of Deb, Delight and Harvey, was coming to California, according to the latest information from home. Mary commented:

I suppose they have heard from Luther by Telegraph at Charlies—as the steamer is in—but it is so wet and muddy that I cant go to hear the news.

Niles came home for a brief visit, and to allow her more time with him, Mary asked Addison to write the next letter home, which he did:

The term of District Court closed yesterday, and Niles has started for Plumas county to hold term there. I have been quite busy   with some tedious cases, and feel quite relieved at the close of the term....

On the return of Senator Waite from the legislature, my duties as Editor closed. I was very glad of it too, for I was heartily tired of the business.... I was in a manner forced to consult him and conduct the paper in accordance with his views, which in many things differed essentially from my own. The result was that during the latter part of the term I wrote but little for the paper, merely managing the paper generally, while the [editorials] were nearly all written by Waite. If I were part owner, and could control the Journal *wholly* myself, I would like the business well....

California begins to seem like a home to me, and I think now it may be a permanent one. California is changing, the population becoming more fixed, and becoming more fit for a home. There is a great chance for improvement yet, however. I think rascality and corruption is more popular here than in any other state in the whole world. San Francisco especially is, without any disguise, a perfect sink of corruption. The whole country is now in a perfect fever of excitement from an event that lately transpired there.

James King of William, Editor of the Evening Bulletin, was shot down in the street a day or two ago by another editor of that city, an escaped convict from Sing Sing. The Bulletin has taken a bold and fearless stand in denouncing villany and villains, and his death (if he dies), is the result of a [preconceived] plan of those whom he has denounced. 5000 of the most respectable and best citizens of San F. are enrolled in a vigilance committee, and we expect every moment a telegraphic despatch that

King is dead, the jail taken by the committee and his assassin hung.

It will be strict justice, and the only way to obtain justice there, for experience has proved that the law is powerless in San F. to convict a murderer. Jas. King is the idol almost of all but southern fire-eaters and gamblers.... I think 500 men would go from Nevada if the call was made to assist the San F. Vigilance Committee.... The prompt action of the vigilance Com. of San F. will do much good, however, and I think no man will dare to draw a revolver in the streets of San F. again soon, except in self defence....

We expect Luther by the steamer which is now about due. Delight has gone to San F. to meet him, and to visit Harriet Backus, and they will all come up to Nevada together.

Addison avoided any mention of the very close connection of Harriet's brother to the excitement at San Francisco. Rodman Backus was represented by the same team of lawyers who were defending Casey (who had shot King), and Cora (who had killed a U.S. Marshal). Hundreds of San Franciscans were clamoring for the vigilance committee to hang Backus, Cora, and Casey.

R. B. Wallace of Nevada County had gone to San Francisco on business and wrote to a Nevada City friend on May 19:

Exciting times here yesterday. About 1 o'clock nearly 3000 of us marched up to the jail and took the prisoners Cora and Casey. It was the grandest sight I ever witnessed. Every man was cool and determined. When we got the prisoners there was no noise or confusion. We have them secured. I select the guard, and if they escape 'twill be no fault of mine. I station one man in the room with Cora and allow no one to enter except Oscar [Smith] and myself. He is chief of the [vigilance committee] police, and I am his deputy.

It keeps us busy—get very little sleep. 'Twas mighty ticklish work yesterday for Oscar and myself, for if the prisoners had been taken by force, we should have been the ones to take them. We started up ahead of the military to the jail and had two carriages on the corner of Dupont and Broadway for the prisoners. There was such a formidable crowd that the outsiders thought they had better yield quietly. So our object was accomplished without bloodshed. The Executive committee have not met yet this morning.

I don't know where this will end. I have not yet attended to any of our business matters. I shall not leave here until this is over. The steamer is not in yet. I must close to attend to duty.

Backus narrowly escaped the fate of Cora and Casey. His uncle's foresight in joining the vigilance committee, plus money in the right hands, allowed Backus to slip away to San Quentin to serve a sentence of 2½ years for manslaughter. He also agreed to pay a $3000 fine and drop further legal action. It was a small price to pay for his life; especially when Warden James Estell, a friend of Casey and Governor Johnson, promised him trusty privileges.

Luther arrived at San Francisco at the conclusion of these events and could scarcely credit his eyes. It seemed to him he had reached the "climax of horrors" after surviving the wreck of a passenger train while crossing the Isthmus of Panama. Fifteen persons died in the accident and sixty were badly injured. Later, Mary recounted the adventures of the young druggist to Cornelia:

Luther's was a narrow escape. From the car next [to] the one he was in, only two persons were taken out alive and they were left to die in the hospital. He made himself useful in various ways—setting bones— binding wounds—administering medicines—there being but one regular physician on board.... When he reached San Francisco ... the first thing he saw ... was two men dangling by the neck from a window, with an immense crowd gathered around them, and ... 15,000 men attending the funeral of James King of Wm.... Delight was in San Fran. through the whole of it....

How does it sound to you at home? What does Pa say to the measures taken by the vigilance Committee? I often wonder. Here but one opinion prevails among the orderly respectable citizens. The idea of justice by Law is a complete farce.... Gamblers and shoulder strikers had every thing their own way—ruled and stuffed the ballot box—and ruled and bribed the officials.

There was but one resort. The whole country has endorsed the course of the Vigilance Committee. They are the best and most substantial of our citizens—the bone and sinew of the country, and have done their work with coolness and deliberation. There has been no mob—no disorder, but the utmost decision and calmness.... James King [was] almost universally known and loved in his capacity as editor, and never did a *state* grieve with such heartfelt sorrow at the death of any one man.

When the bells tolled in Nevada to announce his death here, one would have thought each person he met had lost a near and dear friend, all business was suspended, the streets hung in mourning, and groups of men with sad countenances were seen here and there talking in low tones. All mirth was suspended. A meeting was held and resolutions of sympathy with his family passed—addresses delivered by Mr. Warren, Churchman and others, and a subscription limited to $1 [per person] taken up for the family of King. It is supposed that nearly $50,000 have been raised in the state, $25,000 having been given in San Fran. alone.

A former acquaintance from New York and Nevada City had fallen victim to the vigilance committee, Mary reported:

They *had* Yankee Sullivan, and it was rumored were going to send him back to N.Y. in irons, which trouble, however, he has saved them—yesterday he committed suicide in the Committee rooms.

Yankee Sullivan's crimes, as eventually published in his "confession," were that he and other precinct officers were offered $500 to falsify returns for a candidate in the San Francisco election of 1855. One official was willing, but Sullivan balked because he doubted the man would pay. Another candidate offered $300, and this, too, was turned down because he had treated Sullivan badly in the past. Yankee had knowledge of other deals where from $100 to $500 was paid to change results, but he claimed to have received nothing himself.

Sullivan had gone to New York the previous winter, but came back to San Francisco in March and he announced plans for a $1000-purse prize fight with Steve Simmons. His timing was very bad, for on May 25 he and five others were arrested by vigilance committee police. The were tried and found guilty by the committee on May 27 for disturbing the peace, destroying the "purity" of elections, invading the sanctity of ballot boxes, and being "perfect pests to society." All were sentenced to be transported out of American territory as soon as possible, and ordered not to return under penalty of death.

When Sullivan's lifeless body was discovered in his cell at committee headquarters, many in the Irish community were easily persuaded he had been murdered. The arteries in one arm had been cut with a dinner knife, causing the fighter to bleed to death. Ten thousand people were said to have passed through the coroner's office to view the corpse before it was turned over to his widow and child.

The inquest identified the deceased as Francis Murray, alias James, alias "Yankee" Sullivan, born in Ireland thirty-seven years before. In his cell was a letter from his wife, confiscated by the committee:

Dear James;

I take my pen in hand to write these fue lines to you for I do not no wot to do for I have not got one cent in the world and they will not let me come in to see you   I have been three times to see if they would not let me in to see you; Dear James how are I to folow you When thay Seand you A Way   My heart is almost broke Aboute you   I wishe you to write me a fue lines out so that I can no wot to do   I will wate wile youe rite me a fue lines

So no More at preasent from your Affectionate Wife untill Death

Emily Mary Sullevan

The committee denied any responsibility for Sullivan's death, claiming he was despondent because he expected to be hanged or returned to the Sydney penal colony from which he had escaped in 1840. Distraught and penitent, Sullivan had pleaded with the committee, offering to reform if they would set him free. Being refused, Sullivan took his own life.

Good riddance, according to the Nevada *Journal*:

The *State Journal* and other kindred sheets are making a terrible hellaballo about the suicide of a wretch known over the world as Yankee Sullivan. . . . He became a lawful target, and bid for bullets years ago. The man who had devoted his life to rid society of such pests would be entitled to the gratitude of mankind. No punishment ought to follow him, any more than for the destruction of reptiles, rats and vermin. . . .

Remorse and cowardly fears drove the wretch to end his days, which had he not been a hardened rascal, he would have terminated long ago. Talk about the murder of such a man! Why, if the Vigilance Committee had done nothing else but scare the life out of *him*, they are entitled to lasting gratitude.

II

EDITOR WAITE was infuriated by results of the city election. Democrats had won every contest. Margins were decisive in all but the city marshal race, where Henry Plumer narrowly defeated the popular incumbent, Dave Johnson. Waite blamed the American party's defeat on dishonest tactics, claiming Democrats had brought in Irish voters from outside the city limits:

Such an election is not indigenous to the quiet habits of a mountain population. It properly is the spontaneous growth of such political soil and climate as San Francisco or the Five Points of New York. Bad whisky, bad English and bad temper, were the principal characteristics of the day. A squad of noisy bipeds surrounded the polls at an early hour and remained during the day, to the exclusion of good citizens.

Everything high and low that an enthusiastic phalanx physician could swear was human, was brought up "to assist in preserving the liberties of the country." . . . What with outside pressure, gallons of rot gut, and hard swearing, the phalanxers won the day. Among the quiet, orderly, property holding citizens of the city there has been since the election but one universal sentiment expressed—that of disgust. A celtic horde plundered the citizens of their elective rights. . . .

It was remarked that not a drunken Know Nothing was seen around the polls during the day. . . . The infallible symptoms of democracy— broken English, hiccuping and yelling—were too strong to put any one at a loss to diagnose. . . . Good citizens desirous of order, and not bigoted with so-called Democracy voted the American ticket . . . . of all the men within the city proper who pay to keep up a city organization, two-thirds voted for the American candidate for Marshal. But outsiders from Rough & Ready, Red Dog, Alpha, Rush Creek, and in short from almost every mining camp in the county, would have beaten by hard swearing the "oldest man in the world."

The *Journal* published its first political cartoon, a crude woodcut of an Irishman and an election official. The caption read:

Officer—"Could'nt you swear now that you consider yourself entitled to vote?"
Voter—(holding up his right hand) "I board at Sweeney's, be jabers."
Officer—"MICHAEL O'FLAHERTY"—(sticks the ticket in the box.)

Lewis Sweeney owned a saloon and restaurant on Pine Street. The Irish-born but newly naturalized proprietor had enlarged his establishment two months earlier to provide lodging, thereby adding further competition for the city's financially troubled hotels. The United States Hotel was closed, its owners bankrupt; foreclosure had begun on the Union Hotel, its 1855 taxes still unpaid. The Metropolis (once Phelps) hotel had changed hands again and again—the present owner was being sued, and the sheriff had attached the lot to satisfy a separate judgment against a second party.

The *Journal*'s attitude extended beyond the political and economic scene. In contrast to its normally sympathetic treatment of accidents and personal misfortune, the paper came near to chuckling when a son of Erin was caught beneath a wall of earth that caved in on Cement Hill. A powerful stream of water from a hydraulic hose soon washed away the pile of earth and exposed the unfortunate victim. But all was well, Waite reported: "A little whiskey soon enabled him to declare he wasn't hurt a bit."

III

WIVES OF SEVERAL lawyers spoke of going to Downieville with their husbands on June 2, but most changed their minds at the last minute.

Mary was still undecided as late as June 1; much as she looked forward to accompanying Niles, the fact that her friend Hattie Backus had come to Nevada City with Delight and Charley made her hesitate. Furthermore, taking Fred would make a lot of trouble—"there wouldn't be much fun," she guessed.

By staying home she could save money toward her goal of returning to Durden Cottage. Lately she had worried a good deal about the lack of a rail around the piazza at their boarding house. The unprotected deck was high above the ground and she feared Fred would fall and hurt himself. She told Cornelia, "If they dont build a railing at once we shall leave as soon as our tenants find another house."

In the end Hattie decided matters by inviting herself to Downieville for a week. She was emotionally exhausted and needed to distance herself from the terrifying events at San Francisco.

The stage carried them to within six miles of Downieville, and from there they rode horses. The weather was wonderful, the scenery magnificent, and the ladies of Downieville invited them into their homes on a daily basis. The trip was beneficial to everyone, and Fred was no trouble at all.

When they returned to Nevada City, Hattie helped Mary pack up her belongings, and Addison, Mary, and Fred moved back into Durden Cottage on June 20. Three weeks later Mary wrote Cornelia:

I am glad we came back, as Fred is so much happier and healthier— he can run out doors here whenever he wishes. Our trees have grown finely, shade the yard a great deal. We have some martins that sing very sweetly in our cage, you can see it in the picture of our houses.... My flowers grow finely—blossom all the time. Charlie has a beautiful yard—a sweep of flowers, and it refreshes many eyes beside ours. Scarcely a person ever passes without stopping to admire it, and every day we hear some[one] say "how pleasant it is to see such flowers once more. I have seen none since before I left home." Our trees too are admired-our yards are the pleasantest in town.

During their absence from Nevada City a fight in Lewis and Wright's Main Street Billiard Saloon had resulted in the death of a teamster, and proprietor George Lewis was arrested. His attorneys traveled to Downieville to seek bail, which Judge Searls denied. Until district court opened in the new courthouse on July 21, the popular Nevada City businessman would have to remain in jail.

Criminal activity everywhere seemed to be on the increase—especially the variety of highway robbery practiced by the likes of Tom Bell and his gang. Actions of the vigilance committee encouraged similar efforts in other towns, and citizens were inclined to adopt a tougher stance toward criminals. Nevertheless, the committee was not without critics, particularly in the Democratic party. The San Francisco *Herald* published a letter from a Nevada City correspondent who claimed certain Nevada County politicians had changed their minds since the shooting at Lewis and Wright's saloon:

The perpetrator of the deed was George Lewis, a prominent Know Nothing and a Vigilante. Yesterday, every man of this party was eulogizing the conduct of the Vigilance committee. This morning there is not a man among them that is not for law and order.

The *Journal* indignantly refuted the charge:

Nearly every man of the American party, and the honest portion of the Democracy, are in favor of the Vigilantes. The [recent] homicide ... did not change public sentiment a whit. Did not the District Attorney, who is a warm supporter of the Vigilance Committee, go to Downieville, to use his influence against the liberation of Lewis on bail?—and did not Judge Searls, another Vigilante, refuse to allow such bail? George Lewis himself, asks no other privileges than are accorded to others of his countrymen.

It is a prominent part of the Vigilantees creed, that the laws shall be upheld in all their power. The only complaint is that they have not been so upheld. The District Attorney of this County, and Judge Searls, are exhibiting the prominent feature of the Vigilance Committee's code, put in practice, when they carry out the law in all its force and rigor. The want of such officers in other parts of the State, has created the necessity for Vigilance Committees.

The *Journal's* categorizing of Niles as a vigilante was mostly supposition, for Judge Searls avoided public statements of a political nature. However, it was a supposition shared by the *Democrat*. Although Mary and Addison made no secret of their own opinions in private letters to the east, even they did not presume to speak for or quote Niles.

Criticism of the committee increased when Supreme Court Justice David Terry was arrested for defending himself and friends against an armed attack in San Francisco. Edwin Waite and others argued with dubious logic that Terry had no legitimate business in that city; the vigilante explanation that Terry's friends were being "arrested" for "illegal" acts was equally unconvincing, for they were charged with bringing weapons to San Francisco at the request of California's governor, who was trying to restore government authority.

Judge Terry had cut one of his assailants with a bowie knife, and the committee said it would try him for murder if the man died. Many persons were eager to see Terry hanged, but others thought this would be foolhardy. Hard questions were raised about the committee and the direction it was taking. At Nevada City, *Democrat* editor William Anderson called it a "treasonable organization," and said:

Men have been taken from their own houses in the night time, confined for a day or so in the dungeons of the Vigilance Committee, and before their friends even knew the charges preferred against them, have been shipped on board of vessels, and sent out of the country, and their families left to starve.

As usual, the *Journal* disagreed:

There must be a new hand at the bellows in the shop of our neighbor, or some hope of a reaction in public sentiment must permeate the bosom of the hitherto cautious editor. Had a modicum of the usual caution manifested by that paper, been observed in penning the leader of the latter number, so many sweeping and unauthorized assertions would not have stared its readers in the face....

Now, we ask who have been left to starve, by this forced exodus of villains? We know of none. If there are any such, they have heretofore fed on the wages of sin and iniquity, and it were better to eat the bread of a pauper, than that bought with the stealings of a thief, or the price of blood from the hands of a murderer.

So much for Mrs. Yankee Sullivan and her son.

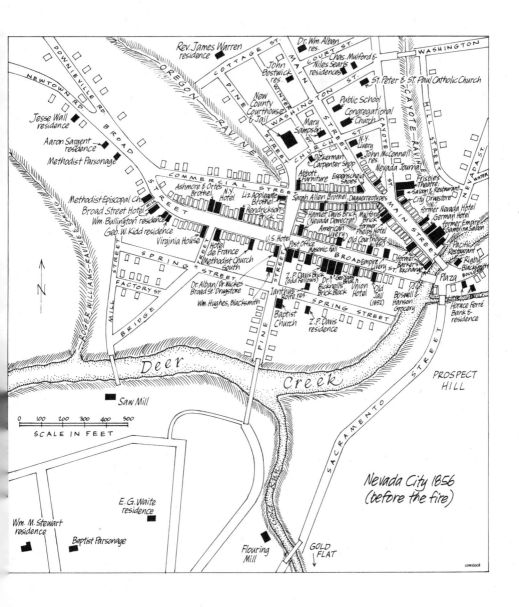

Nevada City 1856 (before the fire)

comstock

Corner Pine and Broad Streets

CHAPTER 27

RUINED DREAMS

July–August 1856

I

*T*HE NEW COURTHOUSE stood on a commanding site and was the first building one saw on approaching the city. The upper stories were of red brick, but the foundation and outer jail walls were of granite, as were the front stairs, pilasters, sills and caps. County offices were on the first floor of the two story building. The top floor contained a 36 by 50 foot courtroom, separated from a pair of jury rooms by sound-deadened walls, finished with three coats of plaster. An immense chandelier hung from the 18-foot ceiling on a lacquered brass hook. The style was said to "approach" the Ionic style of architecture.

A 4-foot high wooden enclosure topped with turned rails separated spectators from the court. Inside it were boxes (3 by 4 feet) for sheriff and prisoners, and these were elevated 2 feet above the main floor, the same as the judge's platform. "Altogether," pronounced the *Journal*, "this room is one of the finest in the state." It had cost $50,000, and the builder swore he hadn't made a cent of profit, although his original contract had been for $41,500.

County officers began moving in on June 30, and by Independence Day were settled in. During the same week Dr. Harvey Wickes took possession of Dr. Alban's drugstore on the corner of Broad and Pine streets and listed among the items he would stock (in addition to drugs and patent medicines): spices, chemicals, wine, brandy, gin, dye stuffs, paint, five varieties of oil (fish, sperm, castor, lard, and polar), and canary seed.

Placerville burned to the ground on July 6, and Georgetown went up in flames a day later. Because some telegraph lines were destroyed and communication disrupted, false rumors circulated at Sacramento that Coloma and Nevada City had burned also. On July 16 Marysville experienced a major fire, and only a few of her "fireproof" buildings lived up to their reputations. The *Journal* took occasion to issue a warning:

FIRES—Too much caution cannot be observed against fires on the part of our citizens. The wooden buildings of the city at the present season of the year are dry as tinder, and but a careless spark is needed to destroy millions of valuable property, and cause a great deal of suffering. The fate of Placerville and Georgetown should be a warning to a town which has several years almost miraculously escaped destructive ravages by fire.

The California Minstrels were replaced at Frisbie's Theater by a dramatic company starring Edwin Booth. It was the young actor's second appearance at Nevada City, but the first in which he took lead roles in such plays as *Taming of the Shrew*, *Richelieu*, *Hamlet*, and the popular new hit, *Iron Chest*. Of Booth's performance as Richelieu, the *Journal* said:

It is the opinion of many ... that Booth personates the great Cardinal more to nature and life than any actor who has appeared on the boards in this city. The house was densely crowded on Wednesday night, and all were delighted with the performance.... Hamlet was produced to a full house last evening, with complete success.... Mr. Edwin Booth takes his benefit this (Friday) evening, on which occasion he will appear in the character of Richelieu, one of his favorite pieces, supported by the entire strength of the company.

Judge Searls was expected from Downieville Friday, in time for Booth's benefit, and was to inaugurate the newly completed courtroom on the following Monday.

II

SATURDAY, JULY 19, began like any other summer day: the sun rose, the temperature climbed, and residents of the city stayed inside or under cover when they could. The only change was a brisk breeze which rose in the west about midday and would have been more welcome had it been less warm, for it was blowing out of the scorching Sacramento Valley.

Niles and Mary were enjoying their first moments together in several weeks, and the first in their own house for many months. Mary wished Niles might rest a little before resuming his work, but already he was anxious to see his office and courtroom and look over the calendar for the term that would begin in two days.

Several blocks away, across from the reopened United States Hotel, Bill Hughes and Jim Selkirk were hard at work in their Pine Street blacksmith shop. It was a busy time of year, and in summer they fired up the forge early to work as long as possible in the predawn coolness. By midday their shop would be the devil's own inferno, but John Blasauf's City Brewery was fortunately next door—a steady supply of iced lager beer in buckets helped Jim and Bill make it through the day.

Next to the brewery was Harvey's drugstore, which occupied a portion of the only brick building on Broad Street above Pine. Most buildings between it and the Methodist Church were new wood-frame structures, rebuilt after last year's fire. It was risky to build with wood, but cheaper and faster than brick. Getting back in business quickly was important, especially for hotel owners.

Fire was on everyone's mind. It was talked about, prayed about, and feared. When the first terrible cry was raised in midafternoon, fear seized the people of Nevada City, but it also made them do what had to be done. The first men to see the flames darting from Hughes' smithy rushed to Pine Street with axes, buckets and blankets, hoping to confine the fire.

But this time the wind was their adversary too, and the stiff breeze flung burning embers into the air and onto roofs like rockets on the Fourth of July; within minutes the brewery was afire. The United States Hotel roof ignited, and burning shakes went flying over Broad Street.

Tallman Rolfe was amazed to see the fire moving as fast as a man could walk. He watched as "vast flakes of flames" played leapfrog, jumping over one building to ignite another, farther away. Mr. Bartol ordered his employees to release sixteen horses from the California Stage Company stable a quarter of a mile away, and they barely managed the task in the five minutes left before the stable caught fire.

Rolfe, T. Ellard Beans, Sherman Fletcher and some others were caught inside Hamlet Davis's fireproof building. Most county officials had moved out two weeks earlier, but it still housed the *Democrat* office and plant, a provision store, and the bank of A. J. Hagan. The occupants ran frantically from window to window, closing heavy iron shutters to seal the building. Before all doors and windows on the street level could be shut, frame buildings on either side were burning.

Fletcher and Beans ran upstairs to shutter the openings. Glancing out a second story window, Beans saw the surrounding fire would cut off their only escape in a matter of seconds. Shouting to his companion to follow, Beans climbed onto the sill and jumped to a shed roof and from there to the alley below. From the ground he saw Fletcher still at the window. "Hurry!" he shouted, but the young attorney shook his head and closed the shutters.

Beans found the Rolfe brothers and learned that three others— Hagan, Johnson and Pearson—were inside also. It was too late to rescue them. They would have to remain there and hope the pioneer fireproof would live up to its name. As the men outside watched, flames and smoke from the three-story United States Hotel spread out and hid the Davis block from view.

Meanwhile, from hills above the city, residents gathered outside their homes to watch in fear and fascination as Nevada City was devoured. At first it seemed unlikely the blaze would threaten their dwellings, because previous fires had been confined to downtown streets. As Mary told her mother:

It commenced on the opposite side of the town from us ... in 10 minutes the flames were beyond all control and sweeping directly towards us. In 30 minutes our houses were on fire, and before reaching them, all the heart of the town had been swept away by the furious flames.

I took Fred and an armful of clothing and my jewelry and spoons, and ran till I was beyond the reach of fire.... In the meantime Niles tried to save the house till all hope was gone, and then seized what trunks, clothing &c he could and threw them down into a ravine back of the house.... I thought I would take Fred to Mr. Walls [on West Broad Street] and return for more clothes, but found their house too was in danger, and dared not leave him.... The wind blew a gale—and whirlwinds carried the dust and fire up in columns and then hurled them in every direction. In two hours from the breaking out of the fire, the whole town was in ashes. It is literally *wiped out....*

[Niles] saved a great deal ... more than I expected to have when I left the house. Had I been there to tell him where things were, he could have saved all that was most valuable—but I dared not stay.... I have saved sufficient clothing of all kinds for myself and Fred to make us very comfortable till I have time to make more . . . but have lost many things that can never be replaced. . . . all my gold and silver thimbles, every article of furniture but the sofa, and nearly all of Niles's clothes. Our beds were carried out but burned afterwards—as did many other things.

Deb Mulford had walked nearly a mile to a friend's house, the friend carrying Fanny and assorted bundles of clothing, silver and jewelry. Others managed to save trunks belonging to Deb, Delight, and Hattie. Deb, a semi-invalid because of a supposed heart condition, had not walked so far in two years, but except for feeling tired for a day or two she was none the worse for her exercise. Wrote Mary:

When I found where she was, I went out to her, and the next morning we rode back and took possession of Mr. Harrison's large pleasant house [on upper Broad Street], which was not burned—though within two buildings of those that were. Mr. and Mrs. Harrison were at the [Sierra] summit, but their brother sent for us and gave us the keys and told us to take possession till they came. Deb had a girl, though a poor one (had she been a good one, she might have saved nearly everything) and we went to housekeeping at once. . . . I have one white spread, one pillow, one tablecloth and two dish towels towards *housekeeping*, and spoons and forks, a broken sofa, and one bureau drawer.

It has of course been a very great loss to us—we will have to begin back at the beginning again. We have just about as [much] capital to commence with as when we were married, but have a *salary* which will at least support us—though the value of scrip is much depreciated now. If it rises again, we can soon retrieve our loss.

Mary referred to the fact that Niles and other state officers were paid not in cash but in scrip issued by the state of California. No one would accept scrip at face value, so the actual salary received was much less than showed on the books.

No, it *cannot* be retrieved—our pleasant home—our *first* house, our beautiful trees and flowers can not be restored—but we ought not to complain—while we are spared to each other and have enough to make us comfortable.

Many have lost their *all*, and worse than all the rest, many lives were lost. 10 of our first citizens were burned in the *"fire proof"* houses, and two others are still suffering and hardly expected to live—one, Mr. Anderson, a friend of Addisons—editor of the Democrat—the other, George Young, his brother-in-law, of whom perhaps you have heard me speak. The owners of brick buildings seemed perfectly infatuated—

some shut themselves in their buildings, thinking to be safe there and perhaps save the buildings—others were shut in by accident. Mr. Fletcher—formerly a student with Niles and Tweed—lately a partner of Tweeds, was among the burned.

Among the Harrison party which had left Nevada City before the fire for a holiday trip in the mountains were Addison, Charley, Delight, and Hattie Backus, who reacted with shock when they saw the blackened ruins.

Those who were at the summit say they can hardly believe there was ever any town here—our beautiful new court house—*all* the churches are gone. The blackened walls of the brick buildings alone remain of the old town. . . . We are glad Charlie was not at home for I have no doubt he would have risked his life to save his brick building—it didnt take fire until 8 in the evening, and would not then, but a dry goods building close by, supposed to have been fire proof, was burning, and the heat being so intense and long continued, heat [passed] through the iron doors and, it is supposed, set fire to some papers &c in the upper story.

If some person could have got in on the opposite side and put out the fire, it could have been saved. That is the way all the brick buildings that were not burned were saved, but there was no possible way to enter except by a door close by the burning building, and Charlie says he should have tried it had he been here. Arthur [Hagadorn] had his hand on the door to open it, and one of the [doctors] here assured him he could not live an instant if he did so; the hot air would strike him with such force. I think there was more than one of the summit party whose lives were saved by their absence, as several [had investments] in the brick buildings. They were all proof against ordinary fires—but *such* a fire was never seen before, even in California.

Two weeks later, the town was rebuilding, and in an optimistic mood. Mary told her mother:

. . . could you see it now, you would hardly know the town had been *burned*. The wooden houses are nearly *all* rebuilt, and brick [is] lying in every direction, ready for replacing the old brick, and building new brick buildings. The walls of Charlies building are not injured, and for $2500 he can make it as good as ever, and has made a contract for doing so. They think some of living in the upper part themselves. . . .

When they all came from the summit, our family was too large, so we chose from among the numerous and pressing offers of homes, one with Bill Stewart . . . [who] has built a fine large house quite out of town, had two large unoccupied rooms [upstairs], one of which he has given to

McConnell's family . . . and the other to us. They are to furnish our room when the furniture comes for which they have sent.

They have a large garden, nice piazza's railed in. An excellent housekeeper, a little Indian girl to take care of their baby and do errands, a man to take care of their gardens, and McConnell has a nurse for his baby. I only came here last night, but as near as I can judge now, shall do very well here. . . .

Niles has talked some of sending me home for two or three years . . . he says it is the only chance of saving a competence from his salary now . . . at present values of scrip. . . . But my dear mother, how *can* I consent to leave him here to toil alone without the comforts of a home or wife or child. . . . two or three years away from my dear husband—and Freddies papa—would be too much. Niles's health is far from good and I should feel as though I might never see him again. . . . We think some of putting up a rude house for present use, and living with great economy. But our course is entirely unsettled now. Perhaps by next mail it will be more clear.

Nevertheless, she urged her parents not to be anxious over their plight, reminding them of the "characteristic coolness" displayed by Californians:

You would have thought to have seen us all at Mr Harrisons that we none of us had lost a dollar, and our cheerfulness was not assumed; we are all young, have enough to start again, and are well and hopeful. I have no doubt you will mourn more for us than we will for ourselves. I dont think a tear has been shed by one of us over the fire. . . .

I havent mentioned Addison. He too was absent with the summit party. His office was in one of the brick buildings saved [the Bicknell Block] . . . [and it] is the "public building" now—court house, lawyers office in general, justices office—everything. His sign reads "Niles, Belden, and several other lawyers." There will be law business enough now. *All* the *county records* lost, but people will be too poor to *pay*. The fire will be felt much more 3 months hence than now.

III

DEBORAH, DELIGHT, HARRIET and little Fanny were going to Rensselaerville, escorted by Arthur Hagadorn. Addison accompanied them as far as San Francisco, where he composed a short letter to his mother on August 19:

I lost but little by the fire. Our office was . . . saved. I held, however, a mortgage on a wooden building for a few hundred dollars, and the building was burned. . . . My principle loss, however, was the almost total destruction of . . . Law business. For two or three months there will be almost a total stagnation, and then we shall probably have it brisker than ever. . . . I would have gone with the rest to see you all, but I cant quite afford it yet. So I have concluded to take advantage of the dull season while Nevada is rebuilding to take a run down to Tahiti and enjoy the fruits and the sea breeze a little while, and then back again to work.

I go on a Clipper Bark, the "General Wool," a fine little vessel, and I anticipate a very pleasant passage and visit. I have a little business which will pay me something, and as it will cost me much less than to stay at Nevada . . . I have determined to go. I . . . shall see the steamer off first with the homeward bound [friends]. I intend to remain about three months—perhaps longer, 4 or 4½ months, and as there are no regular mails from there you may not hear from me until my return. . . .

I am only afraid . . . that you will worry yourself in thinking about my safety while I am gone from Cal. But you must consider that my voyage to the Islands and back again in a sailing vessel is not accompanied with one quarter the danger of a simple steamer passage from San Francisco to Panama. . . . To a Californian, the trip is so usual a thing that we think nothing of it. Its like going to Saratoga or the sea shore. . . .

Mary intends to come home with Charley in the spring. Fred is just of that age when it is impossible to take him safely on a steamer, or she would come now. Fred would be down a hatchway or over the side before he had been aboard a day. He must wait for a little discretion before he goes to see his grandmama.

On August 19 the *Journal* reported:

DEPARTURE. We are not at all glad to announce the sailing of A. C. Niles . . . one day last week on a trip to the islands. The Judge was formerly an Editor of this paper, and his absence has left a blank in our social circle, a not inconsiderable one in the society of the city generally. We hope he will escape the barbecues of cannibals, try the realities of Omoo and Typee and have a glorious time.

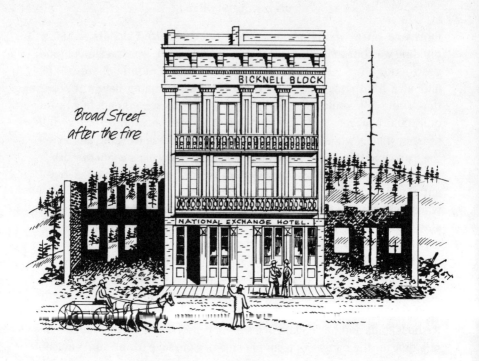

Broad Street
after the fire

CHAPTER 28

CRIMINAL ACTS

September–December 1856

I

*T*HE WORK OF REBUILDING continued at a feverish pace. Gutted ruins were torn down and hauled away, and as new structures filled the empty lots the aroma of freshly-milled fir, cedar, and pine provided welcome relief from the overwhelming stench of charred timbers and burnt cloth. There was little time to think about the grim events of the recent past, for even as they rebuilt, residents became embroiled in an exciting presidential campaign.

It was a hotly contested race between three well-known contenders: Democrat James Buchanan; former President Millard Fillmore, supported by the Whig and American parties; and former Senator John C. Frémont, once an explorer and now the candidate of the upstart Republican party. Those who opposed the spread of slavery referred to Buchanan and Fillmore as "doughfaces," a term used to denote northern men with southern sympathies. But those who believed the Constitution precluded national interference with state laws spoke contemptuously of "Black" Republicans, and called it the "nigger" party.

Most of Fillmore's support came from Whigs and former Whigs, but he hoped also to attract the many Democrats who had crossed over to vote the Know Nothing ticket in 1854 and 1855. One such was Judge Searls, who had been elected on the American party ticket, partly on the advice of Bill Stewart, who correctly predicted the sweeping victories of that party. But now Stewart, McConnell and others were urging Niles to return to the Democratic fold, pointing to many Democratic successes throughout the state in the spring of 1856, including the Nevada City election.

Niles felt a sense of loyalty to men who had helped him gain office, and was uncomfortably aware that to jump the traces again so soon would give him a name for opportunism. Mary could not vote, but she inclined toward Frémont. However, as one who took his politics seriously, Niles took little notice of the Republican party except to decry its apparent willingness to exploit and widen differences in the Union. The party was reputed to be a hotbed of freesoilers, abolitionists, and other such radicals.

To everyone's surprise, Aaron Sargent abruptly withdrew as the Know Nothing candidate for state senate. After failing to get his partners to support the Republicans, Sargent sold the *Journal* interest he had acquired after the fire and said:

In the present crisis of affairs I have no desire to throw away my vote, and shall vote for Fremont and Dayton. My reasons are that I am perfectly convinced that the issue is between the North and South— Fremont and Buchanan—that there is now no considerable conservative party in the Union—no one of sufficient strength to make head against geographical parties—that Mr. Fillmore cannot get a State in the Union with the exception of California, and that votes cast for him are thrown away.

While there was any hope of his election I cordially supported him, because I believed he would yield justice to the North and South, with an impartial hand, and I desired a national party to succeed. Now that the issue has narrowed to a direct struggle between the South and North, and no middle party can keep its footing, my education and principles decide me for the free north and free territory. Southern men of the American party in this county have left us by hundreds, declaring the only issue is the extension of slavery; and upon that they are with the south. . . . They are convinced by the news from the other States that

Fillmore cannot be elected—so am I. They choose, on a sectional issue, to vote for Buchanan—on that issue, I choose to vote for Fremont.

When Niles went to Sierra County in September he took Mary and Fred with him. The Stewart house was overcrowded and no other suitable place had been found for her. From September 12 to October 10 they lived at a Downieville hotel and tried to forget the summer of horrors. A month spent in the deep canyons of the Sierra Nevada alongside the icy, splashing waters of the Yuba was a refreshing change from the heat, dust and confusion of Nevada City.

Upon their return, Niles, Mary, and Fred took up residence in the building which housed Addison's office before and after the fire. Now it was called the National Exchange Hotel, having been refitted by former proprietors of the destroyed United States Hotel. However, Mary thought it was not well suited for the purpose:

Once more I hail from Nevada, but ... I dont feel as though it or any other place were home to me *now*, . . . I don't like it here very well We have a small room, upstairs, and it is so dark that I can neither read or sew in the day time without a candle; the only light is from a ventilator over the door, which opens into a hall. There is a very nice parlor, well furnished, much superior to any there has ever been in Nevada before. But there are several ladies boarding here, among others *Mrs Chubbuck* and her little girl and *Leo*. . . .

The Chubbucks had returned in 1855 after a one year stay at Sonora, where Leopold Chubbuck had managed the Wells, Fargo express office for a while. Now he was a clerk at Nevada City. Mary said of Mrs. Chubbuck:

She did not condescend to speak to me when we first met, and has not since. . . . She is as ignorant and affected as ever. There is also a Mrs Taylor here, who is a fit companion for her; she is very intelligent and agreeable, but *not* very respectable. She is the [same woman] who sang in the Episcopal choir. I supposed for several days that she was the wife of a lawyer who is boarding here, and that the honeymoon was not over with them, they were so loving, [but] I am told she is a [client]. . . . they are the *most* respectable ladies here (myself, I hope, excepted).

Besides all that, there are but few waiters, and they don't understand their business ... my visit to Downieville has spoiled me some, as well as Fred. We had the very best the house afforded all the time—up there—extras without charge, and every waiter in the house ready to spring at a look, to do our bidding. Fred was gratified in every wish, and was happy from morning till night. Here he disputes with Laura Chubbuck, who is as badly spoiled as he, and in addition is selfish and babyish. He will share every thing with her and give her all his playthings, but when he wants hers, she screams and runs to her Mama....

I have been all over town in vain to find a boarding place, and if I cannot succeed in getting a better room here, I think I shall go back to Bopes Ranch when Niles goes up again.... I have never been there longer than to dinner, but know I shall like it. The only objection is it is lonely, and when Niles comes back I'll have to seek board again....

J. B. Bope was proprietor of Plum Valley Ranch, a hotel, store, post office and farm on top of a ridge twelve miles from Freeman's Crossing, on the road from North San Juan to Downieville. The valley took its name from the great number of wild plum trees native to the area. Mr. Bope had terraced the hillside so he could irrigate vegetables and fruit trees with a single stream of water flowing from top to bottom. It was a favorite stopping place for travelers.

Charlie and Harvey board here [at the National Exchange], and I see them every day—often take my meals with them.... Niles and Charlie have sold their lots to Judge Buckner for $500 apiece. Niles talked of buying Charlie's and building a brick house on the centre, which would be comparatively safe from fire, but at last concluded that it would not be *entirely* safe, and he would not run the risk again. He will take his time now and select a lot that suits him.... If we are to remain here the next 5 years, we shall be obliged to build. It will be sure ruin to Fred if we board so long, and it is very unpleasant for me.

On Sunday, November 2, two days before the election, Mary wrote to Cornelia from new quarters. Her new landlady was Mrs. Bullington, whose husband had committed suicide in January. Now she lived with her brother near the lot on which the Methodist Church was being rebuilt.

I am now boarding with a very pleasant widow lady who was burned out and has rebuilt her cottage. Every thing is new and neat—we have a small bedroom opening off the parlor, but as she does her own work ... we have the parlor mostly to ourselves. It is near Mrs Harrisons, and I can run in there at any time. Niles is at home now. We haven't been separated since Deb left, but next week he leaves for Plumas Co. and Downieville, and will be absent 5 or 6 weeks.

Niles had stayed out late to a political rally the night before and consequently had been napping all afternoon. When he awoke Niles carried Mary's letter to the post office, on the way glancing up at the courthouse, which the local firm of Bain and Israel was rebuilding for $18,558. It was supposed to be ready for Niles to hold court in January, and a $100 per week overrun penalty was keeping the work remarkably close to schedule. The basement jail had been in use nearly continuously since the fire, and some of the inmates were hard cases.

II

THE COUNTY JAILER went in to feed his prisoners next morning and found three missing. It was the second escape for all three. The Farnsworth brothers had escaped once during the fire, when Sheriff "Boss" Wright unlocked the jail to save their lives. George Lewis, awaiting trial for killing a man in his saloon, had been released at the same time, but when he saw the sheriff collapse from smoke inhalation, Lewis carried him to safety. Two days later, Judge Searls granted Lewis bail, something he previously had declined to do. Later Lewis had been acquitted and received his permanent freedom.

The Farnsworths were remnants of the Bell gang, which had roamed highways and trails with virtual immunity until a posse caught and hanged Tom Bell on October 6 near the Merced River. The Yuba County sheriff had brought the Farnsworths to Nevada City on his way back from that hanging and now they were loose again. The third escapee was Jim Webster, twenty-one years old; like the Farnsworths, Webster was a well-known highway thief.

City Marshal Henry Plumer, who had caught Webster after a previous escape, offered to find him again, but only if he would be paid. He complained that on the earlier occasion, the sheriff had failed to reimburse him for horse rent. Marshal Plumer claimed to have information that the escaped prisoners might be at a Gold Flat cabin owned by the Farley brothers.

The Farleys were known to have taken care of Jim Webster's mare once, and they had turned it over to Lee Schell, who was arrested at Smartville with Webster. On the way back from that place, Webster had asked Plumer to take him to the Farley cabin, saying their testimony helped him out of a previous scrape, and he hoped they'd raise bail for him. Schell had been released for lack of a complaint; hours after the jail break Plumer's informant had spotted Schell and one of the Farleys carrying a bundle of clothes into the cabin.

Sheriff W. W. Wright hated to part with money, especially to a city employee like Plumer, for whom he had no particular fondness. The money would have to come out of his own pocket, at least until he submitted a bill and was compensated by the county. The Empire Mine at Grass Valley had first claim on whatever money he accumulated; lately he had collected about $19,000 in property taxes that should have been turned over to County Treasurer John Webber. There was time enough for that in the future. He often wondered about Alney Felt, the former public administrator. When the fire burned Nevada City, Alney had been holding about $15,000 belonging to estates he was settling. Alney claimed it went up in smoke and his bondsmen were still negotiating with the county. Because no one would renew his bonds, he was removed from office and a new man appointed to fill his place. None of this seemed to affect Felt, who continued to operate a pistol shooting gallery on Broad Street. Boss Wright doubted any man would let $15,000 burn, no matter what the risk.

Wright was dismayed by the procession of prisoners leaving his jail without permission. Because it was embarrassing, he agreed to pay Plumer $300 for their return. However, he attached a condition of his own: Wright was to go with Plumer. The sheriff would not let the city marshal take all the credit. Plumer had expected to go with his sidekick Bruce Garvey and no one else, but he saw Wright's mind was made up.

They had agreed to meet in the sheriff's office at 5:00 p.m.; Plumer later postponed the meeting half an hour, saying he was too busy to leave. A man stopped Plumer in front of Hirschman's cigar store shortly after five and told him a pair of horses were tied in a ravine at Gold Flat. The man and his friends thought they might have been put there for the escapees.

Plumer and Garvey were outside the sheriff's office at 5:30 when Hamilton McCormick took the marshal to one side and started to tell the same story. Plumer interrupted, said he was in a hurry, knew all about it and was on his way to Gold Flat. McCormick made a point of warning Plumer that another party was there already, watching the horses. Afterwards Plumer couldn't recollect being told about this second party, but McCormick stuck by his story, testifying:

No one could have heard me tell Plumer about the horses except the man who was with me, we were at least ten feet from any other person. . . . I had a reason for telling Plumer that there was a party there, because I knew an instance of that kind once at home, where an innocent man was shot while watching stolen goods; I was afraid of Plumer's party shooting [the others]. . . .

At last the posse rode out of town. To the considerable annoyance of

Plumer and Garvey, who preferred to keep the group small and incon-
spicuous, Sheriff Wright showed up at the last minute with two deputies
and a liquor merchant.

III

LORING WALLACE WILLIAMS and T. L. Baldwin also had observed Lee
Schell carry a valise into the Farley cabin that morning, and they had
watched him take a Farley horse and ride toward Grass Valley. Another
Gold Flat resident saw him turn off the Grass Valley road at Half-Mile
House and head for Wolf Creek.

About five in the afternoon, Williams heard of some horses tied up at
Gold Ravine, through which a small stream known as Gold Run flowed
lazily toward Deer Creek. Williams, Baldwin, and Joe Vanhook decided
to have a look. Because Williams wanted to hobble the horses, he
stopped at George Armstrong's house for a rope, and Armstrong offered
to come along.

The four men located the horses and found A. L. Robinson and a
friend already there. Robinson showed them an Allen's revolver he'd
removed from a saddle bag attached to one animal. They had been
watching the horses since noon, they said, and a third man, McCutchin,
had gone to town to tell the sheriff. McCutchin had wanted to inform
Plumer, but Robinson said he should tell Boss Wright.

With the arrival of replacements, the two men were able to go home
for supper. Besides not having eaten in five hours, they had no weapons.
The newcomers were better prepared: Williams carried a double-barreled
shotgun loaded with three .36 calibre pistol balls in each barrel on top of
small shot; Baldwin's shotgun contained seven pistol balls per barrel; the
others were armed with six-inch Colt's revolvers.

Williams took charge, directing Baldwin into a dry ditch 8 feet deep
and about 40 or 50 feet distant from the horses. Williams, Vanhook and
Armstrong took up positions behind trees on the opposite side of the
ravine, 50 to 70 feet away. Williams told them not to move until someone
tried to mount the horses. Whoever saw them first was to call out
"Halt!" and the others were to jump out and seize the outlaws.

After about twenty minutes, Baldwin heard what sounded like a
person moving through the brush from the north side of the ravine. Later
he did his best to recall what happened:

One man came up close to me, past the ditch where I was squatted
down; it was about 6½ o'clock p.m., and nearly dark. The man passed
within 16 or 18 feet of me ... went up to the horses and spoke in a low

tone and said, "By God, the horses are here yet!" He whistled a low whistle twice.... I answered in a whistle ... [which was] answered by a whistle from ... where I heard the footsteps.

Two other men ... passed within 18 or 20 feet of me, and went up towards the horses where the first man was standing. Then the three men came back to a point right in front of me, within 45 feet of me, [and] I raised up and advanced two steps towards them, I think—I was still in the ditch.

I said to them, "In the name of God Almighty, what are you doing there?" I heard them speaking low to themselves, but could not understand them—some one of the three cried out, "Rush in, boys, we are surrounded!"

Williams thought he heard Armstrong tell someone to halt. Then he heard Armstrong identify himself and repeat his warning not to move. Williams recalled:

... the party at the horses were hailed, and every man of our company told to step forward. These words were hardly spoken before a shot was fired ... one of the party at the horses sung out, "Close up, boys!" and ... fired a shot, which was followed in rapid succession by everybody shooting.

Armstrong, convinced he was surrounded and about to die, fired three pistol shots at someone coming toward him, and heard a man cry out "Oh, I am shot!" Someone fired a shotgun in Baldwin's direction; he was about to shoot back when the man disappeared. He saw another figure and pulled both triggers of his shotgun. The almost simultaneous discharge of fourteen pistol balls nearly bowled him over.

Although the moon had risen, shadows from a thick canopy of trees and brush made it difficult to see anything clearly. When Armstrong heard a voice shout, "Wallace Williams!" he assumed Williams had been shot. All firing ceased and Armstrong hurried to the spot where he expected to find Williams; instead, a lantern disclosed the body of Sheriff Wright, apparently dead.

Upon going to his nearby house, Armstrong found a wounded man sprawled across his front step. He carried the man inside, placed him on a bed, and then learned he was Deputy Sheriff David Johnson, who had lost out to Plumer in the contest for city marshal. Armstrong said he appeared to be in great pain and asked for laudanum, which Armstrong supplied two or three times. Johnson died soon after a doctor arrived.

No escaped felons had been within miles of the tragic shootout. Plumer categorically denied he had been told about the other party, and fierce accusations were exchanged. A coroner's jury concluded that the deaths were caused "accidentally and by mistake."

The *Journal* interviewed Samuel Hargraves, a prisoner who had witnessed the escape, who said the prisoners were able to open the cell doors whenever they pleased. They had invited Hargraves to walk into the hall with them and offered to take him along, but he refused. Jailer William Davidson was on guard duty all night and noticed nothing unusual until morning. The *Journal* said:

There is something very strange about prisoners escaping from a granite jail, as strong as this ... with a guard employed and paid for watching stationed at the only door from which they made a final exit.

The *Democrat* was of the same opinion:

A man has been employed to watch the jail, but he must have been absent or asleep when the escape was made, as he knew nothing of it until Monday morning. There must have been culpable negligence on the part of some one, as with a little care the jail can be kept perfectly secure.

When Sam Hargraves made his own unauthorized exit a few days later, the *Democrat* lamented:

Another prisoner ... under sentence of ten years to the State prison for killing a man near San Juan ... made his escape by breaking through the wall into a cell adjoining ... which was not locked.... When we consider the enormous taxes paid ... for the support of officials, and for erecting expensive Court houses and prisons, is it to be wondered at, that [taxpayers are] eager for a change....

IV

NEWS OF THE TRAGEDY at Gold Ravine interrupted a Democratic torchlight parade on election eve, but did not discourage voters, who turned out next day in record numbers. In the entire state, only San Francisco (12,152) and Sacramento (4,601) exceeded Nevada City's total of 2,085 votes cast. Democrats made a clean sweep. It was a sobering experience for those who had wandered from the Democratic fold. Writing from Quincy on November 9, Niles told Cornelia:

Buchanan has gained a complete victory in this state.... unless some new combination has been formed [in the Atlantic states] since ... our last news, the Know Nothing party is defunct, and we old KNs will have to pitch in anew. For one I have only to say that I shall wait awhile and endeavor to exercise a *sound discretion* in my future course, so far as politics are concerned.

He went on to describe the country around Quincy and spoke with satisfaction of his present circumstances:

Far up the western slope of the Sierra Nevada Mountains, surrounded by high ranges of snow capped hills, is the American Valley, one of the most delightful locations ... upon the face of the globe; luxuriant as the western prairies, surrounded by alpine scenery, and shut out from the rest of the world by high mountains wholly impassible in winter, and in summer only by a tortuous mule path, here is a little world by itself. ...

I love to wander, to visit strange places, and to try the experiment of combatting the world with no advantages save those afforded by my own resources. ... I like my present business and position ... and could May and Fred travel with me through the whole District, I should be perfectly happy. ... I have always felt a degree of contentment [in California] unknown to me in other lands. ...

I am ordinarily accompanied in my travels about the circuit by a number of lawyers who go from one court to another, after the western and southern plan, to practice. This renders the trips more agreeable than they would otherwise prove. Occasionally we have some good jokers along, and notwithstanding my aversion to anything like frivolity, we do have rich times.

On one occasion Niles heard evidence in a non jury case at Nevada City, but before it could be argued and a verdict rendered, it was time to begin the Sierra County term. Lawyers for both sides had come from San Francisco for the trial and were anxious to conclude the case, so Niles agreed to hear arguments enroute to Downieville. When he announced his decision, the losing attorney exclaimed angrily, "Judge Searls, if that mule had known the decision he was carrying, he would have bucked you off into the North Yuba River."

But his relations with the bar were usually cordial. At an oyster dinner in Hosmer's saloon in Nevada City after the election he had been given a polished manzanita walking stick with a massive and elegant gold head. Niles explained the occasion to Cornelia:

In April I held a Term of Court in Placer county, and the Officers and Members of the Bar of that county have presented me with a Magnificent Gold Headed Cane, valued at $125. It is so fine that I dare not carry it, but have laid it aside in Charleys vault, to be used only on special occasions. ... it will be preserved while I live, and then transmitted to Fred as a memento more to be cherished than the wealth of the Indies.

V

LEVI KELLOGG began delivering Mary's mail when he discovered no one else was doing so. He had come to ask about letters from Mrs. Mulford, and Mary said she had received no mail from the post office since Niles went away. Mary wrote her mother:

He says he will attend to me after this. . . . I dont know what I should do if it were not for him. He has been here several times since Niles left, and we have had some sport, as well as some annoyance.

The family I board with are ultra Southerners—prejudiced and ignorant—despise Yankees and all that sort of thing, and Mr Kellogg is all engaged for Fremont, and I must say my own inclinations are all that way. I think I should give three cheers in right good earnest if Fremont were elected. But we are all the time afraid of cutting our heads off by speaking in meeting, and Mrs Bullington takes good care that we are not left alone a moment, or any other persons who happen to call on me. My room is small and we have the parlor in common. She often sits whole days and evenings in the kitchen, but it isnt when *I have company*.

Niles had returned when Mary wrote again on December 18:

I dont know whether I ought to leave him to go home—not that I do him much good, but his health is much better I notice, when he is at home and he has something to take his mind from his business. . . .

All the money we have laid by since Niles was elected . . . is in the form of State Bonds, and those, by a recent decision of the Supreme Court, are reduced perfectly worthless at present, and it cannot be known until the next election whether they shall redeem them or not. At first we were quite discouraged . . . but it seems that the decision will make it a cash business, and the result will be that he will receive the full amount of his salary, instead of from 50 to 75 per cent on it, as he has done heretofore.

It places us in straightened circumstances for the present, but we hope it will all come right in the end. I havent mentioned the subject of going home to Niles in connection with our loss. He seems to avoid speaking of it.

Laird & Chambers hydraulic gold mine at Nevada City

CHAPTER 29

CREEK WATER

January–February 1857

I

ON THE DAY AFTER Christmas the *Journal* announced the return to San Francisco from Tahiti of A. C. Niles, "former editor of this paper. We will be happy to give him the grip cordial on advent to this city, which is expected shortly."

When Addison reached Nevada City Senator Waite asked him to take charge of the *Journal* for a second time. Addison accepted and at the same time formed a partnership with Thomas B. McFarland, a former assemblyman who had been defeated for district attorney in the November election.

Addison had returned reluctantly, for life in the islands suited him better than the rough and tumble world of law and politics. He told Cornelia:

I think ... that you all blame me somewhat for my "wild goose chase."... You cannot judge what feelings or objects influenced me to leave my business and go a cruising. You must rest contented with my assurance that there was an absolute necessity that I should go somewhere and find new scenes and new excitements for awhile....

I have a disgust which is almost hatred, of California and my profession and everything connected with my life here, and I have been where I know I could have lived alone and contentedly, and the temptation was very strong to stay. But here I am, and shall remain here, for a while at least.

He summarized his travels in a letter to his mother:

I . . . reached Tahiti after the long passage of fifty days. We had fine weather, except for three days a little bit of gale, which I enjoyed as well as any part of the voyage—not being troubled with sea sickness in the least.

I found Tahiti a more beautiful spot even than I had supposed, more beautiful than anything I had ever seen before, and enjoyed myself exceedingly while there, running over the whole island, and eating the delicious fruit of it. Staid there six weeks and then went in a small schooner to the island of Huaheine, about 100 miles from Tahiti and similar to it, only smaller.

Staid there ten days and sailed for Honolulu, Sandwich Islands, in a 75 ton Schooner. Had a short passage of 17 days, and stopping only two days at Honolulu, I sailed in a fine Clipper barque for San Francisco, where I arrived a few days since. . . .

You must all take my assurance that, besides the pleasure of the trip, I am enough better in body and spirit to pay for the expense and loss of time from my business ten times over. . . .

I found Nevada a new town when I arrived here—not a trace of the fire left, and handsome and more substantial buildings have taken the place of those destroyed by fire. But our citizens still feel the effects of the calamity, for many of our business men are broken, and others are breaking, and no money can be found anywhere.

Mary had not supposed her brother would return so quickly, she confided to Cornelia:

He took the first boat back, thinking it safest to return while he had the means, and he landed in San Fran. with 2 [shillings] in his pocket. . . . knowing that he did not like Cal, and that the Islands he visited were very charming and would suit his temperament, I thought he would be most likely to stay some time; and he says he would have done so, except for the fear of making Ma and Pa and all of us unhappy about him. . . . He boards with us (at our boarding place, I mean), and Harvey too, so that we have very sociable times now . . . I feel more cheerful and happy on this New Years day than I have before in a long time. I hope it is an omen of better fortune than we had last year. I had a forboding last New Year that there was trouble in store for us. . . .

Addison was less sanguine. "Wealth dont pour in on me as rapidly as on some," he wrote a month after his return. "Lawyers and editors are a poor class in California anyway, poorer if anything now than at home. I shall never be rich till I do something else. . . ." After two months he was advising his younger brother to stay in New York:

I am glad, Ham, that you never took the notion to come to California. It is not a good state for an honest man. Money has been made rapidly here, but no one [realizes] how rapidly it may be lost, or how small the chances of fortune are. You hear only of the big strikes—you dont hear of the misfortunes. . . .

And now it is worse than ever. The state is bankrupt. I fear it will even be disgraced forever by repudiation of its debts. . . . It is a bad state—bad every way. I dont speak from the effects of disappointments of my own—because although I have not made much money, still I do not count money as the only or the chief good of life, and I have acquired at least a fair position among men, and can always make a living at least. But I say it to deter you from ever wishing to come here yourself. . . .. The days of California fever has passed, I hope, and men begin to see that it is not a land where gold is to be had for the picking.

To Cornelia Mary voiced her growing concern regarding Addison's prospects:

He had made some money, tis true, but most of it was not by his profession, and he was quite discouraged, thinking that there was neither pleasure of proffit to *him* in the law business, for he dont like the practices—and he is hardly fitted for anything else. As for his plans for the future, I dont think he has any very definite ones. . . . I think it doubtful whether he ever sticks close enough to its practice to become a first rate lawyer.

When some Nevada County people went to Kansas to settle the newly opened government lands, Mary and Niles were inspired to discuss similar possibilities with their friends:

We talk sometimes of going home, all of us, and buying land at the west, at government price, tilling it some, but just live on it a few years till it rises in value, and thus make money on it. We could then be nearer home and have many advantages we have not now. It would be a good way to bring up Fred. Add is quite anxious to do so, and Harvey says he will go with us. We talk about it a great deal, and if we leave Cal. that is what we will probably do. Add will go on and select the land and get ready for us while I visit home, Niles and Harvey staying here to make a little more money in the meantime. . . .

That is what we thought of doing this spring, that was why Add was coming home with me, but the bonds which Niles was going to sell are worth nothing now, and we shall have to wait a year longer, at any rate, and may all have other plans before that time.

Another Rensselaerville couple joined the Nevada City colony in January. Arthur Hagadorn, who had escorted Deb, Delight and Harriet to New York, arrived with his bride, another Cornelia.

II

BEFORE CHRISTMAS the *Democrat* had praised Niles's first-year performance:

Judge Searls is a most indefatigable officer, and makes steady and summary work upon the bench. Since his accession to the Judgeship of the 14th District he has perhaps worked more assiduously than any judicial officer in the State, and at the same time to his credit he has given as great satisfaction. By the time the term is closed, which will be several weeks yet, he will no doubt clear the calendar of the cases current upon the docket, and also of the complicated fossil remains of former judicial ages.

In January the same paper published a humorous piece that made a serious point about the district court:

COURT HOUSE BELL. The shrewd men of all ages have ever considered punctuality a cardinal virtue in every department of human affairs. . . . Many a luckless mortal has forfeited his rights or sacrificed his property by failing to appear in season to prosecute the one or defend his title to the other.

The last remark is especially true in relation to the proceedings of the District Court of the fourteenth judicial district. This tribunal is presided over by a Judge who always "comes to time," with the Clerk and Sheriff closely in his wake. The admonitory "Oh Yes!" rings out upon the air and the Court is opened, but where are the lawyers, the litigants, the jurors, and the witnesses?

One is preparing an affidavit for a continuance, another is hunting up his witnesses, a third is on his last string at a game of billiards, the last is sawing off a game of "old sledge" for the toddies. . . . But, exclaims one, "his Honor's watch is too fast—mine wants three minutes of ten now." Another declares that he came directly from the jeweller's and that when he left there it lacked just ten minutes of the hour by Charley's huge regulator. A third opens with an equally plausible apology and begins to wax eloquent when he is suddenly brought up standing by an order from the bench which never fails to calm the troubled waters: "Mr. Clerk, enter a fine of five dollars against each of these delinquents."

Well now, gentlemen! seriously speaking, it is simply absurd to suppose that Judge Searls can so regulate his chronometer as to correspond precisely with every old turnip in the country, and I can devise but one remedy for the evil and that is—*a Court House Bell*. Let us prepare a subscription paper—purchase a bell immediately—place it upon the new Court House—have it rung by the Sheriff every morning about ten minutes before the opening of the Court, and there will be no further difficulty. . . . ZED.

The *Journal* said "We chime in with that recommendation."

Addison, looking for some way to raise his spirits, found pleasure in the fraternal order of E Clampsus Vitus, which had existed in Nevada City since 1855. It was a parody of secret societies like the Masons and Odd Fellows (officers of the "Ancient and Honorable Order" bore such titles as Noble Grand Humbug), but not everyone appreciated the humor. Rumors of scandalous practices multiplied as rapidly as its membership.

On January 6 the Nevada City chapter held a rare public event, a complimentary benefit for the ladies of the visiting theatrical company. Prior to the performance, actress Julia Deming received a note warning her not to associate herself with the society. She turned it over to the *Journal* to publish:

Respect for our sex induces me to address this note of warning to you and associates. I believe you enjoy some self respect and to appear on the boards to morrow night in answer to an invitation of that *obscene society* would degrade our sex and reflect great discredit on you.

Believe me you will be disgraced and imposed upon. No matter, they may say what they will, it is true what I say to you.

The newspaper also published The Noble Grand Humbug's comments:

The above *bijou* reached the lady to whom it was addressed, and as such a contemptible missive deserved, was disregarded. Dean Swift says, "a *nice* man is a man of nasty ideas." I think the rule holds good of the lady-like author of the above missive. Her nose must be continually upturned for fear of disagreeable smells.

If the society is a good one, she absurdly and grossly slanders it. If it is a bad one, she has no business to know it. If her idle and depraved curiosity has enabled her to peep into the secrets of an institution not intended for her supervision, she exhibits her own depravity and filthiness, by avowing that knowledge. She is like the old maid who complained of a young man bathing on the beach. The proof showed he was a mile from her dwelling, and the judge asked her how she could see him? "Oh," said she, "I took a spy glass."

According to Addison's presumably unbiased report of the affair, the theater was crowded from floor to ceiling:

The Knights of the Order, in regalia, and [preceeded] by a band of music, went in procession from their hall to the Theatre, marshalled by the C.V., the C.P. and the Most Worshipful N.G.H. . . .

In response to the enthusiastic call of the Knights assembled, David Belden Esq., most worshipful R.P., addressed the audience briefly and eloquently upon the subject of the Order. He entreated outsiders not to judge of our noble fraternity by the absurd reports that have gone out concerning us and our mysteries. He assured them that nothing but good was concealed beneath those sacred and solemn rites which date their origin far beyond the memory of man, and are coeval with the existence of our race. . . .

An appropriate Hymn composed for the occasion was sung by brother J. M. Langdon, whose happy allusions could only be understood by those worthy few, who crowned and girded, have stood in the awful presence of the "Locus Lucis." . . .

We are happy to be able to state that our glorious order is rapidly gaining ground in this portion of the State. The Nevada encampment alone now numbers over three hundred Knights upon its rolls, and at every meeting the hall is thronged with applicants for admission. Speed the good work! our objects are worthy ones. Orphans bless us, and the widows heart is glad.

On January 23 the *Journal* brought to light some "Queer Mistakes" which linked E Clampsus Vitus to the august court of Judge Searls:

The Nevada Encampment of the ancient and honorable order of E.C.V. are accustomed to hold their meetings at the hall occupied by the district court. This circumstance was lately the cause of a pair of rather singular accidents. One evening last week, at a regular and appointed assemblage of the knights a written resolution was adopted as follows:

"No knight except the N.G.H., the C.P., and the C.V. shall leave his seat while the candidates are in the presence of the *Locus Lucis*, under penalty of a fine of two dollars."

Through carelessness, the paper on which the resolution was written was left upon the desk after the adjournment of the meeting. The next morning, the county clerk approaching his desk discovered the document, and very innocently . . . entered it upon the minutes, where it now stands, as *an order of the district court. Query*—Can it be expunged from the record otherwise than by appeal to the supreme court?

On another occasion, a tedious jury trial was occupying the attention of the court until a late hour of the evening. Suddenly, in the midst of a prosy argument of counsel, three loud, distinct raps were heard at the outer portal. Two jurymen woke up, under the delusion that "the case was submitted," and the sheriff, aroused from his slumbers, sleepily staggered to the door.

The magic password was breathed into his ear, and before he could interpose, a gallant knight strode into the centre of the room, and favored the judge upon the bench with the impressive honors of the *grand salute*. As the judge is a worthy member of the E.C.V., the mistake was readily understood, and the zealous brother, being duly enlightened, retired in much confusion.

The *Temperance Mirror*, which considered ECV a disgrace to society, came down hard on the *Journal*, claiming its account of the complimentary benefit was "filled with allusions" that could not be misunderstood by those who knew the secrets of that Society. The *Mirror* said:

The success attending the benificent efforts of the different fraternities such as Masons, Odd Fellows, and the Temperance Orders, has led to the organization of several societies intended to burlesque these noble institutions, into which young men are inveigled under pretence that they are designed for charitable purposes, when, in fact, they are places were the grossest indecencies are practised. The young man who desires to retain his self-respect should shun them as he would the plague or any other pestilence.

Addison pulled no punches in his reply:

To an outsider, the whole article . . . would appear to be an outburst of indignant virtue at some gross outrage upon morality. To those however who are better acquainted with the character of the society to which he alludes, and the class of our citizens who are its members, the whole thing presents a slightly different aspect.

The author of this tirade is undoubtedly a very proper man before the world.... Perhaps his reputation, as far as outward acts are concerned, stands irreproachable before all men. But he has shown that he is filthy and corrupt at heart. His mind is the receptacle of the foulest thoughts. Words and scenes that would only excite the mirth of purer men, in his depraved imagination awaken ideas of obscenity and filth.... His virtue is like a putrifying sore—morbidly sensitive.

He is one of those canting hypocrites, who are the bane of every creed, covering inward vileness with a grave countenance and decorous exterior.... They scent impurity, as a Jackall scents carrion and growl over it, and feast upon it with as keen a relish. We don't admire their taste.

III

WITH MINOR EXCEPTIONS, the district court was occupied with weightier matters than ECV. For one thing, the county was nearly insolvent, thanks to the untimely death of Sheriff Wright and his curious habit of mixing public and private funds. District Attorney Sargent was suing the administrator of Wright's estate, Conrad K. Hotaling. Like the late sheriff, Hotaling was a shareholder in the Empire Mine.

Hotaling claimed the right to hold all money for ten months, the customary time permitted for settling estates. At first the amount of county funds in the late sheriff's possession was supposed to be about $15,000, but a careful audit disclosed a shortage closer to $19,000. Of that amount, $6,000 had been placed in a separate account by Wright, and Hotaling did not object too strenuously when Judge Searls demanded that it be turned over to the district court. Hotaling said he would fight to retain the balance.

The most important suit involved water rights on Deer Creek. One huge consortium, described as George W. Kidd et al., was suing Amos T. Laird and Company, an equally powerful organization. At stake was property worth hundreds of thousands of dollars and future profits that could add up to millions. Kidd retained McConnell, Stewart, and Sargent; Buckner, Hill, and Meredith were defending Laird.

The case had its beginnings in the winter of 1850–1851, when the South Yuba Mining and Sacramento Canal Company was organized to tap the upper South Yuba and take its waters by tunnels and flumes to the Deer Creek watershed. An immense project, it would require large sums of money and years of work to complete. Four years later, the South Yuba Company announced its European agent Dr. R. T. Huddart had arranged for substantial English backing for its scheme. At the same time the company name was changed to the Nevada County and Sacramento Canal Company.

In February 1855 the *Journal* reported:

Dr. Huddart has recently returned after nearly 18 months incessant labor in Europe, after having to battle for months in England against [the belief that] all enterprises having an Australian or Californian origin, [were] swindling transactions....

But he succeeded in bringing together in England a body of gentlemen of large means, willing, upon the examination and favorable opinion of one of their number, to ... furnish the necessary cash capital for the construction of the works.... William Nicholson Esq., a retired gentleman of large fortune, accompanied Dr. Huddart to this country [and] a few days since [gave] his unqualified approval of the undertakings....

A. T. Laird and Co. declared its intention to construct the ditch from the South Yuba to Nevada City, but the announcement was deliberately vague about where the water would be taken out, and the route it would follow.

Mr. Nicholson was on his way home to England when the Sacramento steamer on which he was traveling exploded, fracturing his leg. This unfortunate turn of events changed the picture, for while he recuperated in the Orleans Hotel at Sacramento, others took advantage of the delay.

The *Journal* on February 16, 1855, warned of a possible conflict:

A project seems to be on foot on the part of a company to take the waters of the South Yuba off from the places adjacent, as Alpha, Omega, &c., and throw it into Deer Creek, to feed the ditches already leading from Deer Creek to this city. We think the populous mining neighborhood which is now expecting this water to be speedily brought to the rich placers we have named, will object, and possibly prevent this serious blow to their interests.

A confrontation took place five days later:

We understand that Messrs. Colburn and Smith, members of the Nevada County & Sacramento Canal Company, with about 60 miners of

Omega, proceeded to the South Yuba river on Wednesday for the purpose of erecting the dam of the company. On arriving at the spot they were resisted by Daniel Rich, Charles Marsh, and one Dunn.

Colburn, on behalf of the [N.C.S.C.] Company, ordered them off . . . without effect. . . . The resistance was however sufficient for the purposes of the Company, and legal proceedings will undoubtedly be now commenced . . . to maintain their rights.

By the end of March 1855 both companies had begun construction on rival ditches. Also involved with Rich, Marsh and Dunn in the Rock Creek, Deer Creek and South Yuba Canal Company were James Whartenby and George Kidd, both of Nevada City. In April, Aaron Sargent, then editing the *Journal*, condemned the Rich-Marsh-Dunn combine as interlopers and blackmailers:

Those interested in mining may seriously consider . . . whether it is proper to allow one set of men to own all the water rights that can by any possibility be used to bring water to the most important mining points of the county. . . .

The absolute control in the hands of a few men of all the water . . . would make them millionaires and all others poor dependents.

Though not mentioned by name, George Kidd and James Whartenby responded quickly and angrily to Sargent's remarks. Sargent replied, point by point:

George W. Kidd and James Whartenby say: "We have never intentionally interfered with . . . and have no objections to . . . the [N.C.S.C. Company] . . . building as many Ditches and Canals as they please, but the aggressions are and have been all on their side, and until this time we have taken no notice of them. . . ."

This . . . is falsehood No. 1. They . . . jumped the position for the dam. . . . they refused to yield the position, and by force held it against the [N.C.S.C.] company, compelling the latter to commence suit to gain their rights. . . . they say: "[The N.C.S.C. Co.] has repeatedly made us overtures of purchase, which have been rejected."

The implication from this is that [Kidd and Whartenby] have no idea of a sale. . . . [but] their lawful attorney informed the Secretary of the [N.C.S.C.] Company that his clients would be satisfied with $250,000, and this was the best way to settle the matter. The monopolists themselves proposed to R. T. Huddart to settle for a million, they to finish the ditch and deliver it. Both offers were rejected. . . .

They [own] . . . Snow Mountain Ditch, Deer Creek Ditch, Cayota Ditch, Rock Creek Ditch, Slate Creek Ditch, Deer Creek East. Besides these, confederates in the monopoly own largely in the Randolph Ditch and the Montezuma Ditch, and have mortgages on others ... with the exception of Tomlinson's ditch, they own every other ditch above this place.... George W. Kidd and James Whartenby are known as close-fisted, selfish men, and the latter endeavored to get pay for water three times over at from one to two dollars per inch in 1850. He then cared little for the "interests of miners," for he had control of all the water in the diggings, and he will care as little when he again gets that control.

Now the N.C.S.C. had gone out of business, and Kidd, Marsh et al., was excavating one 3200-foot tunnel between the canyons of Deer Creek and Steep Hollow, and another 300 feet long that would link Steep Hollow to the Bear River. Completion of the entire project was expected in early 1857, but until the dispute over Deer Creek water rights was settled, no water would flow from the South Yuba. Deer Creek was to provide the final conduit to Nevada City, and Sargent had been employed by the "monopolists" to win their suit.

Their principal opponent, Amos Laird, owned major gold claims on Lost Hill, Wet Hill, and American Hill at Nevada City—more than any other man. His operations washed away a half acre of ground each week, and the *Democrat* called him "perhaps the most extensive and successful miner in the state." It was important that his supply of water be cheap, constant, and ample. To this purpose he hired Moore and Foss to build a large reservoir on Deer Creek, seven miles above Nevada City. When finished, the 40-foot dam would flood 200 acres. In January it was nearly complete, and Addison discussed local reactions in the *Journal*:

Some few persons are fearful that the immense mass of water will break the dam, and sweeping down the creek, carry off the lower portion of the city, and all mining operations below it, but from conversation with those who have examined it, we feel satisfied that there is no danger. The dam was constructed by Mr. Moore, of this city, and is said to be a most excellent and substantial piece of workmanship.

If it *should* break one of these fine nights, the slumberers in the lower part of the city would, undoubtedly, have rather a moist time. Trusting in the promise of Noah, and the strength of the dam timbers (and the additional fact that we sleep in the upper part of the town) we shall continue to go to bed with our usual feelings of security.

Two weeks later, as the result of unusually heavy rains, the dam began filling at an alarming rate. Because the flood gate had become choked with debris, workmen began cutting holes in the dam to allow water to escape. On Saturday, notice that the dam might break was given to all persons living downstream; these warnings were generally ignored. At about 4 o'clock Sunday morning, according to the *Journal*:

... a tremendous crash and tumult awakened those of our citizens who reside in the lower part of the town, and on rushing out of doors, they saw a body of water fifteen feet in heighth rushing down toward them, filled with timbers, planks and drift wood, and bearing everything before it in its course. There was no time to think of property or clothing, or anything but life.

Messrs. Boswell and Hanson who were sleeping in their store by the Main street bridge, rushed half naked into the street, leaving their watches and a considerable amount of money in their rooms.... [Their] store ... and [a] boarding house on the opposite side of the creek, were carried bodily along, only falling to pieces when they reached the rapids below. The roaring of the water, the crash of falling houses, the darkness of the night and the howling of the storm, combined to render the scene imposing and magnificent—to one who had no property thereabouts....

One half of the Monumental Hotel ... was undermined and shattered, though not carried entirely away. Wait and Co.'s blacksmith shop, [the] wagon shop of Mr. Whitmarsh, the feed store of L. S. Ely, the houses of David Belden and of Niman and McElroy were swept off and destroyed. All the bridges over Deer Creek except the Pine street bridge, a very high one, were carried off.... We hear rumors of Quartz mills carried away, and dams, flumes and mining claims filled up and otherwise injured. We have as yet received no reliable accounts of lives lost....

S. W. Grush, of the Monumental Hotel ... was also a heavy loser in the fire of July [1856]. Mr. Grush informs us that this is the fourth time he has been ruined by the elements in California. He is obliged to his friends for the patronage they have hitherto extended to him, and means to try it on again.

Bopes' Plum Valley Inn

CHAPTER 30

HARD CASES

January–April 1857

I

JUDGE SEARLS sat on his bench in the new courtroom for the first time on January 28, 1857—six months later than originally intended. There were no visible scars of the fire which had gutted the building and destroyed official documents, but evidence was plentiful on the court calendar—insolvencies, foreclosures, and suits for recovery of money owed. Increased crime was another by-product of the recession induced by the many business and mining failures.

On the evening of January 29, two prisoners escaped from the basement of the courthouse. Wallace Gehr, a former Nevada City policeman awaiting trial for highway robbery, opened the doors for himself and accused thief Daniel Luddington. Luddington had the bad luck to collide with County Clerk John Bostwick outside the jail and was captured, but Gehr got away.

Gehr and an accomplice were awaiting trial for the robbery of Alexander McClanahan, who collected the foreign miner taxes in Grass Valley township. Wallace Gehr had once served as a policeman under the late city marshal, Dave Johnson. When Henry Plumer and new trustees took office in May 1856, his appointment was renewed, but after three weeks he was fired for undisclosed reasons.

Tallman Rolfe, one of the trustees who discharged Gehr, resumed editorial control of the *Democrat* when Bill Anderson resigned at the end of December. On January 28 Rolfe said:

[Gehr] has long been suspected of being connected with the late robberies near this place, and was once arrested for stealing cattle, and examined before Justice Van Hagan, but the evidence not being sufficient to hold him, he was discharged.

Disgusted at this latest escape, Rolfe said:

The Nevada jail is as secure as any in the State, and it seems hardly possible for a prisoner to escape from it except through the carelessness or design of the keepers. We can scarcely believe there was any design in this instance, but such charges are freely made, and many believe them true. It is evident that the jailor is unfit to have charge of the county prisoners, and the Sheriff owes it to his own reputation to appoint some competent person in his place.

County supervisors had appointed deputy William Butterfield to replace the late Sheriff Wright. Unlike the majority of current county officials who were Democrats, Butterfield belonged to the Know Nothing party. Despite its own past criticisms of faulty jail security, the *Journal* now chose to interpret Rolfe's remarks as political:

The Nevada jail is *not* "as secure as any place in the state." Had the bars to the jail doors been properly fastened, Gehr could not have burst the one at his door; and common padlocks are totally unfit to be used about a jail. The account of the *Democrat* ... is colored with the malignity it always evinces when it can get a chance by misrepresentation, to decry a public officer that differs from it politically. It is ... characteristic of the proprietors of that sheet.

The *Journal* described how the escape was effected:

The prisoner was locked into a cell by two locks, and was heavily ironed. Being a blacksmith, he succeeded by the ingenious use of a string in getting off his fetters, dug through the brick partition into the next cell, where there was a common padlock on the door, and a bar of iron outside of the door, which was insecurely fixed into the wall.

The deputy jailor went in as usual to feed the prisoners, passing the food in through a wicket in the iron door.... The fastenings of the cell doors were all in place, and looked firm. After taking his food … Gehr passed through the hole … into the next cell, and when the officer's back was turned burst out of the cell, and with the occupant of the other cell, escaped.

The grand jury investigated and then reported:

We … believe that the occurrence was not in consequence of any carelessness on the part of the officers in charge, but is attributable to the inadequate security afforded by the improper fastenings … to avoid the recurrence of such an accident, [we] would recommend the purchase of a sufficient number of Tab's Patent Locks, or some equally secure fastenings.

The *Journal* gleefully declared:

The report of the grand jury … completely refutes the slanders of the *Democrat* … [and] contradicts completely the tirade in the last issue of that sheet.… [which] referred to the report without announcing its contents, which it dared not do, as it would thus furnish evidence of its carelessness of truth. The *Democrat* is very much accustomed to pick up street stories, and retail them as truth.…

With unusual restraint, Rolfe noted that the findings of "inadequate security" and "improper fastenings" proved his point, and said he would refrain from name-calling.

But Addison continued to attack the other paper, often picking at it for petty details or matters open to honest differences of interpretation. In one case Rolfe had reported:

Information was received in Grass Valley on Saturday that some Chinamen had been robbed by three men of about $500, on Bear River. One of the Chinamen came to Grass Valley and identified one of the men, who was arrested.… Marshal Plumer … arrested one of the others, named Sullivan, in the Theatre on Saturday evening. The other accomplice … was not found. The two were lodged in jail but on Monday were set at liberty by the advice, we are informed, of the District Attorney, without even an examination.

The *Journal* offered a more detailed account, followed by a gratuitous slap at its neighbor:

Sullivan was arrested on Saturday night without warrant, was taken before no magistrate, and kept in jail three days with no commitment. The officer who arrested him, and the ones who detained him were liable for false imprisonment. The one arrested at Grass Valley was brought here to be jugged with no commitment, and ... without any examination....

There was no evidence ... except that of Chinamen. No property of theirs that could be identified ... was found on their persons. The only fact that could be proved by white men was that they were seen about the Chinese camp. The testimony of Chinese against white men was ruled out by the Supreme Court.... Much less would any court admit their hearsay declarations.

As there was no legal testimony.... both prisoners were discharged.... If the *Democrat* can find any authority in the Statute for any proceedings taken in this matter except those by advice of the District Attorney, we should like to see it.

Jim Webster, whose second escape had led to the tragic deaths of Wright and Johnson, was caught and tried at Marysville, where his first trial resulted in a hung jury. On the second try the Yuba County jury found him guilty and he was sentenced to San Quentin for twenty-five years. Lee Schell drew a five-year term.

Wallace Gehr's alleged accomplice in the McClanahan robbery went on trial in Nevada County on February 13. The victim was able to swear that one robber was surely Gehr, but was less confident about the second man. Oddly, it was the testimony of Marshal Henry Plumer that enabled Snodgrass to go free, for he named another man as Gehr's usual confederate.

Wallace Gehr had fled his jail cell with good reason, for it was obvious that McClanahan's strong evidence and the discovery of stolen loot in his cabin would surely send him to prison. But eight days after Snodgrass was acquitted, Gehr's prospects suddenly improved with the news that Alex McClanahan had been killed in a Grass Valley shootout.

The *Journal* said it was a homicide which in any country but California would be called murder. W. Alexander McClanahan, a seven-year resident of Grass Valley, was the victim of Francis Van Moore, "a man of doubtful, or rather of bad reputation."

Moore and some friends had arrived at Heywood's saloon about 11 p.m. on a Saturday night. Moore offered to buy a drink for McClanahan, who turned him down. According to witnesses, Moore then drew his pistol and declared, "You have insulted me, by refusing to drink with me; if you are a gentleman, you will defend yourself."

The saloonkeeper ordered Moore to put away his weapon, which he did despite some urging by a companion to shoot Alex and get it over with. McClanahan then departed, saying he'd see Moore later. In ten or fifteen minutes he was back, and when he approached Moore with a pistol in his hand, the other man fired. The *Journal* reported:

McClannahan's pistol was discharged almost simultaneously with Moore's, the ball lodging in a box, three or four inches above the floor. He then walked a few feet, and saying, "I am a dead man," expired in a minute or two. Moore exclaimed that *he* was shot, and went directly to Dr. Tomkins, who on examination found not a shot wound, but a cut in one of his shoulders. Moore was then arrested and placed under a guard, in Dr. Tomkins' house. . . .

The general opinion among the citizens is that the killing was preconceived by Moore, who had fortified himself by drinking freely on the evening of the occurrence. Ill feeling had existed between the parties for some time. . . . A good deal of sentiment prevailed at Grass Valley, and there was some talk of lynching Moore, but . . . there were not enough ready to take the lead in it. McClannahan was an amiable young man, about twenty-seven years old, and formerly from Baltimore, Md.

The *Democrat* reported several days later on the condition of the killer:

We have heard various and conflicting reports in regard to the condition of Frank Moore, who was stabbed at the time he shot McClanahan in Grass Valley. He is now lying at Dr. Tompkins' office, and it seems to be the general belief in Grass Valley that he cannot live. Although a report was started soon after the affray that Moore had received only a slight scratch, it appears that he received a fearful stab, the knife passing into the cavity of the chest, and coming very near the lungs.

On the evening of March 5 a dry goods merchant was savagely beaten in the town of Alpha. Neighbors hearing cries and loud noises from the inside of Isaac Rich's locked store, broke in and frightened away his assailant. They found Rich lying in a pool of blood, his head "a mass of wounds and gore, the skull broken in several places, and his hands and arms mangled." His attacker apparently had carved him with a bowie knife.

Henry Plumer and Bruce Garvey arrested Charles Nevilles for the crime three nights later in Sacramento. Nevilles had closed his saloon and suddenly departed from Alpha the same night Rich was assaulted. A Belgian, thought by many to be French, Nevilles had been a baker and boarding house proprietor in Nevada City before the fire, after which he had opened a saloon in Alpha. But because no one had seen the attacker and there was no evidence to link him to the crime, he was released a month later.

On March 4, near the town of North San Juan, L. W. Chase killed A. B. Mudge, with whom Chase's teen-aged wife had been living during his short absence. A coroner's jury decided Chase had acted in self-defense and let him go. It had been a violent winter in Nevada County.

II

IN A DOWNIEVILLE newspaper Addison read that someone had taken a toothbrush and several shirts from the hotel room of Judge Searls. The *Journal* editor growled, "We hope the thief will meet the contignest punishment, for we have a strong suspicion that some of those shirts were ours."

While Niles was in Sierra County he learned that Plumas County had been removed from his district. Henceforth he would divide his labors equally between Nevada City and Downieville, and could spend more time with Mary and Fred. Although his financial situation had not improved, prospects for an eventual solution were better, Mary told her sister:

Niles has received not one dollar of salary, except clerk's fees, since last Nov. and has had to borrow money to pay board bills, yet ... we think it will all come right in the end. The Legislature will make some provision, I dont doubt, before they adjourn, for ... Gov., Judges, Legislators, and all other state officers are in the same fix that we are. Add was up this morning with the good news that there had been provision made for the payment of one months salary to all the officers as a temporary relief, and Niles's share is now awaiting his order....

Niles wont listen to the idea of his troubles making any difference about my going home. He says if I *want* to go, I can go, and ... I *do* want to go, on the whole.... I do think [the Mulfords] *will* come back [here]. I have never thought so till quite lately, because I thought Charlie did not want to ... but I see that he *does* ... and Deb says she is willing if he prefers it.... Perhaps if they come back in the winter I can return with them.... It would be most too short a visit for me though, only 3 or 4 months. I would *like* to stay about 6 months.

Mary was boarding again with the Wall family. Jesse Wall's fortunes had improved greatly since the fire: he had built a brick store next to Harvey's drugstore, and improved his residence as well. Mary told her mother:

I am not particularly comfortable, and if I were not coming home, I would think I was quite uncomfortable, but am prepared to get along almost any way until then. There is a railing around the piazza now, and the children are therefore pretty safe now, but are of course very troublesome together, waking each other, teazing each other, and various other annoyances. . . .

Fred had been given a large Newfoundland dog by a Downieville man with whom it had been left. Fred took great pleasure in riding about on the dog, whose name was Frank.

The owner hasnt returned, and his master pro-tem—who I suppose has really as much right to him as any one—says Niles may bring him home to Fred, and we may keep him as long as we want to. He is glossy black with long shaggy hair. He will be a grand playfellow for Fred, and I know I shall never want to part with it. . . .

We have sad news for the [Wickes family]. Poor Luther Carter was killed by the sudden breaking away of a quantity of water in a tunnel, above where he was working. He had not time to escape. Niles sent me the account cut from a paper where he found it, and I sent it over to Harvey. . . . I feel very sad indeed about his death. It is the first serious accident that has ever happened to any of our friends in this country.

Mary had remarked about "a greater number of deaths this winter from accidents than ever before, because there has been more rain, and the ground is so perfectly saturated."

III

Before Francis Moore could be tried for murder there was the matter of an earlier rape charge to be settled. The court of sessions quickly found him guilty of assaulting a Rough and Ready woman and gave him a fifteen-year sentence. This impediment removed, he became one of seventy cases on the district court docket for the term beginning April 20. Tallman Rolfe covered the murder trial for the *Democrat*:

There is perhaps less discrepancy in the evidence in Moore's case than could have been expected. There may be room for doubt as to which shot was first fired, but . . . it is evident that both McClanahan and Moore were raising their pistols at the same time. The weight of evidence would indicate that Moore's pistol was first discharged, but was followed so soon after by McClanahan's that it was difficult to tell. . . .

Some fifteen persons were in the room at the time of the occurrence, but a number of them were so drunk that it was not thought advisable to take their evidence. . . . It will probably always remain a mystery as to how Moore got stabbed. He received a frightful cut in the back, which penetrated the cavity of the lungs. The prosecution set up two theories to account for this wound. One was that his wife stabbed him the morning previous, and the other that he had stabbed himself in order to create sympathy. Neither of these theories was sustained. . . .

The only light in the room was a camphene lamp, and this was extinguished by the concussion caused by the discharge of the pistols. Moore was evidently stabbed by some one about this time. Who it was will probably never be ascertained. Moore has generally been regarded as a bad man, and it is reported that he has been connected with the gang of robbers who have infested this neighborhood for some months past.

McConnell and Stewart defended Frank Moore, but their best efforts failed to impress the jury. Moore was convicted of murdering Alex McClanahan and Judge Searls pronounced the death sentence. The *Journal* commented on Moore's demeanor:

Of the large crowd who listened to the sentence, Moore was apparently the most calm and unmoved. When asked if he had anything to say, he spoke briefly and coolly of the necessity of his act, as one of self-defense, and of the prejudice which he alledged to exist against him. His wife, who has clung to him womanly and faithfully during his imprisonment and trials, was by his side as he received the sentence. We understand that his case will be appealed to the Supreme Court.

Wallace Gehr was captured at San Francisco as Moore was being tried; considerable doubt was expressed that he could be convicted now that Moore had disposed of the principal witness, and the presence of both men in the same jail gave rise to added concern. The *Journal* said:

Since the sentence of Moore, so many threats have been made to fire the town, the citizens have put on an extra police sufficiently strong to keep strict look out at all hours, and in every nook and corner of the city. . . . Moore and [Gehr] . . . have confederates in the vicinity who would stop at no crime, however atrocious, which might, even by a remote possibility, result in their escape. . . . With these two and Myers, now in confinement for an attempt to burn the town, our jail . . . contains about as much villainy as usually finds its way into so small a compass.

The *Journal* bemoaned the fact that "the worst villains" often escaped appropriate punishment because of legal delays and "confederates outside, working with secret and insidious means." Nevertheless, the time for vigilance committees had passed.

Wooden flumes to supply water for mining

CHAPTER 31

SEPARATE PATHS

May–August 1857

I

*S*OME COUNTY OFFICIALS complained that because Judge Searls worked ten and twelve hour days, they and their deputies often had to put in overtime. They wished the legislature would limit daily sessions of district courts to more reasonable hours. But Niles knew that delayed justice often meant no justice at all, and he did everything in his power to clear the calendar in a timely fashion.

Several large damage suits resulted from the Deer Creek flood. The grocery firm of Boswell and Hanson sued Laird, Chambers, Moore and Foss for $25,000 and was awarded $5000. Niman and McElroy sued the same parties and received $1000. Both decisions were appealed because of Judge Searls's instructions to the jury.

Laird and his partners fared better in a suit filed against them by Kidd, Marsh, Whartenby et al., over water rights on Slate and Deer creeks. It was a major defeat for Kidd, and his attorneys appealed to the supreme court.

Although the legislature declined to limit the hours of district court, it responded to the latest request for municipal reform at Nevada City. Some citizens had petitioned for total dissolution of the town corporation, but wiser heads prevailed. As in the past, the chief complaint was the unbalanced budget. To solve .this problem an amendment was approved which authorized the city to attach and sell delinquent property for nonpayment of taxes—a power like that of state and county governments, but one that Judge Searls thought could not be assumed by mining districts.

Oliver Stidger of North San Juan had failed to pay his share of assessments on a mining claim, and in accordance with local mining customs his claim was auctioned off to recover the amount owing. Stidger argued he had been deprived of property without due process, and Judge Searls agreed. Ruling that miners' laws could not override state and national guarantees of due process, Searls declared that before a claim could be attached and sold for delinquent assessments, a clear and distinct agreement to such a practice must be recorded with each claim owner in the district. Because no such contract had been required in the past, the potential consequences were enormous. The losing side announced it would appeal.

Addison traveled to San Francisco on business and was gone for several days. When he returned he wrote his mother about Mary's forthcoming trip to New York:

It will leave a great gap with Niles and I. My lady acquaintances in this state being confined to May, I am afraid it will have a tendency to throw me out of ladies society, and you may expect to see me as rough an old bachelor as the roughest, when I come to the east again.

We shall miss her and Fred very much, but I think it will do [them] good, and that it will do you all good to see them, and I am glad they are going. I wish Rensville Californians were all in a condition to rendezvous at R.Ville this fall. I think we could make the old village seem pleasant for a while. Well, we will all come back to the old nest sometime I hope.

On May 25, outgoing county officers hosted a party at which Judge Searls served as master of ceremonies. Guests consumed enormous quantities of excellent food and chilled champagne while listening to at least twenty speeches, including one by Niles, whose third wedding anniversary coincided with the gala affair.

Mary wrote her mother on June 1. The day had been very warm and she had spent the early evening cooling off on the moonlit piazza with Mrs. John McCoy, Mrs. Wall's newest boarder. Mr. McCoy was the retiring county assessor, and the couple was staying only until their steamer left for home.

Niles had a handsome present the other day from J. R. McConnell, of

"Irving's Life of Washington" in three volumes, beautifully bound in calf. Add. had a *splendid* present, the handsomest gold watch I most ever saw, a hunting case, with a large diamond in the spring, and the workmanship very superior. It was given him by Mr. Bay, for whom he has been doing some business. . . .

I had a present too, last week on the 25th, which was our wedding day. Niles gave me a new dress—a blue tissue—which I made up with three flounces bound with satin ribbon. Fred and I went out to Mr. Stewart's the other day and had a fine visit. A few days since we were all invited to spend the evening at Dr. Overton's to eat ice-cream and strawberries, a rare treat here. Day after tomorrow I am to spend the day at Judge Caswell's. I want to visit a good deal before I start for home. . . . I have some very warm friends here whom I would hate to part with entirely. . . .

Fred and I have many lovely talks about what he will see and do when he gets home, and it would do you good to see what interest he takes in all I tell him, and how well he remembers it. He tells about Uncle Will's kitten, and Grandpa's horse, &c, having something to tell about each one of you.

She also wrote to Cornelia and gave her more specific information about the coming voyage:

I did not know whether you would think it best for Ma to know all about it. If so, you can tell her. We have our passage engaged on the steamer of the 5th of July, which will leave on the 6th in reality—5 weeks from today. [Charlie and I] have staterooms adjoining each other, and the best ones on the boat they say. The reason of our engaging them so long before hand is that there is such a crowd all the time now. McCoy and his wife, who are boarding here now, were all ready to leave by the steamer of this week, and could not get passage—so Charlie sent down at once for ours.

I am drawing my business to a close here, but have a great deal to do yet. I aim principally to make such things as will be necessary for our comfort and neatness on the steamer, and shall depend upon getting nice things after I get home. . . . If you know where [Hattie Backus] is, let her know when we are coming and tell her I want to see her face the first moment after my arrival. Tell Ham too. He said he would go down to N.Y. to meet me.

II

IN A LETTER TO HIS MOTHER Addison described local reaction to news of the massacre of Henry Crabbe's private army of adventurers at Sonora, Mexico:

... the excitement here and through the state was intense. I heard a drum and fife in front of my office, and going down, I found it was a call for recruits to go below and avenge the death of Crabbe and his party. A great crowd was gathered and it served to make an excitement and that we have not had for a long time before. I dont think many volunteered.

Crabbe had been a California filibuster (freebooter), whose career closely paralleled that of William Walker, the so-called "Man of Destiny" who in 1856 had led an armed invasion of Nicaragua. Since declaring independence from Spain in 1821, Nicaraguans had endured a succession of dictators who continued the exploitation of the local populace begun three centuries earlier by representatives of the Spanish crown.

In Nicaragua, as in most other Central American countries, two parties opposed each other: liberals claimed to espouse peasant rights while conservatives spoke for the upper classes. In actual practice there was little difference between them. In the six years before Walker appeared, the country had been subjected to fifteen presidents and countless revolutions. When conservative President Fruto Chamorro defeated Francisco Castellon in 1855, the latter fled to neighboring Honduras and appealed to General Trinidad Cabañas for military assistance.

Cabañas, a dictator backed by the liberal party of his country, sent an army across the border with Castellon and laid siege to the old walled city of Granada. After six months of fighting the city remained in government hands and General Cabañas was forced to recall his troops to defend Hondura's north border against a Guatemalan invasion. In that year the Guatemalan dictator was sympathetic to the Nicaraguan regime, and both spoke for the privileged classes.

The desperate Castellon cast about for new allies and found one in Byron Cole, a former California newspaper publisher who viewed Nicaragua as a plum ripe to be plucked. Castellon offered to hire as many as 300 Americans, who were to be paid in gold and land when Chamorro was ousted. Cole contacted William Walker, an attorney who had edited Cole's paper at San Francisco. After leading an abortive raid into Mexico in 1853, Walker had been tried by the United States government for filibustering.

Although acquitted of the charge, Walker had no wish to repeat the ordeal; therefore he was cautious when Cole showed him the Castellon contract. Sure that it violated the 1818 Neutrality Act, he told Cole to get rid of it and obtain a contract of "colonization." Cole complied. Walker immediately showed the new document to the federal attorney who had prosecuted him, and to General Wool, who had orders to intercept filibustering expeditions. Neither could find a legal basis for interfering with Walker's plan.

While raising funds and recruiting officers, Walker encountered Henry Crabbe, a former classmate from Tennessee who also was negotiating with Nicaraguan agents. In fact, with the assistance of the U.S. Minister to that country, Crabbe's agents had visited government and rebel camps and were considering offers from both sides. Eventually Crabbe went to Mexico and his ultimate demise, while his agents joined Walker and the rebels.

Their campaign succeeded so well that Walker was elected president of Nicaragua in the summer of 1856. Fighting continued in some areas of the country, but Walker confidently revamped the nation's laws, cleverly rewriting them to favor exploitation by American entrepreneurs. Despite a personal aversion to slavery, he restored that institution to a country which long had been free, in order to win support from southerners in the U.S. Congress. But such moves weakened his popularity in Nicaragua and aided the growing opposition throughout Central America.

Perhaps his greatest single error was a decision to revoke Cornelius Vanderbilt's exclusive franchise to transport passengers across Nicaragua. The irate shipping tycoon joined forces with the government of Costa Rica, whose common border with Nicaragua traced the water route Walker had closed. Vanderbilt's two envoys, an American and an Englishman with personal grievances against Walker, crossed the border with Costa Rican troops to begin a quiet takeover of the important waterway.

Addison's own opinion of the Nicaraguan affair had been stated in the *Journal* on January 23, 1857:

WILLIAM WALKER. The world despises little rascals, and respects big ones. Steal five dollars, and you are a thief—worthy of the jail or the whipping post. Steal a million, and we will praise your skill, and call you gentleman, and doff our hats to you as you pass.

Honesty . . . will do for children—that code of old fashioned integrity which our fathers thought was good to live and die by. It will not do for us, "children of a larger growth." We have another code. For "Thou shall not steal" we say, "Thou shall not steal *small amounts*;" and for "Be just, and fear not" we substitute "Be *successful* and fear not."

. . . If William Walker had landed in San Francisco a few months ago, he would have been received with ovations and rejoicings—like a hero returning from a glorious war. There would have been dinners, and presentations, and speeches. . . . What right have Walker and his crew to any such demonstrations of sympathy? . . . without a shadow of claim, by the mere right of the strongest, [they] made themselves for a brief time masters of the state. Over an indolent and degenerate tropical race, the rigor and energy of Anglo-Saxons were of course victorious.

But the natives, inferior in all the appliances of war except numbers, maintain the struggle in spite of defeat, as even an effeminate race will, fighting for liberty and the integrity of their nation. Now, the invaders are rapidly falling before the deadly influences of the climate of Nicaragua, and there is little left to them but a choice between annihilation and retreat, which is disgrace. . . .

We do not care what ends parties or politicians may hope to gain by the theft of Nicaragua; the sympathy and aid which the American people extend to such acts of flagrant wrong is, and should be, a disgrace to us in the eyes of all the world. We cry *"liberty!"* and when a weak people are struggling and suffering in her cause, fighting on their own soil to protect their hearths and altars, we shout for the invaders, and furnish them with money, and arms, and men. We *ought* to be despised and scorned abroad for this—and we *are*.

In February the steamer *Sierra Nevada* left San Francisco with reinforcements for Walker. Men from Grass Valley and Nevada City were said to be among the 200 volunteers on board. As usual, the *Democrat*'s perspective differed from that of the *Journal*. When Walker's fortunes seemed about to improve, Tallman Rolfe wrote:

The intelligence from Nicaragua . . . is of a cheering character. A dispatch from Aspinwall states that Walker has had three battles, in all of which the enemy were repulsed with great loss. . . . The news from Nicaragua, on the whole, is so much more favorable than anticipated, that it may be truly said, the star of Walker is again in the ascendant. May it never go down.

But it was a falling star. On May 16 the U.S. sloop of war *St. Marys* arrived at Panama with Walker and remnants of his staff. He had surrendered and agreed to leave Nicaragua. What was left of his defeated forces struggled through the jungles to San Juan and eventual transportation to the States. The *Journal*, once more edited by Senator Waite, commented:

The day of the "man of destiny" is over, and the star of his fate hath declined. Walker, the freebooter . . . has ignominiously left his slaughter house of Americans in Nicaragua, and seeks an asylum in the country whose laws he has violated and whose honorable name he has wantonly disgraced. The ill-starred ambition of one unscrupulous wretch, aided and abetted by men of like stripe, has dug thousands of gory graves for misguided countrymen of ours on foreign soil.

III

CONVICTED MURDERER Frank Moore made a desperate effort to escape on May 20. He told guards W. C. Asher and William Bidwell his bunk needed repair, and because he was chained at wrist and ankle, they supposed it was safe to enter his cell. As Asher knelt beside the bed, Moore suddenly freed his hands, knocked Bidwell unconscious, and attacked Asher with an iron bar he had filed off his leg shackles.

Though badly injured, Asher fought fiercely to keep the prisoner in his cell. As Bidwell regained consciousness he drew a pistol and began firing, but was unable to see clearly because of the blood flowing from his forehead. As the terrified Asher screamed at his partner to stop shooting, deputies rushed into the jail and overpowered Moore.

Afterwards the *Journal* marvelled:

Altogether it was a daring and fearful affair. We visited the jail the morning after the event. The floor of the corridor and jailor's room were covered with blood, and the clothes worn by the jailors at the time of the conflict were scattered about soaked in gore. Bidwell is seriously injured and is now lying at the house of the Sheriff.

The timing of Charley's departure could scarcely have been worse for Niles and Mary; her ship left San Francisco on the day Niles was to open court in Downieville. Each would have to leave Nevada City no later than Friday, July 3. On the preceding Monday a freak storm hit California and continued all day Tuesday.

Mary, Fred, and Charley began their long journey on muddy roads, accompanied as far as San Francisco by Addison, who was in remarkably high spirits. Addison's career had taken a sudden and spectacular turn for the better—little as he claimed to care for the practice of law, he could not hide his elation at being asked to replace Bill Stewart in the firm of McConnell and Stewart. The busiest law partnership in town was breaking up because Stewart's ambitions beckoned him to Downieville, now a prosperous and growing community.

McConnell's reputation had continued to grow after he stepped down from the post of attorney general. Addison quickly learned why, for his new partner worked hard and long, and McConnell saw to it that his junior partner had little time for leisure. The *Journal* and the *Democrat*, despite political differences, were united in their admiration of McConnell; both thought the next supreme court vacancy should go to him.

Summer always was the busiest season, and this year was no exception: because of the new schedule, district court went to Downieville for only one month before coming back to Nevada City on August 3, and this meant less time for lawyers to prepare cases between court terms. In addition, it was a time for political conventions, rallies, and parades, for the state election was scheduled for on September 1.

John McConnell no longer had time to play an active role in Democratic Party affairs, but Addison managed to chair the Know Nothing county convention and one outdoor rally. Republicans for the first time fielded a full slate of candidates, thus providing voters with three choices for each office. A pair of Nevada City lawyers opposed each other for state attorney general: Tom McFarland for the Americans, and Aaron Sargent for the Republicans.

John B. Weller, the Democratic candidate for governor, was a complex man at the peak of a mostly successful career. Before serving in the Mexican War he had been a three-term congressman from Ohio. He had received a hero's welcome when the war ended and was narrowly defeated for governor of Ohio.

In January 1849 Polk sent Weller to New Orleans to serve on the U.S.-Mexico boundary commission. After waiting several days in vain for his fellow commissioners to appear, Weller joined the rush to California. By the time he reached San Francisco his commission had been revoked by the incoming Whig administration of President Zachary Taylor.

Weller set up a law practice in San Francisco and resumed his politicking. In 1852 he outmaneuvered David C. Broderick in a bid for John Frémont's seat in the U.S. Senate, assisted by Senator William M. Gwin, who controlled California's southern wing of the Democratic party. Learning from this example, Broderick struck his own secret deal with Gwin and took the senate seat away from Weller in 1857.

Addison was not a great admirer of Broderick, but while editing the *Journal* he had complimented Broderick on his victory:

GREAT IS BRODERICK. The six years labor of this gentleman has at length come to an end in his election as the representative of California in the senate of the United States. Whatever we may think of him as the chosen candidate of a party whose principles we oppose ... we cannot refuse to award to him the credit of some high qualities. ...

His success will stand in history as a remarkable instance of the victory of a strong will over opposing circumstances. ... During the six

years of his constant effort, he has met with reverses and disappointments which would have disheartened most men.... Popular opinion
has burthened him with the curse of a multitude of crimes and outrages
committed by worse men than he....

If we must have a democratic senator, he is less objectionable than
any other.... His energy, and his ability to accomplish any object of his
desire, is well enough proven by his very election. We believe that he is
sincerely devoted to the interests of California, and that his efforts will
be devoted to their promotion.

Weller did not take the defeat lightly. At the Democratic state
convention he had retaliated by successfully opposing Broderick's choice
for governor—as a reward he took the nomination for himself.

At the July term of court at Downieville, Bill Stewart asked for a
change of venue for his client, and because Judge Searls already had
noted the strong local prejudice against David Butler, he agreed to move
the trial to Nevada City. Butler had fled to Oregon in 1855 after being
involved in the death of a popular Downieville man. A determined sheriff
had tracked him down and brought Butler back eighteen months later. At
the March 1857 term of district court Colonel Edward Baker had come
from San Francisco to win a delay so lawyers could prepare Butler's case.
Now Stewart and Sargent had teamed up for the defense.

While at Downieville Niles spent a few hours privately with Stewart.
The two friends discussed California prospects, with Stewart arguing
that as a result of the Nevada City fire Downieville now offered superior
opportunities for making money. He agreed with Niles, however, that
Nevada City retained certain advantages for raising a family, and proposed that Niles buy the Stewart house. Niles was interested, for it
represented all the qualities he admired most in a house and location, but
he cautiously reminded Bill of his tangled finances. Stewart let him know
this presented no obstacle. A note for $2500 would suffice, to be paid at
Niles's convenience. Stewart's practice was doing well at the moment.

Clement Fabius Woods, a fledgling attorney and former deputy
sheriff, was engaged to marry Bill's sister-in-law, and had become
Stewart's partner at Nevada City. When court resumed at Nevada City
on August 3, Stewart and his wife were out of town for the wedding of
Clem and Arabella at the Foote family home near Oakland. On Friday of
the same week they had returned to Nevada City, where Addison
notarized papers transferring ownership of the southern-style mansion to
Niles and Mary. When Mary came back to California she would become
mistress of the house built for Senator Foote's daughter.

When the new courthouse bell (installed in July as a result of the months-ago suggestion in the *Democrat*) rang on the morning of August 10, there was an immediate rush for seats to observe Butler's trial for the murder of Robert Moffat.

The *Journal* summary appeared four days later:

... it seems that Butler was in the card room of the Craycroft saloon, when Moffat came in, and accused a Mexican of being a thief—one of a band who intended to rob his quartz mill. The Mexican denied this. Some of the witnesses say Butler then spoke up and said it was a mistake—others [say] that Moffat asked if any one in the room knew the Mexican, and that then Butler replied, "I have known him a long time, it is a mistake," or words of the nature.

Moffat told him he was not speaking to him, he wanted nothing to do with him, or any of his "kind" ... [one witness] adds the words "I don't know that you are any better than he is." Moffat was leaving ... to have the Mexican arrested, when Butler said, "Be sure he is here when you get back."

Moffat, said, "I don't know that you or he either will be here when I get back." Witnesses said Moffat spoke loud and quick, as he usually did, and a stranger might have thought him irritable—and one witness for the prosecution said he thought from his manner there would be a fight. Moffat started for the front saloon. Butler said "I wonder what he meant? ... The next time a man talks to me in that way I'll whip him."

Butler then retreated to the bar, but returned after a few minutes. Butler stood watching Moffat with his arms crossed. His presence appeared to annoy Moffat, who began an exchange of heated words. The *Journal* account went on:

Butler had let his hand drop by his side when Moffat first spoke to him. He now drew his pistol, an eight inch Colt's, and struck at Moffat, without hitting him, Moffat stepping back. He made a second blow, Moffat receiving it on the arm.... Two witnesses for the prosecution said Butler then elevated the pistol ... and fired it at Moffat ... [and stepped] back as Moffat advanced to grasp it....

Two witnesses for the defense swore that Moffat advanced after the second blow, grabbed the pistol [and] Butler stepped back a step, jerking the pistol, and it went off.... Two men say [Butler] held it in both hands [near his] ... waistband, stepping back as Moffat advanced. The other witnesses of the prosecution did not see this ... or say Moffat *might* have had hold of the pistol when it fired ... but don't think he did....

The jury was absent about fifteen minutes, and in the midst of a breathless silence, rendered their verdict "guilty of murder as charged in the indictment." We are told the prisoner quietly remarked, "I shall not have to answer to my God for the crime of murder."

Opinion among the court spectators was entirely against the accused, and the *Journal* quoted one defense lawyer as complaining, "The very air seemed heavy with prejudice against the prisoner, and it would require more courage on the part of the jury to give him the benefit of a reasonable doubt . . . than it would to find him guilty of murder."

The prisoner was brought to court for sentencing on the following Monday; to everyone's surprise Judge Searls appeared distraught and spoke with considerable difficulty. The *Democrat* reported:

The judgment of the Court, which was very impressively and feelingly pronounced, was that David Butler be publicly executed by the Sheriff between the hours of 10 A.M. and 4 P.M. on Friday the 9th day of October next. . . . Judge Searls declared a profound sympathy for the prisoner—a sincere regret for the unfortunate situation in which he had placed himself—alluded to the prejudice which had existed against him at Downieville and the propriety of a change of venue thence—expressed a hope that others might have a warning and example in the awful consequences which intemperance had entailed upon the prisoner.

The *Journal* also made note of the court's unusual demeanor:

The prisoner received his sentence with less emotion than Judge Searls pronounced it. Indeed, the Judge was so deeply moved as to be scarcely able to enunciate the judgement of the court. . . . It was an impressive scene. The court room was crowded. The prisoner, when asked the usual question, replied through his senior counsel, Wm. M. Stewart, that he was under the influence of strong drink at the time Moffit received his death wound, that the shot which afterwards proved fatal was purely accidental, though he was in anger from epithets heaped upon him by the deceased. He also expressed profound sorrow for the deed which had forfeited his life.

John Huyck store, Rensselaerville

CHAPTER 32

SWEET HOME

August–December 1857

I

*A*T THE CONCLUSION OF THEIR two week stay in Rensselaerville, Fred and Mary embarked on an excursion to Sand Lake to visit Will and Cornelia. Once there, Mary and Cornelia launched a marathon conversation to explore events of the past several years. Talking at breakneck speed, they endeavored to make up in a few days for the long separation.

While they talked Mary admired the cleanliness and quiet of Sand Lake, where cultivated gardens and fenced pastures stretched across the landscape. The calm and settled atmosphere contrasted sharply with California's villages. Nevada City was especially ugly now that fires had destroyed the native conifers that once lined its streets. Originally positioned in a great forest, now the city was encircled by stumps, garbage, and the normal debris of a mining camp. Viewing Cornelia's lovely surroundings, Mary hoped the time would arrive when she and Niles might come home to a similar scene.

Will Allen's apparent contentment showed Mary a man could be satisfied without probing the world's frontiers. Nevertheless, it would not do to trade places with Cornelia, whose every move was scrutinized minutely by residents of Sand Lake and Schodac, the townships served by her husband. Mary saw that Mrs. Allen was required to exercise unusual discretion—and in time she discovered aspects of her sister's marriage that were concealed from most outsiders.

Cornelia described a spiritual disagreement between herself and Will that had been a sore point with them until recently. The problem had involved a rather fundamental article of Baptist doctrine stating there was a single path to salvation, each step of which was designated exactly in the Protestant Bible. A dogma known as Close Communion declared that adherents of other faiths could not take part in the Baptist ritual of communion.

Cornelia, born and raised a Presbyterian, had resented the notion of her own unfitness, or that of her family and friends. Sincere and devoted in her religious beliefs, she was unwilling to concede superior virtues or motives to Baptists. Because this disagreement produced a troubling rift in their otherwise agreeable life, Cornelia was relieved when Will appeared to have changed his mind during a conversation with fellow Sand Lake clergymen.

Mr. Doolittle was a Presbyterian minister, and Mr. Ogden conducted a private school. Each had preached guest sermons at Will's church, and he had delivered addresses at their institutions. One afternoon, during a visit to the Baptist parsonage, Ogden asked Will how he could reconcile his recent sermon about Christian brotherhood with the practice of Close Communion. To Cornelia's surprise, Will had replied: "I *cannot* reconcile it. I believe there *must* be something wrong which so separates Christians."

In discussing the matter with her sister, Cornelia assured Mary he was firm in his convictions and would never be a conventional Baptist. "What *time* may do, I cannot tell," she confided, swearing her sister to secrecy—should anyone in his church report this heresy it could result in his removal and excommunication.

Because so many young people had quit the placid farm communities for cities offering greater opportunities, local church pews were occupied mostly by middle-aged and elderly worshippers. Will's parishioners were set in their ways and discouraged innovation, causing Will to talk sometimes of venturing elsewhere, perhaps to the Mississippi valley. Mary perceived that Niles was not so unique as she had supposed.

Abram Searls, her father-in-law, unexpectedly appeared near the end of her visit, determined to escort her and Fred to Canada. Although she had planned to go north sometime, no definite arrangements had been made. Uncle Abram's arrival settled the matter, and on September 25 she wrote to her own parents from the home of Niles's sister Joanna:

It is not easy to write when I am visiting among strangers. . . . We are enjoying our visit very much. Alice [Babbitt] is home with her little boy, and Fred has great times with him and [young] Abram when we are there. We are now at Joanna's and her youngest boy Washington is about as wild as boys often get to be, but he and Fred get along first rate and are very happy together. . . .

I have not been about at all yet. They are all busy thrashing this week, but will be at liberty next week, and then I expect to visit all the cousins. . . . I guess I have some news for you—but you may have heard it. Martha Niles is married to Dr Dorland and is living in Bellville, up the lake or bay somewhere. . . .

I suppose there will be letters from Niles this week. If they come in time to send them up I hope you will do so. It would be very pleasant to hear from him while here. I must stop writing, for Mother wont go to sleep till the candle is out.

II

A BANK PANIC ERUPTED at New York and St. Louis while Mary was in Canada. Banker William Tecumseh Sherman had been transferred by Lucas and Turner from San Francisco to their New York City office. When the crisis came he wrote his St. Louis employers:

Well, all hell has broken loose. . . . There is a run on every bank of the city, many of which have gone in. I see no reason why all must not succumb. Of all excitement heretofore, this exceeds by ten fold.

J. H. Lucas, a partner in the firm, had been wiped out, and Sherman offered condolences, adding, "I hope he will clean out and never again undertake so disreputable a business as banking." Charley Mulford abruptly left New York on the first steamer bound for Panama, leaving behind his family and Mary and Fred. Although he was supposed to have gone with them, Charley believed delay might spell disaster for his bank, now under the temporary management of Arthur Hagadorn and Levi Kellogg.

When Mary learned of his departure, she wrote her mother:

I suppose you will be expecting me this week, but as the question of my returning to Cal. this fall is now settled by Charlie's sudden move, and my friends are very anxious that I should stay, I have concluded to spend another week. I am enjoying my visit much, the weather is charming.

Niles letters were filled with good news. All well, election over, and Niles has taken Stewarts house, they having moved to Downieville. I dont know whether he has rented or bought it. He gave no particulars—only said it was ready for us to go to housekeeping. Add has bought the furniture of one room and is to sleep there and look after the place till I come.

An arrangement to meet Cornelia on her way home went awry, partly due to the arrival of nasty weather. Upon arriving at Rensselaerville Mary wrote her sister:

I was as much disappointed in not meeting you as you were I suppose in not seeing me. Had it not been for my plan to meet you, I should have remained longer in Canada, instead of starting off in a storm of wind and snow, without any thing but my blanket shawl for Fred and that thin cloak for myself. It rained hard Monday morning [October 19] and all day, and as I had 12 miles to ride in an open waggon, I of course did not venture to start....

It stormed hard all day Tuesday, and on account of the roughness of the lake, and the leaky state of the steamer that ran across the river, we were obliged to go in a ferry boat to [Wolf] Island, and then cross the island 7 miles in an open stage and the rest of the way, 1 mile, in a little sail boat. Father Searls came with me to Cape Vincent, and we staid there all night—next morning he put me aboard the cars, and procured through tickets and checks to Albany, so that I had no trouble in coming along. Strange to say, Fred and I took but slight colds. I put all the wrappings I had about him, and had only my duster on while we crossed the island....

Hattie Backus came out [from Troy] Thursday, James Carter is here too, so that if it ever stops raining I shall have some fine times, but it rains right straight along.... [Pa is] sorry he was nominated for the [state] Senate. He thinks there is no chance of election, as the Whigs and Know Nothings have united against the Dem. party.... Had letters from Niles.... Add is doing well. McConnell says he is the smartest young lawyer he has seen in the state.

III

JOHN NILES predicted correctly; although he led the Democratic ticket at Albany and in other communities where he was known, the Know Nothing candidate was elected. Mary spent the next few weeks quietly with her mother and grandmother. They sat and sewed and knitted and talked, and Mary told Cornelia in November:

We take things easily and have good visits every day. Grandma sits in her corner, and we sit by the other windows and can talk as much as we please. I have made today a nice warm sack for Fred to wear out in the yard and to the barn &c. out of that old red sack of mine.

Hattie Backus was detained from coming here this week, but will come next. I wish you could be here. . . . I am impatient for you to come home.

Will brought Cornelia to Rensselaerville, but it was only a short visit because they had to return to Sand Lake for Thanksgiving services. The Bates Tannery at Rensselaerville burned down on the night before Thanksgiving, and the smoke gave Polly Niles such a headache she stayed home from church the next day, despite her wish to hear the new Presbyterian minister. On December 1 Mary added a note to her mother's letter to Cornelia:

I had so many things I wanted to say, but I was invited out and have to write Niles this evening . . . . He is not very well and a good deal homesick; talks some of trying to come after me in Feb. or March. . . . Deb had a letter from Charles at Acapulco, he was well. The panic is not as great in Cal. as was feared, but the [banking] house of Sather and Church was closed—hopes entertained that it would open in a few days. No news from Charles business.

Two weeks later, Mary wrote a long letter, telling her sister she wanted to see her once more:

I intend to visit you this winter if I can. Ma says if it is good sleighing, Pa or Charlie [Niles] can take us in a sleigh. I am almost afraid to take Fred so far, but we can bundle warm and stop often. . . .

[Niles's] stay will of course be short, if he comes. I must say I feel quite sanguine that he will come, but shall know better when he knows of Charlie's arrival in Cal. He will be in Downieville and wont have time to mail a letter by return mail, which will come next week. . . . He asked as a favor that I should write to him weekly, and he has written to me every Sunday for a long time. . . .

[Fred] is busy from morning till night, sawing, building, pounding, preaching, thrashing, pedling, baking, sewing, keeping up through it all a constant stream of talk, and interspersing it with various pieces of mischief and naughtiness. . . . He has been very busy today trying to teach pussy the letters, and is well paid for half an hours patient coaxing if he can get her to look at them and say *mew*.

Will had concluded to find a new church; his fellow clergymen had agreed with his conviction that it was next to impossible to breathe new spirit into Sand Lake. While he traveled about in search of a position, Cornelia would be left alone, a situation Mary proposed to remedy:

Ma and I have been wishing and hoping that you may break up house keeping and come home a few weeks or *months* even before I leave. Wouldnt that be delightful to be all here together once more, long enough to have a *quiet* visit and to make it seem *just like old times.* I shall never feel quite satisfied if it cannot be so that you can be home more than a week.

I think I had better calculate to come to you about the last of Jan. or the middle if it should be good sleighing. Then if Niles comes the last of Feb. I shall be with you. There is a family going back [to California] in May with whom I shall go if there is no other chance. I would like to see you in a new home before I leave, that I might think of you with all your surroundings, but you may go so far that I could not visit you, so I will hope that you remain where you are.

In a couple of days Mary had later news from California to pass on to her sister:

Charlie had just telegraphed of his arrival [at San Francisco]. He had lost nothing, neither had Arthur and his partner [Kellogg]. Sather and Church were still unable to resume but most people thought they would. Niles thought they would not. All our friends are secured against loss except Add. If any one loses he will I fear, as his [bank] draft was drawn at the very worst time.

Charles had formed no plans for the future. I think he will come home soon. I have never *expected* Deb would go back, so that I am not very much disappointed, but it will be a greater loss to me than any one can think. I think Hattie Backus will surely go when I do, and that will be a great comfort, for she is a very sweet girl, but she can not fill Deb's place any more than she could yours.

Niles had not heard of Charlies arrival, but seemed to have a presentiment that I was not coming. He seems very much perplexed to know how I will get back in the event that he cannot come for me. He will come if he can, and if not he proposed that I should start on the 5th of March and meet him at the Isthmus. He can leave [California] at that time and come thus far without leave or license, and without interfering with business, and all the care I would need would be after I arrive at the Isthmus. It is but ten days travel on this side, and he would be there to cross the Isthmus with me. . . .

I know you will be disappointed, so will we all, and I hope and *believe* that he will come for me instead, yet of course I must form my plans to meet that of going in March, until I hear more definitely. . . .

After Christmas Polly pressed Cornelia once more about visiting Rensselaerville during Will's absence:

I feel quite anxious about your matters, but say but little, as I can [not] do good by talking about them. I do hope you will not have to go far away, for when Mary is gone I shall miss you *sadly* but I know you must not stay for me, but go where duty calls and I hope you may do it *cheerfully.*

We have been sitting in counsel this evening upon the subject of visiting and have concluded it will not be prudent for Mary to take Fred over the Hills in an open waggon this cold weather, and you was mistaken in the time of Pa going to Albany; he goes the 2d Monday in January, not the first. Now if you could come out and stay untill that time and go in with him with his own horse if the weather and going will permit, or by stage if bad, are you well enough if nothing else should prevent, or will it make you sick?

. . . Fred is verry well and full of fun, wants to do every thing that he sees done—out doors or in he saws wood and says he is a Carpenter, but sometimes he is a tailor, baker, and butcher, but we are glad he has got a grandpa sometimes, for he gets on the upper shelf—he thinks he is going to take us all home with him, even to kitty. He is as *bright* a *boy* as *I* ever *saw*, but he needs a great deal of careful training and Mary tries hard to do it, but she has got it to do a great while if he lives; I am glad she is *patient* for that is a good quality in a Mother.

Mary added:

I hope it will not be imprudent for you to come. . . . Fred had a merry Christmas, with plenty of candies and nuts, primers &c, and a handsome silver knife and fork I sent to Hammie for. Hammie sent me a beautiful pearl paper knife. Pa gave me a handsome lawn dress (brown), I gave Grandma a new silk Alpacha apron, engaged a pair of mittens for Sarah, which did not get finished, and commenced a collar for Emmie which shared the same fate, but they will do for New Years day. . . . Fred and I went to the Christmas tree at Mr. Washbons.

Broad Street 1857

CHAPTER 33

REVERSED DECISIONS

August–December 1857

I

TEN CONVICTS including Jim Webster and Wallace Gehr escaped from San Quentin on August 24; Lee Schell was caught at once, but nine remained at large. All were accomplished thieves ranging in age from twenty to twenty-eight. A few weeks later the *Journal* warned citizens:

The season for robberies has opened again. . . . We frequently hear of doors being tried of nights, voices heard and other suspicious circumst-ances. . . . Men have on several occasions been stopped evenings in the outskirts of the town and compelled to deliver their money in the face of drawn pistols. The city and the roads leading out of it are infested with thieves and robbers. . . .

[Petitions] have been circulated [asking] for a strong night police to guard the city till after the 9th of October. The threats . . . and the jail deliveries to which we have been subject have warned the people to be on the watch. . . . A number of citizens from each street will alternately guard all the points liable to danger until after execution day has passed.

The execution was to be that of Frank Moore, whose other avenues of escape had been closed—the supreme court refused to intervene, and the governor turned down a request to commute Moore's sentence after receiving a counter-petition bearing signatures of more than 600 prominent citizens. Then, two weeks before the hanging, violence erupted from an entirely unexpected quarter as Marshal Plumer was arrested for the murder of gambler John Vedder. The *Journal* said the city was in "a state of high excitement."

One of only two Democratic candidates to be defeated in the recent election, Henry Plumer's name had been scratched from the party ticket by hundreds of voters in an unusual show of independence. His defeat for the state assembly had pleased the *Journal*, which now stated that Plumer's "course and conduct have been very generally condemned." Having delivered this opinion, the paper went on to say:

For ourselves as journalists it properly belongs to us only [to] give facts. . . . For some months [Vedder] had lived unhappily with his wife, and for some two months the pair have been arranging for a separation. About a week since, the preliminary steps were taken to procure a divorce. . . . While matters were thus pending, Mrs. Vedder [and] her child took lodgings at the Hotel de Paris.

Vedder had taken the child from his wife and left it with friends on a ranch miles from Nevada City. Mrs. Vedder continued to live at the hotel, but often went to her house on Spring street during the day, sometimes remaining there until late in the evening. She was there with Henry Plumer shortly before midnight on the night of the shooting. They were sitting in the kitchen when Mrs. Vedder realized her husband was climbing the back stairs—she said she knew who it was by the sound of his tread, even though it was rare for him to enter the house by this entrance.

According to her testimony, Vedder opened the kitchen door, drew a pistol, announced that Plumer's "time had come" and fired. The *Journal* recounted her description of what followed:

Plumer returned the fire immediately, and following Vedder, who was retreating down the stairs, fired two or three shots more. Plumer then left by the front door. . . . She says she went down the [back] steps . . . and saw her husband lying on the ground with a pistol near him. He was not yet dead. . . . Mrs. Vedder thinks Plumer fired four shots in all.

No bullet marks were found in the kitchen, where Vedder was said to have fired first, but two holes were discovered in the fence and an outhouse, apparently made by bullets coming from the top of the stairs. A trio of doctors disagreed about the direction of bullets which caused Vedder's fatal wounds.

Plumer was released on payment of $8000 bail. When bondsmen later decided the property pledged as security by his friends was insufficient for the purpose, they surrendered him to the sheriff, who placed him in the county jail. The *Journal* fussed:

> It is not too late to offer a remark on straw bail. . . . No blame can be attached to a culprit or his counsel for getting off as easily as possible, but the officer who accepts of bail when he ought to know it is worthless is highly reprehensible. . . .

A grand jury impaneled on October 8 was unable to act on Plumer's indictment because so many jurors had expressed opinions of his guilt. A special grand jury would have to be called to hear the facts.

Meanwhile, when Mrs. Vedder forcibly removed her child from her father-in-law's home near Sacramento, she was followed to her lodging house by people who threatened to take the child by force. Police took mother and child to the station house for safekeeping while a Sacramento judge heard her writ of habeas corpus. When the senior Vedder offered evidence of her bad character he was awarded temporary custody of his grandchild.

II

ON OCTOBER 9 thousands of spectators gathered near the Jewish cemetery to witness Moore's hanging. The sheriff insisted he had taken every precaution to prevent rescue or escape, but he was proved wrong— for the second time in two weeks the city was "thrown into a state of intense excitement" with the embarrassing announcement that the prisoner had taken his own life. The *Journal* recounted the astonishing tale:

> The gallows was taken from the jail this morning at 4 o'clock and erected in the vicinity of Gold Flat, near a mile out of town, where a grave was dug to receive the body. . . . Madam Moore is said to have told the workmen of the utter uselessness of their labor, as Moore would never die upon that scaffold. It was however treated as braggadocio. . . .
>
> The impression has all along prevailed that Moore would not end his career upon the scaffold. So strong has been the idea, and so frequently

expressed, that ... the prisoner has frequently been removed from one cell to another, leaving everything behind in which it was deemed possible a particle of poison could be concealed ... [but] the drug was conveyed to the wretched man and he died by his own hand, cheating the gallows, and the people of an awful spectacle. ...

Mrs. Moore was heard to say ... several times during the night, "Now Frank dont you forget that". ... What the import of the exhortation might be is not known to a certainty, but the repeated declarations of the woman that her husband never would die upon the scaffold, leaves room for inference. ... Moore was engaged in the afternoon of yesterday and a part of the evening in dictating his will, by which he is said to leave property to the amount of six or seven thousand dollars to his wife. ... No woman could be more faithful to a husband under the most trying circumstances. ...

Many of the acquaintances of Moore were admitted to see him on yesterday, and Rev. Father Dalton, his confessor, remained with him until five o'clock this morning. ... His wife left him in the evening, bidding him an affecting and eternal farewell. ... The obdurate heart of the criminal melted and he wept as a child. ... His confessor exhorted him to abstain from liquor and to meet his fate like a sober man and Christian. A bottle of wine was in his cell, and at the earnest exhortations of the Reverend Father ... the prisoner threw it under the grate of his cell. Shortly after 5 o'clock this morning and after the confessor had departed, the prisoner called for a glass of wine which was given him.

[Only] a few moments elapsed [before] a groan was heard to come from the cell. George Lenhart, the jailor, went to the prisoner and found him in the agonies of death. Taking him by the arm, he asked him what was the matter, to which the prisoner made answer that he did not know, and these were the last words he uttered. Dr. Wickes was called, but too late.

Mrs. Moore admitted knowing her husband possessed the poison, but denied furnishing it. She said she had urged him not to kill himself but to die "honorably" in an escape attempt. To prove her assertions she showed the sheriff a file and "other contrivances" Moore had concealed in a crack in the floor. A stiletto improvised from wire was fastened by candlewax to the underside of a backless chair. A packet containing traces of the poison Moore had used was similarly fastened beneath the same chair, which Moore's guard had obligingly moved from the old cell to the new one at the prisoner's request. The *Journal* continued:

A prisoner in the jail says there is not a cell that has not poison concealed somewhere ... for the accommodation of suicides. ... We learn from good authority that the poison was handed into the window, probably on Monday last, and passed to Moore by a fellow prisoner named [Andrew Jackson] Kelly, who at the time was confined in the hall of the jail for some minor offense.

This man Kelly, it is said, had planned an escape of all the prisoners on Wednesday night last, by killing the jailor and seizing the keys. The plan came to light, and a large butcher knife was discovered in the corridor near the cell of Kelly, with which it is supposed he intended to accomplish his horrid purpose.

The body of the deceased was removed this morning at about 10 o'clock to the rear of the jail, where a dense crowd has been pressing for hours to see the corpse. There are probably three thousand people in town. . . . Men are to be seen from Rabbit Creek, Seventy Six, Downieville, Auburn and other places remote. The hotels are full. . . .

We learn that Madam Moore . . . attempted to destroy herself on Monday last by swallowing strychnine. She was discovered . . . and a physician . . . forced open her mouth and an emetic down her throat which succeeded in dislodging the poison. She declares, however, her determination to end her days.

According to a biographical sketch in the *Democrat* Francis Van Moore was born May 5, 1826, in New York City. His father was an American of German descent, and his mother a native of France. When he was two years old his parents removed to Louisville, Kentucky, and afterwards to Missouri. After remaining in St. Louis a year or two, they returned to Louisville.

His father died when he was a boy, and at the age of twelve Moore ran away to New York, Liverpool, Havre, and Frankfurt. After working three years in Germany apprenticed to a gunsmith he returned to France and was married at the age of nineteen. His wife died two years later. After leaving their infant son with an uncle in New York, Moore came to California with Frémont in 1848, and had remained there ever since, mostly in Nevada County.

The Grass Valley *Telegraph* soon reported that Mrs. Moore's spirits had improved after some good ladies and gentlemen intervened on her behalf:

Although she has property in the States, she is absolutely destitute here. She has promised to accept a home which has been tendered her for a winter in a respectable family, where she will be kindly cared for until spring, when she proposes to go to her friends in the East, and take possession of her property there, which will afford her an ample competence. . . .

Andrew Kelly, the prisoner supposed to have supplied poison to Moore, was discharged on October 26. The district attorney said he lacked sufficient evidence to convict Kelly of grand larceny, for which he had been arrested. The freed man promptly demanded that the *Democrat* retract a statement that he stole $20 from a fellow inmate, but Tallman Rolfe was not impressed:

He said he was innocent of the charge, and referred us to the jailors, who would substantiate his statement. We conversed with the jailors yesterday on the subject, and they not only confirm our former statement, but from the circumstances as related, we should judge there would be no difficulty in convicting Kelly of petty larceny.

The next issue chronicled Kelly's subsequent activities:

He left Nevada immediately after his discharge and went to Grass Valley, where he had the misfortune to be again charged with stealing, for which he was convicted of petty larceny, and was sentenced by Justice Spofford to imprisonment in the county jail for six months. It seems he went into a shooting gallery, and picked up a pistol which he carried off. He says he only took the pistol in joke, and that if he had had half a chance to have defended himself he might have cleared himself of the charge. Kelly is certainly an unfortunate man. He can console himself with the reflection, however, that the county is responsible for his board.

Henry Plumer posted acceptable bonds on October 27 and was released from jail. Judge Searls refused a motion for change of venue and set trial for December. Wallace Gehr, who had been recaptured after escaping San Quentin, was granted a new trial by the supreme court, which said Judge Caswell had erred in permitting a juror to sit on the case after expressing an opinion.

III

NEWS OF BANK failures in the east reached California in October—the last steamer of the month carried a list of 200 failed institutions. On November 5 the Nevada City telegraph office reported that Sather and Church had suspended operations at San Francisco. The *Journal* said:

From the best information we can gather, from forty to fifty thousand dollars in drafts are holden by our citizens drawn on the concern ... [and] about half was issued from the office of Hagadorn & Kellogg of this city.... Whatever may be the fate of Sather & Church, we deem the parties who sold the checks here at home, perfectly responsible. Besides being responsible, we are quite certain they are honorable men. Therefore there need be little fear of loss on the part of depositors or draft holders ... we are fully in the belief that the banking house of Sather & Church is perfectly solvent.

A story headlined "Splendid Act!" told of the daring rescue of Nevada County gold:

The express of last night filled the city with joy. Drafts to a large amount had been drawn on Sather & Church by Hagadorn & Kellogg, and the dust sent by Wells, Fargo & Co. to meet them. [Sather & Church] had suspended, the telegraph was down, and no orders could be transmitted to stop the gold from going into the hands of the suspended firm.

In this crisis there was found an old Nevadan at San Francisco, who like General Jackson, was willing to take responsibilities. Knowing the fact that a large sum, over $11,000, was on its way from Hagadorn & Kellogg, J. R. Whitney Esq. watched its arrival. Before it came it was garnisheed by the creditors of Sather & Church. Mr. Whitney made his appearance as soon as the funds came and demanded them as the agent of Hagadorn & Kellogg.

Not obtaining the money he went farther and replevined it and had it transfered to the assay office of Kellogg & Humbert, where the checks of our principal Banking House will be duly paid. There's an act for you.

Charley Mulford arrived soon after and resumed control of his bank. Tallman Rolfe wondered if lost confidence in banks might account for an unusual discovery:

A search warrant was procured last Sunday to search a house occupied by some Spanish people, near the court house. The search was made by Mr. Tompkins, the Deputy Marshall, who found in the house, according to his estimate, between $10,000 and $15,000 in gold coin, a large quantity of jewelry, and some four or five thousand dollars of Adams & Co's. certificates of deposit. The experience of the owners of the coin in making deposits, doubtless induced them to become their own bankers. The stolen property for which the warrant was procured was not found.

David Butler's scheduled hanging was postponed from December to February, provoking a storm of protest from Downieville citizens. The *Journal* endeavored to calm their fears:

The indignation in Sierra is natural. A citizen very much respected was slain, they believe, without sufficient provocation. The individual who committed the deed has been arrested at great expense, tried, convicted and sentenced by an unbiased jury. The people of Sierra, like all other good citizens, desire to see the laws executed and the convicted punished. . . .

They have . . . a groundless apprehension that Governor Johnson intends to pardon Butler before the expiration of his term of office. There is no foundation for such a surmise. . . . no petition in behalf of Butler has been circulated either here or elsewhere . . . the leniency extended . . . by the Governor has been mostly obtained by the efforts of a minister of the Gospel and the prisoner's counsel. . . .

The *Bulletin* raises a howl about the money of Butler having its influence! This will be news to his counsel, who . . . would like to know where the case or property may be found to remunerate themselves out of it.

The proprietors of the *Democrat* could not resist a sly dig:

The men who have been the most active in endeavoring to procure Butler's pardon were all the vigilance sympathisers, and have heretofore delighted in holding forth to the people on the inadequacy of the laws to punish crime . . . the only object they can have in thus endeavoring to defeat the ends of justice, in by far the worst murder case ever tried in this county, is to give them an excuse to denounce the legal authorities hereafter.

Men who set themselves up as patterns of morality, and are the most fierce in their denunciations of the faults of others, will generally bear watching.

Wallace Gehr was found guilty a second time, but his sentence was reduced from ten to four and half years in prison. No extra penalties were imposed for his numerous escapes.

Addison's letter to Cornelia on December 18 said he and McConnell had received unwelcome news: the supreme court had reversed a ruling by Judge Searls that favored their clients. The suit was one of several against Laird and Chambers for damages incurred when the Deer Creek dam failed. Laird and Chambers had contracted with Moore and Foss to build the dam, which had not been completed or accepted when it gave way. Defense lawyers requested Judge Searls to instruct the jury that if in their opinion Moore and Foss had (1) acted independently, (2) had sole control of the work, and (3) through their negligence damage occurred before it had been accepted, the jury should find for Laird and Chambers.

Judge Searls instead instructed the jury that Moore and Foss had been employed by Laird and Chambers; if the dam gave way because of imperfect construction Laird and Chambers were liable for whatever injury might result. Justice Stephen Field, writing for the supreme court, sided with defense lawyers who argued that during construction only the contractors were liable.

Several cases against Laird and Chambers was based on the same principle, and each would have to be retried. Unfortunately, the grocery firm of Boswell and Hanson and the contracting firm of Moore and Foss had been forced into bankruptcy, so it was unlikely any new trials would follow. Addison described the atmosphere in his office as tense:

My partner is chafing and tearing about the room in a huge rage . . . . I think he is half inclined to be angry with me because I wont get angry too—but I cant afford to waste good anger on what I cant help; so while I am as calm as a summers day—I am writing in the midst of a thunder storm.

I suppose you are shivering with the cold of mid winter now. Here it is one of the finest pleasantest days of the whole year. The sun shines warm, and though the rains ceased only two days ago, the ground is almost perfectly dry. Yet I would almost as soon it rained, for there is no one to enjoy the pleasant weather with—and no time to enjoy it if there was.

You cant think how lonesome I get here sometimes. Niles is always busy. My friends are lawyers—good men, some of them, and intelligent—pleasant men to talk with—but not companions after all. I wish May would come back—and Fred. We miss his Royal Highness and his Royal Highness' Mother. . . .

I dont know a woman in the whole state now—only just well enough to say good morning, and touch my hat. What chance do you think I have to find the "good girl" you wish for me? I could not find one here if I wished—and I dont wish it. I look forward to old bachelorhood with tolerable content—and you must be content to have one old bachelor brother.

I am looking and waiting for the time when I can come home and visit you—and mother. I have not made a fortune, you know. I dont think I ever shall. . . . whenever I get a few hundred ahead, it takes to itself wings and flies away. I dont care [about] that, but it puts off the time when I can come and see you. . . .

Corner Broad and Bridge Streets

CHAPTER 34

UNHAPPY HUSBANDS

December 1857–February 1858

I

WHEN A HUNDRED MEN were summoned to try Henry Plumer, only seven could say they had formed no opinion. A hundred more were brought in from greater distances and eventually a full jury was found to hear the case. Plumer was being defended by McConnell and Niles, George Hupp, and David Belden. Soon after the trial began, assistant prosecutor Henry Meredith protested that Hupp was providing the *Journal* with a one-sided version of the proceedings. Editor Waite replied he surely hadn't meant to distort the facts, but he and his staff were too busy setting type to read the story and discover Hupp had been defending Plumer.

Much testimony repeated what had been developed at the coroner's inquest and was already well known. H. W. Rice, a friend of the deceased since 1850, had visited Mr. and Mrs. Vedder on Independence Day. Rice did not mention it to the court, but on July 4th Vedder had been injured when a rocket struck him in the face during a fireworks display. Two splinters entered his forehead, one so deep it had to be removed by a surgeon. At the time it was supposed he might lose the sight of one eye.

A few days later Vedder described to him the details of a serious domestic quarrel in which words had been exchanged that "could never be retracted." Rice told the court that on other occasions he had seen Vedder knock his wife down and pinch her nose "until she could scarcely get her breath." Vedder boasted of whipping her, "which made her behave pretty well for a few months."

David Belden, one of Plumer's own lawyers, took the stand to tell how John Vedder visited him three or four weeks before the killing and said his wife wanted a divorce. Vedder would not contest the action if he received custody of their child. Belden asked what her grounds for divorce would be, and was told it was because he had slapped her a few times. Several days passed before Vedder informed Belden his wife had changed her mind.

Next to visit Belden was Henry Plumer, who said Lucinda Vedder wished to see him about a divorce. Lucinda told Belden her husband was cruel and abusive and often "abandoned" her—meaning he would not stay with her when she was ill. Afterwards Vedder wondered who had arranged the meeting with his wife, but Belden refused to say. Vedder assured him the couple had reconciled, but in a few days he returned and told Belden to get on with the suit. He would not "be fooled with any longer."

Plumer's life had been threatened by Vedder, according to what the marshal told E. H. Barker. However, Plumer swore he wouldn't let Vedder have the first shot. Plumer also told Barker he was aware of everything Vedder said and did. Vedder himself told Barker a different story: he could have killed Plumer twenty different times had he wished, but he had no desire to become an assassin.

N. F. Scott remembered Vedder saying he and Plumer "walked the streets with their hands on their pistols." Vedder had showed Scott a knife he thought more of than any pistol. Nevertheless, Vedder had asked Rice for the loan of a pistol, and on being informed Plumer had gone to the Vedder house with Lucinda, said that was all he wanted to know. Rice continued:

[He] quickened his pace and drew out his pistol and knife and said that he would make a funeral pile of Plumer and his wife on the spot. He told me the next morning that it was a lucky thing for Plumer that he did not find him there, as he would have killed them both. He said he took his wife by the hair of her head, drew his bowie knife and threatened to cut her throat—that he ought to have done so long ago.

On the afternoon of the fatal day, Vedder gave his wife $25, which she handed over to Belden in exchange for the divorce papers. Vedder exclaimed, "I want no more fooling . . . she can go to hell her own way!"

Rice had written Vedder's father to say trouble was brewing, and urged him to get his son away from Nevada City. But Rice also agreed to loan Vedder a pistol, and on the day of the killing Vedder told Rice he was going to kill Plumer:

He said that he would try to get under the floor and catch Plumer and his wife together, and kill them both at once. Vedder told me that [not] Plumer nor any other man could be intimate with his wife until he married her.

About midnight Thomas Couch heard screams outside his Pine Street residence, which was about 60 feet from the Vedder house. A glance from his window revealed Lucinda Vedder running from house to house and crying for help—her husband had been shot. Couch quickly dressed and hurried to the Vedder's steep lot on the south side of Spring Street. The front door was at street level, but a staircase connected the rear of the house to a lower level where outhouses were located. It was at the foot of these stairs that he discovered his neighbor's lifeless body. After noting there was no sign of a weapon in the near vicinity, he entered the empty house.

Plumer's deputies, Bruce Garvey and Pat Corbett, arrived a few minutes later, at which time Couch went back for a second look at Vedder. To his surprise, this time he noticed a 6-inch Colt's revolver in plain sight alongside the dead man's hand. Couch testified:

I picked it up and saw it was loaded, and was about examining it more closely when Pat Corbett took it out of my hands. "I'll take that pistol," said he, coming up to me abruptly, and reaching out his hand, he took it and placed it in his bosom. . . . I saw three caps upon the pistol. I was near the body about five minutes when I first went there, and at that time I saw no pistol lying upon the ground. . . .

Corbett returned to the house and left the premises a few minutes later with Garvey and Mrs. Vedder and the pistol. Plumer had by this time turned himself in to the sheriff, and as soon as the marshal was arraigned, both Garvey and Corbett had resigned from the police. Garvey's replacement on the force was James Malbon, who had served more than one term as city marshal, but was an ordinary patrolman on the night of the killing.

City lawmen communicated with whistles, and Malbon testified that on the night in question he heard both gunshots and whistles while on patrol near the Methodist Church. Said Malbon:

I heard four reports of firearms, and directly after, I heard a whistle blow. I heard it again ... and it was then blown impatiently. ... I heard [a total of] three whistles blow. ... I met two men running from Spring street and they told me that a man had been killed around there. I then went to the place and found Mrs. Vedder crying, who told me that Plumer had killed her husband.

Malbon testified that Corbett followed him to Vedder's body. Half an hour later, when Corbett had departed with the weapon found by Vedder, Malbon heard a pistol discharge once in the vicinity of the Methodist Church. The pistol confiscated by Corbett was later shown to have fired a single shot. Plumer's story that Vedder had fired a weapon in the house was not borne out by a careful examination of the interior. Tom Holmes, on the premises ten minutes after the shooting, swore he could find no mark of a bullet. There were no cracks in the floor through which a ball could have passed without making a mark, he said, adding, "There was no pistol loose about Vedder when I went there."

A milkman testified that Plumer owned the house before selling it to the Vedders. Ovid Chauvel, owner of the Hotel de Paris, described Mrs. Vedder's room at his establishment as being located directly across the hall from that of Henry Plumer and Pat Corbett; he could not recall seeing Plumer and Mrs. Vedder "alone in her room together."

Finally Lucinda Vedder took the stand and described a dismal history of estrangement, physical abuse and jealousy, candidly admitting both she and her husband were bad-tempered. After repeating her earlier testimony at the coroner's inquest, Mrs. Vedder blamed her father-in-law for Plumer's current predicament:

Mr. Vedder, senior [has been] talking to me about the circumstances of the killing. He said he would spend the last dollar he had and the last drop of blood if necessary, in order to convict Henry Plumer. I have been advised by my friends that old Mr. Vedder was trying to entrap me—that he was a treacherous man and was seeking the advantage of me.

Mr. V. Vedder rebutted her testimony, saying Lucinda confessed to him that she stood within a few feet of her husband when he was shot, and that John Vedder would be alive were it not for her. The victim's father explained:

She told me afterwards that Plumer was asleep when John entered the house. She said she had invited Plumer and Corbett to the house on the evening of the killing. She told me also that she knew that Vedder would be back that night, and that Plumer stood in the door with his head and right hand outside and fired down at John, killing him at the foot of the stairs. She said that she was sorry that she had sworn as she did here at the preliminary examination, but could not help it now.

I asked Rice what they wanted to kill my boy for when they knew he was going to Sacramento, and he said he believed they wanted to get her into a house of ill-fame.

Judge Searls recessed court on Christmas eve, and the trial resumed on Saturday, December 26. The jury went out at 9:30 p.m. and returned at 1 a.m. with a verdict of second degree murder. On December 30 John McConnell requested a new trial, claiming three jurors had expressed prior opinions of his client's guilt.

Judge Searls gave attorneys on both sides until January 2 to prepare statements, at which time McConnell offered evidence that before the trial jury foreman George Getchel had said Plumer was guilty and ought to be hung. Similar testimony was presented about jurors from North San Juan and Red Dog.

After postponing the case another week, Judge Searls and Isaac Williamson left Nevada City with $400 in relief funds to be delivered to Downieville, which had been destroyed by fire the day before.

On January 3, Addison wrote his mother:

As usual, I have allowed the time for writing to pass till the last day—we have been busy for a fortnight with a murder case—which we defended. Public prejudice has convicted our man of murder—but we hope to get him a new trial—and we are so interested and occupied with it that we can hardly find room in our minds for other thoughts.

But I must write a line or two to you—if only to wish you all a happy new year. Tell May that our new years day was a glorious sun shining one—and that I crawled out of my shell, and called upon all the ladies in town, for which—as it is the first time in my life—I deserve some credit. Many inquiries were made everywhere for her—and of her return.

But I forget that perhaps even before this reaches you, May and Fred may be on their way to us. I hope so, for we have grown lonesome without them.

II

WHEREAS CORNELIA'S VISIT in January occasioned much pleasure at Rensselaerville, complaints were voiced at Sand Lake, for Will had arrived home sooner than expected. Cornelia hurried to his side, causing Mary to remark it was too bad Will had "such a lonely sad time," but her sympathy was unconvincing. Writing to Cornelia, she said:

Poor fellow, he did have a hard time, but how does he think Niles gets along all this time. True, Niles has active business, but then he is without his little Fred too. I need not explain to you after this why I am impatient to get back to him. . . .

Our plans remain just as when you left, I believe—about times of starting &c. We are very much relieved by John Russ's opinion of March as the time for sailing. Deb received a letter from Hattie [Backus] last night which was very desponding indeed. She would go, [Hattie] said, but felt as though she were signing her own death warrant. I do not think it strange if we all feel apprehensive.

We have always had some one to decide for us all important questions, and cannot help shrinking from the responsibility of naming the time when so many shall start on a long and of course at all times somewhat perilous journey. For this reason we hardly dare to go in opposition to the advice of so many, and I have had many anxious hours about it, but I find Pa and Robert [Mulford] both think as Russ does about the weather, and I find my superstitious fears have nearly all vanished.

These fears reflected the recent disaster off Cape Hatteras when the steamer *Central America*, bearing passengers from California, sank with the loss of 400 lives and two million dollars in gold. Nearly all the women and children had been saved, but most of the men, including several from Nevada County, had drowned. It was the same vessel, then known as the *George Law*, which had carried Addison, Harvey, and Delight to Central America two years before.

A subsequent inquiry showed the ship was poorly equipped and undermanned; no carpenter was on board, nor were there tools for making necessary repairs. The most serious fault appeared to be the lack of a single chain of command on the vessel, all too common on passenger steamers of the time. Each department on the ship acted independently instead of being subordinate to the captain.

Mary continued her letter to Cornelia:

By the way, what would you think of my taking my [gold] specimens and buying me a plated tea service. Robert [Mulford] says I can get a set like Ma's. Coffee, Tea, sugar, cream, & slop for $23. and I have $30. worth of specimens—beside those that were here, which I shall not use.

Can you think of any thing that would be of more use, that I could keep? I can pack them with my clothes, he says. I dont know but it would be wiser to pay towards my spoons &c, and save my money, but I shall probably use it for furnishing my house if I save it, and I dont know whether to use it towards furnishing the table, or the parlor, which would you?

From Canada came word that Lydia Jane, Niles's youngest sister, had married without her father's consent and was living with her sister and brother-in-law. Wishing to learn more about this new alliance, Mary wrote to Lydia, who was eighteen, and received this reply:

You wished to know the particulars of my marriage and why so sudden, it was nothing very new as we had been engaged nearly a year. James had a long talk with Father a few weeks before we were married, and he would give him no reason for opposing it so much but my age. We both told him we would willingly wait a while if he would consent to it, but no, he called us both all the fools in the world, said I should never go with [James] again, or he would kick me out of the house.

And now Mary, do you think that he acted as a parent should act with a child, [even] if I did do wrong. And I am so positive that it was not my age he objected to, for there was another person that he would willingly have seen me marry any moment, simply because he possessed more wealth. But Mary, I never loved him nor never could.

Mother said nothing against it of any consequence. I have not seen Father since I left home. Mother sent for me to come home last Saturday, father was away and I went—you may depend I was glad enough to see her. Theresa was here last night and stayed with us. Alex had gone [away] and she dared not stay alone; they are both well and wish me to give there love to you. It is only about a mile from here to Alex, so I can go there any time.

Referring to her married sisters, Lydia went on:

Joana has a young daughter, quite a rarity with her. . . . They have not decided upon any name as yet I believe. Alice is staying at Joana's. Oh I nearly forgot to tell you its age: 2 weeks old today, nearly old enough to marry is it not. George is in a great hurry for a piano now but Joana wants him to wait till next fall. Oh dear, I am sorry you are going back so soon, for I do want to see you so bad before you go. I could say so much to you that I can not write.

Polly Niles wrote Cornelia on January 31, describing preparations for Mary's coming trip:

Freds coat and panties fit nicely, I wish you could see them. Mr Jarvis told him he must ring the bell when they are done and he would come and see them, so we gave him the bell and they all came to the door; of course he was delighted—he is busy now cutting apples today to take with him. He thinks we must all go with him. I told him that I must stay to take care of old grandma. After thinking sometime, he said he could fixe it, she could sleep in the low birth and he would help me take care of her, for he dont think he *can do* without *me anyway*. He thinks we may just as well leave this house emty—(and we think it will seem verry much so)—

I think Mary felt quite at rest about going in March after your letter, until last night she had a letter from Hattie B. [who] feels so low spirited about going then that it makes [Mary and the others] feel down too.

Like Mary, Polly expressed little sympathy for men who complained of wifely neglect:

Mary had letters from Niles last night; it is evident [he and Charles] are expecting them earlier.... I suppose Will will say Husbands are doomed to *disappointments*; if so they must learn to bear it manfully. Has *he* quite recovered from his *wrongs*? [Too] bad to joke him I know, but I have known men to get over such trials without serious damage....

Only 4 weeks longer before they go—how short the time seems ... if *one was made sorry, many* was made *glad.*

As the time for leavetaking neared, Mary wrote her sister again:

I did not receive the package you left for me till the stage before Ham came. I was suited with every thing. The ginghams are beautiful, all of them, and the silk matches well. I think some of making my dress after a new fashion that has appeared here—a grecian waist—plain except some bias folds like the side stripes, put on the front from the shoulder to the centre, an old fashion resurected. Delight is having one made so—havent seen it.

My last piece of white work will be done this week, havent a [quarter] yard left of that piece of cloth.... Im glad you told me about not buttoning the sacks for Fred—twill save much work and look much better.... Have his coat made, and some pants, but have several more to make, as several pairs white ones have given out.

Meant to have a miniature [taken] of him with his new suit on, but had not trimming for his coat, and today he fell and cut a gash in his forehead—on the kitchen stove—and I fear it will not be well in time. Have an excellent one with his dress on, which can be copied. Have not succeeded *at all* with mine yet—but shall try again. None looks as well as the little old one Ma has. Ambrotypes dont do well for me....

I have bought a silver set. Had specimens enough to pay for coffee-pot, milk, sugar, slop, castor, and 9 ivory knives, and ivory carving knife and fork....

I do not feel particularly anxious about sailing in March ... Hattie almost concluded to wait and go with her brother Rodman, who was going in May, but tonight wrote that he would try to go in March too with us.

Rodman Backus had obtained early parole from San Quentin and immediately left California. Before his release Backus had enjoyed privileged trusty status. Once, during a period when the new warden, John F. McCauley, became notorious for starving his prisoners on short rations, Rodman Backus was observed roaming about the prison grounds with a shotgun, shooting birds for his dinner; he was said to look fat, brown, and healthy. Now he intended to ask for a full pardon from incoming Governor John Weller.

Stamp mill for crushing gold ore, Grass Valley

CHAPTER 35

UNPLEASANT SURPRISES

January–February 1858

I

*J*UDGE SEARLS DENIED McConnell's motion for a new trial and sentenced Plumer to twelve years in prison. The judge had misgivings about the grand jury indictment, but was powerless to interfere. He reasoned that if he granted McConnell's present motion, a third trial might be granted at a later time. He preferred an immediate review by the supreme court to eliminate future causes for appeal. McConnell promptly appealed.

On the eve of his decision, Niles wrote his wife's father, hoping Mary would be gone when the letter arrived:

I have thought a good deal of trying to obtain leave of absence to come home, but all things considered, leads me to conclude the plan devised for May and Deb to come with Luther [Wickes] is better, provided it will work, or if he cannot come it has struck me that possibly James Carter might return.

There are several reasons why it is not best for me to come just now. It is more than probable that in a year or two our state constitution will be abolished and a new one formed, the effect of which will be to set me at liberty to go and come when I please. Again I fear somewhat that were I to come home now, *Philipsville* or some other good location for an "economical young man of industrious habits and correct principles," would so attract me that I could not summon enough of firmness to return.

Addison and I are still thinking in good earnest of going to some point in the western states in a year or two and purchasing two or three thousand acres of new lands and turning farmer. It is the business to which I was educated and I know we could make a good living and the rise in land would ultimately make us well off.

Addison is doing very well, and as the state now pays me punctually every month in cash, we hope to make some money. Addison received a draft which was returned to him from New York protested. It will be paid without doubt in a few months.

I received letters from May, night before last, bearing date December 15th, and by the next arrival we hope to know the issue of our plans for their return here. My court is in session at present, though I shall take a vacation of a month now soon, nominally for the purpose of giving the lawyers time to attend a term of the Supreme Court, for which they are very grateful, but really for the purpose of resting myself, which I have scarcely done for two years.

The weather thus far this winter has been altogether too fine, and not rain enough to facilitate mining. Downieville, the county seat of Sierra County, was almost entirely consumed by fire on the 1st day of January. If May is still home, tell her that the houses of Spear, Taylor, Musser, Green, Helm, Rev Mr Ponds, and Wm Stewart are all saved, and that they are nearly all that were saved. The court house is safe but somewhat injured by an explosion of 100 kegs of powder. We raised some $400 in an hour or so on hearing of the fire, and I went up in company with Mr Williamson, and took it to those who were left destitute.

Add and I board together and sleep together most of the time, and when May and Freddie get back, he is going to live with us, as we have plenty of room in our new house for him.

Two weeks later, Niles wrote an angry letter to Cornelia. It was a rare act, explainable only by his extreme frustration:

I feel this evening as though I would like to torment you a little just to remind you of old times, but it is doubtful if I can so well effect the object by letter as when personally present. The fact is though, Nelly, I am out of humor and would be most happy to do something *mean*.

Last night was the evening for the arrival of the Atlantic Mail, and I staid up to get my letters until three o'clock this morning, and for my pains was rewarded by *"nary one."* Whether May failed to write or not is more than I can tell. Charley Mulford however received one from Deb and one from Robert [Mulford] saying they had received our letters in reference to coming out with Luther, and had concluded to come, but that instead of coming Jan 20th as we wrote, or as I did to May, it was uncertain when they would start, but probably Feb 20th or March 5th, and Robert in his stated that he had seen you and that you and he thought the latter date the preferable one.

Now do you know, Nelly, that this will spoil all my arrangements and that I would infinitely rather they would not start until the 20th of April unless they can leave earlier than March.

Fully confident that they would start the 20th of Jan, I have adjourned court until the 1st of March in order to get our houses put in order, and to meet them in San Francsico, but now I will have to hold court, and on the 1st [Monday] of April have to open court in Sierra county and remain there for nearly two months. All this May well knows, and I still hope that in the language of Sparkler, "she has no nonsense" and will insist on coming sooner.

If she does not, I shall conclude it is just like a womans calculation, and only regret the whole affair was not entrusted to Freddie, who would have managed it with that peculiar wisdom which he has inherited from his paternal ancestor.

The fact is, Nelly, I am becoming very arbitrary, and do not make that allowance for a difference of opinion which I should. This disposition is in part natural to me and partly, I think, acquired from my present pursuit, which really requires me in hundreds of instances, nay always, to express my opinions without consulting others. The result of this will be in time to make me illiberal enough for a minister. I mean an Episcopal or Methodist minister and not a *Paptist* of course. Please impress this last remark on the mind of Will.

Addison and I have been hard at work for three days past over at the house, setting out fruit trees and fixing up the gardens. I am having the house repainted also and put in order. Harvey, Jerome and Arthur are all quite well. U. E. Allen was down two or three weeks ago, and was in good health. My regards to Will and tell him I mean to write him some of these days.

I am and shall be anxious about my pets until they arrive. Having succeeded in saying not much of anything in a great many words, I remain, dear Nelly, your affectionate brother Niles.

II

MARY SAT BESIDE a small table in New York's Metropolitan Hotel on the night before she was to leave for California with Luther Wickes, Hattie Backus, Deb, Delight, Fannie, and Fred. She was composing a last letter to her mother.

It is [Thursday] the night before sailing, the rest have retired, the last business is arranged and . . . We have every thing ready to start at 11 A.M. for the steamer, though it is possible we may not sail until Sat. Tickets are $200 for the upper deck rooms, $175, first cabin. Hattie Backus and I have done my shopping today. The rest did theirs yesterday. I bought a dressing gown for Niles, and materials for a little coat for Fred—blouse, they call it. . . . They asked $4.50 for one ready made, I found material much handsomer for $1.50, will make it on the steamer.

The children have got on nicely, they play *well* together, and will be much company for each other. Now I have something to tell you that you may think strange: I am going to take *Laura* back with me. She came to see me yesterday and is so anxious to go with me, she says if I will advance money to pay such part of her passage as she cannot pay, she will repay it all when I get there by working for me, or otherwise. Her little girl is very quiet—cannot talk a word of English, and seems very good natured.

Laura had been Mary's housemaid at Nevada City until Fred was a year old. Since then she had married, lost her husband, and gained a child. She had gone to New York to live with her German inlaws, but now she and they begged Mary to help Laura and the child Ettie return to California, where she would have a better chance to succeed.

The fare will be so much less for me and for her that I concluded to take her. . . . Mr and Mrs Shuman came today and pleaded so hard I could not refuse. It need cost me nothing unless something should happen to her, that she should be sick or something. I think she will be very useful to me on the way, and is such a faithful trusty person that I am anxious to retain her in my service as long as I need any one.

About the time Mary went aboard the ship, her husband and brother were taking positions in the ranks of the military escort for David Butler. Sheriff Boring had requested the assistance of the newly organized Nevada Rifle Company in maintaining order among spectators who jammed the city's streets and paths. They had come to Nevada City to see Butler hanged.

The *Journal* had published Butler's memoirs and confession in book form, revealing his true identity as Mr. Major C. Bolin. Aaron Sargent, his co-counsel, helped prepare the manuscript on the theory the book might become a best seller and pay his legal fees. Thanks to the prisoner's cooperative attitude, there were no unpleasant surprises to spoil the occasion.

Butler went to his death with astounding equanimity and resolve, according to the *Journal*'s detailed report. He breakfasted heartily at 7 a.m., smoked, and cheerfully received friends until noon. Escorted by a mounted guard of Sheriff Irwin and Deputy Proctor of Sierra County, as well as ex-Sheriff Butterfield and Deputy Van Hagan of Nevada County, Butler was driven in a closed barouche through the throng to the gallows half a mile west of town on Lost Hill.

Four divisions of the Nevada Rifles accompanied the carriage and helped disperse the dense crowd surrounding the execution site. Once there, Butler "nimbly" ascended the platform, along with Sheriffs Boring and Irwin, Deputy Van Hagan, Aaron Sargent, and the Methodist and Congregational ministers. The *Journal* account concluded:

The death warrant was read, as also the respite of the Governor postponing the sentence to that day. The prisoner then spoke a few words in a low tone of voice to the Sheriff, and immediately turned to the vast assemblage and addressed it for the larger part of an hour. He spoke of his resignation and willingness to die, of his lively hope of a future life, his sufferings which had been to him worse than the stings of death, and the prospect of at last resting in peace....

He desired his spiritual adviser to make a few remarks, which he did. A number of his friends one by one then ascended the scaffold, to each of which he extended his hand, gave them words of earnest advice and bid them a last farewell. Embracing his counsel he told him he had been a true friend, and he loved him as a brother....

He then signified his readiness, and pulled off his shoes with his own hands, saying he was glad he could help himself. He placed himself upon the trap with a firmness and heroism never excelled. Not a muscle moved, nor was the least sign of emotion discoverable on his countenance, which remained as for some days past with a slight trace of sadness, or perhaps, intense earnestness it should be called.

After the cap had been drawn over his face, he requested to be buried as he was with the letter of a friend in Oregon in his pocket. As the rope was being adjusted around his neck, he charged them to fix it properly

337

to do its work, and then desired Sheriff Irwin to give his love to the lady at Downieville who treated him so kindly while he was in prison there.

Rev. Mr. Dryden then made a short and earnest prayer. On pronouncing the word "Amen" the rope was severed that held the drop, and the soul of M. C. Bolin was launched into eternity. The unfortunate man died without a struggle. Signs of a pulse were observable for 14 minutes when it entirely ceased. The body was allowed to hang 28 minutes when it was cut down and removed to Riley's brick, corner of Broad and Pine streets, where it was visited by many during the afternoon. The funeral takes place today at 2 o'clock P.M.

The utmost order and decorum were observed at the execution and through the day. No rows or disturbances of any kind disgraced the day. Thus ended a scene, the like of which may we never again be called upon to witness.

The *Journal* estimated the crowd at 2500, but the *Democrat* disagreed:

As the crowd returned into town they were counted, and numbered 4516. Quite a number left for their homes without coming back [through town], and probably not less than 5000 people witnessed the execution, among whom were about twenty women.

III

THE HANGING MARKED an end not only to Major Bolin's career, but to a week of violence that left Nevada County residents dazed. Six days before the execution Eldred Northup shot and killed stage driver Bill Reynolds at North San Juan, apparently aided and abetted by Constable George Moore. Northup's wife had been discovered in bed with Reynolds a couple of weeks before, and there was reason to believe it was not the first time they had been together. Northup's boss had found the couple, and word of the affair spread quickly.

Some were annoyed when Northup failed to act on the information— in fact, he behaved as if nothing important had occurred. On February 20 Constable Moore decided to provoke a response from Northup, and brought matters to a head by inserting a card in the San Juan *Star* that pretended Reynolds had offered a $500 reward for information leading to the source of rumors about him. The advertisement suggested Moore would reveal all for a lesser amount.

When Reynolds drove his stage up from Marysville that day and saw Moore's card, he confronted Northup's boss and threatened to thrash him. Moore and Northup came along and said he had the wrong man.

Moments later Reynolds was dead, with six bullets in his body—at least, so said the doctors. Northup's pistol had five empty chambers and Moore's had been fired once. Both men were arrested the next day, but Moore was released on his own recognizance. Northup was placed in the custody of Moore's deputies, one of whom shared his bed that night, but never noticed when Northup left the house.

On the same day Northup disappeared, mining superintendent Michael Brenan committed suicide; his was not the only suicide that season, but he had taken the further step of killing his entire family. It was not the sort of behavior expected from a gentleman, which Mr. Brenan was. Before coming to Grass Valley he had graduated from Dublin's Trinity College, and edited newspapers in New York City.

Brenan was one of the original investors in the Rocky Bar Mining Company organized at New York by James Delavan to finance the purchase and operation of Alonzo Delano's Massachusetts Hill Mine in 1851. Delavan was better at extracting funds from city dwellers than at taking gold from quartz, with the consequence that stockholders soon removed him from management of the mine. Mr. Whitney, who replaced him, was scarcely better, and was followed in short order by Charles Seyton.

Michael Brenan, whose arrival coincided with a change in the company name from "Rocky Bar" to "Mount Hope," was sent to replace Seyton, who had coaxed a respectable amount of gold from the mine but spent most of the proceeds on himself. Brenan was picked to succeed him because he had a reputation for honesty, but he knew as little about the mining business as those who went before. However, the New York and London backers of the company persisted in believing that only educated gentlemen of their own class could be trusted to run things, despite their high rate of failure.

Mr. and Mrs. Brenan quickly took their places among Grass Valley's elite. By paying a dividend to shareholders, Brenan restored confidence— enough so they agreed to let him invest substantial sums in new machinery and exploration. This gave an immediate boost to Grass Valley's prosperity, and cheered everyone so much that local people were persuaded (despite their knowledge of its sorry past performance) to invest in the New Hope Company.

Alonzo Delano, "Old Block," no longer an agent for Wells, Fargo and Co., had started his own bank. He had sentimental as well as monetary reasons for extending loans to the growing enterprise, having been one of the original locators of the Massachusetts Hill Mine. Another man who helped Brenan was André Chavanne, who came to California from France in 1851. André, his brother Louis, and Jules Fricot had come to

Grass Valley and built a quartz-crushing mill at Boston Ravine which made them very rich.

Quartz mining required a lot of capital to start up, and years might pass before these expenses could be amortized. But foreign shareholders had waited long enough before Brenan came on the scene and they wanted results. In order to keep the operation going, Brenan was forced to rely on local borrowing. Like every speculator he hoped for a lucky break—a rich vein that would solve his problems. By the time his creditors began to press him, he was ready to settle for a not-so-rich vein.

André Chavanne in particular worried that Brenan's company would go bankrupt. Chavanne needed the money for his own operations, and he exerted steady pressure on Brenan to pay. Finally the bank panic forced him to foreclose on Massachusetts Hill, New York Hill, and Cincinnati Hill, the Mount Hope properties. In December Judge Searls ordered the mines turned over to Chavanne.

During the next two months Brenan pleaded with the Frenchman for time and help. Chavanne offered to lease the properties back to Brenan on a cash basis, but Brenan was broke and without the mines his credit was worthless. Brenan grew ever more despondent, and on February 21 he made a final, irrevocable decision.

In a long and carefully composed letter, he gave instructions to his secretary, Mr. Martineau:

I leave you power of attorney, will and bill of sale of all my personal effects, and the house. The power [of attorney] that you may do the best you can for yourself, the other two papers that you may have the house, which is justly yours, and that you may turn anything that is mine into money, which send to Robert Thallon, Hanover Bank Building, N.Y. city, for the use of my mother and sister, who are left destitute. This is my only regret in leaving—otherwise I am very happy in going with my beloved wife and children to where I have no doubt we shall have a better fate than any possible for us here.

I have written to Thallon and Satterthwaite, 38 Throgmorton street, London, about my mother and sister. One thousand pounds at 7 per cent. would make them comfortable. They and a few friends might do something for them—the richer English stockholders. The money the Company owes me would be a fortune to them. Suppose you write Sattherwaite a line and tell him what I have risked and lost. Do anything you can that way—'tis my only sorrow. I could continue here could I help them, but I feel it is quite impossible henceforth. For ten years they have had nothing but what I have sent them. If any money of mine can be got out of the concern, send it to Mr. Thallon for [the] same purpose.

You will find lists of attachments, confessions and notes in my pocket memorandum book. See that Mr. Judd loses nothing by the Woodville affair. I would not have him lose a dollar on my account. Tell him I remember him as a true and noble hearted friend. I am glad you remain to tell all the world that I have, in all, done what was right and honorable, as far as I could see it, at the time. "The proof is to die." No other would ever clear me. Did I live and ever do well, many would believe I had acted basely here—and this would make life bitter.

There is a little money, the last I have, in the left hand drawer of this desk. Send it to Thallon for my mother and sister—don't mind burial expenses. Grass Valley owes me and my family enough earth to cover us, and that is all we want. Tell Chavanne I do not blame him—poor fellow! He has a great risk, and is trying to save it; he would have done better by being more precise to his word.... But I do not blame him. I think his acts of the last few weeks have been done under half madness—

I would like to mention many whose kindness I have felt. Mr. and Mrs. Rush; that good little Mrs. Solomon—her sweet good face cut me to the heart, knowing the loss I had, in some sort brought on her interest; although, like others—like you and *myself*—I thought all would be well. I do not feel that I have misled or deceived any one, (Massachusetts Hill is the deceiver), but they would all feel that *I* had done it, which I could not bear.

This end I have foreseen for many weeks, but as long as there was a chance of seeing all, I could not leave. That is spoilt. I feel deeply for you too; but there is no use in it—there are so many and so much.... I myself had to leave, and it was cowardly to leave my poor wife and children behind—so they come with me.

Henry Silvester, Abraham Solomon's partner in a Grass Valley grocery, had urged Brenan to "take care of" himself, inferring Brenan should cover his losses and get out. Brenan found this advice repugnant and he told Martineau:

It almost makes me smile—now, that phrase of his—what a vast difference between his ideas and mine! ... One thing pleases me for your sake ... that *you* did not [take care of yourself]. In this your exculpation may be found.

Then he wrote to John D. Boyd:

Massachusetts Hill has fairly beaten me, and I am tired out and doubtful of the future, so that I take a sudden leave of all. I don't see anything worth struggling for. There is close on $100,000 due.... No man knows what I have suffered the last few weeks—meeting so many I owed and unable to pay.

I have drawn so many into this—poor old Delano—no one can know the pain I suffered in reflecting on him and others. He was always so good natured and cheerful. I don't blame Chavanne much. He has a great deal risked, and a poor show for it. But he has broken faith with me—better he had not. I am grieved about you too. I hope you may get your money, though I fear it. Mr. Martineau will attend to the business.... God bless you, my dear old school fellow. I must stop this or I will get too weak.

For miner John Judd there was an urgent request:

Do not bury us until you are sure we are dead. Let decomposition take place. Friend Judd, will you see to this.

A special edition of the Grass Valley *Telegraph* reported:

The last that was seen of any of the parties about the house was about 11 A.M. on Sunday. Mr. Brenan ... managed to get all the members of the family into the house and closed and securely fastened the doors and windows from all communication from the outside, or from the servant's apartments. They thus remained until after dark, supposed by the servants to be asleep.

Not being able at that time to arouse them, the door was forced open when one of the most appalling and heartrending sights was disclosed.... One of the children was found on a bed in the bed-room, another on the bed in the nursery, and in the sitting room, upon a lounge, reclining as if in sleep, lay the body of Mrs. B., her husband lay upon the floor by her side, and immediately at his feet, also upon the floor, lay the body of the little boy....

[Prussic] acid, which is almost instantaneous in its effects, had been administered to each one separately, in different rooms, and a pillow, no doubt, immediately pressed upon their faces to smother any possible outcry. When found, the face of each body, with the exception of that of Mr. B.'s, was covered with a pillow. Mrs. B. Was undoubtedly the first victim—then the children one after the other, the tragedy finally closing with the unfortunate man himself.

The children's ages were four and a half, three and two. The wife was thirty, and the husband about thirty-eight.

Simmon P. Storms

CHAPTER 36

WEMA: PART IV

1857–1858

CALIFORNIA'S NOME LACKEE Indian Reservation was said to contain about 4000 Indians in the Spring of 1857, and the farm at Nome Cult was credited with having an equal number. Most were native to the area, members of what was called the *yuki* tribe by their *wintun* neighbors. 'Yuki' was merely the wintun word for stranger or enemy, but it was an apt designation for this unique group which made a virtue of being unfriendly and warlike, and had a particular reluctance to share information with outsiders.

The wintun also called them by another name, the *noam-kekl*, or western tribe, just as they called the tribe near the other reservation *noam-lakki*, western tongue. Storms had this is mind when he christened the valley Nome Cult, his best approximation of the Indian sounds.

The yukis bore little physical resemblance to other California tribes, for they had short bodies and very long heads. Their skin color could be yellowish-buff, brown, or nearly black. Even their language was unlike others, but what made them notorious was their use of warfare as a competitive sport. Battles were prearranged with a traditional enemy, and before each confrontation the men danced all night, clad only in tar and feathers.

Once the warriors left for the battlefield, the women took over the dancing and did not cease until their men returned, in order to assure the men's endurance. Each man carried as many as 300 arrows; the two sides faced each other from opposite ends of the field, and after fighting fiercely for hours, one or the other would signal that casualties were sufficient for one day. A truce would be declared and everyone went home. Bodies were collected later for suitable burial.

The yuki were notorious for their persistence in seeking revenge—they would go to great lengths to achieve it. But on the reservation they were looked down upon by *nisenan* and other *maidu*, who called them stupid. Of the yuki it was said, "They do not want to know anything."

Some time in the summer of 1857 Wema left the reservation and came back to Grass Valley. Although he had an important position as an overseer at Nome Cult and had received many gifts from Simmon Storms, he was unhappy. Storms had told Wema's daughter she could live with him no longer—a white Boston lady was coming soon to Nome Cult to marry him and bear his children. He had a great affection for Wema's daughter, the nisenan woman who had served him well and faithfully, but it was not seemly that a white man should live forever with a squaw.

On August 21, 1857, the mutilated body of a miner was found in a cabin at Jefferson Canyon in Nevada County. The *Democrat* reported:

[Mr. Gilbert's] head and neck had been literally cut to pieces with an axe—there being no less than nine mortal gashes—and his head was nearly severed from his body. Suspicion rests upon some Indians who had been stopping for some time in the neighborhood, and who left the evening of the murder and came to Nevada.

Indian tracks were seen about the house, and a powder horn and two shot-pouches were taken from the cabin. Gilbert was in Washington on Friday morning, where he got intoxicated, and was taken home drunk and left by his friends lying on the floor. The night previous to the murder, the house of Mr. Jones, which is near Gilbert's cabin, was robbed of a lot of women and children's clothing, a black frock coat, and an accordeon. Indian tracks were also found about Jones's house.

Bruce Garvey was deputy marshal at Nevada City then, and he told the *Journal* about an attempt to capture the guilty Indians:

An Indian named Mose came to town on Saturday morning, and informed [Garvey] that the murderers of Gilbert were at an Indian Camp about a mile and a half from town, and offered to go with him and point them out.

He (Garvey) took three men with him and repaired to the camp, and saw an Indian called Jack, who had the powder horn and shot-pouch which were taken from Gilbert's cabin in his possession. They immediately caught hold of Jack, and as they did so, about a hundred other Indians, the most of them armed with guns and pistols, interfered and compelled them to desist. They then returned to town, and got ten or fifteen men to go out with them, but found the camp deserted by all except a few squaws and children.

The next morning a marshal's posse went to the camp, about six miles below Grass Valley, and succeeded in arresting thirty Indians who were brought to town. The Chief, Wemeh, and three others were lodged in jail a short time. Mr. Bovyer was sent for by the Marshal, to talk with them. They were discharged on promising to apprehend and deliver up the murderers. Wemeh gave his opinion that Jack was one of the two murderers.

The *Journal* also received an anonymous letter charging some Nevada Indians with having killed ten others near Indian Springs, below Rough and Ready. This was thought to have happened on September 20, and the victims were supposed to have included two men, four women, and four children. Later information tended to confirm the substance of the story, but exact details were not forthcoming.

In that same month an Indian killed a white man at North San Juan. The white man, husband of a nisenan, had broken Indian Jim's bow. Jim retaliated by shooting two arrows into the head of the man's son. He then seized the youth by the heels and smashed his head against a tree. Constable George Moore (who had helped Northup settle scores with a stage driver) went to the Indian camp to arrest Jim, in company with an Indian and two white men.

Their guide identified one man as Jim's confederate. The man tried to escape, and when Moore ordered him to halt, the suspect produced a gun. A member of Moore's posse shot and killed him, and at the same time a woman fled from the camp. When Moore ordered Indians to stop her, they killed the woman. Afterwards Moore said the Indians misunderstood—he had not meant to harm her. The posse never found Jim.

In November, Simmon Storms traveled to San Francisco to meet Sarah Jane Stevens, daughter of the Boston merchant for whom he had clerked in 1848. She came with her brother Henry, and became Simmon's wife on November 18, 1857. He took his bride to the ranch he and Charles Bourne had located next to the reservation. A house was under

345

construction, but not ready to be lived in. Until it was finished she and
Storms shared a log cabin with Bourne.

The Storms-Bourne spread employed twenty men, who lived and took
their meals in the reservation mess hall. In fact, everyone ate there,
including a contractor hired to build a new barn for Storms. At the end of
eighteen months Sarah Jane wrote that she and her husband had never
eaten by themselves in all that time. Communal living was the order of
the day, with no distinctions made between government and private
property.

In May 1858, a correspondent for the pioneer San Francisco daily
Alta California visited Nome Cult reservation and described it in glowing
terms. But, according to his report, there were only half the previously
reported number of Indians at Nome Cult. And Wema had returned:

The present Reservation ... numbers over two thousand bucks,
squaws, and papooses, most of whom are known as "Yukas." ... In
addition to these, at an early day after the establishment of this colony,
Mr. Storms transferred hither from Nome Lackee most of the Nevada
tribe who were located on the latter Reservation.

The veteran Chief "Weimer," who has figured in the annals of
California journalism so extensively, in days gone by, as Digger Arbitra-
tor, pacificator, and commissioner, is now here, the reigning Mogul of the
Nevadas. A few of the Yuba, Bear and Feather river Indians are likewise
encamped in the immediate vicinity of the station.... One hundred
acres of ground have been set apart as a garden, and over this
department old Weimer presides with ability and strict watchfulness.
Only yesterday I observed him instructing his copper colored laborers
in the *modus operandi* of planting corn, and was much amused at the
pompous dignity with which he strutted through the furrows, scattering
the yellow kernels with mathematical precision.

Weimar, by the way, is the most valuable Indian on the Reservation,
and as faithful and honest as he is industrious. He owns some seven or
eight horses, which he constantly loans to the government, disdaining to
receive any compensation for their services. Besides corn, the garden
plot abounds in vegetables of every variety, but owing to the late season
here, will not ripen for a month. In other portions of the valley, Indians
are plowing prior to the planting of more corn, of which not less than
two hundred and fifty acres will be put in this year....

Whilst the "bucks" are thus employed, the vast field is chequered
with the homely, yet picturesque, garbs of the squaws, who may be seen
squatting on the ground, and raking through the grass for roots and

seeds, which, when picked, are pitched into their big cone shaped baskets. The papooses invariably assist their maternal ancestors, if large enough to walk, whilst the infantiles are lashed securely to flat boards, and swing on their backs, enduring their close confinement without a whimper.

A federal investigation of California's reservations was underway, and Storms was asked his advice concerning the best method of controlling Indians. He replied on August 14, 1858:

To govern Indians, it is of the first importance to gain their confidence—in order to attain this result one must be very careful never to promise them anything which one cannot perform. Firmness is necessary—no order should ever be allowed to be neglected. At the same time they should be treated kindly, encouraged and praised whenever they deserve it. They should be taught to feel the Agent is their friend and go to him whenever they are in trouble, with the assurance that their wrongs will be redressed.

With good management, corporeal punishment is seldom needed. When given, it should be severe, and in the presence of others that it may operate as a warning. . . . to keep Indians quiet and contented, they should have abundance of occupation, and this can always be done on a Reserve, where improvements should be constantly made. When Indians are unoccupied they are always plotting mischief. Each tribe of Indians should be kept separate. There is always jealousy between the different tribes and when it is not prevented, the more intelligent will impose upon the ignorant.

In removing Indians to Reservations, it is very important that the entire tribe should be taken to their new home, otherwise there is dissatisfaction and a strong desire to return to their old home and friends.

For Wema there was no turning back this time. Despite Storms' rejection of his daughter, the old chief knew that of all whites only Storms had behaved with honor. He believed the Indian agent bore genuine affection for Wema's people and was doing his best to make their lives tolerable. What Storms had created at Nome Cult was a refuge, not a home, but home no longer existed. The ancestral lands had been trampled upon and ruined, the nisenan way of life outlawed, and Wema's people forced to beg and steal and sell their bodies to stay alive. Nome Cult was no Paradise, except perhaps for the whites who lived there, but Wema saw that it was better than any alternative.

He had done what was possible. In the end it was not enough. Outside the reservation there was nothing for the nisenan but humiliation and poverty. Here he could live among real people. Here he would not be thrown into jail at the whim of some pompous white sheriff. Here, in this peculiar sanctuary, this prison without walls, at least he was treated with respect. Wema knew of worse ways to live and die.

Congregational brick church and Catholic Church of St. Peter and St. Paul

CHAPTER 37

NEW HOME

January–May 1858

I

URING MARY'S ABSENCE Niles and Addison found much to occupy their spare time. In addition to renovating the Stewart house and grounds, each took an active role in the creation of a public library and formation of a volunteer rifle company at Nevada City.

In December the Library Association met twice in the grand jury room of the courthouse. Niles chaired both meetings. In addition to an initial fee of five dollars, there was a monthly charge of one dollar for borrowing privileges. Forty members signed up. One hundred and twenty books were donated, half by Rev. Warren, and Addison provided eight. John Birdseye was elected president at the January meeting. Birdseye, a mine and mill owner, was a pioneer resident whose future seemed particularly bright at a time when others were failing. In August he had foreclosed against the bank of Williamson and Dawley, and was preparing to open his own on the same premises.

Dr. F. E. Bailey, who took over Dr. Harvey Hunt's practice, acted as librarian two nights a week in the upstairs room at Crittenden's brick building at the corner of Main and Coyote streets. The association adopted Niles's motion to give honorary library memberships to Nevada

City's five clergymen. In February Sargent purchased 300 new books in San Francisco.

In the latter part of January sixty-nine men agreed to form a volunteer militia at Nevada City. On February 13 they organized themselves formally as the Nevada Rifle Company and elected Henry Meredith captain. But demand for his legal services was so great that Meredith resigned a month later and was replaced by Rufus Shoemaker. Addison was named third corporal, Justice John Anderson was official drummer, and sign painter Tom Marsh the fifer. Niles was a lowly private.

Each church society had suffered great losses in the 1856 fire. The Methodists were the first to rebuild, completing their new building in December of the same year. For a while the Baptist lot was used for a lumber yard, but in 1857 the church was rebuilt.

Before the fire the Catholics had been meeting in a house at the corner of Washington and Coyote streets. In 1857 they erected a church at the same location, close to where Mary's "Durden Cottage" had once stood. In June Archbishop Alemany and Father Gallagher came up from San Francisco to dedicate the church of Saint Peter and Paul. The Episcopalians had never owned a building, and continued to hold services in rented facilities.

Rev. Warren's Congregational Society took its time before rebuilding. A decision was made to build with brick this time, which required a longer period to raise the necessary funds. In the interim they met in Mr. Chittenden's private schoolhouse at the head of Main and Broad streets. The foundation of the brick church was laid in June as the nearby Catholic church was being dedicated. The cornerstone was laid with elaborate ceremonies on July 4.

The *Journal* listed items that were placed in a metal box and sealed shut with solder and boiling pitch: a Bible, the Confession of Faith and Covenant of the Church, the history of the church (listing officers, board of trustees, building committee, architect, and contractors); an 1851 engraving of the first church and the original subscription papers for its erection.

Also included were a lithograph of Nevada City before the fire, a map drawn by J. Chittenden of Nevada after the fire, the Constitution of California, the Nevada *Journal*, the Nevada *Democrat*, the Grass Valley *Telegraph*, the *California Mining Journal*, the *Pacific*, the *Christian Advocate*, the *Pacific Methodist*, the *Weekly Gleaner*, the New York *Independent*, the *Nevada Directory*, and the *Home Missionary* of April 1852.

The last item was a fragment of the "Pioneer Church bell of the mountains," which had been destroyed in the fire of 1856—wrapped in the original bill of lading. As the box was sealed and placed in the cornerstone, the young ladies' choir sang the National Anthem. The first service in the new sanctuary took place on January 3, 1858.

Two lecture courses had been announced in December and January; one was to raise funds for work on the Methodist parsonage and the other benefited Grass Valley's Young Men's Literary Association, and both featured a lecture by Sargent on the "Life and Times of Martin Luther," and another by David Belden about "Facts and Fancies."

Now a third series of weekly lectures was scheduled for February and March to benefit the "Brick Church," as the Congregational church was popularly known. The first, on the subject of India, was delivered by Rev. Brayton of San Francisco. A week later Rev. Walsworth of Marysville discussed "Ancient Ninevah," and the remaining lectures were delivered by local men. Mary's friend Levi Kellogg analyzed Napoleon, Aaron Sargent dissected Mormonism, and Addison told everything he knew on the subject of "Bores." Edwin Waite, whose own lecture would follow, said of Addison's effort:

Whoever heard it will hereafter be at no loss to classify bores of every description. They were individually marked in the lecture so as not to be able to escape being properly placed each in his appropriate class. The lecture was well read. In fact Mr. Niles made a good hit all around. As the lecturer frankly admitted himself to be a bore, of course his audience good humoredly received the punches in the ribs he bestowed upon them.

II

NILES AND CHARLEY reached San Francisco on Friday, two days before their families were due to arrive. But on Sunday, when the *J. L. Stephens* should have appeared in the Golden Gate, Mary was writing:

Had we made the usual time on our trip we should have arrived at San Francisco today. As it is we shall not arrive before Wednesday noon; but, as we are all very well, and as comfortable as we can be on a slow steamer with head winds that keep us all sea sick, we bear the suspense quite cheerfully. . . .

We have the greatest crowd ever taken to Cal. on one steamer. The crowd however is not in the 1st cabin—but in the steerage and 2nd cabin. . . . There has been no serious illness on board, a few have had symptoms of fever, but all have recovered. We have all been very well. Fannie is happy enough since she has a supply of milk. She has grown thin though, while Fred is so fat and hearty as ever, and as black as he was when he came home—none of the children have had sores, as Fred and Fannie had going home. . . .

Our provisions have been very useful on this side, as we have not been able to eat the ship lunches at all. The last of them disappeared yesterday—except the pickles and cream. We have had milk all the way on this side—*the ladies* have. . . .

Sometimes [Fred] gets quite homesick to go back, and insists that he wants to see Grandpa and Grandma more than papa, and would rather go back, but it is only when he is tired and fretted. He is as untiring and determined as ever. The passengers say he was born to command. . . .

Wednesday 6 o'clock P.M.—International Hotel, *San Francisco.*

. . . We arrived within one hours sail of San Francisco last night at 3 o'clock, and the fog was so dense that we had to lie outside the Gate until 12 N. today. Niles and Charlie had been waiting on the wharf more than 2 hours—as the steamer had been seen and telegraphed at 9 A.M.

Fred knew his papa when he saw him on the wharf in the crowd—and is happy as he can be. . . . Niles is well—but looks thin—he has been waiting here for us since Friday. We have but one drawback to our happiness—Niles has to start for Downieville Monday. He has our house all, or nearly all furnished. Charlie has rented a beautiful place out of town, but in another direction from ours—and has it too, all furnished, and a washwoman engaged. He has a place for Luther to go into business. . . .

—Thursday evening. We bought our curtains this morning—they are very handsome—but I'll tell you about that some other time. Niles wants something to ornament our parlor, and proposed getting pictures. I have persuaded him to wait till I can get those written directions Nellie promised me, and I will try to paint some. Will you tell her to send them to me as soon as possible. I have not written her, because I dont know where to send. . . .

Happily for Mary and Niles and the miners, a storm followed them to the mountains, filling rivers and streams, muddying roads and shutting off access to Downieville for a few days. Niles telegraphed ahead that court would be postponed a week, and his normally good spirits reappeared. As the weeklong second honeymoon neared its end, he joined the Nevada Rifles for a morning of maneuvers and target practice on Aristocracy Hill, described by the *Democrat* on April 10:

There was barely room enough for the Rifles to display their efficiency in drill, but ample to show their skill in shooting and their carelessness for rough ground while executing rapid evolutions.... The company were dressed in their tasteful "fatigue dress," to wit: black pants, grey overshirt, and navy caps....

The shooting was excellent, considering that the guns used were U.S. muskets, under a suspicion by the members of the company that they had been condemned years ago. The distance was sixty paces.... A. C. Niles, in a neat and appropriate speech, presented the first prize; Geo. S. Hupp presented the second, and David Belden the leather medal [for poorest score].... Our report would be imperfect did we not mention that Private Searls (His Honor the District Judge) and Captain Shoemaker made desperate efforts to win the leather medal, and each lost it only by a very small distance.

III

WHILE NILES was in Downieville, Mary found time to answer the mail that followed her from New York. Cornelia had written about Niles's angry outburst, and though she said she wasn't angry, Mary knew better and tried to soothe her ruffled feelings:

I have felt very unhappy about you ever since Niles told me what he had written you. I knew it would be the "last feather" and I would have given a great deal to have recalled those unkind words before they reached you. You may be sure that I *did* defend you *warmly* . . . and I soon succeeded in making him regret very much that he had written it....

I do not wonder that he was vexed when he heard from Robert that *he* and *you* had decided for us. That was just like Robert Mulford to say that. He wanted some one to help shoulder the responsibility, and it was very mean of him. In the first place, he misrepresented it to you through the coloring of his own prejudice, and then took advantage of your assent....

Fortunately the snow was so deep that Niles could not go up [to Downieville] until a week after the term should have begun, so I had him here just a week after I arrived. He had got over his anger and did not scold me at all. I think he determined to not mar the happiness of our reunion by reproaches, and you may well believe we were happy enough for one week, and are still happy in knowing that we are so near each other.

I think I may well be proud of the pains he took to have every thing in readiness for us.... He had made his arrangements to start for Sac. the next morning after the mail that brought that letter from Robert, intending to buy furniture &c and have it sent up ready for my arrival by next steamer, and thought we would have a month, most of which was leisure time with him, to put our home in order. Of course his disappointment was great. The letter that I wrote him did not arrive, and the only explanation of our delay was what Robert wrote.

He went to Sac. as he had planned to do, and when I came, my house had been in order, carpets down, beds up, &c for a whole month. He and Addison [had been] sleeping here and working in the garden &c. I am glad that you were not angry at what Niles wrote. I think you had good reason to be at what he wrote about ministers. It was very unkind, and I can excuse him for all but that. He would not have said that if he had not been very angry.

Mary described her furnishings in loving detail: the parlor with its Brussels carpet, sofa, matching rocker, large easy chair, ottomans, a "handsome" table, and mantel ornaments consisting of a cigar stand and perfume bottles made of china. All the parlor furniture was black walnut, and Niles had selected "beautiful" damask curtains and a gilt cornice, already in place.

One upstairs bedroom (the other was Addison's) contained a "handsome ingrain carpet" like that in her own downstairs bedroom. The "spare room" upstairs contained a set of mahogany furniture—bed, table, two chairs, sink-wash stand and towel rack—a matching bureau would stay in her own bedroom for the present.

The dining room floor was bare and contained only a large cherry table and oak armchairs. She told Cornelia:

Stewarts had had a door cut through from the dining room [to the kitchen], also cellar stairs to go down from the kitchen, where is a large woodhouse, with a bath room back, a cellar back of that, and still farther back is an ice house.

The yard is well filled with fruit and shade trees, and a great many climbing and other roses, some of which are as high now as the floor of the upper piazza. We should have had more than 20 bushels of peaches this summer if the frost had not killed all the blossoms about two weeks ago. We shall have a great abundance of strawberries if nothing happens.

Add has set out some grape vines to make an arbor, and I think in 2 years we shall have as pretty a home as one need wish any where. Of course if I had been here I should have selected less expensive furniture, but Niles said he made up his mind he could afford to spend $1,000 in fitting up, and wanted every thing complete. He spent about $300 of it in painting outside and in—and in fitting up the water works which were going to decay. Our well had been drained by a [mine] tunnel, and we shall have to dig deeper.

We have bought some very fine chickens, and may make arrangements to have a cow this summer when Niles gets back. Oh, my dishes are beautiful—of French china, thin and clear, and most of them very handsome shape—though they dont all match—some are oval and some octagon. . . .

[Addison] is doing very well now, attends closely to his business, and has a good deal of it, though as usual complains of not getting half he earns. His draft will be payed in N.Y. I suppose, as soon as it gets back there, and he thinks he will be able to pay off all he owes by this months profits from Downieville (his partner is up there). . . .

[The Mulfords] have rented a beautiful place about 1/2 a mile from us, the other side of town, and it is furnished very nearly like ours. Their furniture is green plush instead of hair cloth—and they have gilded oak for bed room furniture. [Deb and Delight] are doing their own work, and Deb is happy as she can be—looks younger and happier than she has since I went home. They are all well. I am very sorry we live so far apart, we cannot see each other often. Delight is really a good girl, and I have become quite attached to her since we left home.

Fred had a new wagon to ride in, and he dug cellars and hauled dirt to and from his own garden patch. He enjoyed his father's company when Niles was home, but in his absence he longed to see the folks at Rensselaerville:

I read him Ma's letter and some of yours, and he listened very quietly till I finished and then he said in the most determined tone, "I am going right back—tell Grandpa when you write that I am coming back the *next week.*" Oh, said I, what will papa do. "He can get some little boy out of the street, my Grandpa wants me, and [the cat] mews about the house for me, and I *must* go," said he, and his eyes flashed. . . .

He wanted to know if Charlie [Niles] took Grandma's letter to the [post] office, and then with tears in his voice he said, "Charlie is a good boy, he used to bring me lots of raw eggs and do a great many things for me."

Mary enclosed Cornelia's letter with one of her own to Niles at Downieville, where he took time to write her an apology on April 25:

Now for what I said to you—and first I think you attributed a degree of unkindness to me which I certainly never felt. But instead of justifying, I desire humbly to confess that I was radically wrong, and to implore pardon for having wounded your feelings. I need not say that I esteem and love you, that your uniform kindness of heart toward your wicked brother is ever remembered and cherished as among the brightest recollections of bygone years; but this much I will say, dear Nelly, in all seriousness, if you will forgive me this time, no words of unkindness from me shall ever again be written you.

On the contrary, I will follow the promptings of my own heart and treat you with consideration which I know full well you deserve at my hands, and when in bad humor with myself or the world, will try and exercise that forbearance which becomes every man laying claim to ordinary sense. If you have decided upon making a home in the great west, I have only to hope you and Will may find it as congenial to your feelings and wishes as I have done, and maybe some day May and I will turn our steps in your direction and become your neighbors.

IV

BANKER WILLIAM TECUMSEH SHERMAN was in California to collect money owed to his employers, who had closed their bank at San Francisco. For security on a loan, a Captain Stone had given the bank two mortgages on Sierra County property. One was for $5000 and the other for $12,500. Before going east in 1857, Sherman had arranged for the Downieville law firm of Spear and Thornton to collect payments on the notes for his bank.

Since then he had written more than once to William Spear, who did not reply. Sherman heard rumors that the smaller note had been settled, and he tried to see Spear when the lawyer came to San Francisco with his wife in March 1858. Spear's brother refused Sherman admittance, saying the attorney was very ill with typhus. When Harry Thornton Jr., the district attorney of Sierra County and Spear's partner, came to the city, Sherman asked him to look into the matter. Thornton, the same man who tried once to kill Addison at Frisbie's Saloon, said he would.

Several other clients were of the opinion that Spear had misappropriated their funds, and Thornton's father thought his son's partner must have gone insane. But Sherman was skeptical, telling his employers: "No doubt [Spear] feels bad enough and it is the highest compliment I can offer him, that he has sensibility enough to go crazy, after having so basely betrayed his trust."

Sherman arranged to have the steamers watched so Spear and his wife could not leave the state—"a steamer ticket is the cheapest mode of paying debts here." Spear, claiming to have lost his mind, returned to Downieville to face several lawsuits. Sherman followed, and when he saw

Spear disposing of his furniture and assets while Thornton showed no inclination to bring charges, Sherman filed a criminal complaint against Spear.

Oddly, despite his contempt for the man, Sherman sympathized with Spear and thought he knew the cause of his predicament:

No man should have a wife in California. . . . Unless she be a working woman, no man can by his own labor support her. Trying to keep my family in California has ruined me. It will ruin Bowman and was in my judgment the cause of Spear's downfall. He had the largest and most lucrative practice here, but no amount of money can maintain a family when servants are from $35 to $60 a month, wood, coal, and washing in proportion. Spear is not a drinking man . . . did not gamble . . . [there is] no other cause to which I can attribute . . . the expenditure of our $3,700 but the accumulated expense of his family.

When in November he heard of the failures in the East, he thought we had gone in like Page & Bacon and other banks, and flattered himself we would not miss the money. In January and February, finding out his mistake, it . . . preyed on his mind till it made him reckless. . . . Now he affects insanity. . . . he is no more insane than any other man who was fool enough to attempt to live in California with a family. . . .

Had Spear come out, acknowledged it, and pitched in to help Thornton earn the money, I would not have preferred a criminal charge. . . . Were his friends here to come forward and undertake to pay this money or any considerable part . . . I might relent, but I have no hope of this. People here are generous with the money of others . . . but not their own.

Niles and Mary knew and liked Mrs. Spear, and when he saw that she was nearly destitute, Niles arranged for her to go to Nevada City. Mary wrote on May 2:

I intended to have commenced 3 days before [steamer] time and write a letter each evening, but received a letter from Niles Wednesday evening saying that he had invited Mrs Spear of Downieville (of whom you have heard me speak) to come and stay a long time with me, and I had to be very busy indeed to prepare her room &c, as I had neglected everything almost, because I liked to work in the garden, and did not feel hurried in the house.

She arrived yesterday, and I anticipate much pleasure from her visit. She laid down this afternoon and insisted upon my writing while she did so, and I had just prepared to do so when Fred upset the ink on his clothes and my bedroom carpet, and it has taken me an hour to clean it up. He feels very sorry about it, and begs that I wont tell papa.

Mary went on to mention the Spears' financial difficulties and destitution, and Mr. Spear's derangement, continuing:

I find she retains the same quiet dignity in her adversity that she had when I first knew her, and I respect her more than ever. She has most perfect confidence in her husband yet. She thinks this has been growing upon him for a long time and that he has done all that seems wrong under the influence. I hope it will be proved as she thinks, but I fear not, even if it be true, as most people seem to think his insanity feigned to cover his crime.

I am glad I can entertain her pleasantly, as I can here, without much trouble. She is a delicate nervous woman, and has, added to all her other misfortunes, the knowledge that many who have appeared [to be] her friends have now turned against [the Spears] and do all in their power to injure them.

Stewart-Searls house

CHAPTER 38

MORE SURPRISES

May 1858

I

HE HOME OF Mr. and Mrs. W. K. Rigby occupied the lot north of
Niles and Mary's new house. The Rigbys had owned a pretty
place on Prospect Hill until creditors foreclosed the year before. Prospect
was one of seven hills that overlooked the city—the one on which they
now lived was Piety Hill, so called in part because of the Baptist
parsonage across the street from Mary's house. Another Piety Hill
resident was *Journal* editor Waite, brother-in-law of the Baptist preacher.

The Rigbys were not the sort Mary would have chosen for neighbors,
although Mrs. Rigby was good-hearted and helpful, despite her lack of
style. Mrs. Rigby and Annie Stewart had not got along well, but Mary
found she could tolerate either until the time Annie came down from
Downieville to visit Mrs. Spear. Then Mary wrote:

> Mrs Stewart is down from Downieville, and she and Mrs Rigby talk
> dreadfully about each other, but from all I learn I think Mrs Stewart most
> to blame, and am beginning to think that what *every body* says must be
> true, and that she is at least not a woman to be relied upon. Very few
> have ever liked her, which caused me to take her part as long as I could,

but no one likes her now, either here or in Downieville; her best friends have felt the influence of her bitterness when the least thing crosses her will. I am sorry to find one whom I had valued as a friend is not worthy, but I have to give it up and believe it so.

Mary's current dilemma was houseflies, which disgusted her greatly:

There are 23 doors in my house, and it is no small days work to keep them all closed after so many who leave them open . . . Laura and Ettie need more teaching than [Fred] does, they seldom put any thing in place and shut any doors.

It was gradually dawning on Mary that Laura was not nearly so competent as she once supposed, but Laura owed Mary $80 for steamer fare, and she meant to make the best of the situation:

I find there is a great difference between Laura and Sarah, for all Laura is such a good girl, she is *not* very *neat*, and it troubles me very much indeed to have her kitchen always so dirty, and every thing uncovered in the pantry, meat and bread left out of the cellar and all such things, which I never noticed in her before, because I had to take care of Fred and was not in the kitchen much. . . .

I had about concluded to get another place for Laura and do my own work, but shall keep her while Mrs Spear stays, and I think while the hot weather lasts. We have a fine lot of chickens, and talk of keeping a cow this summer, all of which pleasures add much to the work, and she does not expect, I think, more than $25 per month, with the board of her child, and the child is no trouble at all. She is always dirty and looks dreadfully with her faded ragged dresses, but she is very good indeed, and Fred is not half the trouble he would be without her. . . .

Still I know she is much better than most girls, and feel much more safe to have her in the country, even if she were not with me, for I know if I would be sick she would be sure to come if I wanted her, and I can trust her perfectly, just as I could Sarah. I would prefer Sarah on many accounts, and you must tell her I often think of her neat pantry and kitchen and neat calico morning dresses. . . . [However,] Laura is better fitted for me than Sarah in some respects. She is strong and healthy, and has a strong mind and good sound sense. She is used to Cal. and can take care of herself and me too). . . .

Deb and Charlie, Harvey, Luther and Fannie were here to dinner last week one day. We live so far apart that it makes us sick every time we go to each others house. Isnt it too bad. The children teaze so much to be together, and it is too far for either to walk. Fred did walk once, but it took him several days to recover from it. It is more than a mile. The walk from town here, or there, is nothing; I do not mind it at all, but we have to go the length of town beside both the other distances, they live [on] the opposite side. Deb has walked over here twice and back.

II

MRS. SPEAR REMAINED in the Searls home long after Niles came back from Downieville, Mary told her parents on May 16:

Her husband has recovered his reason—if indeed he has ever lost it.... He has to finish out his business in Downieville, and she will remain here in the mean time. We are enjoying her visit very much....

[Niles] is quite unwell and had to adjourn court more than a week before the close of the term. I suspect he was as much *homesick* as any thing. He is improving now every day. The garden is a good thing for him, it keeps him out doors, and I think he will be healthier. We take a great deal of pride in our garden. The strawberries are beginning to ripen; we had a few for lunch today. I am afraid people didnt know how many *we could* use when they said we would have more than we would want....

I have some sad news to tell you concerning our friends the Harrisons, of whom you have heard me often speak. Mr [Joseph S.] Harrison was killed very suddenly ten days ago, by the falling of his house. He had been having it raised by means of jack screws to an even grade with [Broad] street, and went under the corner of it to assist in adjusting some rocks, when the house slipped from the foundation and crushed him in an instant.

Mrs Harrison was in the house at the time, and rushed out and saw her husband as they lifted his mangled corpse. I was within a few feet of the house, and heard the crack, but did not know what had happened till I saw them leading or carrying Mrs H out. I went with her into the next house, and held and soothed her a long time, but I hope it may never be my lot again to witness such agony of mind as was hers. We thought she would go into convulsions, and her strength was so utterly prostrated that she has not been able to walk one step since until this morning.... I was with her two days and one night, and have the satisfaction of feeling that I was able to be of some comfort to her.... They were among our warmest friends, and she is a devoted Christian and a pillar in the church....

I have been with another scene of suffering within the last week. Arthur [Hagadorn]s wife has a little boy 4 days old, and he had a terrible time coming to town. I was with her all one day, and I have no desire to live over again the last week of my life, in which I have witnessed the greatest suffering in mind and body which mortals can endure and live. Arthur's wife is doing very well indeed now, and has a fine boy.

William Spear joined his wife later in the month and stayed with Mary and Niles for several days. On June 1 Mrs. Spear went to San Francisco and her husband returned to Downieville. An accommodation had been reached for repayment of the embezzled sums. Mary said of his prospects:

... he can of course do nothing in Downieville after the course he has pursued, [but] he hopes to get business in some other place. He is a fine looking man, very agreeable and gentlemanly, intelligent, generous and kind hearted, but extremely fond of spending money freely, and not very scrupulous about the way in which it is obtained.

She is a sweet little woman, cheerful, amiable, and affectionate, ladylike and refined. I have enjoyed her visit very much and miss her greatly.... [Fred] was very fond of Mrs Spear and she of him. He told her one day, "he wanted her to stay here till we all die, and God takes the skin off of us and takes us to live with him." What an idea for such a boy. I dont know where he got it, I am sure.

William Sherman told his employers, "I will be forced to leave behind ... important interests in the hands of lawyers. If they cheat us, they will have at least the fear of exposure such as now overwhelms Spear."

III

HER NEW HOUSE was so remote that Mary did not get around to mentioning the latest fire until after she had completed the telling of more personal matters; had she been living in town it would have counted as a major catastrophe. Mary wrote:

There was a great fire in town a week ago last Sunday, nearly all the wooden houses on Broad St, Commercial, Pine, and Main Sts. were burned, and parts of several small streets. Nearly the same district was burned over as before, but the brick houses were all saved, as were the churches and all public buildings. There was no suffering caused by the fire—few families burned out, but some of our best citizens have lost more than all they were worth, having mortgaged their houses for the money raised to build them.

It was the second time her house had escaped a major Nevada City conflagration because of its remote location.

We can see the whole town, but there is no danger of fire, without we burn ourselves, and it relieves us from that constant fear that those in town experience. Arthurs people went down to Charlies and are still there. The wood part of [Arthur's] house was torn away and burned, but I think they will rebuild and return there. She has a good girl who takes care of her and baby (Frank, the boy's name is), and I suppose helps the girls some, though they do the cooking still.

The May 23 fire differed markedly from its predecessors. At first it had seemed insignificant—the sort of minor blaze that happened all too frequently, frightening to be sure, but capable of easy containment. And so this should have been, said the *Journal*, except for the scandalous lack of organization:

Had any considerable associated effort been made the first half hour after the fire broke out ... we would not have to mourn the loss of the town. The progress of the flames was so tardy that few imagined the fire would cross Pine street at all.... we were on the ground early and never entertained the idea for a moment that any great amount of property would be destroyed, till we saw the almost perfect *nonchalance* of the crowd in the streets.

There were plenty of buckets to be had for the picking up, and an abundance of water back of the Hotel de Paris to have extinguished the fire in a few minutes ... could a score or two of men been found to work systematically together.

There was no order or discipline. Every man who did work did so on his own hook, and those who didn't were in the way of those who were trying to render service. Had the efforts put forth on the New York Hotel by Ed. Wheaton, Sargent and others, been expended earlier on the first buildings on fire, the destruction of property would have counted nothing....

A body of men has been found in our midst patriotic enough to form themselves into a company to "strut *en militaire*." Cannot an equal number be discovered with patriotism oozing from their finger ends to get hold of the brake, the hose, hooks and ladders, instead of swords, muskets, cartridge boxes and bayonets? ... We are ready to jump in and "run wid der masheen" at the tap of a bell.

The fire broke out at 4:30 p.m. in Win Kee's opium house and brothel across from the Methodist Church. Unlike the fire of 1856, this time the air was calm. Before it was over the new gas works had been destroyed, along with most of the wooden structures on the downtown streets.

Every one of the brick buildings, thirty in all, survived, and a great deal of merchandise was kept safe in fireproof cellars. The court house and all the churches escaped burning, but Frisbie's splendid theater was reduced to a pile of ashes and charred timbers.

The *Journal* declared that because the fire originated "from the carelessness of opium smoking Chinamen," orientals should be barred from occupying buildings in the city. The *Democrat* agreed:

No more than two or three lots are owned by [the Chinese], and if white men will refuse to rent them houses, they can be kept out without trouble. If they must live in towns, let them build a town of their own. But few of them have been seen around town since the conflagration, and possibly they have already taken the hint that their presence in our midst is not very desirable. The house in which the fire originated, we are informed, has been found on fire several times within the past few months.

The *Democrat* building had been saved, but it was a close call. The Rolfe brothers thanked volunteers who had removed materials and equipment from the building:

We are under many obligations to Messrs. E. G. Waite, S. H. Chase, A. B. Paul, Geo. [Hearst], and a number of others, for their timely services, in assisting to remove the materials of our office at the time of the fire. But little hopes were at first entertained of saving the building, consequently every thing of value, except a press, was removed.

We are also indebted to some forty or fifty other citizens, who worked for nearly an hour with unflagging energy to save the building.... By the desperate and untiring exertions of a large number of citizens, who worked with a hearty will for nearly an hour, the *Democrat* Building, and Lampe's barber shop adjoining were saved from the devouring element.... Had they taken fire, the flames would have crossed over to Spring street, and consumed the Baptist Church and a large number of residences on that street.

But a critical hour had arrived for Nevada City's businessmen, whose resiliance had been stretched to the breaking point. Many were denied aid by the same persons who offered willing assistance in 1856. San Francisco wholesalers and bankers, aware the city had failed to organize even the semblance of a fire protection system, were disgusted and said Nevada City deserved to burn. If local residents would not look out for themselves, why should outsiders underwrite their risks?

As Mary put it, "I am afraid Nevada will never recover from this fire."

Stage leaving town

CHAPTER 39

WARREN'S FAREWELL

May–June 1858

I

*T*HE ANNUAL CAMPAIGN to eliminate the Nevada City government once again produced tax reform instead. This time the legislature abolished the recorder's court and authorized a one-half per cent tax on all able-bodied males to be used to offset up to $1000 of new indebtedness.

Town trustees announced revised pay rates for police: the marshal and policemen would receive $100 per month, plus $3 for each arrest or court appearance leading to conviction and paid up fines. The marshal also received a commission of 15 per cent on poll taxes and 5 per cent of other city revenues collected by him.

Harvey Wickes took charge of the county hospital in February; in his first three months on the job he cared for nineteen patients whose infirmities included rheumatism, paralysis, indolent ulcers, insanity, sore eyes, erysipelas, tertiary syphilis, and phthsis pulmonalis (consumption).

New diggings in western Canada caused a mass exodus from California in May and June. Every day scores of hopeful miners left Nevada County towns and camps for the Fraser River, and stage companies added extra runs to meet demand. But mixed reports came back, some attesting to rich finds, while others accused merchants and shipping interests of fostering a hoax. Most Nevada City businessmen went on rebuilding and restocking shelves, confident the economy would rebound another time.

On June 3 Addison told the folks at Rensselaerville:

I finished a letter to Pa this morning and set down to write to you—when in came three chinamen with wooden shoes and tails, who had to explain to me in extremely broken English how "one, two 'Melican men, jumpee their claims—no good men—no good john, muchee no shabee"—and when they had gone, came an Irishman, very drunk, and with a very black eye, who wanted another Irishman prosecuted for assault and battery—and then came others—and so the result io I have had a busy day, and am very tired, and it is growing late. . . .

I dont know what Nevada will come to. People cant go on forever building houses and having them burned down again. They are building with a great deal of spirit—but when pay day comes, I am afraid they will find the burthen too heavy to bear. I am glad that Niles' house is out of reach of fire, and am glad that [McConnell and I] were in a fire proof building, and lost nothing—though we had to do some famous work to save it.

Fred is thriving. He is so full of life that he scarcely rests, I should think, from morning till supper time, when he generally falls asleep at the table. It is amusing to see him sometimes with his eyes shut, and a mouthfull of strawberries. His father got him a pair of boots, which he wore out in about three weeks—stout calf skins. He is as black almost as a Digger, and very healthy. . . .

It is court time and we are very busy in our law business—have hardly time to think of anything else. Niles is busy too—is trying a murder case now, which is creating considerable excitement in the county.

The case was that of Constable George Moore, accused of aiding Eldred Northup in the killing at North San Juan. Moore was defended by Henry Meredith, Frank Dunn, and McConnell and Niles. The trial lasted all week, and McConnell felt relieved when Judge Searls instructed the jury that if they believed Northup (not yet tried) was guilty only of manslaughter, they must acquit Moore—there was no such crime as "accessory to manslaughter." The jury, guessing at the result of Northup's forthcoming trial, deliberated three hours before returning a verdict of not guilty.

Two stages had been stopped by highwaymen on May 2. One had been robbed of gold entrusted to Wells, Fargo, and Co., but Isaac Dawley saved an equally large sum he was carrying for Marx Zellerbach's bank at Orleans Flat. The *Journal* reported:

Two stages started out in company about 1 o'clock. I. N. Dawley who was riding with the driver on the foremost stage discovered a man ahead staggering towards the stage and supposed him drunk. Coming alongside the horses, he reeled towards them and suddenly caught hold of the reins. The stage stopped. Dawley asked him sharply what he was about. The robber dropped the reins and presented a double barrel shot gun.

Dawley felt for his pistol, but while doing so the muzzle of another gun appeared close to his breast from the other side of the stage, and he was ordered to desist from his purpose. The robbers demanded the express boxes. The driver told them that was not the express stage. They told him they knew better, to pass out the boxes and be quick about it.

Dawley examined the boot under the seat and after a moment told them they might [as well] shoot, as there was no express box aboard. The robbers then said, "drive on." Dawley had $20,000 belonging to Marx & Co., in his possession.

The other stage by this time was not far behind and the robbers made for it. Dawley urged some of the passengers to go back to the assistance of the other stage, but without success. [Sheriff's deputy] John O'Brien was riding with the driver on the other stage and was unarmed. The demand for the specie box was complied with.... The box was split open with an axe ... and $21,000 in charge of Wells, Fargo & Co., taken. The treasure consisted in two bars of over $7,000 each, and the remainder in coin and dust....

On arriving at Grass Valley, Dawley and O'Brien returned to Nevada and gave the necessary information. Under Sheriff Van Hagan started in pursuit [and] ... found the box rifled of its contents, and at daylight attempted to track the robbers.

The *Democrat* provided details of Van Hagan's subsequent search:

He discovered tracks where three or four men had left the place. One of the tracks was easily distinguished, and he followed it to McCarty's ranch, but was not able to trace it any further. He then went to a cabin between the ranch and Grass Valley occupied by [Daniel] Luddington and a man called One Eyed Tom. He found the two men in bed, arrested them, and sent them to Nevada, where they were lodged in jail.

On searching the cabin, Mr. Van Hagan found a dozen or more skeleton keys, a large silver watch and a revolver, which both of the men protested did not belong to them. The watch was doubtless stolen property, and can be seen at the Sheriff's office. A gold watch and some forty dollars in money was found on Luddington's person.

The miners who live in the vicinity of the cabin have long suspected that Luddington and his comrade were robbers. It is said they were in the habit of sleeping during the day, and were generally absent from the cabin at night. After Van Hagan left the place, the miners set fire to the cabin and burned it down. Yesterday, another watch was brought to the Sheriff's office, which Luddington sold some time ago to a Chinaman for five dollars, and which is also supposed to have been stolen.

A description of the gold bars appeared on Wells, Fargo and Co. handbills which offered a $3,000 reward for apprehension of the robbers.

1 Gold Bar, made by Schotte, No. 1683; value $7,598.28; 846ths fine, weighing 435 ozs. 1 Gold Bar, same make, No. 1684; value $7,217.01; 866ths fine; weighing 403.14 ozs.

San Francisco police arrested former Nevada City saloonkeeper R. Dutton as he was boarding the steamer *Golden Gate*, enroute for the Atlantic states. Dutton admitted knowledge of the robbery, but denied taking part. On May 31 Deputy Sheriff Van Hagan picked up John Hope, Aaron Bridgeport, and a Spanish woman at Marysville. Hope had a good reputation and said he had left Nevada City to live with a brother in Sonoma county; Bridgeport was known as a Nevada City idler who complained constantly of being sick; the woman was not even charged, but was held as a witness nevertheless.

Continued investigation failed to link Dan Luddington and One-Eyed Tom Williams to the stage robbery, but evidence found in their cabin caused authorities to hold them for other crimes. During Van Hagan's absence at Marysville, the pair broke through the brick wall between their cells and made an opening large enough for a man to crawl through. Sheriff Boring ordered them chained to the floor by hands and feet.

Benicia authorities had arrested William Marshall, and the *Democrat* heard rumors Billy Marshall had confessed to the stage holdup and was naming confederates. He was indicted and the case put over to the next court of sessions.

Luddington and Williams were convicted of burglary and sentenced to short terms in prison, and the supreme court decided Henry Plumer was entitled to a new trial. The *Democrat* explained:

Judge Searls [had] overruled the [defense] motion for a new trial, intimating at the time that the indictment was defective, and [he wanted] all the objections [to] go at once to the Supreme Court, thus avoiding the possibility of two more trials. The Supreme Court overruled the objections to the indictment, but held that the jurors who had thus expressed opinions [of Plumer's guilt] . . . were incompetent.

The high court questioned whether such persons ought to sit in any case "involving the life or liberty of a citizen," saying:

A man who could so far forget his duty as a citizen, and his allegiance to the Constitution, as to openly advocate taking the life of a citizen without the form of law, and deprive him of the chance of a jury trial, would not be likely to stop at any means to secure, under the forms of a legal trial, a result which he had openly declared ought to be accomplished by an open violation of the law.

McConnell and Niles had submitted affidavits and testimony to the supreme court showing several jurors had favored hanging Plumer before hearing testimony. Of J. G. Denny they said:

This man appears to have resided in San Francisco during a period of its history which every honest citizen ought to blush to think of—and to have imbibed, in that hot-bed of treason and lawless violence, all the bitter prejudice against a man accused of crime which at that time prevailed there, together with an ardent admiration for their new and summary modes of procedure and punishment. Such men as he and Getchel ought not to live in a free and civilized country—much less to sit in judgment upon the lives and liberties of its citizens. With such men, to accuse is to convict—

Unless this portion of the appeal was written by McConnell, or at his insistence, it represented a change in attitude for Addison. Two years earlier he had said of the expected executions:

It will be strict justice, and the only way to obtain justice there, for experience has proved that the law is powerless in San F. to convict a murderer. . . . I think 500 men would go from Nevada if the call was made to assist the San F. Vigilance Committee. . . . The prompt action . . . will do much good. . . .

II

AFTER MRS. SPEAR WAS GONE, Mary concentrated her full attention on Emily Warren, whose family was moving to San Francisco. James H. Warren, the city's pioneer preacher, had been named editor of the *Pacific*, the west coast Congregational missionary journal. On June 17, after the Warren family departed on the morning stage, Mary wrote to Emily, her youngest sister:

I visited at other places with them, had them to dinner, and helped Mrs Warren sew. I made and gave the two girls each a white Marseilles Talma with a hood, trimmed all around with fringe. They were very pretty. We hated to have them go; I shall miss them very much. Mrs Warren is without exception the most intellectual and the most estimable woman I have known in Cal. I dont expect to find her like again.

On June 13 the Reverend Warren delivered his farewell sermon, which the *Journal* printed on June 25. Many who did not usually attend the Brick Church came to hear him—they were paying their respects to a pioneer. Warren's talk amounted to a capsule history of Nevada City, and many of the stories he told were known only to other old timers:

Seven years is not a long time, but in California long enough to make a chapter in life—extraordinary in incident and interest, long enough almost to make a life of itself. I first arrived here April 14th, 1851. I was told before coming that the place contained some 30,000 inhabitants—there could not have been less than 10,000—there might have been as many as 15,000. Every house in town was then crowded, as well as every cabin on the hills, on the flats and in the ravines for one or two miles around. . . .

It boasted then a mayor, common council, marshal and police, city attorney and recorder, and all other officers necessary for a city government, and sufficient to plunge it into debt, which to this day remains unpaid. . . . many of the diggings were not paying anything like the fabulous rates of '49 and '50. Men got angry and sold their claims because they were not turning out more than an ounce per day to the hand. . . . the great fire of March 11th had just swept over the city, causing an enormous sacrifice of fortune, as well as of property. . . .

Nearly opposite the Nevada Hotel, where I stopped and was kept for weeks without charge, a large and, for the times, a splendid saloon called the Exchange was nearly completed. It was built for a permanent institution. The proprietors, Smith and Barker, intended it to last as long as the city itself. It was a place of Exchange truly—the exchange of hard earned wages for the poverties and curses of faro and monte, the exchange of virtuous principles, better memories [and] good habits for the desperate chances of the cut throat and the gambler.

Opposite Barker's Exchange was the Empire. Gamblers were kings in those days. Political and money kings—California was their *Empire*, their *El Dorado*, their *Golden Gate*, their *Exchange*, their *Bella Union*, &c. They were about the only ones that could afford to wear a polished boot and hat; and perhaps it was chiefly owing to my black coat and hat that some of the miners on Little Deer Creek asked me if I was not a broken-down monte dealer when I applied to them for a church subscription.

I remember how Ad Smith came to the Hotel and invited some of the ladies (as a matter of special favor to them), to go over and see and admire his new saloon before he opened those fine *glass stained* doors for the benefit of the vulgar herd—and I remember how the ladies went and admired. Scott, of the Empire, envied his rivals, but then he too was respectable. Dr. Brown was not only very rich, but reputed to be a very honorable gambler—honorable, no doubt, as the man once said to me, with all gravity, that Tom Bell was the most honorable robber he had ever seen or known in the country....

In that same month [April 1851] a religious society was organized, chiefly for the purpose of building a church edifice. Horace Everett of Charlestown, Mass., was President, and Dr. Dexter Clark of Rockford, Illinois, Treasurer. There was no church organization here then. A class of the [Methodist Episcopal Church] and one of the Methodist South church held occasional meetings, while a Gold Flat miner preached to them on the Sabbath.

Dr. Clark, as nearly as I can recollect, was the only professional man that pretended to adhere strictly to his profession. Lawyers, physicians and preachers were, all of them, for a time miners or traders. Law, medicine and gospel were simply incidentals; they came into important note, however, very soon after.

The building of the church commenced in June, and it stood on this very spot, surrounded by lofty evergreen pines, which gave it quite a forest-like appearance. In September, the church was done; a full and crowded house met together for a joyful and delightful dedication.... The [charter] membership was 21. One lady, the rest men.... it was a membership for the times.... In February the entire debt was paid off, chiefly by the ladies, who by their efforts raised $2,700. In April '52 I was installed in due form as pastor.

But all this time, from my arrival to my installation, what of the times? Indeed that year will ever be a long, long remembered year. We worshipped, till we had a house of our own, in the Dramatic Hall on Broad street, by permission of Dr. Robinson. The Theatre at night however had always by far the largest crowd. The Sabbath was the day of days, not for worship and spiritual refreshings, however. With the exception of the 4th of July 1851, bull and bear fights, theatrical exhibitions, circus performances, all paid better on the Sabbath than any other day.... The Sabbath was the set time for the pandemonium of passion....

Society was just divided into two classes: those who were actually going, and those who were intending to go away as soon as possible. There was but little confidence in the mines—quartz was set down as humbug, and placer diggings about used up. Men did not think it worth their while to buy Sunday clothes—it was throwing money away; white shirts were useless....

Well, in that year, two churches were organized and two church buildings dedicated. A day school and Sabbath school were opened for the children, and a press, the *Nevada Journal* was established, and since then how many interests have risen up to mark our progress, and how many have gone down; ... Another press, four churches; three Sabbath schools, 2 divisions of the order of the Sons of Temperance, public and private schools, eleemosynary societies, a library association, hospitals, factories, mills.... There are houses now, cottages with neat and green surroundings show the longing of the heart for rest, and its settlement into rest....

We have not the wealthiest city in the mines; we might have had, but *six* fires have proved more than our match; five consumed property, the last and sixth wasted our confidence; it has done damage more by breaking up our intentions, upsetting our plans, making us uneasy, unsettled, to look somewhere else for a home, than if it had only burned five times the property it did. This feeling is bound to exist, it is bound to keep families and capitalists away, until waterworks, fire companies, &c. guarantee some safety against these dreadful fires.

A state law to outlaw Sunday business had gone into effect two weeks before, and Warren spoke warmly of this innovation:

If nothing else but this partial restoration of the idea of rest on one day in seven had been accomplished, this would have been enough to repay the years of anxious prayer and effort. You remember, some of you, the first meeting in the old church in '53, to request the merchants to close on the Sabbath, promising our patronage to those who did.

A day of small things; then the agreements and disagreements of the merchants about closing, then the petitions to the Council, then to the

Legislature for three years in succession, how only inch by inch, the great work has progressed, till today we rejoice in a quiet Sabbath, a Sabbath some of you never expected to see this side of the Rocky Mountains.

The new quiet would not last for long. Within the month the supreme court declared the Sabbath law unconstitutional because it referred specifically to a *Christian* Sabbath—opponents successfully argued that its unfairness would be obvious had the legislature called for a day of rest on the *Hebrew* Sabbath.

Of the host of lawyers that were here [at the beginning], only [McConnell, Searls and Buckner] remain. One who used to turn the windlass has since filled the office of attorney general of the state and has quite distinguished himself in his profession; another, who used to sell books somewhat tinged with yellow covers, for three years has been a district judge equal to any in the state for industry, executive ability and dispatch; the third is still pursuing the even tenor of his way, breaking from it only once to figure as a candidate for the office of Supreme Judge.

Of the whole tribe of doctors, only two, Knox and Overton, remain to remind us of pioneer days. Of ministers who have preached to you in different churches as stated supplies for a longer or a shorter time, I have counted 19. Only two, beside myself, remain to preach ... their farewell sermons. This church has renewed its membership twice since its organization. Of the original members, beside my family, only two remain. So it has been from the first—friends, acquaintances and strangers have kept coming and going, with the coming and going of every day.

And here I must turn to the sad record of your dead.... The dead, oh how many, taken off in the prime of life, in the gloryings of hope and in the full strength of manhood. How many strangers have lain down before your eyes and you have gathered them to their long homes. I have preached funeral sermons over the remains of 55 who died of sickness, of 17 who were stricken down in a moment without any warning, of four who by their own hands ended life and sought the refuge of the tomb, two who clutched to life but lost it in the throes and horrors of a drunkard's delirium [and] nine little children, whose sleep I could not call death.... Only two above the age of 50 have I buried, the rest, nearly all of them at least, not quite 35....

Yes, seven years ago I came among you with all the rawness, inexperience, and unfitness of a student, fresh from the seminary. Though you had not much confidence or much care as to the work

373

which brought me here, you were willing that I should have a chance and try the experiment. I had fair warning that I should have to toil pretty much alone, and while you hoped or wished me success, you were not willing to risk your time or chances. Dr. Clark, himself a right-hand man, gave me a hundred dollars, to be released from a note of a few hundred which had his name, in connection with two or three others.

But you have in my case verified the rule of helping those who help themselves, and when I think of the many enterprises I have undertaken in your name, and in none have been left finally in the lurch, I cannot but feel a pride in a people whose prompt and generous impulses have these many years justified every expectation, and earned to themselves a true and honorable name.

Go where you please, and under the sun you will not find a people, taking all the circumstances together, more liberal, more free-hearted and generous than this, and many places with ten times the ability not one-tenth part the heart and will. Your kindness to my family, that night in which our little cottage on the hill was burnt, the heartiness with which you supplied the wants of my little children, then totally destitute of raiment and food, and the fact that in about 24 hours you had subscribed enough to erect over our heads the spacious and beautiful home . . . we never shall forget it.

I feel deeply also, the patience with which you have borne with my blunders . . . the fortitude with which you have stood my incessant begging. From the first I have been almost a professional beggar. . . . A long time ago I voted myself a bore, and wondered the people did not drive me off. Show me another minister who has begged . . . some $10,000 in the same time from the same persons, and I think I will show you a man who has been driven from the face of his fellow; but you have *endured* me. . . .

Friday morning next I leave this place with all its interests and attachment, the birthplace of all my children but one. . . . Farewell, finally brethren, farewell. Be perfect, be of good comfort, be of one mind. Live in peace, and the God of love and peace shall be with you. The Lord bless and keep thee; the Lord make his face shine upon thee and be gracious unto thee and give thee peace. Amen.

Political street rally

CHAPTER 40

TWO DEMOCRACIES

July–September 1858

I

*T*HE NEVADA RIFLES paraded at North San Juan on the Fourth of July—their uniforms were brand new and exactly conformed to the latest United States Army regulations. The rifle company traveled first to Sebastopol on horseback and was met by a citizens' committee and twenty-two-piece band directed by Major S. S. Lewis, marshal of the day. The volunteers led a procession to North San Juan and marched with local residents to the picnic grove.

Band music and orators entertained 400 guests until dinner was served. Afterwards the militia showed off by marching in close drill. Toasts were offered, speeches read, and finally everyone marched back to San Juan for a ball at the Union Hotel. A like celebration took place at Alpha, under the auspices of the Sons of Temperance, who substituted sparkling water for liquor. Speeches by Aaron Sargent, Dr. Wixom, Rev. Dryden, and Major William Downie, had similar zest. Major Downie, founder of Downieville, was on his way north to Canada and the Fraser River, where he hoped to better himself.

It was a more subdued occasion at Grass Valley, where a respected citizen had been murdered at Osborn Hill on July 1. The firms of McConnell and Niles, and Meredith and Hawley were employed to defend the accused parties. The Grass Valley *Telegraph* headlined its account: "The Tragedy at Grass Valley. Seven Men Killed and Wounded—Arrest of the Murderers—Committal to Jail—Talk of Lynching—Excitement, Etc." As it turned out, only one man was dead, although another died in a few days.

After an Irish company had jumped the claims of Dr. McMurtry, his brother James, and Richard Kimball, the two parties had come together to try to settle the dispute. After some talk it was agreed to hold another meeting in the morning—on this occasion only the principals were to be present, for a large number of kibitzers had arrive on the scene, hopeful for excitement.

The Irish contingent included Michael McGee, Alexander Griffin, Patrick Harrington, John McCabe, Michael Casey, Phillip Shields, John Collogan, Jerry Harrington, Paddy McGee, Shea, Holland, and a brother of Shields. They withdrew first, leaving the McMurtrys and Kimball at the mineshaft. But after a few moments Alex Griffin rode back to deliver an ultimatum: they must reach a settlement immediately or his party would return. Told there was nothing to settle, Griffin summoned his friends, who stationed themselves behind trees and logs with shotguns and rifles.

The Irish appeared to number from seventeen to twenty-five persons, and when one of them began filling in the mineshaft, Dr. McMurtry seized his brother by the arm and suggested they leave before someone got hurt. As the trio started climbing the hill to their cabin a single shot was fired, followed quickly by a series of discharges.

Dr. McMurtry drew his derringer when he saw his brother holding a shotgun that had been left behind earlier by someone in the invading party. Kimball had no weapon at all, and James McMurtry quickly discovered the weapon he had found would not fire. Only the doctor was able to return fire. When the shooting ended, James McMurtry was dead and Kimball was wounded. The *Telegraph* reported:

The affair naturally created great excitement at Grass Valley, and some talk of lynching Griffin, the supposed ring leader.... On an examination before Justice Richardson five of those under arrest were committed to jail, one admitted to bail and four discharged. The following are those committed to jail: Michael McGee, Alexander Griffin, Patrick Harrington, Jno. McCabe, Michael Casey. Admitted to bail in $2,000: Phillip Shields....

A late report has it that but two are dead and five wounded. Michael

Casey is severely wounded in "that ill-starred spot where mothers smite their young."

On the same day, several Chinese were arrested in Nevada City and brought before Justice Clark for having violated a new city ordinance prohibiting their race from residing inside the city limits. Clark said the ordinance was unconstitutional and discharged the men. Both newspapers agreed with his decision, and the *Democrat* proposed another way to accomplish the same purpose:

We believe ... there is but one lot in the town owned by Chinamen, and the only effectual way to keep them out of the business part of the town is for property holders to refuse to sell or lease them ground. The interests of the community require that they should be kept out, and we trust that owners of property will not so far forget their duty as citizens as to allow any of them to again come among us.

II

SUMMER MEANT political conventions, and politics in 1858 was influenced strongly by events in Kansas and the nation's capitol. The fight over slavery had become so complex that each scheme and counterscheme created more confusion, and each measure designed to calm the country had the opposite effect. The greatest fights were taking place within the majority party, where supporters of the president were opposed by a coalition of northern and western Democrats led by Illinois Senator Stephen Douglas.

California's Senator Broderick had allied himself with Douglas and antislavery opinion, a stance admired by many not in his party, but decried by many who were. The Know Nothing Party had collapsed entirely—some of its former adherents now backed the Administration, some liked Douglas, and still others had joined the Republican party.

Managers of the Democratic county convention vainly strove to achieve unity. Nominations had scarcely begun when fighting broke out and a deputy sheriff extinguished the lights. When they were relit, the only possible bargain had been struck: Administration men gathered on the right side of the room and all others caucused on the left. Each group picked its own rival Democratic slate.

An "Independent" convention met to select men beholden to no party, but this, too, failed when experienced politicians said straw polls showed no strong sentiment among the voters for such a ticket. The Republicans, encouraged by the Democratic split, nominated candidates for every state and local office.

The odd result was that for a change both Nevada City papers were friendly to the same candidates. The *Democrat* was controlled by pro-Douglas people, and the *Journal*, though it had never supported Democratic administrations, was unwilling to back "abolition" Republicans. This left Buchanan Democrats without a voice until they bought control of Warren Ewer's Grass Valley *Telegraph*, renaming it the *Nevada National*. Warren Ewer retained an interest, but George Roberts became the new editor.

Roberts, a Grass Valley mine owner, could write as mean a story as Waite or Rolfe, which was saying a lot in the campaign season. In short order the rhetoric was hot enough to suit the wildest firebrand, and at first it made Niles thankful he wasn't involved—which made it all the harder to accept when Governor Weller unexpectedly called for elections in every judicial district. According to the constitution, each district judge served a six year term, and Niles had been in office only three. But the legislature passed a bill in 1854 requiring all district judges to be elected in 1858 and every six years thereafter.

Niles thought the constitution would prevail, and most lawyers agreed. If so, it was unnecessary for him to run again. But a test could not occur until after the election, and if the decision went the other way, and some candidate chose to run, Niles would be out of a job. Niles had distanced himself from politics since becoming a judge, and he was not anxious to choose sides in this year particularly.

At the moment he was everybody's favorite—the *Democrat* said, "Judge Searls, since his election, has made a popular judge, and gives very general satisfaction throughout the district, and it is not likely that any candidate will be run against him." Niles was in Downieville when he heard the bad news, and he naturally turned to Bill Stewart for advice—his counsel had been invaluable in the past.

When he returned on August 2 and announced his support of the Administration, both Nevada City papers were stunned. Edwin Waite, his running mate in 1855, exploded with indignation:

> Our District Judge played leap frog over the backs of friends to whom he owes his position, not long since, and met with a melancholy landing among the authors of sprightly referee reports, dirt eaters, bummers, F.F.V.'s [First Families of Virginia], lovers of African musk, *et id omne genus*.... Judge Searls turned a very clumsy somersault the other day and struck, to the serious damage of the supposed spinal column, flat on the trapdoor of Lecomptonism. He has made a decision this time that will probably not be overruled by the Supreme court.
> ... the Judge of the 14th Judicial District has dropped body (we'll say

nothing about soul), boots and breeches into the befouled nest of Buchananites.... Why can't Weller correct his election proclamation and leave this District out? He certainly ought to do it, since the recent miraculous conversion.... Once again, let pardon be granted.

One day after the surprise conversion of Niles Searls, Governor John Weller did indeed grant a pardon—to Rodman M. Backus. Weller, titular head of California's Administration Democrats, was also something of a prison reformer. On assuming office he informed the legislature of his intention to use the pardoning power whenever a sentence seemed too severe. He also meant to remove all juvenile offenders from San Quentin, which he termed a "school of villainy." Backus, now twenty-eight, seemed to fit neither category after serving only eighteen months for a manslaughter conviction, but something had persuaded the governor of his fitness for consideration.

When pressed for an explanation of his unusual political alliance, Niles was silent, and so he remained throughout the campaign. Douglas Democrats angrily nominated Robert H. Taylor of Downieville to oppose him. At first the *Democrat* treated Niles gently:

It is a mooted question as to whether or not the successful candidate will be entitled to wear the judicial robes, but the Governor has ordered an election for this District and it is proper to vote for a candidate in order that the question may be settled by the Supreme Court.

Judge Searls, the present incumbent, has given very good satisfaction to the people of the District, but he was elected as a Know Nothing, and has been identified with that party until about three weeks since, when he transferred his allegiance from the Know Nothing to the Lecompton party. Such being the case, it would be requiring too much of Democrats to ask them to give him their support.

Lecompton referred to the controversial constitution enacted in 1857 at Lecompton, Kansas, in accordance with provisions of Douglas's Kansas-Nebraska bill calling for the inhabitants of that region to decide whether to be free or slave states. The Lecompton delegates, largely supported by proslavery forces from Missouri and opposed by abolitionist guerilla bands known as "Jayhawkers," voted to make Kansas a slave state. The result was a new fight in Congress over the legitimacy of the Lecompton constitution, and whether Kansas should be admitted to the Union. Within the Democratic Party Buchanan was supporting the Lecomptonites and Douglas was in opposition.

In the same issue of the paper, Rolfe discussed Douglas's Republican rival in Illinois:

We heard a prominent Lecomptonite express the hope the other day that Douglas would be defeated . . . .and that Lincoln . . . would be elected to the Senate in his place. We believe that such is the wish of nearly all the Lecompton leaders, though at present, from motives of policy they may conceal their real feelings. They now pretend that they agree with Douglas, but as soon as the election is over the mask will be thrown off, and he will again be denounced by every pap-eating Federal official in the State.

On the eve of the election, the *Journal* published an editorial entitled, "Judge Searls—His Antecedents," which attacked him on the basis of his political record. It was the first time any such document had been compiled, and some of what it said was true. Waite intended it as an embarassment, if not quite a revelation. Mary and Addison were indignant, but Niles took it in stride. Waite's exposé read:

What the political or other opinions of Judge Searls were before coming to California we do not know, but looking at his course here, we can shrewdly guess. The first positive knowledge we have of him, he was a self-nominated candidate for Justice of the Peace a few days after his arrival in this city. Next a vender, according to the authority of a late divine of this place, of "yellow covered literature" on Main street. From this the transition was easy to the law. Then we hear of him as an aspirant for the office of District Attorney, which he succeeded in obtaining.

Politically, he was known to favor the Broderick wing as soon as, or before, a split in the Democratic ranks occurred. In 1853, late in the year, he assumed to edit the *Young American*, which soon after became the Nevada *Democrat*. For about six months the name of Niles Searls was displayed as Editor. . . .

Circumstances apart from editorial labors showed him to be as warm a Broderick man as his nature would admit; for so soon as he could clear himself of an interest in a newspaper, he was found one of the most stirring of the getters up and voters of the celebrated "Blue Ticket," a ticket whose design avowedly was "to exterminate the chivalry," and whose success threw the Democratic County Convention into the hands of Mr. Broderick.

As a reward . . . Searls was made Chairman of that Convention. The want of back-bone in . . . that Convention . . . caused the nomination of two or three chivalry men. This was not according to the card agreed upon by the "Blue Ticket" men, and an expedient must be devised to destroy these few chivalry nominees before the people. Noiselessly and secretly, a few choice spirits assembled in an obscure chamber, chief among them, we are assured on substantial authority, were Judge Searls (now Lecompton candidate for District Judge), [Christopher] Lansing (candidate for the Senate on the same ticket), and Wm. M. Stewart of Downieville (who is now challenging all the world and the rest of mankind to meet him on the stump, he taking the chivalry side).

Here an institution commonly known as the "North Star" had its origin in this county. We have no personal knowledge of the obligations taken by its members, but we believe it can be substantiated on good evidence that a binding oath not to support any southern man for office was imposed upon every member. But one thing is not denied—the institution was sworn to hostility against the chivalry of Nevada county, and among the latter were many with whom the North Star Trinity are now cheek by jowl.

Presumably the "blue ticket" referred to an unofficial list of candidates printed on blue paper and distributed to voters in 1854. If there was such a campaign to eliminate chivalry (southern or proslavery) candidates that year it was not very effective. Three men with southern origins were elected to important offices, and of the five Democrats who were defeated, two came from New York, one from Pennsylvania, and the origins of the remaining two were not recorded. The only certifiable southerner actually defeated was a candidate for public administrator—a profitable but politically unimportant office.

North Star was the name of an abolitionist newspaper then being published by former slave Frederick Douglass at Rochester, New York. Although a secret organization opposed to the spread of slavery might have used that name, Waite's editorial was the only evidence that it did in fact exist.

At the time, Mary had written that Niles was pleased with the 1854 results: "It would make considerable difference with his business which men were elected. . . . the election was rather *small* business this year. Many of the candidates acted so like fools that I was glad Niles had no part with them."

Waite continued:

A little later and the Know Nothings gained a foot-hold among us and soon promised to be powerful. Hundreds flocked to their councils. The North Stars are reputed to have thrown themselves in a body into the Know Nothings to control that organization against the chivalry. Whether this be so or not, Judge Searls about that time was a prominent member of the so-called dark-lanternites, and oblivious to his implied pledges to the Democratic Convention over which he had recently presided, and unmindful of the claims upon his political sympathy of the foreigners—the larger half of the Democratic party—he bound himself solemnly to be their political enemy.

The paragraph following was full of errors: Waite claimed Searls had voted the Know Nothing ticket in 1854—no such party existed in the county at that time, and Waite had Niles "running a blue ticket" within the Democratic party in that same year. Waite continued:

... by the indefatigable exertions of his late friends, [he] was a successful candidate by a small majority before a Know Nothing Convention of the District. He was elected to the position he now occupies at the general election of 1855. Since that time he is known to have boasted of his Democracy with staunch Democrats, and declares that he "only went into the wigwam to clean out the chivalry and get the office he now holds—that he triumphed in both objects and was satisfied."

... True to what were supposed to be former instincts, when the primary Democratic election came off in this city with a victory to the [Douglas] Mud-Sills, Searls rejoiced exceedingly, and remarked to an old comrade, "I never wanted to be a Democrat so bad in my life—I'd help you run another Blue Ticket on 'em."

In this frame of mind he left Nevada to hold a term at Downieville. The next we hear of him he was representing Nevada county in the Lecompton Convention at Sacramento, by trading a Sierra proxy with a delegate from this county. Thus endeth the chapter till the first of September writes "finis" to the history of the man.

On August 18 Mary wrote to brother Hamilton:

Election times are *hot, hot*, this fall, and I am vexed enough that Niles has been obliged to have any voice in the matter. By some hocus pocus or other the Governor has made some wonderful discovery in the constitution which he thinks calls for an election of Dist. Judge in this and certain other Districts this fall, and it thereupon became necessary for Niles to announce his politics.

Since elected he had taken no sides whatever, considering it the duty of a judge to leave politics alone as much as possible. Well, of course all the friends who were on the other side from the one he chose are vexed and ready to do him any thing but a friendly turn because he didnt join *their* party, and so he has more enemies than he ever had before in his life.

But he dont seem to care. He says they will get over it after election, and after consulting the best lawyers in the state he has concluded the call for an election is illegal, and he will not [campaign], so that if any other person is elected, he will have to contest the position, and there is a *chance* of his losing his office, but he thinks it a small chance.

I cant explain all about it very well. I might better have said nothing till after election, when it will all be settled one way or other. I am glad he dont run, for I dont want him to be mixed up in the strife this fall. It is more bitter than ever. We and [Addison] belong to opposite parties. Add is a Douglass Democrat, and Niles a Lecompton. What is Pa and what are you? I wish I knew, for I cant help feeling still that I am just what my father is.

The Douglas wing was known variously as "Mudsills," "Anti-Lecompton," and "Popular Sovereignty" Democrats. Among their number were Addison Niles, Tallman Rolfe, David Belden, and Dr. William Knox. On election day the *Democrat* reminded foreign-born citizens:

The Democratic nominee for District Judge, Col. R. H. Taylor, was formerly an old-line Whig, but has acted with the Democracy since the downfall of the Whig party. Unlike most of the Whigs, Col. Taylor never had anything to do with Know Nothingism. . . .

In the year 1855—the same year . . . Judge Searls was elected on the K. N. ticket—Col. Taylor . . . stumped Sierra county for the Democratic ticket, and stood up manfully for the rights of foreign-born citizens. . . . Will you vote for Judge Searls who took advantage of the temporary furore against foreigners to ride into office, or will you vote for the man who stood up for your rights at a time when it was popular to join in the crusade against you?

In another column the *Democrat* defended its earlier remarks:

The Grass Valley organ, in speaking of the course of the *Democrat* and *Journal* towards Judge Searls, says: "But a few weeks since, the *Democrat* spoke of Judge Searls in the highest terms, and said in case of his being a candidate for District Judge, that it would be folly for any man to run against him." Some three weeks ago we spoke of Judge Searls as having made a popular Judge, but never said or intimated that it would be folly for any man to run against him . . . we stated that it was not probable any candidate would be run against the present incumbent.

We had nothing to say about the political summersaults which Judge Searls has made within the past few years. He has certainly been as consistent as a majority of the candidates now running on the Lecompton ticket, which is saying but little in his favor.

Judge Searls is peculiarly objectionable to us as a Judge. When the

Vigilance Committee excitement was raging, two years ago, he chimed in with the excitement of the day, and carried the weight of his influence as a Judge, in favor of that treasonable organization. A man so easily carried off by such a momentary excitement is not possessed of a sufficiently well balanced mind to qualify him for a high judicial station.

Ironically, William Anderson, the editor who had penned the *Democrat*'s bitterest denunciations of the Vigilance Committee, now supported Niles Searls and the Administration ticket. Rolfe's last minute appeal to foreigners failed, in part because President Buchanan himself was the son of a poor Irish immigrant. When the votes were counted Judge Searls and the Administration ticket emerged victorious.

Only three county offices had gone to the Douglas faction. By the margin of a single vote David Belden was elected county judge over Henry Moore of Moore's Flat; John Caldwell, a widely respected legislator, edged out a less popular colleague for one of the county's five seats in the assembly, and John Grier was elected to the board of supervisors.

Mary was elated:

The excitement has been intense this campaign, and in this town more bitter against Niles than any one else.... Well, they have done what they could and have said every thing in the way of blackguard that could be thought of, and he has staid at home and let them talk, never denying a statement however false, and the result shows he has a majority even in this town, where opposition was strongest, and it was supposed he would certainly be beaten—and in the county his majority is great.

In Downieville he had, as far as heard from—a majority of 3 to 1. In precincts where the opposition had the majority he had sometimes nearly *all* the votes. We are delighted, I can assure you.

Not that we think it will make any difference in his term of office. It is generally supposed that the election will be pronounced uncalled for by the constitution, though called by the Governor. If the Supreme Court should pronounce the election valid, he will hold his office for 6 years longer. But it is not at all probable. I am glad he has got the election in spite of them....

Niles has just come in, and says he has gained nearly 1000 majority in this county—and 300 in this town. Good. He has run way ahead of his ticket right in town here—and some of his rich opponents have lost $1000 in bets on his election.

Later Mary told Cornelia what they thought of Waite's editorial on the "Antecedents" of Judge Searls:

You need not think we felt no indignation over them. I passed some sleepless nights in any thing but holy thoughts, and could have abused that editor most heartily too. All things are *not* fair in politics, and that was most atrociously mean. The Editor had been a personal friend of Niles for years, and had owed his present standing partly to Niles's influence, and Niles will *never* forgive him for that article and others that he wrote, though they did Niles no harm. They are near neighbors of ours, and we of necessity meet now and then, but meet as the most perfect strangers.

She was glad he would remain in office:

He could make more money practicing [law], I suppose, but it is such unsteady uncertain proffit, and so difficult to collect. Besides, I am afraid we would be likely to move to Downieville, as he could do much better there than here. I think if the good people there could have their way they would make him President.

Courthouse at Downieville

CHAPTER 41
MURDERER'S ROW
August–November 1858

I

FRED SEARLS WAS nearly four years old when Mary caught him staring at the large grandfather clock Niles had purchased. Fred told her he would go home to Rensselaerville when he was a "large man" and tell Grandma all about it. Mary suggested that he write a letter instead of waiting, but Fred explained that because it was a very large clock, he'd need a *great large* sheet of paper.

He came home from a neighbor's house very excited because their dog had "laid some little bits of puppies." Sometimes he was permitted to go to Harvey's drug store for two or three hours, but after one such visit he came home so "wild and unmanageable" that Mary tied a rope to him until he calmed down. It was about time he had a brother or sister, she supposed, and that made her feel better about her situation.

On August 1 Mary told Cornelia she was pregnant again:

I hope the climate [at Keokuk] will agree with you. I shouldnt wonder if you should be much better—and perhaps—it would not be at all strange—if you should raise some little Freds of your own there. I have

386

heard the Mississippi was as famous for its effect in that way as even Cal. I hope it will prove so in your case. I want every one to be in the same fix *I* am. It is delightful to go moping around from morning till night, just sick enough to turn up your nose at everything—Bah. I hope you'll have a chance to try it.

But then I *know* Fred will be spoiled if he is an only child, and hoping it will prove a benefit to him, and a future pleasure to us, I am content with the prospect. Dont tell Ma, not a soul knows it here, not even Niles, who has been absent a month, and will return tomorrow.

In April the Baptist Society of Keokuk, Iowa, had invited Will Allen to be its pastor. Cornelia had said of her new home in the west:

I often wonder, when I think of myself west of the Mississippi; and as I go about the city, and catch now and then a glimpse of the river, it seems like the Hudson, and I could easily fancy myself in Albany, only this is a pleasanter place to be in, than Albany.

It is a larger city than I supposed, and yet the houses have so much space between them, and are built so much like country houses, that it does not seem close and confined, but like a village. There are more handsome houses than I first thought. I did not really like the town till I took a walk on the bluff, not more than 3 blocks from where we are boarding, and saw so many elegant houses, with beautiful yards around them, looking out on the river, and then I made up my mind Keokuk was already a beautiful city.

They were boarding until they could find a place to rent at a price they could afford. But everything was expensive, including their boarding house, which cost $12 per week, exclusive of washing and gas. It was very nice, however, and boasted

... excellent company at table, some of the first young men in town, and very pleasant ladies, and such a table as you do not often find. Our meals are every day *excellent*, perfectly neat, and the best kind of food in abundance: sweet potatoes, chickens, oyster plant [salsify], pie plant [rhubarb], custards, brown bread, and fine meats, every day.

They hunted in vain for affordable housing until, fortunately, the problem was solved by their landlady:

Mrs McChain ... came to us, and said she wanted us to stay very much indeed, with her.... She said she would so much rather have us take her front rooms, when the present occupants leave ... the middle of this month, than to have a family with children ... and offered the two rooms, a large high parlor, front upstairs, and large bedroom with gas, and our washing, if I would iron the shirts and dresses, for $45 pr month, to commence when we first came. .

This covers all expenses and we can store our goods in her barn, furnish our own room, and secure a good cool place for the summer. We found no *poor* house could be got for less than $25 pr month, and Will was anxious I should rest this summer, and I fear the heat would affect me, if I worked hard, so I gladly assented. . . . Will will use one end of the parlor for a study. There are 5 large windows in the 2 rooms and it is a high brick house, and all say one of the coolest places.

She had formed a friendship with Mrs. Eaton, who occupied the rooms Cornelia and Will would inherit when she left:

She is a lovely young wife, married this spring. Her husband is somewhat older, and they are pleasant, kind people. . . . We sew together, and do all kinds of friendly things for each other, and I really am contented to wait some time for our front rooms, as when we take them, she leaves. She is going East, and will go into a beautiful new house of her own, when she returns.

Our goods have not come yet, but we hear the canal was not opened early, so we do not wonder. Mrs Eaton . . . wants me to let her furniture and carpets remain and leave my furniture [packed], as she has no place to store hers, and so if my goods dont come early, we shall still be well off. Her rooms are beautifully furnished with marble topped rosewood, and everything neat as wax.

On September 2 Addison boasted to his father that he and McConnell had the largest and best law business of any firm in Sierra and Nevada counties:

We are employed in nearly all the important suits. For instance, we are retained for the defence of *seven* murder cases in this county for the October term. That speaks better for our business than for the morals of the county. This is a kind of business however which we do not covet.

Niles and May and Fred are well. They all go to Sierra [County] Saturday, to remain there during the September term (a month). . . . Charley Mulford, Deb and Delight have gone below to San Francisco, San Jose &c, to be gone two or three weeks.

Actually, according to Mary, the Mulfords and Delight were going first to the bay area and then on a pack trip to the famous big trees and falls at Yosemite; Fannie would remain at Nevada City with a neighbor. Mary would have liked to go with them, but Niles could not absent himself from the bench. Before leaving for Downieville, she wrote her mother:

I shall start on Sat. this week. I hope it will become cooler in that time. I would not go, only for the pleasure of being with Niles. He has been away a good deal this Nevada term, and has succeeded in procuring rooms that bid fair to be comfortable. We shall be gone between 4 and 5 weeks. Laura will stay in the house and take care of things, unless she finds a place to work, which is not likely. If she does, Mr Rigby has offered to take care of the chickens and flowers.

In response to queries about the Fraser gold rush, Mary guessed there had been more excitement in New York:

The thing was mostly understood to be gotten up by the steamship companies, and none of those who had any business in Cal. started. I believe there was a week or so, too, when the fever was highest that every body tried to go, but the papers made it much more than it really was.

Two weeks later she described life at Downieville:

We board at a restaurant, have a large parlor and small bedroom, comfortably furnished—our meals, which are very good, are sent to our rooms, and we are quite retired here, except we are opposite all the drinking saloons in town ... and I cant walk out on the piazza without meeting the gaze of a doz. idlers.

The ladies are not at all social. I have seen but few.... I am making my last visit at Downieville, I suppose, as next summer we shall have a cow, and no one knows what else to keep me at home. I care not a fig for the place, and little more for the people. It is a horrid ride up, in the best state of the roads. I had but one inducement to come, except the hope it would improve my health, as it has done. Niles and I have had more long talks about home than we have before, since I came back. At home ... we dont get a chance to talk....

I am sewing a good deal, making Freds winter flannels, night shirts for Niles, transfering the cuffs to match my collar, netting on my everlasting mat, &c. When I get home I shall be very busy indeed, for I have discharged Laura, and shall try to do my own work. I dont think I could endure to have [Ettie] in the house this winter. She is good, but very disagreeable, and Fred is not very good to her. She teazes, and he fights her. I need exercise and shall have none now the garden needs no more care....

She spoke again of the election campaign, which had upset her greatly:

[Niles] has received the greatest majority that has ever been given in either county for any candidate. He ran 1286 votes ahead of his ticket in this county ... yet there was a great deal more said against him than has ever been in all his political career before. But the lies told about him were so well known to be lies that they worked rather in his favor than against him. ...

He spent no time and little money on the election. The vote was the spontaneous voice of the people, yet I was greatly disappointed to find that he had so many bitter enemies. I was not aware that he had *one* before, but many who have had important suits decided against them vented their spite in doing and saying all they could against him. I am glad that some of them have lost large bets by his being elected. They had no business to make them. ...

Fred ... amuses the men here very much by the earnestness with which he resents his father or himself being called a *muasin*. He says he is a Democrat, and his pa is an "*administration* man." He has a gimlet and saw and a large pile of blocks. He gets up in the morning, sometimes two hours before we do, puts on his clothes, climbs on the bed for me to fasten them, puts on his red top boots, brushes his hair, and *travels*. He sometimes sits quietly working with his tools, and [sometimes] goes over to see the carpenters at work on a house. ... He blistered his hand with his gimlet, and I tried to persuade him to not work with it today, but he said, "Oh, I can slip the gimlet down low and make a sore in *another* place," and he perseveres in it yet. ...

Mary wrote once more when it came time to leave:

I am waiting to know whether Niles will succeed in getting off today or whether I must unpack and stay another night. A tedious state of suspense to remain in for several hours. ... The gentlemen here are more agreeable than the ladies, I think. ... I wish you could have seen the great heaping dishes of fruit a gentleman sent me one day—a lawyer of this place. There was a large glass fruit stand, placed on an oval platter, and both filled with grapes, apples, pears and oranges. The fruit must have cost at least $5 here.

Fred has enjoyed his visit. He has been stuffed with fruit and candies till he would have been sick if he had not been so very healthy. He has not learned much good however, and I dont think I will bring him again, or come myself again very soon. ...

I feel anxious enough to get home. I am all the time troubled for fear some one will steal my chickens, or my preserves, or my garden will be neglected and die—or some other great trouble. Mr Rigby was to have the care of the garden while we were absent—if Laura did not stay all the time—and unless restrained by policy (as I judged he would be) I have no doubt he would live on eggs and chickens while we were gone, for he is known to be any thing rather than honest, but they are so extremely anxious to be on good terms with us—and to place us under obligations to them, that I suspect there will be extra care taken of every thing.

II

A NEW THEATER had opened at Nevada City. The Metropolitan Theatre was located not where Frisbie's had always been, but on Main Street and closer to the creek. Nat P. Brown, Edwin Waite's partner at the *Journal*, was part owner of the new venture, and Tallman Rolfe annoyed his rival by unloading some heavy criticism at theater manager John S. Potter:

Our New Theater has been in operation about one week, and fully demonstrates that any institution which charges one dollar admisssion to witness the burlesque of tragedy and butchery of comedy can be supported here. It is needless to mention that J. S. Potter, better known as "Old Potter," is the Tamerlane who leads the present troupe of Histrionic Tartars, to the desecration of the Drama.

It is only for the purposes of incubation that Potter occasionally relieves Nevada of his presence. When landlords and printers become clamorous, and actors frantic for their pay, this astute manager frees himself from the one by dismissal, and the other by flight, and in the regions of San Andreas, or some such favored locality, brings forth a new brood of dramatic artists for the special benefit of Nevada. To this regular advent we are becoming resigned; it is all we can be. We would as soon think of changing the course of the comet as of this stage manager.

Finances cannot get low enough to stop him. Curses are the meat on which he feeds, and the only meat which is not given grudgingly. At each return those who will pay a dollar can see him represent on the stage the new way to pay old debts; while those who credit him get a parting rehearsal of his old way of paying new debts.

As would be expected, such a manager can never command the

service of sufficient talent to prevent tragedy becoming farce and farce tragedy.... and from the drop of the curtain to the fall of a king, some ridiculous blunder characterizes the entire performance. The rendition ... of a "Tale of Mantua" was replete with absurdities.... The only redeeming feature of the first three acts was an unlooked for descent of the curtain by which Antonio's (Potter) soliloquy was most ludicrously abreviated. Antonio had just commenced a confidential talk with himself when the curtain came down just far enough to leave his digestive organs in focus before an admiring audience.

Judge Searls approved a change of venue to Marysville for Henry Plumer's second trial, and in September the ex-marshal again was convicted of second degree murder. Judge Barbour sentenced Plumer to ten years at San Quentin, but a ten-day stay of sentence was granted so McConnell and Niles could file another appeal.

The trial of John McCabe for the murder of James McMurtry began in Judge Searls's court on October 7. McConnell's efforts failed to convince the jury, which found McCabe guilty of second degree murder. Alex Griffin was convicted of the same crime, but before trying the remaining defendants, Judge Searls took up the case of Eldred Northup, who was acquitted of murdering his wife's lover. The verdict surprised no one.

The remaining defendants in the McMurtry killing (Harrington, Casey and McGee) were then tried and convicted of murder in the second degree. Judge Searls sent all but Griffin to prison for ten years, and sentenced the ringleader to fifteen.

The next trials were those of L. P. Stone, Spanish John, and Benjamin Pascoe for the murder of a Chinese miner. Stone had been acquitted of highway robbery for lack of evidence, but there was a chance he would be convicted this time, for although Chinese testimony was useless by itself, another defendant had accepted immunity in exchange for his testimony. The *Journal* reported:

Considerable difficulty was experienced in procuring a jury, and over 100 persons were examined before the panel was completed.... The District Attorney entered a *nolle prosequi* against Benjamin Pascoe ... offered him as a witness against the others. The coolness with which this witness, a mere boy, testified to his own connection with a most heinous crime, created a deep sensation in the crowded Court Room. His testimony ... condensed, is as follows:

"[I] am 19 years of age [and] have been associated with Stone two months. We left Grass Valley to rob Chinamen on Bear River with the intent of killing. . . . We intended to go on the robbing expedition a week before we started. I proposed the place and Stone assented."

After reciting a litany of other robberies and mayhem, Pascoe got down to the case in hand:

A half mile below Little York we robbed a camp on Saturday; camped in a board cabin over night [and] went up the river Sunday afternoon. I went to a cabin and asked for water . . . with the Spaniard. A Chinaman tried to come out I pushed him back. A Chinaman behind . . . struck me with an axe in the thigh, which is the cause of my lameness. Stone was about ten feet behind me. A Chinaman shot at [him, and] Spanish John and I ran away as fast as we could. . . . The Chinamen fired first at Stone. Stone tried to leave after they shot at him. . . .

[I] heard a great many shots—I fired five shots and Stone five . . . there were twenty shots fired. . . . Stone tried to get away from the Chinamen but couldn't. . . . Stone was 25 yards from camp when he fired. The Spaniard took no part in the affair. When I looked back [I] saw Stone down and Chinamen shooting and stoning him. . . . When I left, several of the Chinamen had fallen. . . ."

Stone and Pascoe were literally tracked by the blood of the latter to the place where they were arrested. The defence offered no testimony and the case was submitted to the jury about 3 o'clock on Wednesday. The defendants' counsel admitted the truth of Pascoe's statement and the villainy of Stone, but [said] the prisoners had abandoned their attempt at robbery, and were endeavoring to escape, and that the Chinese were not attempting to capture but to kill the defendant.

The jury were out about three hours and returned a verdict of guilty of murder in the second degree. Great surprise is manifested . . . as it was thought the jury must find Stone guilty . . . in the first degree. . . . Yesterday morning Spanish John . . . plead guilty to murder in the second degree.

When called up for sentencing on October 30, Stone said he had been raised by religious parents, but had strayed from their teachings. Although he acknowledged himself to be a bad man, he denied he had committed murder. Stone, about 30 years old, had long been suspected of being connected with a gang of robbers. He was said to have one wife somewhere in the east and another in California.

Judge Searls gave Stone a short lecture, saying if he had been a juror he would have voted for a verdict of first degree murder. The judge declared he was convinced that if the dead could speak, other victims would point to Stone as their murderer. He then sentenced Stone to thirty years in prison and gave Spanish John a fifteen-year term.

The remarks of Fred, who went to the Stone trial with Mr. Rigby, were being quoted widely, according to his mother:

A lawyer who has very black eyes and is cross-eyed gave him two shillings, and when [Fred] got home he described him as "the man who looked both sides," suiting his gestures to his language, so that every one who knows Mr [C. Wilson] Hill can tell at once who he means. He gave the particulars of the case that was being tried (a man who had killed some Chinamen), and said his pa preached a short sermon, and the lawyers preached long ones.

The *Democrat* commented that Ben Pascoe had been observed hanging about the jail after the trial:

... for the past few days [he] has taken up his residence on the south-east corner of the Court House steps. It is generally believed that his former companions would handle him rather roughly if they had an opportunity, and for this reason it is said he intends to leave the State at an early day. . . . we are informed his parents reside near Grass Valley.

William Marshall was tried in the court of sessions for robbing Wells, Fargo's box from the Sacramento stage, but the evidence was entirely circumstantial and he was acquitted. On November 2 Sheriff Boring started for San Quentin at four in the morning with Griffin, McGee, Harrington, McCabe, Casey, Stone, and Spanish John. The stage was escorted until daylight by four armed horsemen. At Sacramento the sheriff was served with an order for the return of Alex Griffin, McConnell and Niles having obtained a suspension of sentence until the application for a new trial could be heard by the supreme court.

Until Griffin was put back in his cell, the county jail had been empty for twenty-four hours—the first such occasion in more than three years.

St. Patrick's Catholic Church,
Grass Valley 1858

CHAPTER 42

JUDGE BARBOUR

November–December 1858

I

ℱOR THE FIRST TIME in more than two years Mary was keeping house by herself. She could not bear the thought of a winter with Laura's child and Fred in the same house, and she supposed the exercise would benefit her health. She admitted to Cornelia that Niles did not like her plan:

I have been alone now three weeks, and enjoy it very much thus far.... My trip to Downieville did me much good I think. I never *felt* better in my life, have not even a headache when I am tired, but I have Deb's old difficulty when I walk far, and sometimes when I work too hard....

I have a great mind to get a sewing machine. Many of the ladies here have them, and like them very much, and as Niles has promised me $35 per month *wages*, and Add insists on paying me for his board, I think I can easily save money enough above my current expenses to get one. Do you know anything about them? Wheeler & Wilsons is considered best here, and has a *hemmer* attached which turns down the hems. . . .

This morning Niles went to Downieville again. I am so lonely without him. I have cried all the afternoon and must not talk about it or I shall go at it again. He is so good and thoughtful, and takes such good care of me when he is here, and I love him so dearly that it seems like tearing my heartstrings to have to part with him so much. He will be gone 5 or 6 weeks, and will then be home until the 1st of April, about which time we expect a great but *welcome* event.

Have you been expending sympathy on me all this time Nellie? If you have, be assured it is unnecessary, for though we were both somewhat sorry at first, we have concluded to be very much pleased, and to think that *if* we can have a little *girl* we shall be *perfectly delighted* and shall be satisfied and pleased any way. I dread the care, it is true, but am better fitted to endure it, and Niles is fitted to aid and sympathize with me more than when Fred came to demand our attention.

Tuesday evening [Nov 2]. Nellie: I have been out all the afternoon with Deb and Delight in a carriage—making calls. I left Fred to take care of the house, as he would not consent to my going unless I did. He thinks it very smart to *keep house*, alone, and it is pleasant weather, and Mr and Mrs Rigby watch him and take care of him, I know that he is safe. . . . I think he would be very happy with a little girl or boy baby. He is very fond of a little girl baby there is near here, and often wishes he had a little sister like Hattie Turner.

Wallace Caldwell's sister had accompanied his fiancee to California that summer, and Addison was showing unusual interest in the young woman. Mary made a point of looking into the matter:

We have been out today about 2 miles to see a young lady, recently from the states—a Miss Caldwell, who seems like one of our sort of girls, and Add has taken quite a fancy to her. I am glad he has found some one worth calling upon, for it is better for him to call on the ladies now and then, and there is no longer any danger of his being *fooled*; he is too old and indifferent for that. This lady is not at all handsome or stylish, but a plain unassuming sensible girl. . . .

I hope to get letters from home tonight, but Add is always out so late, I think I will not wait for them. He is as tardy about going to bed and getting up as ever. He wants to go to bed at 2 and get up at 10, and actually does when he boards at a restaurant and there is no court to call him earlier.

Mary still had not revealed her pregnancy to her mother, despite the promise made after Fred was born—but she did tell all about Lizzie Caldwell:

Add has not been home tonight; I suppose he was busy until late, and so took dinner in town. We teaze him a great deal about a young lady who recently arrived from the states, and to whom he has taken a slight fancy—that is, he has called on her two or three times, and taken her riding once. It is enough to render their engagement an established fact in the minds of the good people here, whereas I do not consider that there is the slightest prospect that it will ever be. I am glad he has found some one with whom he can now and then spend an hour pleasantly. She is a good sensible girl, and they are by no means common here.

After two weeks in Downieville, Niles traded courts with the Butte County judge. He spent two days with Mary on his way to Oroville, which made his absence easier to bear. Niles would arrive home the first week in December and stay there till the first of April. Her father was pleased with Niles's political course; "I thought he would be," she told her mother.

II

JUDGE WILLIAM BARBOUR was making news again. In addition to being defeated in his district, an old and nagging problem refused to go away. An item in the *Journal* read:

The *Trinity Journal* says four years ago Wm. T. Barbour, Judge of Marysville District, assaulted a man with a deadly weapon; his case has been continued from term to term ever since. If the assault had been made by some fellow with a broken-down shirt collar, we apprehend justice had not been so drowsy. This law is a curious thing, and doesn't always furnish sauce suitable for both goose and gander.

A week later the *Journal* published a letter from Oliver Perry Stidger of North San Juan:

[The article] in your paper ... contains a few errors [and] I propose ... to give you and your readers a full history of this case.... [In] 1854, a man by the name of Plummer W. Thurston.... attacked Doctor [J. W.] Winter [in Marysville] ... beat him severely with an axe or pick helve over the head and body, breaking one of his arms and one or two of his fingers, and otherwise bruising him severely.

Stidger went on to explain that after Thurston was found guilty and sentenced to pay $500 and spend six months in prison he appealed the case to Judge Barbour's district court. The district attorney argued that the district court had no appelate jurisdiction, but as late as October 1854 Judge Barbour still had not rendered his decision in the matter; and many, Stidger included, thought Barbour did not intend to do so if he could help it.

At this same time a dispute arose between Judge Barbour and Yuba County Judge Bliss concerning a man convicted in Barbour's court of murder or manslaughter (Stidger couldn't remember which). Owing to Barbour's "negligence and his too frequent use in those days (he has reformed now) of the *O, be joyful,*" this culprit was never sentenced. The term of district court having expired, the county judge took it upon himself to discharge the convicted criminal, "not finding anything in the law authorizing his detention." Barbour was understandably upset and he denounced Judge Bliss with vigor. Stidger continued:

The excitement ... became intense and led to a newspaper controversy between Judge Bliss and Judge Barbour. At that time I was engaged in the *Herald* Office in the capacity of Reporter; and in consequence of my position became intimate with all the facts in the cases under consideration.... During this excitement ... much was said by many of the best citizens of Marysville against Judge Barbour's conduct.... threats were made that he should be impeached, not only for his utter neglect of his duties but also for his drunkness and debauchery.

All sorts of things were said of and against him ... and more than one person intimated ... that he had been bribed by Thurston to smother his case if possible. Feeling it to be my duty ... to keep the citizens of Marysville and Yuba county apprised ... I addressed a communication to the Editor of the *Herald*, asking in polite and moderate language what had become of Thurston's case, and also about another case....

On Saturday morning Oct. 14, 1854, the *Herald* appeared, containing my communication. That day I was attacked by Thurston and Barbour—the former armed with a revolver and the latter with a large bowie-knife—and between the two I was badly beaten. But for the interference of a friend, I probably would have been killed....

Barbour was indicted for assaulting Stidger in November 1854. He pleaded not guilty and asked for a change of venue. His petition was granted by the court of sessions, which ordered the papers certified to Nevada County. Shortly before the case ought to have been heard, Stidger received information that he would not have to travel to Nevada

City then or in the forseeable future, for the file on Barbour's indictment had been stolen from the Yuba County Clerk's office.

Stidger notified the district attorney, who discovered the papers had disappeared on the same day they had been ordered transferred to Nevada County. Barbour was indicted a second time, but before he could be brought to trial, the first papers mysteriously reappeared. Stidger wrote:

Here was a dilemma. Two indictments for the same offense were hanging over his head; one of them was ordered to be tried in Nevada county, the other was not. Barbour ... preferred Nevada, and elected to be tried there.... In 1855, I think at the February term, the case was called up in the Court of Sessions of Nevada county. I was on hand as a matter of course. Buckner & Hill appeared as counsel for Barbour, and that indefatigable and able lawyer, A. A. Sargent, Esq., in behalf of the People.

Every impediment which the learned counsel for Barbour could invent was thrown in the way to prevent a trial; but the Court being composed of honest, sensible men, overruled every objection, quirk and quibble ... and ordered the case to proceed. Finding that ... he had either to go to trial before such a court ... or remove the case to some other county, he [chose] the latter course....

Mr. Sargent being, no doubt, anxious to be rid of the case, and ... save Nevada county a large expenditure of money, consented to Barbour's proposition, and the case was ordered back for trial in Yuba. This ended the second act of the great drama.... The 3d, 4th and 5th Acts I will give you next week.

The *Journal* apologized for the absence of Stidger's second communication in its next issue "owing to the whole force of the office being employed in putting in type a most extraordinarily lengthy delinquent tax list." The delayed installment appeared a week later and described how Barbour, represented by former adversary Stephen Field, tried to have the charges dismissed on a legal technicality. The court overruled him and Field appealed the court's decision.

Despite frequent inquiries from Stidger, nothing more was heard of the case until January 1858, when the new clerk of the supreme court (a personal friend) told him the papers had vanished a second time. As soon as Stidger demanded an investigation the papers reappeared, and the supreme court upheld the lower court's ruling.

The remainder of Oliver Stidger's saga appeared on December 3, although it was a story without a conclusion. When the case was called on the first Tuesday in July 1858, Barbour asked for and was given a two-week postponement. Another was granted at the next hearing, when Barbour claimed he could not proceed without two witnesses, one in Sacramento and the other in bed with a broken leg.

Barbour won another week's delay in October because one of the witnesses failed to appear. At the next court date the witness was there but told Barbour his testimony would not be what had been expected. If the trial proceeded, Dr. Zabriskie's testimony would convict him even if no other witness was questioned. Pressure then was exerted on Stidger to agree to drop the charge of attempted murder and permit Barbour to plead guilty to a the lesser count of assault and battery.

Stidger refused, saying the matter now was in the hands of the court and the district attorney. Barbour then made the same request of the court. The district attorney called it a novel proceeding, Judge Bliss denied the motion, and Barbour's attorney asked for and received a continuance. Lamented Stidger:

The case is still pending in the Court of Sessions of Yuba county, and for aught I know it will remain there for all time to come. I have no confidence that it ever will be brought to trial ... because I believe Barbour will stave it off until his term of District Judge expires ... on the 1st day of January 1859—and then he will probably leave the State.

III

DOCTOR E. STONE was furious. A person she described as "a professed Physician of Nevada" had slandered her reputation. A woman with Mrs. Stone's will and determination had no intention of sitting idly while rumormongers did their damage. Instead, she issued a challenge. Her card appeared in the *Journal* on November 26 and every Friday thereafter for several months. It read:

In all my professional career I have not had occasion to defend myself against slander intended to injure my professional reputation before; I have practiced for some time as Physician and Midwife in Germany, my native home; in N.Y. City & in Buffalo, N.Y., and have been in the high estimation of the profession and the public, so far as I am known, which a reference to Dr. L. A. Wolfe of N.Y., or Professor White of Buffalo will testify.

The circumstance which calls forth this card is certain false and slanderous remarks which have come to my ears from one calling himself a physician. The last I heard was a sarcastic remark that "he would like to see me in a difficult case of midwifery." Now it is sympathy with my sex at the cruelties practiced on them by men in medical practice for want of knowledge in the profession, that chiefly induced me to remain here, and if that gentleman or any other will be kind enough to present me a difficult case, I will attend it with a great deal of pleasure, that he and the public may form an estimate of my capacity.

I have attended 2000 cases of midwifery, among which, I presume I have had as difficult cases as has fallen to the share of any physician in this country, but how I performed my duties and with what results, I leave others and time in this country to testify; suffice it to say, I challenge any one or number of physicians to prove me inferior in female practice to any physician in California.

My diploma can be seen at my residence, which will testify that in midwifery, medical operations, and the use of instruments in all forms required in medical practice, I have perfected my studies to the satisfaction and unanimous approbation of the whole board of professors. Medicines and supporting instruments of all kinds required by females to be had at my residence.

A. Peyser's Santa Claus Headquarters at 47 Broad Street had a wonderful array of toys, dolls, and holiday gifts. Peyser boasted he had the largest and best selected stock of fancy goods and toys ever exposed in the mountains:

Nobody will leave the store without purchasing, as it comprises large invoices of India Rubber Dolls, Doll Heads ... Wax, Kid, China and Paper Dolls, China sets, Baskets, Buckets, Wagons, Wheelbarrows, Guns, Swords, Cannons, Drums, Horses, and Musical Instruments of all kinds, and a thousand other articles too numerous to mention.

Snow fell on the day before Christmas, and Nevada City youngsters beheld a new and exciting treat at the Methodist Church that evening: a Christmas Tree decorated with toys, candies and other gifts from the good saint. The tree was erected on a platform in front of the pulpit, surrounded by children of all ages, "from yearlings to full grown," according to the *Democrat*, which went on to say:

Some three hours was consumed in giving out the presents, during which a continual clatter was kept up by little tongues and feet. Such scenes are calculated to make one think better of the world in which he lives, and years hence, when the little boys and girls take our places, and are occupied with the more serious cares and duties of life, their minds will often wander back to the pleasant Christmas sports of their childhood days.

The Searls family was invited to Christmas dinner some distance out of town. The snow had turned to rain, making the roads nearly impass-able, according to Mary:

Our horse fell where the mud was up to the hubbs of the wheel, broke the shaft, and I got out and went into a house. Niles got another carriage and two horses and we went on, had a pleasant visit.... Fred had innumerable presents Christmas and New Years too—too many for his good. He dont appreciate them as well....

He was over loaded with presents by Santa Claus, and a happier boy never was seen than he on Christmas morning. He had been quite irritable for a week, and had been told several times that Santa Claus would not bring him any thing if he were not better, so that he feared there would be nothing for him, but he found both stockings and an arm chair full of toys. A soldiers cap and feather, a sword and belt, a box of toy tools, a locomotive that winds with a key and runs all about the room by machinery, various other toys, and a pretty book and a note from St Nick. (alias Deb) which was best of all.

It was very prettily written, and had the effect to induce him to be very good till next Christmas. I will write what I remember of it. It is mislaid and I cant hunt it now. It commenced thus:

"I am glad to find you in bed like a good boy. I find that you have been a very good boy *most* of the time since last Christmas. Some traces of mischief I find, it is true—marks of hatchet on the apple trees, glass taken out of dining room stove, and tracks of boots on the flour sacks (all very bad indeed, my boy)—but I find that you have tried so hard to be good, and have helped your Ma so much, and been so good to your little cousin Fannie, that I shall excuse you this time, but mind that I do not see one such naughty thing next Christmas, for you will be so much older then that I cannot excuse you again. This pretty red covered book I give you because you have been so kind to your cousin Fannie &c &c."

I have not time to copy more of it. He knows it by heart, and is trying hard to deserve more presents when Christmas comes again.

Earlier in the month there had been enough snow for good sleighing. Luther Wickes's partner, A. B. Gregory, came to the Searls house with a sleigh improvised from planks and a crockery crate from his and Luther's grocery. He insisted on taking Mary and Fred for a ride to Charley's house, she told Cornelia:

We left the dishes washed and unwiped, the rooms unswept and hastened to obey the summons. I thought of you and wondered if *you* would have left things in such a plight. They left us there for 2 hours, and I induced Deb to return with us and stay all night. It was a *freezing bitter* cold night, such as has been known here but once before since we lived here, and Charlie and Harvey came over in the evening to play whist, and we made Charlie stay all night to keep Deb from freezing.

Next morning we had ... a grand visit. I wouldnt [begin] to clear the breakfast table for fear the boys would start to go, and so there we sat, talking and laughing in real *home* fashion until nearly noon. Deb and I laid our plans for the Holidays after the boys went out, not expecting to see each other again till they are over. The roads are almost impassable now with mud, a long rain having removed the snow.

We intend to be prepared for N. Years calls this year, as it is the custom here for every one to call, and we have never been prepared. I have been preparing the fruit today for a loaf of fruit cake—and shall make it tomorrow. Most people buy it, but I have plenty of eggs, and thought I would like to try my luck. I shall make some jumbles next week, and a loaf of plain cake, and my silver will be *"mighty nice"* wont it, to set off my table.

Dont think I am doing all this without help. After various attempts, and frequent disappointments, I have succeeded in securing a "Catholic Irish girl," and as nearly as I can judge from 3 days service I shall get on very well with her, though it is an unwelcome dose, and I find myself trying many times each day to contrive some way to avoid it.

She is very pleasant and willing, and I can order her about and make a *servant* of her as I could not Laura, but I dont like the kind, and she is *such* a talker. If it wasn't for Ettie, I should wish Laura back, though she has been so untidy and slack this summer that I was tired of her too.

My two months housework has been of much use to me. I could not get along with an Irish girl at all if I had not learned a little more about work myself. I think too that I have saved all of $100 by it. What a pity I cant *continue* to save it, every two months, but I *cant*, and shall not try any longer. I dont suppose I shall ever be able to do my work again, there will be such an increase in the amount of sewing &c....

Niles admires your energy in providing for your household, and pretends to regret the choice he made. He too finds it a great care to provide for his family. He has double the care while home that he would have if he were here all the time, and he has to purchase and plan for his absence too. Add is a noble good fellow, but without any intention of complaining of him, I will admit to you that he is *not* a very good *family man.* If he ever has a wife, I *pity* her. With the kindest intentions in the world, I am sure he will neglect her....

He ought to be rich, and have an active business like woman, to plan and order every thing. Then he would worry her life out by staying out late and *never* getting up in the morning. I dont believe though that he will ever get married.

Kidd-Knox building, Pine and Broad Streets

CHAPTER 43

BOLD INTRUDERS

January–February 1859

I

SHORTLY AFTER MIDNIGHT on the morning of December 29, 1858, four thieves entered the house of William Davis on Piety Hill. They ate four mince pies, a quantity of cake and crackers, and pocketed three cans of oysters before Mrs. Davis's sister saw a light at her door and called to know who was there.

Her cry woke Mr. Davis, who then heard someone running down the stairs, followed by the crash of a table being upset and articles tumbling on the floor. Mrs. Davis peered out of her upstairs window in time to see four men rush from her house and vanish. At Mr. Brown's house a dog barked, but Edwin Waite's family next door was undisturbed.

Around the corner and down the street, Mary and Niles were asleep when intruders entered their house at 3 a.m. A sudden noise caused Mary to wake, but supposing it was her new girl Maggi getting up to clean floors before breakfast, she made a mental note to scold her for not being more quiet. Mary had slept poorly that night and was annoyed at this latest interruption.

I heard some one try our bedroom door softly, and raising my head, I saw a light at the crack. I called out to know who was there, thinking it might be Add or Maggi. The light instantly disappeared and all was still. Niles had been awakened by my calling and thought I was mistaken about hearing anything, but after a little reflection I knew I could not be mistaken, and knowing there was neither pistol, knife or matches in the room, I determined to go myself to get matches from the kitchen, thinking they would not attack me if any one was there.

The door they tried was in front, and I concluded there was no one likely to be in the kitchen. I found matches, lit a candle, and returned. Niles took the candle and opened the door and called [up the stairs] to Add, to know if he was up. There was no answer, but he heard some hard breathing on the stairs, and after standing a moment, a man with a black veil over his face came down a few steps and said, "If you'll get out of the way we'll come down."

There was no alternative, and Niles stepped back [inside the bed-room] and bolted the door again, and the man rushed out. He would have been in Adds room in a moment more. There is little danger to be apprehended from these burglars—*except* robbery. They never hurt any one if they can avoid it, as it increases the danger of discovery. Several other houses were entered before ours, clothing and provision stolen, and a trunk was stolen off the stage and robbed the same night.

Niles immediately had bolts installed on all the doors and obtained two pistols; despite these precautions, someone entered the house on the following night and was frightened off when Mary lit a candle. Mary told Cornelia:

We know there was but one man last night, and think there was not before. He was more frightened than Niles the night they *compromised*, as Niles calls it. We had a great deal of fun about it the day after the first attempt, and Niles was well laughed at, though every one said he took the only possible, or available course. We have said nothing about last nights visit, thinking they would be more apt to return if there was nothing said.

By the way, they took Niles over coat and cane from the hall. Niles will deposit our watches at Charlie's safe today. You need not think I am frightened to death or any where near it, even at the time. I am of course somewhat alarmed, and it is very annoying to be disturbed in this way, time after time. It would doubtless make me very nervous after a while.

Niles was supposed to have gone to Sacramento the day after the second attempt, but he cancelled the trip. Unfortunately, he would have to spend several days in Auburn, but otherwise would be home until April. By that time, as Mary phrased it, "the season for burglary is over here, and the peculiar danger to me will be over too, I trust," referring to the expected birth of her second child.

Niles obtained a double-barreled shotgun and arranged with Addison and a neighbor to stand watches during the night. Despite Mary's wish to keep it quiet, word of the second burglary found its way into local papers. Nothing happened for several days, and during Niles's absence in Auburn, Mary stayed with Deb and Charley. While they were away Addison found the outside doors open one morning, though he distinctly remembered bolting them the night before.

Rocks were thrown through Mary's bedroom window on the last night before Niles came home. The shutters, glass and a portion of the sash were driven in, and two rocks, each four or five inches in diameter, were found on the floor. A small lamp had been kept burning in the room throughout the night. Edwin Waite speculated it might have been the work of personal enemies, unintentionally positioning himself as a prime suspect.

When Mary moved back she brought a companion who had "blue eyes, dark eyelashes, brown, smooth hair, clear but not very light complexion, large mouth but beautiful teeth, a little taller than I am, but larger a great deal; broad shouldered, well formed and graceful." She explained to her mother why she had invited Lizzie Caldwell to come home with her:

She is an intelligent sensible girl, in some respects reminds me of Nellie, in her looks and manner. She is very amiable and warm hearted, and all we R Ville people set her down at first sight as one of *our sort of girls*, and determined to cultivate her acquaintance.

They all accuse Add of being *particularly* taken up with her, and as he does seem somewhat attentive, I thought I would take some pains to become acquainted with her myself, and have made an excuse to send for her to spend some days with me. The result of my observations is very favorable. She is one whom I think would make an *excellent wife*, if Add *should* take a decided fancy to her, and I think I may safely let things take their own course.

Add is old enough to judge for himself, is able to support a wife if he wants one, and I think would be much happier if he had one. I have seen no one who seems better fitted to make him happy than Lizzie. Perhaps I ought not to say this to you, for I doubt if Add would like it if he knew it, but he need not know that I have said it, and I thought you would be glad to know it.

Having revealed so much about Addison's affairs to her mother, Mary then decided it was only fair to be more candid about her own:

I am very busy indeed nowadays. I think I have an *excellent* girl, and she does all the housework, but I have an immense amount of sewing to do, and am only "as well as could be expected." You wont be anxious about me now because I have told you this, will you? You need not, for I am as well provided for in every respect as any one could be, and we are well pleased with the prospect.

Fred often wishes for a little brother or sister, and I think it will find a cordial welcome from all. I thought I would not try to keep it from your knowledge this time, because you are healthier, and I think it would be a pleasure to you, rather than a trouble—wont it?

On February 1 Addison wrote home and confirmed Mary's guesses:

I dont suppose Mary has told you quite all of my doings, however— perhaps for the very simple reason that she did'nt know them all—and I suppose when I come to tell you (as I am going to) the sort of extras I have been engaged in, you will be about as completely astonished as you ever were in your life.

You see it so happened, a few months since, that I discovered a girl here (or lady, I suppose I ought to call her, since she is 25)—who was such a good sort of a girl—and resembled our Rens. Ville style of girls so much—that I thought it would be pleasant to you to have her for a daughter. You know Mary is so far away from you, that she is'nt much more than half a daughter to you—and I thought Lizzy would just about make up the deficiency.

Of course I dont care anything about her myself—only on your account. So I asked her one day if she would take our name, and she said she would (foolish, was'nt she?), and some time in April next—if nothing happens—she is to come and live with us, and be one of us.

Now aint you astonished! You did'nt imagine I would be doing such things away off her in Cal. did you? . . .

She (Lizzy) is called good looking (I am no judge you know, under the circumstances)—but I know she is intelligent—and a lady—and I believe she will make a good wife for me. She has been staying with May a few days last week, and May has become very much attached to her, and likes her, I know. And to tell the truth, I rather like her myself—and we think (Lizzy and I) that we shall be happy together. . . .

All here are pretty well but Deb Mulford. She is not very sick, but ailing.

Mary wrote her own version of Addison's news to Cornelia:

Addison is engaged and is to be married soon. He only waits until I am well enough to have him bring his bride here, which I hope will be about the last of April. . . .

She is certainly a very loveable girl. She is from Byfield Mass., is the only daughter among a family of 8 children, and has been much petted by the brothers. One of them we have known in Nevada since we first came here. He is a steady industrious young man, made some money when he first came and immediately sent [it] home to put his sister at boarding school, and gave her a good education (it is *said* to be good—I have had no opportunity to judge much of her acquirements). . . .

He of course, like all ardent lovers, is in a great hurry, and she, like all modest maidens, is coy, and thinks next fall would look better than this spring, since their acquaintance has been so short—but long engagements in Cal. (and 6 months would seem a *very* long one here) are not at all pleasant. I advise them if there is nothing else to hinder (and there seems to be nothing else) to not postpone the matter for the mere sake of appearance. To the friends at home I am afraid it *will* seem hasty, but it will be pleasanter for all parties here, I think.

They will fit up Addison's room and board here during the summer, and longer if we all like it, , , , They will be married quietly at her brothers [place], with only *our folks*, the boys &c, and their friends, and will come directly here. There would be no pleasure in a trip any where at that season, and there is not much fun in a stage ride here any way. I am glad they are too sensible to wish to go.

Addison had called attention to Deborah's ailing condition, and Mary made further comments:

I dont see Deb more than once or twice a month now. She is very poorly indeed, but I hope she will be better soon. I dont know as you ought to speak of this to RVille people, as her mother would be worried. It is nothing serious and I think she will soon recover.

Deb's ailment was the same as Mary's: she was pregnant. However, it was commonly supposed that Deb's health was more delicate and thus required greater protection. Despite the precarious nature of her system, Deb managed to exhibit considerable physical endurance whenever it was required, much to everyone's surprise.

II

MARY'S OWN BEST NEWS concerned the new district court boundaries, which had been reduced to embrace only Nevada County. "Isn't that grand," she told Cornelia; "It will save much expense, besides the great trial of having [Niles] absent so much. It comes in such a good time too."

She thought of her sister's husband, and that reminded her of how badly a good minister was wanted at Nevada City, no one having been found to replace James Warren at the Congregational church.

We have one Methodist, an Episcopal, and a kind of Baptist exhorter, and I suppose 3 poorer preachers were never heard in one decent community. We need a good smart sensible man, he would be well supported, but these poor miserable drones can scarcely get their bread.

She compared Laura with Maggi, whom she had grown to appreciate more than ever:

I have a good girl—a good natured, stout, active Irish girl, who can do more work and *make* more work in one day than Laura could in two. She is a pretty good cook, and I think as neat as Catholic Irish get to be; a *very* good washer and ironer, neat about her person and tries to be economical. *Can* an Irish girl be taught to be saving? In many respects she is better for me than Laura, and in some she is not. . . .

[Fred] went with me to town today and stopped at Harvey's [drug store], and when he came to Arthur's he was loaded down with toys. You would have laughed to see him strut along the street with a small hoe, rake, and shovel on his shoulder, and a gun in his hand, and when he got in the house he had a ball, a book, a knife and some marbles in his pocket.

He had a pick given him the other day, and he has been working with all his strength ever since at mining. He has two sets of diggings, one over at Rigby's and one in his little garden, and this morning a young man who has been stopping here for a short time, went out early and put a piece of quartz with gold in it into his mines. Fred found it, and a prouder boy you never saw. He has told half the men in town that "he struck gold in his diggings this morning," and he insists on taking it into Charlies to be made into money. Says he will build a bank of his own when he gets out gold enough.

He has too many presents. He does not value them half as much as he would a few, but he is a great favorite with a number of men about town, besides [David] Belden and our boys, and each one has to give him something whenever they see him.

Some men who once had occupied positions of respect and trust were not so well thought of these days: ex-Judge Barbour had been tried and found guilty of committing assault and battery on Oliver Stidger; the grand jury accused Nevada County Treasurer Thaddeus Sigourney of gross neglect or outright dishonesty (you could take your pick), and Public Administrator Frank Nicholson had left town with $2,000 in trust funds.

Sigourney was charged with irregularities in the issuance of business licenses. He had failed to provide receipts or gave receipts for incorrect amounts, according to complaints. Discrepancies were alleged to exist between what had been collected and what was in the treasury, and Sigourney was faulted for deducting a 5 per cent commission instead of the 3 per cent authorized by law. Finally, his security bond was said to be insufficient.

When the *Journal* reported a widespread belief that the treasurer had pocketed a large share of the money collected, Sigourney denied all charges and attacked his accusers:

The Grand Jury, through super-officious zeal and industrious malice of a few of its members, have not only transcended the requirements of official duty, but the plainest rules of justice and moral propriety in reporting to the public 'as facts,' their own conclusions, ignorantly jumped at upon a partial and prejudiced investigation.

He called the grand jury system "a secret and one-sided inquisition—a relic of barbarism, which in these modern days is too often made the means of concealment for personal malice or craven revenge, and a lever to oppress, malign and injure."

On December 17 the treasurer went with his attorney to the county clerk's office and asked to see license receipts which had been requisitioned by the grand jury and then placed in the auditor's hands for safekeeping. After a cursory examination the lawyer advised Sigourney to confiscate the material, which he did.

The auditor protested to the district attorney, who got an order from the county judge requiring the treasurer to return the papers or face contempt. Sigourney refused and went to jail. Judge Searls released him that same night on a writ of habeas corpus, reasoning that because the full court of sessions had issued the order to put the licenses in the care of the auditor, the county judge, acting alone, could not find Sigourney in contempt.

Later Judge Searls ordered the indictment set aside because certain members of the grand jury had a conflict of interest in the case, which should be presented to the next grand jury.

Frank Nicholson's problems began in December when he was ordered by the probate court to hand over the estate of S. N. Palmer. Instead, the public administrator closed his account at Birdseye's bank, left a note at the court house saying he would be delayed, and caught a stage to Grass

Valley. From there he hired a buggy as far as Iowa Hill, and then dropped from sight. The *Journal* blamed Judge Caswell for not removing Nicholson from office before that happened:

Several times have the securities of Nicholson been called in question. The Board of Supervisors demanded of him additional bonds about a year since. The bonds were to be forthcoming within a certain time. [When Nicholson failed] to comply the Board declared the office vacant.

The Probate Judge interfered and the Board, doubtful of their powers in the premises, did not pursue the matter further. Two grand juries afterwards examined the bonds of the Administrator and pronounced them insufficient in the eye of the law. The grand juries recommended additional bonds. We believe little attention was given to these recommendations.

Here we have another lesson on the evil of electing irresponsible men to office. Mr. Nicholson never should have been elected to a position of trust. By good luck he has had several small fortunes fall into his hands, all of which he wasted in vice. When he became a candidate before the people two years ago we asked the pertinent question through these columns, if a man should be trusted with dead men's money who couldn't or wouldn't take care of his own. The question was propounded solely from a sense of duty we owed the public, for personally we have been on good terms with the candidate.

On January 18 the probate court declared the office of public administrator vacant for failure to give an additional bond of $10,000 and the board of supervisors was directed to fill the vacancy at its next meeting.

III

ON THE NIGHT OF February 2 Alex Griffin broke a bar loose from his cell and, with the aid of this and a saw fashioned from a watch spring and a vial of acid, removed two bars from a window on the outside wall and made his escape. Before leaving he took the precaution of drugging the only other inmate with opium-laced whiskey.

Four guards were asleep nearby—one heard a noise he guessed was rats. It was the first escape since Sheriff Boring assumed office, and the *Democrat* asked embarrassing questions. The *Journal* hurried to Boring's defense:

While the acts of a public officer are open to legitimate criticism ...

the spirit that induces a public print to pile up inferences and baseless insinuations against such an officer, is contemptible. It is abusing the position of an editor, and prostituting his means of access to the public ear, to the vilest uses. . . .

The Democrat . . . says that Griffin "had been permitted at times to walk about town on parole, to see his friends, and had always returned to the jail according to his promise." Again it says, "The negligence of the officers in allowing Griffin to walk about town, unattended and unwatched seems unaccountable. . . . He had undoubtedly procured the necessary tools for cutting off the iron bars while running at large about town."

Now the statements in the above quotations are totally false. . . . On two occasions only was he ever outside of the bars, and then did not leave the jail three hundred yards, and on each occasion was attended and closely watched by the jailor, Mr. Lenhart. . . .

[The *Democrat*] also says "It is believed by many that he left while out on parole, and that he never broke out of jail." The insinuation amounts to this—that Mr. Boring, finding he had let out his prisoner on parole, and that he would not return, broke off the bar of the cell, and sawed two bars out of a window, to create the impression that Griffin had broke jail!

The *Democrat* replied:

For giving a few facts connected with Griffin's escape, it seems that we have raised the ire of somebody, who gave his rage in a long article . . . in that receptacle of billingsgate, the Nevada *Journal*. The foul language of the *Journal* we shall pass over, for we are not disposed to insult our readers by answering it in kind, but shall devote a short space to the elucidation of facts. . . .

McConnell & Niles are the attorneys for Griffin. Their office is on the second floor of Kidd & Knox's brick building, which has [two entrances, one each] from Broad and Pine streets. One day while Mr. Niles was writing in his office, he heard the door open, and on looking round saw Griffin enter; he came in, sat down, talked about his case, and informed Mr. Niles that he was out on parole. After talking a few minutes he left. No officer was with him.

At another time Griffin was seen by J. C. Malbon [former city marshal], standing in front of the Post Office. Malbon looked expressly to see whether or not an officer was in attendance, but saw none. . . .

At another time Griffin went to Shellhorn's brewery, remained some time, and drank six or seven glasses of ale. This brewery is more than "three hundred yards" from the jail, and on this "occasion" he was not "attended and closely watched by the jailor, Mr. Lenhart." Some one accompanied Griffin to the brewery, but who he was we cannot learn. Griffin told Mr. Shellhorn that he had hired the man to go with him as a guard.

About two weeks before his escape, Alex. Griffin came alone to the meat market of Charles Kent, on Pine street, where he remained fifteen or twenty minutes. As he left, he borrowed half a dollar of John O'Brien, "to get something to drink." John O'Brien [a former policeman and deputy sheriff] watched him as he went to Blaze's Saloon, looked particularly for an officer, but saw none. Griffin met a Grass Valley friend in front of the saloon, with whom he talked for some time, after which they went in, and we presume "imbibed."

At one time Griffin was allowed to remain outside of the jail and saw wood, while Mr. Lenhart went over to Main street and ate his dinner, and no one was watching him. He was seen by Henry Knerr and Geo. Kendall. The latter asked Lenhart if it was safe to leave Griffin there; Lenhart said it was.

At another time Griffin was in a house of ill-fame, on Commercial street, where he remained for half or three-quarters of an hour. No officer was with him; we are not at liberty to publish the names of the parties who saw him there, but the fact can be substantiated if necessary....

The statement of the *Journal* that we insinuated that Mr. Boring had sawed off the bars to "create the impression" that Griffin had broke jail, is entirely gratuitous.... Of all the men that ever held office in the county, Mr. Boring is the last whom we should suspect of attempting such a deception. But he is liable to be deceived, and we believe he is even now ignorant of the many liberties which have been allowed Griffin. He has given but little personal attention to the jail, but his deputies who had charge of that institution, to use a mild term, have been slightly remiss in their duty....

CHAPTER 11

NEW LIVES

February—May 1859

I

AFTER THE PUBLIC SCHOOL burned in 1856, a new one had been constructed on land purchased from the Rev. Mr. Warren; for that reason it was ironic that an angry debate now raged over use of the Bible in the public school. It began when the school board interviewed teacher applicants for the 1859 term and chose Mr. J. A. Jennings and Miss Lizzie C. Farrell.

James Stratton told Rev. D. A. Dryden he had been rejected because of the Bible. In 1853 Stratton had founded a private academy and female institute at Sacramento, charging $250 board and tuition for a twenty-four week session. In 1857 he opened an academy and boarding school in Nevada City, behind the National Exchange Hotel. An anonymous writer (presumably Dryden) informed the *Journal* on April 8, 1859:

> The truth has been forced upon me at last. *The Bible is banished from the school....* on being asked [by the board] if he would use the Bible in school, [Stratton] replied that he would use the Gospels or portions of the New Testament, and he would not [take] the school if deprived of that privilege.

The committee applied to Mr. Jennings to take the school, and receiving from him a promise to banish the Testament from the school room, he was elected to the post.... The gentlemen participating [in the decision] are reported to be Wm. F. Anderson, Dr. Overton and I. J. Rolfe, and from them the public expect a defense of their course.

District Attorney Anderson replied in the *Democrat*, offering several objections to use of the Bible:

As a Protestant I [would] object to the introduction of the Catholic testament into the public schools; as a Catholic I [would] object to the introduction of the Protestant version into them; as a Jew I [would] object to the new testament altogether.

As a lover of peace and good will to men, I object to any book which will lead to strife and angry discussion upon all subjects, including religion; as a lover of justice I protest against the public money, contributed by tax-payers of all creeds and denominations, being used to promote the peculiar views of particular sects; as a friend of the innocence of childhood and the kindly sentiments which should be engrafted upon their minds, I protest against the system.

[Suppose we] let the children daily be called to read the new testament—one half the school refusing perhaps, in accordance with their parents wishes, and such daily exercise marks the distinctions of sect, and implants the seed of discord. Suppose the spectacle of one third armed with the Protestant version—another third with the Catholic version and the other with no version of the Christian scripture, but with the Bible of the Jewish dispensation. These distinctions thus introduced cannot but do evil; for children are not naturally sectarian.

James Stratton promptly replied in the pages of *Journal*:

Till the evening of the 20th ult. I had not thought of applying for the Public School.... Nor should I have applied at all, much as I desired the situation, had not Mr. Rolfe ... urged me.... [He] promised to vote for me ... and expressed much confidence that Mr. Anderson would do the same....

Messrs Anderson and Rolfe, assisted by Dr. Overton, County Superintendent of Public Schools, formed the august Committee before whom we four trembling supplicants for public patronage must pass the dreadful ordeal of an examination.

[Mr. Anderson] says, "Upon examination ... the qualifications of Mr. Jennings were in every respect equal to those of Mr. Stratton." ... What examination? pray let me ask. When—how and where did it take place? How was it conducted? and what dreadful blunder did I make? Like the old lady who became painfully excited when made aware of having talked foolishly in her sleep without knowing what she said, I feel terribly conscious of having had my whole intellectual being overhauled, weighed and measured by this astute committee without an idea when it occurred. . . .

Not a question was asked us in arithmetic, grammar, geography, or any of the higher branches; nor was Mr. Jennings questioned at all upon his methods of teaching. . . . True, they asked me several questions as to what text books I used in school, in a sort of "beating round the bush" manner, to get at the Bible question, which we soon reached, and spent the rest of the time in discussing.

But the only practical question even bearing upon our "qualifications" as teachers was a simple sentence in spelling given us to write as they pronounced . . . and lest it might contain some mystic signification . . . by which the Committee were enabled to [decide] . . . I will give it as nearly as I can recollect for the benefit of the community:

"John, traveling in a baggage wagon to save expense, ate plum pudding out of a cobbler's basin.". . .

Permit me in self defense to add that the Trustees decided that I was the only one who spelled the words correctly. . . .

[Anderson] says they were governed in their selection by the price. . . . both before and after the examination, if such we might call so palpable a farce, Mr. Rolfe expressed his willingness to engage me at my price. On the Saturday following, he frankly told me, in the presence of others, that his only reason for voting against me was the Bible question. He said unhesitatingly that both he and Mr. Anderson would have voted for me if I would give up the Bible. . . .

Ianthus Rolfe rebutted Stratton in the *Democrat*:

I never told Mr. Stratton that I would vote for him. I did tell him that the difference of $25 a month more than we had been in the habit of paying would, with me, be no objection . . . [but Mr. Stratton's] demands were deemed so unreasonable that they could not give their consent to employ him. The use of the Bible was by no means the principle objection to Mr. Stratton. He was determined to have charge of both [boys and girls] schools. . . . We wished the schools to be kept separate. . . .

I shall not consent to have the management of the public schools dragged in the mire of religious intolerance, or be made the vehicle of propagating the peculiar tenets of any one religious sect. If the people of Nevada are not satisfied with my course as School Trustee, I should advise them to meet on the first Saturday in April, 1860, and elect some man in my place who will carry out their wishes.

Now Mr. Jennings thought he should reply to Mr. Stratton:

There has been no "expulsion of the Bible from school," as Mr. Stratton would have known from an article in the Democrat of last week, if it had suited his purposes to know it. Though I have received directions not to put the Bible forward as a text book, I have been also directed to have regard to the conscientious scruples of parents who insist on having their children read it in school. . . .

Some days before the meeting of the Trustees, March 31st, I had a conversation with Dr. Overton on the subject of the Bible in schools, in which I told him I had always used it to some extent. I never had known evil to result from it in school except when devotional exercises were made tedious. Then they may produce habits of irreverence. Children seldom take a sectarian view of the Bible till after their public school days are over. . . .

Mr. Stratton says it was all "beating around the bush" to get at the Bible question. I confess my faculties were not acute enough to perceive it. . . . Almost at the first of it he declared that he would not teach a school unless he could have the Bible among its books. This was entirely voluntary on his part and not called for in answer to any questions put to him. At the close of the discussion, some one asked the question: "Do you say you would not teach a school unless you could have the Bible in it?" Mr. Stratton's answer was "Yes, some portions of it—the Gospels." . . .

I told a friend that if there were any trouble about it, I should consider it in a great degree due to Mr. Stratton's ill timed and over zealous discussion of the question. . . . Mr. Stratton also modestly assures the public that *he* was the only one who stood the test of scholarship imposed by the Trustees. The only difference between my orthography and his, was in the preterit tense of the verb *eat* and in the word *travelling;* the former I wrote *eat* and he wrote it *ate.* The latter I wrote with *two* l's and he with but *one.* In each case there are high authorities for both ways of spelling the words, so that neither can be justly called wrong.

On April 29 the *Journal* published an anonymous attack against Mr. Jenning's fellow teacher, Miss Lizzie C. Farrell:

Notwithstanding much has been said about our public school lately, we ask for light on one other matter: In selecting a female teacher for our children could the Trustees find no Protestant lady qualified for the position; and is it from the necessity of the case that we have to send to a Catholic teacher?

Perhaps our excellent agent can give us some information on this point. From his avowed hostility to all sects and sectarianism we could scarcely suspect anything sectarian about this selection of a teacher; but really, when taken in connection with the attempted expulsion of the Bible out of our school, it looks a little Jesuitically sectarian. SEVERAL PARENTS.

This resulted in an acid response from "One Who Knows" in the *Democrat*:

Of all the ill feeling called forth about the public school within the last month, the meanest is that ... signed "Several Parents." No wonder they keep back their names. As a Protestant I am ashamed of them and their coward bigotry.

I should wish all such to turn Catholic at once. They might be improved by the change—they could hardly be made worse. Will Protestants never cease to turn pale and quake in their shoes at the bugbear of Jesuitism? The lady teacher is doing her duty thoroughly, and it is a disgrace that she should be thus assaulted for a matter of opinion, which does not affect her usefulness as a teacher.

With quiet humor and good sense, Editor Tallman Rolfe offered his own view of things:

Our religious community are very much exercised about the exclusion of the Bible from the Public Schools, by our Town committee. In our opinion this action of the committee is uncalled for and unwise. The Bible is accepted by the majority of our citizens as the basis of morality and system of salvation, and although the Jewish portion of our community regard the New Testament as a humbug, and the Catholic portion the King James translation as a heresy, yet these are mere trivial objections....

If it is *the Bible* that our community wish used, they cannot object to the Douay version, should it chance to be selected. [But] if it is *their* Bible they are anxious about and are only desirous or willing that the particular work on which *their* salvation is based, should be used, then the charge of intolerance and illiberality which they raise against the Committee must return upon themselves.

If the Bible is to be read as part of a system of salvation, let the instructor understand it as *such*, as he does the other branches which he pretends to teach. If this work is introduced for its elegance as a composition, the splendor of its imagery, or its poetic beauties, we see no reason why the Koran should not become part of our common school system, as possessing these same excellencies.

But as a quietus to all this discussion we would suggest that at the several schools, the teachers be permitted to use such books as they see fit, and let the parents then select the school for their children, instead of as now, prescribing their own religious opinions as the rule for others.

Because of their Mormon upbringing, Tallman and Ianthus had excellent reasons for urging tolerance and sensitivity in religious matters. Recent events in the west had brought Latter Day Saints and their leaders into greater conflict with competing religions than at any time past, which was saying a good deal.

The United States government was exerting increased military pressure on Mormon leader Brigham Young to submit to federal control within the Utah Territory. Young had ordered all Mormon colonists in other states to return to Salt Lake, and by the winter of 1858-1859 nearly $4 million had been spent by the federal government to force compliance.*

The Rolfes had seen what infamous acts could be performed in the name of religion.

II

THE WINTER OF 1858–1859 was one of the severest in Nevada County history. Snow collected to 10 and 12 feet deep on the high ridges above Nevada City and near Little York. During February it stormed almost every day, and Mary complained there had not been two consecutive pleasant days all month. Because of the coming baby, she told Cornelia she didn't expect to get out of her house before summer, and by then she would be quite an old woman:

I shall have such a family to attend to, but I think Lizzie is such a domestic sort of girl that she will rather aid in the care, than add to it.... Addison went to Sac. last week and was admitted to [practice before] the Supreme Court, went on to San Francisco and spent a few days, and says he is now ready to *settle down*, and be contented.... Lizzie has not been in town to stay any since the visit of which I wrote you. She has merely called here once. She says people talk so much about her when she is in town that she dont intend to come any more till she comes to remain....

*See appendix for more about this and other Rolfe family experiences in Utah and San Bernardino.

419

My neighbor Mrs Rigby is very kind and social and I dont know what I should do without her, but is one of the kind who are of no use in sickness, and I place no dependence upon her for any thing of that kind. She will take the best care of Fred, though, at any time, if it is needed. I have engaged Laura to stay a week with me when I am sick. She will put Ettie out to board. So you see I have every thing arranged.

Adding to her concern was the fact that the neighborhood continued to be "infested" with robbers:

I have many sleepless nights or wakeful hours at least, in consequence. They have not tried our house in some time, at least if they have been around the dog has frightened them away—and they do not succeed in getting in or getting any thing valuable any where. Still, they are frequently heard of, and I am most in fear now that they will poison the dog. They have poisoned several large dogs recently.

One gang has however been scattered last week, by one of the number being wounded and made prisoner, and the others are known but have escaped. I think that will perhaps put an end to their depredations. I am not frightened about them, but anxious to have them meet a *warm* reception if ever they do come here again, for it is time an end was put to such annoyance. Niles keeps a pistol under his pillow and a shot gun and bowie knife within reach. We get used to it.

She finished the letter on March 2, remarking she was "all well as usual." No sooner was the letter posted than she felt unwell, and continued so for several days. On March 5 Mary woke at midnight in severe pain. Niles fetched Harvey Wickes and Mrs. Turner, and three hours later Mary's child was dressed and lying at her side. To Addison fell the honor of communicating the news to Rensselaerville:

May has met with a little accident—and has not quite recovered enough to write to you. Niles is in court and cant write. I am very busy today and cant write much. But there is news which must be told by someone, and it is the last mail day, and so I suppose I must tell it.

Well then—we (that is Niles and May) have had a slight addition to our family. There is a little fellow out at the house, kicking up his heels and crowing, and crying, and doubling up his fists at the world, who rejoices in the name of "Addison Niles Searles." We were all very much disappointed that we could'nt call him "Cornelia," but we could'nt well do it under the circumstances. Deb proposed that we call him "Cornelius" by way of compromise, but we decided not. . . .

Well—the aforesaid A. N. Searles is a fine healthy little fellow. He has not been weighed yet, but is rather larger than Fred at his age, and looks much as he did. Fred, of course, is nearly tickled to death with his new brother. May is doing finely. She had no trouble and is getting well fast. It is fine Spring weather—warm and pleasant—and she will be out and quite well soon, we hope.

After this important item of news, I hardly know what more to say. . . . I shall probably marry about the middle of April, and we (Lizzie and I) shall live with Niles and May for a short time, and then I hope to have a home of my own. Our wedding will be very quiet—such as suits two very quiet people.

On April 1 Mary began a letter to her mother. Contrary to what Addison had written, the weather had not been particularly pleasant:

. . . very unfavorable for me—cold and rainy nearly all the time, and I have gained *strength* slowly, but have suffered very little, and had no serious drawbacks. I did not expect the little stranger so soon by several weeks, but am glad enough that I am now nearly well instead of being just now taken sick. . . .

I had intended to have Laura to take care of me, but she had gone out of town and not supposing I would want her so soon, had left no word where she was going, so I sent for an old lady who was recommended to me, and was glad Laura was gone, as Mrs. Atkins was an old experienced nurse and did much better. . . .

I am writing now with "little Addison" on my lap, and am not sure of five minutes time to write even in that way. Not that the new baby is so troublesome, indeed he is a very good baby and sleeps a great deal, but I am not very strong yet, and the few cares that I have as yet resumed, take a great deal of time, as I have to calculate my own strength, and rest a good deal while baby sleeps. . . .

Fred has slept with Niles, and has learned to look to him almost entirely for attention of all kinds. I wish you could see what a patient, kind, and in fact what a *model* of a *family man* Niles has become. He spends nearly all his evenings at home, dresses and undresses Fred, gets up in the night to wait on us all, and in many things excites my wonder and admiration daily by his improvement. I never expected him to be *such* a husband, for it seemed so far from his nature, but his love for his family has changed him in some respects.

Deb was expecting her own baby in July—in fact, Harvey suspected twins and advised Charley to take her to New York quickly:

You will be surprised again I know, and think surprises never will cease, when I tell you that Charlie's folks are all going home in May. Harvey too is going. They have talked of it a long time, but have recently decided. Deb is not well—that is she expects to be *worse* sometime *next Summer* and is anxious to get home first, and as Charlie has made money beyond his highest calculations since he came back this time, there is nothing to prevent their going except Deborah's health.

She has been quite unwell for a while, but has been and is improving very rapidly, and they think that with Charlie, Harvey and Delight to take care of her it will be safe for her to attempt the trip home, so they are laying their plans to start on the 5th of May.

Addison will take their house and furniture just as it is; he gets it at a bargain, as Charlie did when he bought it. It is the finest house in the place and a pleasant place—but a lonesome neighborhood. Deb can tell you *every* thing about *every* thing when she gets home, if they go—if not, I shall have time to write you more particulars hereafter. . . .

We all take everything *California fashion*, very coolly. I shall miss Charlies folks and the Dr. very much, but shall have Lizzie to take their place in a measure, and little Addie too will be a great solace as well as care. He is a tiny little baby, but I *hope* he will have eyes like yours, and be very pretty. He is homely now.

Addison and Elizabeth Caldwell were married April 13 at Wallace Caldwell's house at Selby Flat by the Rev. James Warren, who had come from San Francisco to put his house up for sale. On the following Sunday he preached again at the Brick Church, which still lacked a regular minister.

On April 20 Luther Wickes withdrew from the firm of Gregory and Wickes, Grocers, in order to go home with his brother and sister. Arthur Hagadorn became a full partner in the firm of Chas. W. Mulford and Co., Bankers, on April 22.

The final surprise came when Delight changed her mind about going home and instead became the bride of Levi Kellogg in San Francisco's Grace Church; four days later she watched her friends and relations sail out of San Francisco Bay. Harvey and Luther would return, they said, but the Mulfords were leaving California forever.

In June, after Jerome Moore had gone home too, Addison told his mother:

I suppose it will seem amusing to you—as it always did to me—to hear a married man of two months talk of his happiness, and what a good wife he has—and how pleasantly and happily he is situated. And I suppose you will say that ten or twenty years hence we could talk of our happiness with better authority. But we are right happy now at all events, and I cant see now why we shall not continue to be. . . .

Lizzie and I are keeping house alone. Delight and her husband stayed with us for a while, but have left us and moved near Mr. Kellogg's diggings .... We have, I think, the pleasantest place in town, and I bought it on such terms that I could easily afford it. I busy myself mornings and evenings with my trees and flowers, and like the work better than I used to when I was a boy. My business is flourishing, and I am perfectly contented and happy.

Today Lizzy is at May's—and I go there to dinner. May and Fred and Niles are all well. Young Addie is growing finely—is handsome and good natured—and an honor to his namesake.... I wish Lizzie and I could be [in Rensselaerville] for a while with Harvey and Deb and all the rest, but I have'nt been as lucky as they have, and I cant afford to visit yet. It will all come around some time, I hope.

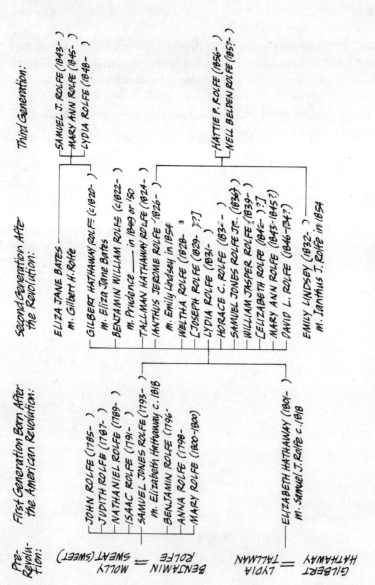

Rolfe family genealogy to 1854

APPENDIX

*T*HE FIRST ROLFE had emigrated to America from England in the early seventeenth century. The family resided in Massachusetts for several generations before going to New Hampshire in the late 1700s. On March 4, 1818, Samuel Jones Rolfe married Elizabeth Hathaway in a section of Massachusetts which soon became the state of Maine.

Gilbert, Benjamin, Tallman, Ianthus, Weltha, Joseph, Lydia, and Horace were born at Rumford, Maine. In 1834, when Horace was ten months old, the Rolfes followed a Mormon missionary to Kirtland, Ohio, to begin a new way of life.

Samuel, named for his father, was born at Kirtland before the colony broke into two bitterly feuding groups. The Rolfes went with Brigham Young to another colony in Missouri, but growing friction between the Latter Day Saints and non-Mormons exploded into violence, and the family joined another migration, this time eastward to Nauvoo, Illinois. William Rolfe was born during the exodus.

At Nauvoo the father became a carpenter and joiner, and the two oldest sons worked as plasterers. When prophet Joseph Smith called for volunteers to erect the great Temple, all three took part. Tallman was appprenticed to a printer and Ianthus became a cabin boy on a riverboat. When he was eighteen Tallman began reading law.

A combination of internal disputes and conflicts with settlers outside the colony resulted in the jailing and subsequent lynching of Joseph and Hyrum Smith. The loss of leadership and the hostility of the neighborhood fragmented the group; Brigham Young announced a new westward migration, but not all were willing to follow. In the midst of this confusion, Tallman decided to join an Oregon-bound wagon train and Ianthus was sent to live with relatives in New England. The year was 1845.

In 1847 Samuel Rolfe was picked by Brigham Young to be in the advance party that would locate Zion, the promised land. But Ben Rolfe argued that his father lacked the strength for the long ordeal, and asked to be sent in his place. Young agreed, despite the fact that Ben was not then a member of the church. The lead group consisted of 143 men and boys, two small children, and three women. Behind them a huge migration of impoverished saints struggled across the plains, including the remaining members of the Rolfe family.

Meanwhile, Tallman was in Oregon City, setting type on the first newspaper on the west coast. By the time the Mormon vanguard arrived at the Great Salt Lake, Tallman had gone south to Yerba Buena, where he found work on Sam Brannan's weekly. In a few months gold had been discovered and Yerba Buena became San Francisco. After mining a while, Tallman returned to the newspaper trade, working for a time at Sacramento before settling in Nevada City in 1851.

Ianthus was in Nevada City, too. After receiving an education in Massachusetts, he had set out for California, coming overland through Utah. There he learned that his family was about to embark on yet another journey, this time to establish a new Mormon colony in California. Ianthus continued on to Nevada City.

When Horace Rolfe joined his brothers in 1853 he described the ordeal of the long trek across the desert, and the first years of the colony. According to Horace the city of San Bernardino began as a fort 300 feet wide by 700 feet long, with palisade walls made of split cottonwood and willow tree trunks sunk in the ground.

Rows of mud-caulked log cabins were built along three walls of the fort; a number of cabins that had been erected previously were realigned to form a fourth wall. Many apartments were linked together, a series of connecting rooms with end partitions between families. People slept in the beds of wagons in order to have more room.

In addition to unmarried adults, more than a hundred families lived at San Bernardino. In the southeast corner of the fort, two teen-aged brothers of Horace shared a cabin with him and his parents. Gilbert, his oldest brother, lived in a nearby cabin with his wife Eliza Jane, a son, and two daughters. Benjamin and his wife Prudence had remained at Salt Lake City.

In 1853 Los Angeles County was divided to create the new county of San Bernardino at the behest of Assemblyman Jefferson Hunt. Brigham Young had designated Hunt as the colony's leader, and asked H. G. Sherwood, the planner of Salt Lake City, to lay out a smaller but similar version at San Bernardino City. Ten streets in the mile-square city were to be numbered; cross streets would bear names full of meaning for the Mormon pioneers: Kirtland, Independence, Far West, Nauvoo, Salt Lake, Utah, California.

In 1857 Young ordered all Mormons to return to Salt Lake. The U.S. government was threatening to use force against Mormon territorial leaders because of their refusal to comply with federal directives. Most

Mormons abandoned the colonies, but some, like Horace and Sam Rolfe, Jr., chose to remain.

In November 1857, as their parents and relatives were making the long pilgimage back across the desert, Tallman and Ianthus printed two related stories in the *Democrat*. The first said:

By the recent arrival at Los Angeles of an immigrant train, which came by the southern route from Salt Lake ... there is reason to believe that the Mormons design resisting the government troops now on their way to Utah; and it is quite certain that they are leagued with the Indians for the purpose of annoying and robbing the immigrant trains that pass through their country. . . .

The Mormons cannot be so insane as to suppose they can successfully resist the authority of the Federal government. . . . The Mormon leaders have the credit of being shrewd men, and they certainly must know how utterly futile all their attempts would be. . . . The Mormon population is composed to a great extent of ignorant foreigners, who know nothing of our institutions and laws, and it may be well enough for the government to teach them that there is a "higher law" than that which issues from the mouth of their prophet.

The second article related to the massacre of 118 California-bound emigrants near the outskirts of Mormon settlements in Utah on September 18, 1857:

The train that was so cruelly massacred was under the charge of Capt. Baker, from Carroll county, Arkansas. . . . It is stated that Wm. Baker [son of the Captain] escaped from the massacre, but was afterwards murdered on the Muddy by some Indians, in the presence of three Mormons, who represented that they were unable to save his life.

The fifteen children whose lives were saved were taken to Cedar City, a Mormon town not far from the place of the massacre. The eldest of these is a little girl only six years old, and it was probably the intention not to spare the life of any one old enough to give any particulars of the butchery. . . .

The train stopped some weeks near Salt Lake City, and the men were very free in expressing their opinion of the Mormons. Feeling perfectly secure in their arms and numbers, they are said to have been reckless, and would commit little acts of annoyance for the purpose of provoking the Saints. . . . These imprudences were doubtless the cause of the whole company, with the exception of the fifteen infants, being slaughtered. . . . The Mormons were on the most friendly terms with the Indians, which goes far to implicate them in this horrid work.

By the winter of 1858-1859 the United States government had spent nearly four million dollars to outfit a military expedition against the Mormons.

After leaving Nevada City in 1854, Horace Rolfe had joined a small company organized by Mormons to fight Indians. At one time he was fined $5 and costs for riding a horse through the schoolhouse during classes. In 1858 Horace Rolfe began to study law with William Pickett, newly arrived at San Bernardino with his wife and stepdaughter.

Pickett was not a Mormon, but his wife had been—in fact she was the widow of a younger brother of Joseph Smith, founder of the Mormon faith. Agnes Coolbrith, a convert from Maine, had married Don Carlos Smith, who died shortly after the birth of their daughter Josephine. In later years the daughter went by the name of Ina Coolbrith.

BIBLIOGRAPHY

BOOKS, MONOGRAPHS AND ARTICLES:

ADLER, MORTIMER J., CHARLES VAN DOREN and other editors. *The Annals of America.* 18 vols. Chicago: Encyclopaedia Britannica, 1968.

ASBURY, HERBERT. *Sucker's Progress: An Informal History of Gambling in America from the Colonies to Canfield.* New York: Dodd, Mead, 1938.

BANCROFT, HUBERT HOWE. *History of California.* 7 vols. San Francisco: The History Company, 1884–1890.

BANCROFT, HUBERT HOWE. *Popular Tribunals.* 2 vols. San Francisco: The History Company, 1887.

BEALS, RALPH L. "Ethnology of the Nisenan," *University of California Publications in American Archaeology and Ethnology,* 31 (1933), 335–413.

BEAN, EDWIN F. *History and Directory of Nevada County, California.* Nevada City: Daily Gazette, 1867.

BENTON, JOSEPH A. *The California Pilgrim: A Series of Lectures.* Sacramento: Solomon Alter, 1853.

BERRY, JOHN J., ed. *The Life of David Belden.* New York: Belden Brothers, 1891.

BILLINGTON, RAY ALLEN. *The Far Western Frontier 1830–1860.* New York: Harper and Row, 1956.

BILLINGTON, RAY ALLEN. *The Protestant Crusade 1800–1860: A Study of the Origins of American Nativism.* New York: MacMillan, 1938.

BLAIR, HARRY C., and REBECCA TARSHIS. *Lincoln's Constant Ally: The Life of Colonel Edward D. Baker.* Portland: Oregon Historical Society, 1960.

BOGGS, MAE HELENE BACON. *My Playhouse Was a Concord Coach.* Oakland: Mae Helene Bacon Boggs, 1942.

BOWMAN, ALAN P. *Index to the 1850 Census of the State of California.* Baltimore: Genealogical Publishing Company, 1972.

BROWN, NAT P., and JOHN K. DALLISON. *Nevada, Grass Valley, and Rough and Ready Directory, 1856.* San Francisco: Town Talk Office, 1856.

BROWNE, LINA FERGUSSON, ed. *J. Ross Browne: His Letters, Journals and Writings.* Albuquerque: University of New Mexico Press, 1969.

CALIFORNIA STATE AGRICULTURAL SOCIETY. *Transactions During the Year 1858.* Sacramento: State Printer, 1859.

CARRANCO, LYNWOOD, and ESTLE BEARD. *Genocide and Vendetta: The Round Valley Wars of Northern California.* Norman: University of Oklahoma Press, 1981.

CARTER, KATE B., comp. *Our Pioneer Heritage.* Vol. 6. Salt Lake: Daughters of Utah Pioneers, 1963.

CARTER, KATE B., comp. *Treasures of Pioneer History.* Vol. 3. Salt Lake: Daughters of Utah Pioneers, 1954.

CAUGHEY, JOHN WALTON. *California.* New York: Prentice-Hall, 1940.

CHAMBERLAIN, WILLIAM H., and HARRY L. WELLS. *History of Yuba County, California.* Oakland: Thompson and West, 1879.

CLARKE, DWIGHT L. *William Tecumseh Sherman: Gold Rush Banker.* San Francisco: California Historical Society, 1969.

COLEMAN, CHARLES M. *P. G. and E. of California: The Centennial Story of Pacific Gas and Electric Company 1852–1952*. New York: McGraw-Hill, 1952.

COMSTOCK, DAVID A. *Gold Diggers and Camp Followers 1845–1851*. Grass Valley: Comstock Bonanza Press, 1982.

COMSTOCK, DAVID A. "Proper Women at the Mines: Life at Nevada City in the 1850s." *The Pacific Historian*, 28:3 (Fall 1984), 65–73.

COMSTOCK, DAVID A., and ARDIS H. COMSTOCK, comp. *Index to 1880 History of Nevada County, California, published by Thompson and West*. Grass Valley: Comstock Bonanza Press, 1979.

COMSTOCK, DAVID A., and ARDIS H. COMSTOCK, comp. *Nevada County Vital Statistics, June 1850 to June 1859*. Grass Valley: Comstock Bonanza Press, 1986.

CRANDALL, HENRY SARGENT. *Love and Nuggets*. Old Greenwich, CT: Stable Books, 1967.

DAVIDSON, MARSHALL B. *Life in America*. 2 vols. Boston: Houghton Mifflin and the Metropolitan Museum of Art, 1951.

DAVIS, H. P. *Gold Rush Days in Nevada City*. Nevada City: Berliner and McGinnis, 1948.

DELANO, ALONZO. "A Live Woman in the Mines," *The Minor Drama: The Acting Edition*, Vol. CXXX. New York: Samuel French, 1857.

DELANO, ALONZO. *Old Block's Sketch Book*. Sacramento: Union Office, 1856.

DELANO, ALONZO. *Pen-Knife Sketches or Chips of the Old Block*. Sacramento: Union Office, 1853.

DELANO, ALONZO. *A Sojourn with Royalty*. San Francisco: George Fields, 1936.

DOTEN, ALFRED R. *Journals, 1849–1903*. 3 vols. Reno: University of Nevada Press, 1973.

ESSHOM, FRANK. *Pioneers and Prominent Men of Utah*. Salt Lake: Western Epics, 1966.

FERRIER, WILLIAM WARREN. *Henry Durant: First President University of California*. Berkeley: William Warren Ferrier, 1942.

FERRIER, WILLIAM WARREN. *Origin and Development of the University of California*. Berkeley: Sather Gate Book Shop, 1930.

FERRIS, HELEN. *Here Comes Barnum: P. T. Barnum's Own Story*. New York: Harcourt, Brace, 1932.

FIELD, STEPHEN J. *California Alcalde: Personal Reminiscences of Early Days in California*. Oakland: Biobooks, 1950 (orig. pub. 1893).

FISCHER, CHRISTIANE, ed. *Let Them Speak for Themselves: Women in the American West, 1849–1900*. Hamden, CT: The Shoe String Press, 1977.

FOLEY, DORIS. *The Divine Eccentric: Lola Montez and the Newspapers*. Los Angeles: Westernlore Press, 1969.

GARD, ROBERT E., and DAVID SEMMES. *America's Players*. New York: The Seabury Press, 1967.

GILBERT, FRANK T., HARRY L. WELLS, et al. *Illustrated History of Plumas, Lassen and Sierra Counties, with California from 1513 to 1850*. San Francisco: Fariss and Smith, 1882.

GREENE, LAURENCE. *The Filibuster: The Career of William Walker*. New York: Bobbs-Merrill, 1937.

GUDDE, ERWIN G. *California Gold Camps*. Berkeley: University of California Press, 1975.

HANSON, GLADYS. *San Francisco Almanac*. San Francisco: Chronicle Books, 1975.

HEIZER, ROBERT F., and ALAN J. ALMQUIST. *The Other Californians: Prejudice and Discrimination under Spain, Mexico, and the United States to 1920*. Berkeley: University of California Press, 1971.

HEIZER, ROBERT F., and MARY ANNE WHIPPLE. *The California Indians: A Source Book*. Second Edition. Berkeley: University of California Press, 1971.

HERMANN, RUTH. *Gold and Silver Colossus: William Morris Stewart and his Southern Bride*. Sparks, NV: Dave's Printing and Publishing, 1975.

HERMANN, RUTH. *More Than Gold: An Authentic Story Never Before Told*. Grass Valley: The Union, 1966.

HOEXTER, CORINNE K. *From Canton to California: The Epic of Chinese Immigration*. New York: Four Winds Press, 1976.

HUTCHINSON, W. H. *California: The Golden Shore by the Sundown Sea*. Palo Alto: Star Publishing, 1980.

INGERSOLL, LUTHER A. *Century Annals of San Bernardino County, 1769 to 1904*. Los Angeles: L. A. Ingersoll, 1905.

JONES, PAT. *The Chicago Park Connection: A History of Chicago Park and Peardale*. Chicago Park, CA: Pat Jones, 1983.

JONES, PAT. *The Colfax Connection: A History of Colfax*. Chicago Park, CA: Pat Jones, 1980.

JONES, PAT. "Nevada County's Black Pioneers," *Nevada County Historical Society Bulletin*, 39:3 (July 1985).

JONES, PAT. "The Forgotten Pioneer: Simmon Peña Storms," *Nevada County Historical Society Bulletin*, 37:4 (October 1983).

KIP, WILLIAM INGRAHAM. *Early Days of My Episcopate*. New York: Thomas Whittaker, 1892.

KROEBER, ALFRED L. *Handbook of the Indians of California*. New York: Dover, 1976 (orig. pub. U.S. Government Printing Office, Washington, D.C., 1925).

LAMOTT, KENNETH. *Chronicles of San Quentin: The Biography of a Prison*. New York: Ballantine Books, 1972.

LAPP, RUDOLPH M. *Blacks in Gold Rush California*. New Haven: Yale University Press, 1977.

LAVENDER, DAVID. *Nothing Seemed Impossible: William C. Ralston and Early San Francisco*. New York: Crown, 1975.

LEVINSON, ROBERT E. *The Jews in the California Gold Rush*. New York: KTAV Publishing House, and Berkeley: Commission for the Preservation of Pioneer Jewish Cemeteries and Landmarks of the Judah L. Magnes Memorial Museum, 1978.

LOOMIS, NOEL M. *Wells Fargo*. New York: Bramhall House, 1968.

M----., L. "The Indians of Nevada County," *The Overland Monthly*, March 1884, 275–279.

MacMINN, GEORGE R. *The Theater of the Golden Era in California*. Caldwell: Caxton Printers, 1941.

MANN, RALPH. *After the Gold Rush: Society in Grass Valley and Nevada City, California 1849–1870*. Stanford: Stanford University Press, 1982.

MARKS, EDWARD B. *They All Had Glamour: From the Swedish Nightingale to the Naked Lady*. New York: Julian Messner, 1944.

MAY, PHILIP ROSS. *Origins of Hydraulic Mining in California*. Oakland: Holmes Book Company, 1970.

MELENDY, H. BRETT, and BENJAMIN F. GILBERT. *The Governors of California*. Georgetown: Talisman Press, 1965.

MORLEY, JIM, and DORIS FOLEY. *Gold Cities: Grass Valley and Nevada City*. Berkeley: Howell-North, 1965.

MORRIS, WILLIAM GOUVERNEUR. *California Reports*, Vol. V, 1855. Sacramento: B. B. Redding, 1857.

MORSE, EDWIN FRANKLIN. "The Story of a Gold Miner," *California Historical Society Quarterly*, Vol. VL, 339–341.

MUIR, LEO J. *A Century of Mormon Activities in California*. 2 vols. Salt Lake City: Deseret News Press, 1952.

NEASHAM, V. AUBREY, and JAMES E. HENLEY. *The City of the Plain: Sacramento in the Nineteenth Century*. Sacramento: Sacramento Pioneer Foundation and Sacramento Historic Landmarks Commission, 1969.

OLMSTEAD, R. R., ed. *Scenes of Wonder and Curiosity from Hutchings' California Magazine 1856–1861*. Berkeley: Howell-North, 1962.

POND, WILLIAM C. *Gospel Pioneering in California*. Oberlin, Ohio: News Printing Company, 1921.

POWELL, SUMNER CHILTON. *Puritan Village. The Formation of a New England Town*. Middletown: Wesleyan University, 1963.

POWERS, STEPHEN. *Tribes of California*. Berkeley: University of California Press, 1976.

PRESTON, R. N. *Early California: Northern Edition*. Corvallis: Western Guide Publishers, 1974.

REIDT, THEO. "Lola Montez' Ill-fated Trip to the Truckee River," *Nevada County Historical Society Bulletin*, 37:2 (April 1983).

RITER, HENRIETTA, ed. *People Made It Happen Here: History of the Town of Rensselaerville ca 1788–1950*. Rensselaerville, NY: The Rensselaerville Historical Society, 1977.

ROSS, ISHBEL. *The Uncrowned Queen: Life of Lola Montez*. New York: Harper and Row, 1972.

ROYCE, SARAH. *A Frontier Lady: Recollections of the Gold Rush and Early California*. New Haven: Yale University Press, 1932.

RUGGLES, ELEANOR. *Prince of Players: Edwin Booth*. New York: W. W. Norton, 1953.

SARGENT, AARON A. "Sketch of Nevada County." *Nevada, Grass Valley, and Rough and Ready Directory, 1856*, Brown and Dallison. San Francisco: Town Talk Office, 1856.

SEVERSON, THOR. *Sacramento: An Illustrated History 1839–1874*. San Francisco: California Historical Society, 1973.

SHERMAN, WILLIAM TECUMSEH. *Memoirs*. 2 vols. New York: D. Appleton, 1875.

SHUCK, OSCAR T., ed. *Representative and Leading Men of the Pacific*. San Francisco: Bacon, 1870.

STERNE, MADELEINE B. *Purple Passage: The Life of Mrs. Frank Leslie*. Norman: University of Oklahoma Press, 1953.

STEWART, GEORGE R., Jr. "The Drama in a Frontier Theater," *Essays in Dramatic Literature, The Parrott Presentation Volume*. Princeton: Princeton University Press, 1935.

STEWART, WILLIAM MORRIS. *Reminiscences.* New York: Neale Publishing, 1908.

STRONG, FRANK, and JOSEPH SCHAFER. *The Government of the American People.* Boston: Houghton, Mifflin, 1901

SWISHER, CARL BRENT. *Stephen J. Field: Craftsman of the Law.* Washington: The Brookings Institution, 1930.

ULDALL, HANS JORGEN, and WILLIAM SHIPLEY. *Nisenan Texts and Dictionary.* Berkeley: University of California Press, 1966.

VANDENHOFF, ANNE. *Edward Dickinson Baker: Western Gentleman, Frontier Lawyer, American Statesman.* Auburn, CA: Anne Vandenhoff, 1979.

WALKER, FRANKLIN. *San Francisco's Literary Frontier.* New York: Alfred A. Knopf, 1939.

WEBB, CATHERINE J. *A Family History of California.* Berkeley: Catherine Webb, 1975.

WEBB, CATHERINE J. *History Reconstructed: Stories of Tallman, Ianthus, Horace and Samuel.* Berkeley: Catherine Webb, 1978.

WELLS, HARRY L., ALLEN M. FREEMAN, H. B. RICE, and J. ALBERT WILSON. *History of Nevada County, California.* Oakland: Thompson and West, 1880.

WHITSELL, LEON O. *One Hundred Years of Freemasonry in California.* 3 vols. San Francisco: Grand Lodge, Free and Accepted Masons of California, 1950.

WILLEY, SAMUEL H. *A History of the College of California.* San Francisco: Samuel Carson, 1887.

WISTAR, ISAAC JONES. *Autobiography.* New York: Harper and Bros., 1937.

WRAY, KEN, ed. *100 Years of Nevada County.* Nevada City: Nevada City Nugget, 1951.

DOCUMENTARY SOURCES:

Newspapers:

Alta California, 1855–1858.
Grass Valley Telegraph, 1853–1858.
Nevada Democrat, 1854–1859.
Nevada Journal, 1851–1859.
San Francisco Daily Herald, 1855.
Young America, 1853–1854.

Private Correspondence:

The Rensselaerville Correspondence, 1800–1859.

UNPUBLISHED MATERIALS:

California. Register and Descriptive List of Convicts under Sentence of Imprisonment in the State Prison of California. MF2:1(59). California State Archives, Office of the Secretary of State, Sacramento.

New York. Rensselaerville Township, Albany County, Minutes 1795–1869.

Washington, D.C. Record Group 75 (Series M-234), Rolls 33–42, National Archives.

INDEX

THIS BOOK WAS DESIGNED
AND ILLUSTRATED BY THE AUTHOR.
TYPE COMPOSITION BY COMSTOCK
BONANZA PRESS AND DWAN TYPOGRAPHY.
TEXT SET IN SABON, EXTRACTS IN
ITC CHELTENHAM BOOK, TITLES AND SUBHEADS IN
POSTER BODONI ITALIC, INITIALS IN ALBUM SCRIPT.
PRINTED ON HURON NATURAL TEXT PAPER, BASIS 55,
AND BOUND IN HOLLISTON ROXITE BLACK VELLUM
CLOTH BY THOMSON-SHORE, INC.